# AGENT PROVOCATEUR

by
## Edmund Charles

**U.S. Library of Congress Registration Number** TXu 1-888-134

- Registration Date: August 26, 2013

- Author: Edmund Charles

First published in Great Britain as an ebook in 2014

Typeset in Minion Pro and Yanone Kaffeesatz

Editing, Design and Publishing by UK Book Publishing

UK Book Publishing is a trading name of Consilience Media

www.ukbookpublishing.com

ISBN 978-1-910223-16-1

Cover photos:

Edith Cavell
http://commons.wikimedia.org/wiki/File:Nurse_Edith_Cavell_1865-1915_Q15064B.jpg

Philippe Baucq
http://commons.wikimedia.org/wiki/File:Philippe_Baucq_(1880-1915).jpg

Germans marching through Ostend WW1 - 1914/1915
Library of Congress, Prints & Photographs Division LC-DIG-ggbain-18681
http://www.loc.gov/pictures/item/ggb2005017381/

Wounded Belgians, Antwerp Hospital, 18 May 1915, Underwood & Underwood
http://commons.wikimedia.org/wiki/World_war_1#mediaviewer/File:WWIAntwerpHospital.jpg

German invasion of Belgium 1914
http://it.wikipedia.org/wiki/Invasione_tedesca_del_Belgio_(1914)

German Cuirassier Guards parade in Berlin 1916, Underwood & Underwood
http://commons.wikimedia.org/wiki/World_war_1#mediaviewer/File:WWICuirassierBerlin.jpg

# Dedication

As this novel is being published, we stand at the centennial commemoration of the commencement of events, which led up to the horrific spectacle of 'The Great War' as WW I was most commonly termed up until the advent of the Second World War. It is perhaps an opportune time to reflect through the long lens of history of the events and people who contributed and often sacrificed their lives for the causes in which they felt were patriotic and true. While much has been written about the public heroes of the conflict, to include the leading politicians, generals and solitary brave soldiers, far fewer works have been composed about the people whose lives were most directly affected by the unexpected modern war – the average civilian. Unlike most wars fought since the time of the European Age of Enlightenment in the seventeenth century and continuing through until the early twentieth century, civilian populaces often lay at the mere periphery of war, yet modern industrial warfare denounced this sterile concept and 'The Great War' witnessed the re-introduction of the ancient phenomena known as 'total war', an event in which civilians became equally engaged in and suffered enormously the consequences akin to those soldiers serving on the battlefield in military uniform. The technology and industry of the modern nation-state changed warfare forever in its scope, scale, intensity and operational tenets. Conversely there was a lack of change in the nature of its human protagonists and antagonists; women and men remained the same creatures of both elevated nobility and savage vice. It is on the average citizens of the modern industrial-scientific age, who are often caught-up and made helpless in nationalistic and global forces beyond their control or influence, that this novel is focused.

This book was specifically inspired by the brave civilian women and men who sacrificed their lives and freedoms during 'The Great War' in order that succeeding generations of free people may live and continue the fight against any future aggressive and savage militant enemy. Over nine million soldiers perished, half of whom have no known graves and at least another five million civilians died through starvation, war actions, disease and outright genocide. I want to praise the efforts of Prince Reginald de Croy, Princess Marie de Croy, Directress Nurse Edith Cavell, Philippe Baucq, Countess Jeanne de Belleville and Marie Depage who personally sacrificed their fortunes, reputations and in some cases their very lives, to assist in courageous acts of freedom for the stranded Allied soldiers and for their personal beliefs. In final devotion to the cause of freedom, Nurse Edith Cavell and Monsieur Philippe Baucq sacrificed their promising lives so that hundreds of Allied soldiers could escape the clutches of death, starvation, imprisonment and possible execution. Many more civilian men and women, both known and unknown to history, also sacrificed their lives or endured long prison sentences of hard labour to help liberate their countries from Imperial German military oppression. While many silently wished for liberation, only a select handful acted to obtain it.

NOTE: The general contents of this story, characters and events portrayed in this novel are true and noted in recorded history. While the author has made a 'best attempt' to remain true to the facts and to preserve the characters, sequence and actual events that have occurred as a matter of record, some events and dialogue have been added or modified for literary purposes. Much of the official German files and information concerning the de Croy underground network that operated to assist Allied soldiers escape from occupied Belgium, were destroyed during World War II, thus only those personal stories left behind by select de Croy network participants serve as the 'best evidence' of the activities that have occurred; many more events and details exist that are peripheral to and complementary to this story that have no recorded or first-hand accounts.

# About the author:

Edmund Charles is a retired U.S. Army officer with over 34 years of service, including numerous assignments, both foreign and domestic. He holds several advanced degrees and professional certificates. He has worked in the telecommunications, engineering and management consulting fields and he has written several defense-related articles. He has published two previous novels, an action-drama involving Hot Shots battling the wildfires called "Satan's Pitchfork" and crime-suspense story called "Two-Faced". This is his third commercial novel. Edmund Charles is in semi-retirement and resides in Tampa, Florida.

Edmund can be reached via email at:

edmund.charles@me.com
edmundcharles.55@gmail.com

Oprah C
Please accept with my complements, my novel on Wolf MacRae and the story of the brave women and patriotic men who fought the German Army through their resistance and rescue efforts.

Best Wishes.

Edmund Charles

# Table of contents

# Chapter 1:
# 'A Mysterious Summons'

*"Our citizens need help getting out of Europe! We need
to get food to the starving neutral European countries! I
need good analysis and intelligence on this war!"*

The constant methodological, rhythmic clanging of powerful metal-on-metal sounds of the massive steam locomotive was akin to that of a mythical fire-exhaling dragon of medieval legend. The Baldwin 4-6-0 wheel-configured, seventy-two ton machine clanked and clattered along a pale silver ribbon that bisected the lush green Maryland countryside. Externally, the matt black metal steam engine was periodically accented with bright red paint outlines that ran across the horizontal length of the steel monster, further serving to render visual power to a machine that was already formidable from both a mechanical and engineering perspective. Without warning, the roaring mechanical beast bellowed forth a shrill cry, its steam powered whistle alerting both man and beast that a powerful force was coming their way and for all who heard to make clear a path or be crushed under its mighty steel body. From its smokestack there exited a hell-like black acrid smoke that gradually was transformed and diffused into a light grey and then finally a soft white coloured smoke trail. The massive engine and coal tender weight bearing upon the steel railroad tracks made for a constant vibration that was continually heralded throughout the cluttered railroad passenger compartments. The inevitable vibrations impacted upon the evenly spaced metal rail joints and thus created a constant and predictable sound interruption every two seconds and it had become an almost illusionary sound unto the train passengers who had endured the quick five hour journey which had originated in New York City's 'Grand Central Terminal' through the states of Pennsylvania, Delaware, Maryland and finally culminating at the end of the line at Union Station, Washington DC, the heart of the young nation, the Capital of the United States. At speeds averaging seventy miles per hour, the train bellowed across the green spring landscape like a determined black snake slithering through a rich emerald jungle. There was a strict time schedule to maintain and the steel monster was not going to be deterred in its journey.

The steam train was the infamous and very extravagant 'Royal Blue' line of the most prolific and profitable Baltimore and Ohio (B&O) rail line. The name of the exclusive line was aptly deserved from both a function and form perspective. The massively powered ten-wheeled engine called a 4-6-0 or more commonly referred to as a 'Ten-wheeler', possessed extra heavy 78-inch diameter steel driving wheels for additional momentum to achieve passenger and freight speed-of- delivery. This special 'Royal Blue' line also had its custom-made Pullman coach cars painted in dark, rich royal blue exterior paint accented in rich gold-gilt outline painting, the interior compartments from club car to the passenger cars were equally befitting with attunements in various shades of Royal and powder blue leather and cloth work throughout the cabin to include exclusive patterns of blue silk wallpaper and gold-plated heavy brass fittings and accents throughout.

The two dining cars, appropriately named the 'Queen' and the 'Waldorf', were equally grand in design, each outfitted in splendid array with rich honey-toned mahogany and tiger-maple wood panelling, buttery soft chilli-burgundy coloured leather chairs, Wedgewood china and heavy sterling silver flat wear beneath which was attired the finest powder blue coloured linen table covers. The epicurean fare boasted such delights as roasted pheasant, New England lobster, king crab, terrapin and roast beef – all served by expensively recruited French-trained chefs. Exotic drinks and fine, aged brandy, wines and whiskies all served in heavy lead crystal glasses, tantalised the palates of the discriminating and wealthy diners. A complement of highly-groomed and well-mannered serving staff were in abundance; all of the waiters were dutifully outfitted in short-cut white dinner jackets, complete with starched white wing-collar shirts and black bow-ties; the staff eagerly attended to the slightest anticipated whim of their pampered dining patrons. This was the zenith of the Gilded Age and the US railroads were the uncontested champions of the recently industrialized American transportation system that ferried both cargo material and people efficiently and in comfort across the vast rich nation. All the luxury of the B&O Royal Blue line between New York City and Washington, DC, was lavished exclusively on those privileged passengers who could so afford the premium fare between the two powerful cities: the wealthy citizens of the financial community and the politically connected sect.

"Next stop Annapolis Junction, ten minutes, ladies and gentlemen! Annapolis Junction next stop!" loudly bellowed a fiftyish, white, portly, grey-haired man. He was neatly attired in the traditional B&O cabin uniform of dark royal blue single-breasted wool suit graced with brass buttons and complementary matching wool vest and peaked-visor cap badged with the B&O railroad insignia beneath which the gold lettering of 'Conductor' was prominently displayed. Throughout the symmetrically arrayed identical set of royal blue paired-seats there was the traditional walking corridor or aisle; it neatly separated the passenger train compartment in half and it was through this conveyance corridor that the various gentlemen and ladies were making ready their exit for the Annapolis Junction stop. The acrid odour of gentlemen smoking various strong cigars and unfiltered cigarettes was intermixed with the sweet fragrant smell of the ladies' strong perfume. As befitted the custom of the day and their expected station in life, every man and woman travelled in their finest adornment possible; every woman wore her mandatory gloves, while the men were smartly enrobed in various styles of single and double-breasted suits. Each of the sexes wore their mandatory head wear with the ladies displaying a dizzying forest of feather encrusted hats, while others preferred the more modest linen or silk variety. The gentlemen contented themselves with the atypical fedora, traditional round bowler, simple throw-on cap and the ever-popular straw boater hat with accompanying hat ribbon. At Annapolis Junction, Maryland there was the typical jockeying of those hastily departing passengers rushing to get out of the humid, stuffy passenger compartment, while boarding passengers desperately struggled to enter the compartment and find a seat for the final journey on to Washington, DC.

A finely dressed man in a plain grey suit sat crumpled-up against the side of the passenger seat. His slumped body was propped up against the side panel of the Pullman car, his head and eyes strategically covered over with his matching grey fedora as a practical type of eye cover. He was medium-framed and in his early thirties. His black cashmere coat served as a self-made comforter against the mild spring weather. The man was fast asleep, an obvious indication that this was one of the original passengers who had taken the first of the morning Royal Blue trains out of Grand Central Station in New York City. He slept oblivious to the various train stops in Philadelphia, Wilmington, Baltimore and now Annapolis Junction; he was in this ride until the end-of-the-line, to the nation's capital and the conductor was expected to awaken him upon reaching his final destination. Such behaviour was de rigeur for the train travelling public.

"Hey there, excuse me sir, is this seat taken?" a stranger asked as he stood in the corridor of the passenger car, hoping to avoid the movement of other passengers lining up to either exit or take their seats. Not a word was uttered, not even a slight body movement was detected from the slumbering passenger. "Excuse me, is this seat taken?" the stranger inquired again, this time in a more urgent and frustrated voice. Again there was no discernible reply, so the stranger shrugged his shoulders, placed his well-worn, small leather attaché case on the seat and took his place upon a double-seat that was positioned directly opposite and facing the sleeping gentlemen.

"Next stop, Union Station, Washington, DC…the end-of-the-line folks!", yelled the conductor, as the massive Baldwin 'Ten-wheeler' lurched forward once again with a great mechanical grumble from the releasing steam valve exhaust manifold and from the slow metallic grinding of massive steel wheels upon equally strong steel railroad tracks. The metal-on-metal sounds and the oily-scented fumes were the unmistakable manifestations of the modern 20th Century innovations that were overtaking the old pre-industrial 'horse & buggy' world and transforming it dramatically and permanently.

The stranger began to make himself comfortable for the short 30-minute journey to the Union Station terminal; there was still ample time remaining, however, to enjoy his newspaper and have the languorous pleasure of a hand-rolled Cuban cigar. It was mid-Spring and the weather was pleasant, the temperature being in the mid-70 degrees Fahrenheit. The decorum of the day dictated that he ask permission of his seat companion to smoke – however, the gentleman was fast asleep to the world and there were no other passengers nearby, especially ladies, from whom social permission needed to be requested. With forthrightness, the stranger opened up the window to that of one-quarter opening; he took out a friction match and struck it heartily against a conveniently available metal sideboard abrasive surface. Immediately, the strong scent of phosphorus and sulphur became discernible, yet the odour was quickly diffused by the ample circulating air draught. He lit his dark brown cigar, puffed vigorously and proceeded to sit comfortably down to read his morning newspaper 'The Sun' of Baltimore, Maryland. The stranger wore a light brown-gold checkered suit that was topped off with a practical, breathable beige-coloured straw boater hat, complete with an encircling vibrant red and blue silk hatband. He carried no coat or luggage aside from the attaché case, indicating that the stranger was a local daily commuter, known colloquially as a day-tripper.

The young slumbering gentleman was suddenly engulfed with a cool flow of an airstream across his torso and face, this accompanied by the sweet pungent aroma of a fine, strong cigar. The combination of both scent and temperature conspired to awaken the gentlemen from his mid-day slumber. Ever so slowly he raised his right hand to gently elevate the fedora that had shielded him from the visual confrontations of the small world within the social confines of the Pullman car. His pale blue eyes gazed wearily at the nameless stranger whose face was now conveniently hidden behind the pages of the Sun newspaper that was held up high to the stranger's face. Headlines from around the world boldly accented the front page in big bold black lettering. The headlines outlined the improved US economic conditions, local politics and the raging war in Europe, now in its second bloody year and with no victory in sight for either of the warring sides.

"Hummm, I'm sorry, I must have dozed off, sir!" the gentleman muttered slowly and in a low tone – this as his informal introduction to the stranger who sat indifferently, smoking his pungent stogie directly opposite to him. The stranger slowly lowered his newspaper from in front of his face. "Well hello, I tried not to wake you at Annapolis Junction, that's where I got aboard you know, I hope you don't mind the cigar, but you were sleeping and no one else was around, so I lit this tasteful little baby up, you don't mind, do you Mister, Mister ah…ah," the stranger awkwardly inquired as to the gentlemen's name in an obvious leading manner.

"No sir, not at all, go right ahead and puff away! The cigar aroma is rather pleasant. When the mood strikes me I sometimes indulge myself – and my name is William, William J Donovan!" the gentlemen replied with a weary smile and still half-asleep from his interrupted nap.

"It's a pleasure to meet you, Mr Donovan, my name is Sanders… Jeffrey Lionel Sanders, I'm a representative for the Maryland farming and livestock association. I've an appointment to see some of those Washington Big Shots to try and get the Government to buy more of our great agriculture and meat products for those idiots fighting the war in Europe – you know they're calling it the Great War over there! To me, it sure does not sound that great either, from the headlines I read that a lot of young soldiers are dying and I cannot say for what express purpose. What do you think about that mess over there, that is, if you do not mind my asking you, Mr Donovan?" the stranger stated in a rather forward, but innocent manner. He was typical of an American personality, somewhat crude, socially forward, but always direct and well meaning.

"That's quite all right, Mr Sanders, I don't mind at all, in fact, it would be good to discuss these worldly matters with my countrymen. Yes well about the war question, well I think that for the moment at least, we should stay out of this conflict; I think that it's a European issue for the time being. Of course, if Germany attacks US citizens or interests, then we must take action and defend ourselves," Mr Donovan replied with a response that was shared among the vast majority of United States citizens and its elected members.

"Amen brother! I could not agree more, Mr Donovan; those Europeans are crazy. Some rinky-dink Arch Duke and his wife get themselves shot in some half-assed, no-name country and all of a sudden: boom! Everything goes up in smoke and one country after another declares war on the other and before you know it the entire continent is at war and soldiers are dying in the millions! To make it worse, no one can stop it. I can't even pronounce, never mind locate some of those countries on a map! Yep...you're darn right, Mr Donovan, stay out of European affairs – after all, no one came to our aid in the great US Civil War, so we should not come to anyone's aid either!" concluded the stranger in a smug manner as he anxiously puffed on his cigar, which was now half-burnt down and the nicotine juice from the strong cigar was getting to upset Mr Sanders' stomach and probably his temper too. Yet most Americans and politicians shared Mr Sanders' sentiments, including President Woodrow Wilson.

"Have you ever been to Europe, Mister Sanders?" Mr Donovan inquired to further along the conversation.

"No sir, afraid to say that I have not. I was planning to take my wife there for our ten year wedding anniversary, but now that plan is shot to hell – she will have to settle for seeing San Francisco or New York instead of Paris and London I guess, but maybe that's for the best – there's no language difficulties in America," Mr Sanders replied with a sigh of resignation and arrogance in his voice.

William Donovan merely smiled in polite acknowledgment and the men soon turned their discussions to the fair spring weather and the booming economic conditions. Yet, in his mind, Donovan's deeper thoughts were focused on the war in Europe, for it was in his character to dwell upon the wider affairs of his country, for he was a brilliant and successful lawyer from Buffalo, New York and a National Guard officer in the US Cavalry Corps. People and places fascinated him immensely. In this year of 1916, he too believed that American neutrality was the best option and so too thought his peers and family.

"I did not quite get your business, Mr Donovan, that is, if I'm not being too intrusive in your affairs sir," Mr Sanders boldly inquired, more as a mere social chitchat inquiry and to help pass along the time.

"No sir, not at all Mr Sanders, I'm a corporate lawyer from upstate New York and an old college friend of mine from Columbia University asked that I meet with him and his friends and that's the extent of my business down here – a quite dull affair I'm afraid to say!" Donovan remarked in a very honest and forthcoming manner.

Suddenly their lighthearted banter was again interrupted by a familiar barking voice. "Next Stop…Union Station, Washington, DC, the end of the line! Union Station…the end of the line in five minutes, ladies and gentlemen!" yelled the lurid conductor as the Royal Blue journey had come to its conclusion.

"Well, good luck, Mr Donovan, it was great meeting you and I hope you have a happy reunion with your old friend," Mr Sanders remarked as he carelessly tossed his well consumed cigar stub out of the train window with a simple flick of his finger. The Royal Blue had arrived into the sheltered steel and concrete cocoon of Washington DC's massive and ornate Union Station. William grabbed his coat and threw it casually over his left shoulder, being mindful to affix and straighten out his hat to get the proper flap-down look. From beneath the Royal Blue cloth seat, he withdrew a sturdy and rich almond-coloured leather suitcase. He had packed light, hoping that his meeting with his university friend would be a short one, as urgent business awaited him in Buffalo. The war had made his legal business profitable; for the fortunate few, the European war was one of opportunity and reward. As all contracts in business needed legal review for correctness and terms of agreement, his private law practice of Donovan & Goodyear was bulging with business and both he and his partner were considering taking on additional associates at their firm.

Yet within his personality, there was a longing for things beyond his own experiences and circumstances. Since his youth, he possessed a raging intellectual hunger for things of the greater world. Catholic by both birth and practice, he was educated by Catholic parochial schools, the Baltimore catechism and the discipline of his teachers and parents. He possessed an individualized Celtic form of fatalism which manifested itself in him as a total lack of fear for danger and death. Despite his religious upbringing and faith, he was quite liberal to new ideas, people and places. For him, life was an adventure to be experienced fully, not just to be vicariously experienced through books or the tales of others. He was a keen judge of character and he chose his friends and clients with discretion and attention, a habit that served him well throughout his life.

He patiently waited until the bulk of the train passengers had vacated the cloistered luxury of the Royal Blue, as there was no exigent business scheduled that immediately awaited him this pleasant afternoon – his appointment was for the early evening to meet his friend at a location that was obscure to him, but his Columbia law school friend did confide that he would be in contact with his old college friend sometime during the afternoon. It was now 12:00 noon and he yearned for a short nap and a quick snack. After a span of ten minutes, the Union Station crowds were now well dispersed, so William Donovan grabbed his coat and light suitcase and departed the train and passed through the rich marble and brass encrusted lobby of the massively ornate and cavernous Union Station atrium. He raised his open free right arm and waved furiously for a vacant taxi, which were preponderant and hungry for passenger fares.

"Good afternoon, where to, Mister?" a cabbie dressed in a dark black suit and matching peaked chauffeur-styled cap loudly barked as he quickly turned around and looked into the face of his new passenger. The hectic taxi business and the rush of the passengers had enforced a very pedestrian-type protocol relationship between the cabbie and his fare; the politeness of holding open doors and greeting the client outside of the cab had become a recent victim to the modernity of the increasingly busy Washington, DC atmosphere.

"Hello, please take me to the Willard Hotel, cabbie, thank you very much," Donovan replied with a politeness that bespoke of his superior manners and inner character.

"Yes sir! You got business with the government? It seems like just about anyone these days that comes to this town does, ya know Mister!" the cabbie exhorted in an innocent, but not unusual chit-chat inquiry and not intending any social faux pas.

William smiled back slightly; he relished the good-natured character of America's 'common man' and he took no offence at the cabbie's bold inquisitive verbal banter, unlike so many other uppity aspiring Americans. "No I'm here in town to see my old law school friend; we haven't seen one another for many years, but he sounded a bit desperate to me, so here I am in the nation's capital," Bill Donovan remarked quite casually and with honesty. This was the second time this morning he had informed a stranger of his business and he desperately hoped that there would be no third inquiry.

"It's a nice Spring day here, it came early for us! The winter was mild and I just hope that the scorching summer humidity does not come early this year." The cabbie referred to the terribly humid summers that were the bane of Washington, DC.

Bill merely smiled politely and remained quiet in the recluse of his thoughts about his friend, John Lord O'Brien. The last time that Donovan had heard of his old friend John O'Brien, he was working as a corporate lawyer for the big Robber Baron companies such as Standard Oil, Union

Pacific, and US Steel. O'Brien was a young, ambitious lawyer in a hurry and he was after the big money clients. It seemed a bit odd that O'Brien wanted to meet him and in Washington DC, instead of the corporate nerve centre of the United States, that of New York City. 'Oh well, maybe good old John had a deal working as a lobbyist or something,' Bill amusingly thought to himself as he temporarily shrugged off his passing concern.

"Here it is Mister, the Crown Jewel of Pennsylvania Avenue – the grand old lady herself, the famous old Willard Hotel! There's none finer in the city, a real fancy place that I want to take my wife to someday for dinner; that is, once we can afford such an extravagance! They say all the famous people in American history since the time of the Civil War stayed here: Grant, Sherman, Sheridan, Buffalo Bill, Charles Dickens, Mark Twain, Ambassadors, kings, princesses and every US President since Franklin Pierce in 1853 – they all stayed at the Willard! You're a lucky and privileged man!" the cabbie mouthed as if in a recitation of a tourist guide and his remarks bordering on those of familiarity.

"Well thank you, sir, that's very fascinating indeed; I'm just a New York lawyer though, so I guess my name is safe from being included on that prestigious list of personalities," Donovan replied smartly, as the cabbie removed his cap and scratched his head in bewildered ignorance of whether or not he had just been insulted by his fare.

Bill smiled and handed the cabbie a US Morgan silver dollar, which was an enormously generous tip for the short two-mile drive from the Union Station train terminal. "Anytime sir, anytime! Maybe I'll get to eat here after all one day!" the nameless cabbie smilingly remarked and forgetting his verbal decorum.

A waiting hotel attendant opened the door for him and beamed a wide smile. As the sun's gentle rays pierced the darkness of the cab's interior, before him was presented a magnificent gleaming white, limestone Grecian styled edifice that rose up from the ground to a towering ten stories in height. A tall black man dressed in a bright red uniform abbreviated with eight polished brass buttons immediately opened the cabbie's door, and offered an extended white-gloved hand to the debarking guest. "Welcome to the Willard Hotel and our nation's capital sir, my name is Henry...both myself and the entire Willard staff stand ready to assist your every need, please follow me this way to the lobby, sir," the head bell captain announced in a low baritone and polite manner that was quite the opposite of the familiar manners presented by the cabbie.

"Hello sir, my name is James, the Willard Hotel Register, and may I inquire as to your name and reservations please?" a middle aged and slightly balding white man, smiling, inquired of his new guest.

"Yes, the name is Donovan, William Donovan Esquire... my friend, John O'Brien was to have made reservations for me, I believe," William pronounced in a short, definitive business-like reply.

The hotel front desk clerk smiled, as his long fingers rifled swiftly through a neatly scribed listing of journal entries, which was arranged by the name of the guest, dates of the reservation and the reservation sponsor. The Willard Hotel lobby was the epitome of refinement and luxurious taste. The visitor's eyes became bedazzled by the rich light caramel and gold coloured paint, silk wallpaper and cream-coloured marble columns. A small forest of potted lush green palm trees adorned the lobby and hallway, giving one the impression of closeness to nature amid opulent human-crafted splendour. Salmon and plum floral pattern silk chairs and sofas filled the two storey, vaulted lobby atrium area, further presenting the décor of exclusiveness and pomp. Ornate and high-density stitch Persian silk-wool rugs in alternating patterns of gold and maroon furnished the finishing touch to the décor and one's feet almost sank a quarter-inch into the lush carpeting.

"Ah yes, Mr Donovan, here it is, but it seems that the reservation is annotated differently from that which you have described," the hotel front desk clerk added. A puzzled look came over Bill Donovan's usually placid complexion. The desk clerk saw the distressed look on Mr Donovan's face and he was quick to dispel any anxiety. "Oh my apologies, sir, you should not be disturbed at all, it's just that the reservation sponsor is listed as, my goodness, pardon my expression, the Rockefeller Foundation, expenses paid-in-full and the reservation date is indefinite; this is very interesting and very extravagant – however, given the name of Rockefeller, naturally there's absolutely no question at all, sir!" exclaimed the gleeful desk clerk. He and everyone in America knew that John D Rockefeller was the richest man in the world and that his Foundation was unequalled in wealth and prestige, so anything that Mr Donovan wanted was to be at his mere request.

"Yes, that is very interesting and a bit strange too! I'll find out more later, but right now I'd like to go to my room, freshen-up and perhaps take a quick nap," Donovan remarked as he made the obligatory signature in the hotel register as proof of his arrival.

"Of course, anything you say, Mr Donovan and you'll be staying in the Executive suite – it's one of our most opulent and expensive and it overlooks Lafayette Square and the US Treasury building and part of the South Lawn of the Executive Mansion," the positively agitated front desk clerk announced proudly as he conveniently snapped his finger and a dark grey suited bellman appeared to take Mr Donovan's coat and suitcase to the 10th floor suite. He handed the bellman a generous 50-cent tip and closed the door to the suite. The 1,000 square foot room was fit for a king; in fact, most Americans had their entire extended families living under less spacious conditions, not to mention the newly installed electricity system, central heating, hot and cold running water and the latest modern marvel, the telephone. The furniture was classic American colonial, subdued and elegant with furnishings in American walnut and New England honey maple. Having been awake since 4:30 am and having half slept on the noisy train, Donovan had little appreciation for the ornate surroundings; he unpacked his clothing and took a leisurely relaxing shower. He made a quick call back to his Buffalo office and to his wife Ruth. Sitting down upon the soft inviting bed, he grabbed a pillow and was immediately fast asleep. He slept for three blissful hours.

The dreamy slumber was all too soon rudely interrupted, as the annoying intrusion of the ringing telephone brought forth a shrill ringing tone that could neither be squelched or ignored without human intervention. Slowly and with hesitation, Bill got up from the seductive comfort repose of the soft bed. "Hello, who is it please?" he grumbled back into the telephone receiver, still in a half-conscious state.

"Well it sounds as if the sandman has visited you a bit early in the day, huh Bill, in case you haven't already guessed, it's John O'Brien, your Columbia Law school pal. I guess I woke you up, but hey old buddy, its 3:30 pm and the day is burning away. How about I come by in an hour and see you?" the old friend cajoled in a cheerful tone.

"Well John, sure, but what is this all about? I mean the cryptic letters asking for my help on some vague project and now I suspect you're involved somehow with the Rockefellers! What gives here, old buddy? I mean, I just left my law partner and wife on the most flimsy excuses that I have ever given to anyone to come down here and visit you! So are you going to let me in on your little secret, John?" Donovan spouted out as much in naked inquiry as also in a polite demand.

"You're right, Bill, absolutely spot-on, I have been vague, but this matter is something that I had to speak with you about in-person, so how about it? Our meeting was scheduled for later this evening, but I had to move our meeting up a bit. See you in the lobby in a hour sharp then!" O'Brien requested in a friendly manner.

"Sure, old buddy; after all, I'm at your mercy and in a strange town – besides what else do I have to do today! One hour in the lobby it is!"

Donovan placed down the heavy telephone apparatus. He took the hour to order a pot of strong hot coffee and some pastry from the kitchen via the room service menu; he needed a strong cup of stimulus and some light subsistence. He riffled through the complimentary copy of the Washington Post newspaper morning edition. The pot of hot coffee and relaxation rejuvenated his spirits. He took out his spare black single-breasted cashmere suit with matching vest, a dark blue four-in-hand tie and a clean white shirt. He washed his face and shaved again to remove any afternoon face hair shadows. He splashed on some Old Bay spice scented after-shave lotion. He looked at his watch; the time had flown – it was almost time to meet his old university friend. Again his curiosity was aroused by this mysterious meeting and its shrouded purpose. All this smacked of intrigue and Bill hated such things; he was a down to earth type of man, who both thought and spoke his mind directly. Still friends were friends.

The Willard's lobby was as good a place as any to spend a pleasant afternoon and wait for an old acquaintance. He sat quietly in a comfortable deep-cushioned leather chair, which spied out the lobby entrance to quickly spot his friend; he did not want to place anyone in an awkward situation of eyeing-up a room in the desperate search for a friend. He hoped the past ten years since law school had been visually kind to both of their eyes. A tall, slim, well-built man about six feet tall entered the Willard lobby. He took off his black fedora hat to reveal a thick head of jet-black hair, his eyes were large and friendly, 'smiling', as the Irish termed these 'smiling eyes'. The two men recognized one another instantly, even after ten years and across the massive hotel lobby; the years had indeed been kind to both men. They shook hands and embraced one another briefly.

"Hello Bill! It's been a long time since Columbia! You look great, Bill; I see that Ruth's cooking has not yet spoiled your athletic former bachelor frame!" John O'Brien spoke flatteringly to his friend.

Bill smiled back with a perfect, full-smile grin. "John, it's been far too long, you look like you're still playing half-back in college. I hear that you became quite a successful and wealthy man with the big Robber Baron companies!" Donovan replied in a manner designed to flush-out his present position.

John O'Brien drew back slightly and became a bit more serious. "Well Bill, I'm working for the Rockefeller Foundation the past few years, it's the reason why I contacted you, Bill!"

Donovan was a bit perplexed and he stated his feelings plainly. "That's fine, John, but you did not have to bring me all the way down to Washington,

DC – after all the Rockefeller Foundation is located in NYC!" he charged and still somewhat agitated about being kept in the dark about their meeting.

John O'Brien anxiously looked away at his Hamilton gold pocket watch; he seemed to be carefully calculating the time. He looked back up at his friend again. "It's a fine sunny early spring day: how about we go for a short walk and further discuss the future proposal that I have for you, Bill?"

Donovan nodded in positive agreement; the two men put on their top coats and fedoras, as they walked out in the middle of the mild late afternoon day. John led the way as the two men walked at a very moderate pace. O'Brien checked his watch every few minutes, of which the eagle-eyed Donovan took note, but decided wisely to say nothing; he preferred to let the situation develop. Everyone in Washington DC whether they be male or female, gentlemen or worker, on leisure or actively employed, were attired in their finest clothes, hats adorned the heads of women and men alike and rudeness and street crime were vestiges for the more cloistered inner recesses of the city.

"I know that you are a very successful lawyer in up-state New York, Bill, but what exactly do you think about the world Bill? I mean things like the economy and the war in Europe?" O'Brien asked quite bluntly and unexpectedly.

"Funny you should ask me that, John – that same question arose between a stranger on the Royal Blue and myself this very morning! My opinion is the same now as it was this morning: I think the United States needs to be watchful over affairs in Europe and ensure these do not spill over onto our shores or interests. However, I firmly believe that until we are physically threatened, we should maintain our isolation and mind our own business. Our wars should remain our own affair and so let Europe's wars be those of Europe's affairs!" Donovan concluded without hesitation or evasion.

O'Brien thought on these words quietly for a few minutes, pondering the implications carefully. He smiled and patted Donovan firmly on the back of his coat. "Bill, that's great, a logical and honest answer spoken as a practical man and not some flunky lawyer, lobbyist or politician, of which in this town there is an over-abundance." O'Brien admired his friend's honest words that were remarkably simple and clear to understand; there was no grey-area or middle-ground when his friend Bill Donovan spoke. Bill too was glad to see his old friend, but still puzzled by the summons. Once again O'Brien looked nervously down at his watch. Without warning, O'Brien picked up the walking pace in silent determination as if he had a strict schedule to keep. They had walked about two city blocks at a brisk pace and Bill was prepared to interject and inquire about the purpose of their still vague meeting. Suddenly O'Brien stopped in his quick stride, and Bill followed his lead.

"Well Bill, we're here! Don't be nervous!" O'Brien spoke out loudly to his bewildered friend.

"Just exactly is this 'where' to which you are mysteriously referring to, John? Nervous about what exactly?" Donovan replied anxiously and at his wits' end at this boondoggle of a meeting. O'Brien broadly smiled and pointed his right arm directly in front of them. Towering in front of them was the majestic Executive Mansion commonly known to the public as the White House to most Americans. "John, that's the White House, by God! You must be crazy, John! We can't go in there; good grief we'll get arrested! Besides, you work for the Rockefeller Foundation and I'm just a lawyer from Buffalo, New York. Just what in the dickens is going on here, John?" Donovan shouted frantically as the two men approached the fenceless mansion that had some farm animals treading on the front lawn. The two men approached a small, non-distinct white masonry structure from which a tall, well-built civilian gentleman appeared with a humourless face. Bill correctly suspected that this gentleman was a member of the US Secret Service, which protected the executive mansion since the days of the assassinated President William McKinley in 1901 over a decade earlier.

"Good day, gentlemen, please state your names, business affiliation and the party sponsoring your visit today at the Executive Mansion?" the emotionless agent stated sternly and carefully eyed up the two gentlemen to assure a visual check as to their sanity and intentions. Since President McKinley's assassination, the White House was no longer generously open to any citizen desiring to meet with the President of the United States; now visiting guests needed a valid reason and a person to sponsor the visit.

"Yes sir, I am Mr John Lord O'Brien of the Rockefeller Foundation and this is my friend Mr William Donovan, Esquire – we have an official appointment for 4:45 pm please."

Donovan was in obvious shock. The agent picked up the telephone and made a phone call to another party in the mansion. It was obvious that O'Brien's continued checking of the time was intended to precisely plan their arrival at the White House at the appointed hour, yet the purpose of their meeting and his role in any meeting was completely baffling to Donovan.

"You are both on time and expected, gentlemen; please proceed to the side door of the mansion. Someone will meet you and escort you to the meeting room," the agent replied as both men walked along a modest gravel walk-path that led to one of the side entrances to the Executive Mansion.

For the first time in his life, William Donovan was both speechless and profoundly impressed. Whatever his friend John O'Brien had planned, it was indeed big, very big indeed. Donovan now started to appreciate the mysteriousness and secrecy that engulfed his friend's strange invitation, to include the perplexing location of Washington, DC. This meeting by its mere location of being conducted in the Presidential Executive Mansion automatically implied something that involved the US Government at the very apex of its power. Being a wise and observant man who kept his counsel to himself, Donovan said nothing and observed all.

"Right this way, gentlemen! May I take your coats and hats please?" a middle-aged, well-mannered black valet greeted them warmly as two more burly looking white gentlemen in dark suits and the same serious-looking faces observed the two guests carefully. 'More Secret Service agents,' Bill thought to himself.

Another black valet in a finely tailored formal morning cutaway suit greeted O'Brien and Donovan. "Messers O'Brien and Donovan, please accompany me, this way please," the valet instructed in a crusty southern accented mellow voice, as he led the two men down ornate hallways decorated also in adorning potted palm plants that accented the ornate rooms with a touch of green nature in much the same decorative style as the Willard Hotel. Numerous paintings of past US Presidents and American historical events graced the hallways of the mansion. The two visitors said nothing to one another. They were escorted down several corridors that were devoid of people; however, their every move was being shadowed at precisely three paces behind them by the ever-watchful and stealthy muscular Secret Service agents. The white silk-gloved valet came to a plain white coloured door and knocked exactly three times. A male voice was clearly discerned to utter, "Come in please!" The White House usher turned and stood erect as Donovan and O'Brien opened the door and walked slowly through the doorway. The usher discreetly closed the door behind them. The two Secret Service agents remained outside the door should any emergency or situation so arise, even if so remote was this possibility, the US Secret Service maintained its professional decorum as the 'Silent Service'.

The two men had been brought to one of the more private and publically unknown rooms located on the first floor of the Executive Mansion and directly adjacent to the south portico area. Unofficially known as the 'Billiard Room', it had been re-designed by President Teddy Roosevelt some few years earlier as a place of relaxation and private meetings for the US President and his guests. The room was lit with the soft golden glow of incandescent lighting and the fireplace was lit to provide for both heating and theatrics of the moment. It was discovered over the years that visitors relaxed at meetings in which the atmosphere was casual and inviting. John O'Brien and Bill Donovan stood silently in the archway of the white painted, ornately carved door arc; the 30' by 26' room had a huge, ornate billiard table with a green felt covering, while two hand-made Tiffany overhead lamps provided ample and focused lighting onto the pool table surface. From the dispersion of the billiard balls, it was apparent that the two men occupying the room had been at play for a period of time. There were only two men present in the room, both were middle-aged, one looked to be in his early forties, the other man with the wire-rimmed glasses, with grey hair appeared to be in his late-fifties or early sixties. The older gentleman was dressed in a three-piece, grey pin-stripe suit, while the younger man was attired in a double-breasted black suit of perfect fit. The older man was hunched over the billiard table and he had just made a miss of placing the number 3 ball in a corner pocket. He looked up and smiled at the two visitors standing innocuously in the doorway.

"Ah well I guess that I'll never make it as a pool shark, I had better stick to politics! Ah hello there! Herbert, it seems as if our visitors have arrived! Welcome gentlemen, please come on in!", the older man exclaimed with a faint smile, as he placed down his pool cue and walked toward his two visitors and extended his right arm in customary social protocol manner. "Hello gentlemen, I'm President Woodrow Wilson and over there is Mr Herbert Hoover and you two gentlemen are John Lord O'Brien of the Rockefeller Foundation and his Columbia University lawyer friend, Mr William Donovan of Buffalo, New York!" the President warmly exclaimed and obviously knowing the background of each man from sources not verbally advertised.

"Welcome to the White House Billiard Room, gentlemen. May I interest either of you in a game of billiards, a drink or perhaps a fine cigar?" the President cordially invited of his two visibly reserved guests who were mindful of the personage and office of the President of the United States – neither man wanted to display any social indiscretion; both men politely gave a soft, reserved 'no thank you, Mr President'. President Wilson immediately set to place both men at ease; it seemed that every guest that came to the White House was like a lamb going to the slaughter. A man of refinement and reserved manners, the President sought to place both men at ease.

"Hello my name is Mr Herbert Hoover. It is a pleasure to meet you gentlemen!" the younger man announced as he too smiled and extended his hand out to greet the Messers O'Brien and Donovan.

"Well gentlemen, I for one am going to have a cocktail, an aged American rye whiskey and ice, please join me!" Wilson stated as a matter of order rather than request. The President knew that people acted best when they were relaxed and he wanted everyone relaxed for the discussion at hand. He prepared each drink personally and handed each man about half a glass of fine aged American rye. "Here's to the United States of America!" the President toasted as each man was obliged to raise his glass and partake of at least a sip of whiskey. Bill Donovan was almost a teetotaller, yet he too took a slight sip of the light amber coloured whiskey, which tasted somewhat bitter to his virgin palate. He did not wish to offend his hosts and barely any alcohol was consumed by him as he merely let the drink touch his lips, but he did not ingest it.

"Let's sit down, gentlemen. My experience has instructed me that people talk best when they are seated and I want to speak with you, gentlemen, about some serious, vital US Government business," President Wilson pronounced as all four gentlemen took their places on the two multi-coloured silk sofas that were arrayed next to the idyllically lit fireplace.

"Well now, gentlemen, I know that you are wondering the reason why private citizens of this great country are being asked to meet with their Commander in Chief! Your backgrounds are quite diverse and commercially successful in their own rights, I dare say. Mr Hoover is a successful engineer and has a proven reputation for large scale management and organization, he's self-motivated and a self-made man to boot, a multi-millionaire in fact!" The President thus unintentionally encouraged Hoover to volunteer his own bombastic remark: "I think a man who does not make a million dollars before his thirtieth birthday is a financial failure." Bill Donovan received this remark in quiet, subdued rejection as being very ill-mannered and inappropriate to the discussion at hand. Calmly the President ignored Hoover's wise-crack remark; instantly he gave Hoover a jaunted look of disapproval. However, before Wilson could speak further, Donovan fired off a verbal salvo at Mr Hoover's bad manners and air of social superiority.

"Well then, I hope that I'm not too big of a failure, gentlemen, I'm just a working man! I hope that my humble presence is indeed worthy for this mysterious summons," Bill Donovan immediately retorted in reply to Mr Hoover's insensitive remark giving an indication of Bill Donovan's very middle-class status and quick acumen.

With Donovan's remark, it was now Mr Hoover's turn to feel

embarrassed. The President interjected to once again to act as the ice-breaker for the tension between the two men and he tried to move forward the conversation. "Mr O'Brien is a highly successful corporate lawyer and a esteemed member of the recently formed and singularly wealthy Rockefeller Foundation; in fact, I have to thank Mr O'Brien for recommending to Mr Hoover the name of Mr William Donovan for this mission that I have in mind, gentlemen," the President remarked. The President then went on to mention the last member and least known member of this select meeting: "Finally everyone, Mr Donavon is a man of discretion, honesty and a keen analytical mind. That which I am about to propose, and request, is that I need your personal best efforts and skills in helping my office and the United States of America. It will be a mission of self-sacrifice, family hardship and strictly on a volunteer basis!" Woodrow Wilson stated more in a form of a definitive sentence than an outright inquisitive type of a query, yet each man knew exactly of which the President had spoken. He wanted the time and talents of each man present. Bill felt both humbled and elated at the President's recognition of his background and personage; he knew that he was in privileged company well beyond his meagre accomplishments in life thus far.

"I, for one, would be honoured to help you and the United States in any way possible!" Mr Hoover remarked first and earnestly.

"Count me in too!" Bill Donovan and John O'Brien added in unison and also nodding their heads in positive affirmation.

The President knew from their personal and immediate reactions that he had picked the right men for this job: they were all young, vigorous, intelligent and of independent mind, not the run-of-the-mill 'yes men' type who prolifically flooded the corridors of power in Washington, DC. It was a refreshing sight to see for the over-burdened President who now wore the years of his Presidency as a greying, burdensome crown upon his head.

"Thank you, gentlemen, I knew that I had selected the right people for this mission!" the President replied, as everyone was on the edge of their seats in anticipation of more information. It was forthcoming immediately. "My loyal opponents in Congress seem to believe that the war is a very good financial thing for the neutral United States' business interests. They contend that we get the best of both worlds – continued peace and plenty of money from the Europeans who spill their resources and riches and we reap their money like greedy opportunists. I realize that many Europeans benefited from this same type of war commerce during our Civil War; however, I for one, think that the United States is made of higher moral fabric than mere money making off the dead young men of Europe – although JP Morgan strongly opposes my sheepish-type views." There was utter silence as all ears in the Billiard Room hinged on the President's every word. He was a wise man as bespoke his thoughts into seemingly extemporaneous words.

Wilson continued with his preparatory remarks. "Once upon a time, only a generation ago, Morgan might have been right in his views, but in this new 20th Century the Gilded Age and the advent of the great Industrial Revolution have brought about a dynamic change in world affairs today, in which neither the United States or any other nation in the world can remain isolated by either sheer desire or blissful ignorance. The world has become smaller due to advances in transportation and communications; it is impossible to remain unfettered from the affairs of one's neighbours situated across the expanse of mere oceans. No, gentlemen, the world is getting much too small to afford the United States the luxury to sit idle in its rich cocoon of continental isolation, to only remain blissfully ignorant of the affairs in Europe. As a minimum we must know from a personal, unfiltered perspective, the true state of affairs on all sides of this conflict before we can make realistic cognitive plans for our country just in case trouble comes courting at our doors. We must be prepared and to be prepared one must have knowledge and to have this knowledge I need to have my own people on the ground in Europe working directly on my behalf. This means no political hacks or office holder types! Also prominent named men cannot be employed, as they draw undue attention and receive filtered words! I need to have and trust non-political emissaries, men of private self-made success – and thus your requested presence here today."

All in attendance were mesmerized by President Wilson's keen and honest appraisal of the world situation. It was sobering for the men to hear this from their national leader. All three men were honoured by President Wilson's summons.

"How can we assist you, Mr President?" John O'Brien spoke out in earnest inquiry and as a deflection to Hoover's continued dominance of the conversation.

The President merely smiled and drove into the heart of his inquiry. "From a pragmatic sense, we need to take care of our US citizens, who, through no fault of their own, have been caught suddenly off-guard by this European war and who now remain stranded in various countries throughout Europe and who are in very desperate and deteriorating conditions, as witnessed by the various diplomatic cables that I am receiving from all my Ambassadors and Ministers across the continent.

"First, we need to get our stranded citizens out of these European countries and back to America, gentlemen. Second, I also want to assist those starving European civilians who, through no fault of their own, have had the bad luck of being either invaded or are now under forced occupation of the Austro-Hungarian Empire military forces. The British blockade is working so successfully that basic foodstuffs, medical items and especially grains are being cut-off from the people that need these items the most. Mass starvation of the civilian populace in Europe is becoming a reality, as the most fertile cropland goes untilled and the German military takes first priority of all food production. As an American I cannot in good conscience sit back in the fat of the land and merely let those innocent people in Europe starve to death. In Belgium alone, there's 10 million starving civilians; across the rest of Europe tens of millions more; and if history proves one-thing, gentlemen, it is that hungry people breed revolution and social change. This is often the change that we do not welcome and of a nature which is more destructive than starvation itself. As a Christian I cannot allow this mass starvation to become a stain on my soul. It is a problem that morally and pragmatically as the President, I can positively influence to a successful conclusion."

There was utter silence in the White House Billiard room; everyone was humbled by President Wilson's infallible reasoning and moral justification.

Bill Donovan had lost all of his previous passivity and his pragmatic personality emerged having been inspired by the President's remarks. "Mr President, may I ask exactly how this mission is to be accomplished? Will we have diplomatic cover or do we do this as private citizens?" Donovan inquired.

Wilson smiled in anticipation of the question. "Good questions, Bill and that is the reason for the presence of Mr John O'Brien here. Through the good graces and auspices of the John D Rockefeller Foundation, the US War Relief Commission has been established to assist the starving nations of Europe with United States foodstuffs. As a neutral country and with the world renowned Rockefeller philanthropic name, this is a perfect canard for my other mission, gentlemen."

"Other missions, Mr President?" Hoover interjected, looking confused.

President Wilson continued to further elaborate. "Yes, this is the third part of this mission. I want Messers Hoover and Donovan to act as my personal 'observers' and emissaries concerning the conduct of the war in Europe to include all aspects of this conflict. You are both being sent on a Grand European Tour by your Commander-in-Chief to make visits to every country in Europe that is engaged, both directly and peripherally, to this insane war. I want all information, analysis and evaluation of the political, military, social, technology, business and economic events happening across the continent of Europe! I need information on all these tenets of the war and from all parties waging war, Allied and Central Powers alike! I cannot take a future policy stance for our nation, especially our potential war participation, if I remain ignorant in these matters. Only a fool makes decisions based on willful ignorance! Believe me, gentlemen, none of my political opponents or the American public are fools; they will both demand and I must be prepared to give them, the reasons for our continued neutrality or for any decision for taking a side in this war. I will not risk the blood and treasure of this nation in a bloody foreign war that is predicated on faulty information or that of rampant newspaper headlines that spurt forth various rants of 'yellow journalism', as was the case in our last war with Spain! I made a pledge to the American people to stay out of this European conflict and I mean to keep that promise too, unless US interests are directly threatened."

"Excuse me, sir, what, may I inquire, is going to be the roles of Mr Hoover and myself in this affair, Mr President?" Bill Donovan quickly cut to the chase.

"My, you are a sharp lawyer of deserved repute, Bill. You get to the point neat and fast without talking around an idea! Quite unusual for a young man, very unusual in a town like Washington DC too! Thank you for getting to the heart of the matter." Mr Wilson smiled back in a cajoling tone.

"Well, here it is, gentlemen," the President continued in a monotone voice to his captivated guests. "Mr Hoover is an excellent businessman, engineer and organizer – he is my hand-picked man to lead the War Relief Commission under the Rockefeller Foundation charitable trust. While you, Mr Donovan, are a highly skilled lawyer, noted for his skills in observation, information analysis and unbiased judgment. I want 'Wild Bill' here to be my unofficial intelligence gathering man. You'll work under Mr Hoover, but make your reports directly to me with a courtesy copy naturally to Mr Hoover. There is no competition in this mission gentleman! Mr Donovan's role will be of more limited duration than Mr Hoover's and I'll personally recall 'Wild Bill' after an appropriate amount of time. Oh, Bill is also a Captain in the US Army National Guard, so this background will make him especially useful in this mission from a military perspective as well.

"This mission is strictly 'unofficial', yet vitally important. With our neutrality at stake, I do not want any open US Government involvement or bureaucracy involved; personal emissaries work best in this type of mission. I'll back-brief the Secretary of State on the general aspects of your mission and I'll have him transmit the various Embassy and Consulate cables informing all my Ambassadors and Ministers to afford both of you the utmost of cooperation as my personal representative on a unspecified confidential mission on my behalf," the intellectual US President concluded in a scholarly summary.

"Our citizens need help getting out of Europe! We need to get food to the starving neutral European countries! I need good analysis and intelligence on this war! That's it in a nutshell, gentlemen; you will need to start quickly on this! Any more questions, gentlemen?" Wilson concluded matter-of-factly.

The silence was palpable; all three men knew the challenges and sacrifices implied and so amply stated in the President's charge to them, yet out of all the American citizens at his disposal, he chose these three men to implement his plan – they were helpless to refuse. The President rose and the three men knew instinctively that the meeting was concluded. The implementation details were to be communicated through various aides and other entities as needed. The world of 1916 moved in a more intimate, if not more efficient manner than those of succeeding decades as so revealed through the long focused mirror of hindsight.

Wilson shook all of their hands before issuing a final salutation: "Thank you once again, gentlemen. I hope to be getting progress reports from you all shortly. May God bless you and your success!"

As the men left the Billiard room, a personal aide of the President greeted them; each man was handed an envelope that contained various contact information and a summary sheet of various US personages in various European countries, to include US Embassy and Consulate names. Other information and details would be funnelled and communicated through the auspices of the Rockefeller Foundation and John O'Brien became the de facto communication link with the White House. Once overseas, confidential communications and periodic messages were to be sent through contacting the US Embassy or Consulate in each country in Europe and utilizing the tried and true secure messaging protocol of diplomatic courier services. The international telegraphy system was not deemed totally secure enough for the transmission of every national secret by any country of the time. Telegraph messages were encoded and sent at the peril of the telegram being intercepted and deciphered; it was a transmission type that was fast and vulnerable. Diplomatic couriers were slow, but very secure. Also, any compromise of a diplomatic pouch, although rare, could quickly and efficiently be evaluated and damage mitigation implemented quietly. It was also the more gentlemanly means of communication, although such communications took days to reach the intended audience.

★ ★ ★ ★ ★ ★ ★ ★ ★ ★ ★

# Chapter 2:
# A New Century Awakens

*"It was a singular war in the sense that no military experiences
gained before it contributed substantially on the conduct of the
strategies employed and any resulting war experiences gleamed
from it were to be hopelessly irrelevant for the future"*

The new twentieth century was barely over a decade old, yet in this
remarkable short time it had witnessed the birth of the airplane,
motorized transportation, dominance of the telephone, and the
predominance of the modern manufacturing plants. While the United
States was comfortably nestled in the cocoon of both its geographical and
political isolationism, the modern European nation-states emerged as a new
entity. Europe threw off the shackles of laborious, feudal agriculture and
embraced the new manufacturing paradigm. Europe was anxiously looking
outward for growth and added wealth – inevitably toward their respective
neighbouring countries and under-developed foreign colonies. The sources
of this European-wide nationalism was a potpourri of growing wealth,
the industrial revolution, exponential population growth, agricultural
efficiencies, the rise of modern transportation and the classic rivalries among
disparate countries.

Aside from the Franco-Prussian War in the 1870s, there had been
relative calm in Europe since the defeat of Napoleon at Waterloo. France,
which had previously been the main protagonist on the continent, was now
replaced by a new entity – the German state. Formed from a loose alliance
of principalities, Bismarck united the states into a single nation-state with
an Emperor, Kaiser Wilhelm I. In the four generations since Napoleon's
defeat, Germany was now the country that others had begun to fear, for its
military-oriented Prussian and titled land baron aristocrats, referred to as
'Junkers', who were oriented toward nationalism – and nationalism often
breeds the preparation for war and sometimes even the conduct of war itself.
Just as the British noble elder sons went into politics, the elder sons of the
German Junkers went into the military; over time the Prussian-German
military became an elite which dominated all aspects of German society.

The main Empires on the continent were the Austrian-Hungarian Habsburg dynasty and the ancient Russian Empire. Great Britain, a mighty empire in her own right, was not traditionally continental-oriented; instead her power was maritime and her interests were the far-flung colonial vistas such as India, China, Indonesia and Hong Kong. In the far recesses of Asia Minor, the Ottomans ruled the Middle East and Arab peoples under a mighty hard hand from the Empire's capital in Istanbul. To these grand old Empires, Germany was as a mere upstart young child, yet that which it lacked in ancient lineage, Germany more than aptly compensated for in nationalism and fervent militarism.

As the European countries so distrusted one another out of historical discord and for the pragmatic purpose of self-security, the nations each created and entered into a series of inter-locking treaties that offered mutual support to one another if one country was attacked by a belligerent country. The ironic, if not sad aspect to these interlocking treaties, was that most of the countries signing these treaties were, in fact, not historically or overtly friendly with their aligned partners; it was all so much like a pre-arranged marriage, a phenomena quite natural to European heads of state for countless centuries. It was all such fanciful and intertwined 'paper statecraft' and no country actually believed that in this modern age, the actual occurrence of a large-scale war was possible. Yet the old ways of thinking and acting for the nobility and commoner alike were quickly fading into the recesses of history, though ignorant be all parties to this reality. The kings and generals proclaimed that all wars henceforth were to be short, quick and decisive – this was only logical given the industrial and economic developments that had taken place in the last one hundred years and long wars were a hazard to business success and prosperity. Wars had to be short and decisive for practical nationalistic resource purposes; long wars were impractical and cost prohibitive. This was the reasoning of the theorists, yet theories needed to be placed into experimentation for verification and no one in Europe wanted to be the 'first man' to declare war. Yet the hopes and desires of aged statesmen were often trumped by the realities that could not hoped to be imagined. No one had seriously bothered to consult the advancements being realized in the fields of science, technology and the modern manufacturing bases to appreciate that the aggregate and convergence of such fields of endeavour could lead to the exact opposite of short, limited warfare. Ignorance was a mighty and most prolific master to ignore, yet it was an almost innate trait characterized within the species, which could better master the pragmatic fields of science and technology than the inherent flawed proclivities for self-deceit, death and destruction.

Modern education had made Europe's population literate to the stage where most children attended eight years of formal state-sponsored education, which resulted in children being able to read, write and perform basic mathematics; thus a middle class of workers emerged to resource the modern industrial base, save for that of the Empire of Russia, which was so vast and diverse that only those living in the urban centres had any semblance of a modern education. As basic discoveries in science led to a fundamental understanding of physics, chemistry and electricity, an industrial base was rapidly built upon these basic sciences. Soon technology and mechanical engineering were applied to communications and transportation and new industries were born. Better health care was emerging based on medical science and populations grew rapidly and more healthy. Agriculture was transformed through new fertilizers from the chemical plants, more food could successfully be grown and in greater abundance than any time previously.

The Industrial Revolution and concept of mass production resulted in a great migration from rural farms to urban centres, where the location of factories took root due to the lines of transportation, communications and modern finance. Soon there was a steady and plentiful supply of food and clothing, along with the growth of small shops and merchants to cater to these workers. A new labour middle class emerged for the first time in history. Yet all classes of society were rewarded by the dramatic changes, even the poor, who were now taken care of through a budding system of church and state sponsored programmes that provided for the minimal human requirement of food, shelter and drink. More resources translated into more Europeans rising out of poverty and rural farms into a solid, productive middle-class that rewarded skill, labour and innate ability over noble blood and inheritance.

The social and political changes were knocking at the door of modernity as well, albeit at a pace slightly slower than the march of science and technology. This was being driven by the triumphant power of a swelling, more healthy populace; agricultural emancipation from the land cultivation; and finally mass education that lifted the veil of ignorance and which levied equality of intellect among the classes. The landed nobles and gentry classes were about to collapse, torn apart by the modern scientific and industrial world that pierced their entrenched world order. No longer was the estate a refuge from slavery of the land; the industrial revolution had now made the cities and factories a haven for wages and a standard of living that far surpassed the security and splendid isolation of the landed estate-tenant relationship. For society as a whole, this new revolution also meant that large standing armies could be fielded without great loss in manufacturing productivity, as more machines could be added to replace draftee and volunteer nationalistic armies. When the men were drafted, women could replace them.

Unbeknownst to the national leaders was the reality that the limited wars of the Napoleon era had already been replaced with a modern industrial model that could furnish an almost limitless supply of material and human fodder for the potential slaughter. The lessons of the American Civil War some fifty years earlier was a harbinger of things to come, yet any lessons from it had either never been learned or else these had long since been consigned to the musty bookshelves in the library. Although all nations prudently kept war plans in hand for their national security, all nations had envisioned and planned for a rapid, short, limited duration war, yet this predicated that the element of perfection was not discounted. Yet in all wars, the best laid plans became muted upon the opening salvos of the rifles and cannons. The folly of their imperfect planning resulted in four long bloody years of muddy trench warfare in which many millions perished.

With each battle and campaign, the invested costs of the war for every nation became more intractable; no nation wanted to concede that their young soldiers had died for either a worthless or non-victorious war. The solution of this false illusion was to continue the war, have more soldiers die in vain and hope that victory was right around the corner. Failure reinforced failure. As illustrated in the American Civil War and the recent Russian-Japanese War, technology had changed war forever; however, neither politician nor general could hope to appreciate or understand the novelties of the new warfare. The Great War became one of the few wars in history where the defence was king and the offence was pointless. It was a singular war in the sense that no military experiences gained before it contributed substantially to the conduct of the strategies employed and any resulting war experiences gleamed from it were to be hopelessly irrelevant for the future. In modern terms, it was to be categorized as a catastrophic systems failure, in which the war problems became too great or unacceptable for those in power to solve and for which there were no viable devices to halt disastrous actions once a decision had been made and events were set forth into intractable motion. The dynamics for the way the war was fought, the intensity level and duration of the conflict and the huge numbers of causalities, all combined to make this a 'different kind of war'.

Yet all this lay in the future, for everything seemed well in the Europe of 1913-14 – there was prosperity, no mass starvation and relatively stable, but changing social conditions. There may have been loose talk on the far fringes of society in some intellectual circles about Marx, Engels and the new political system known as communism, yet talk was all that there was except for the boiling ferment in the remote Russian Empire. All remained calm, for there was nothing to provide the catalyst for socio-political change for only wars and revolution breed such unwelcome beasts. The powerful rulers and their ministers believed that it was absurd for the modern, enlightened European nation to even consider going to war with one of their neighbours. Yet they failed to conceive that even neighbours have disputes over seemingly ridiculous and petty issues. Woe to those who live in the times when that which they either think or believe becomes irrelevant due to the intractable power of external factors. Slowly over time, however, the complacency of peace produced a distortion and distant fable-like perception of actual war; as peace continued to prevail across Europe, several generations of leaders and generals had come to forget or even experience the first-hand horrors of a massive continental war and its devastating effects. In paintings, poems and stories – war became glamorized to an almost universal extent, with the colourful collage of images depicting charging cavalry, handsome sabre-wielding officers and sterile looking battlefields. War and battle became a romantic thing of the imagination and the landed gentry estate drawing rooms.

\* \* \* \* \* \* \* \* \* \* \* \*

The axiom that prosperous nations do not go to war against each other continued to infect the minds and attitudes of citizen and statesmen alike. National economic prosperity, instead of breeding contentment, produced the opposite effect: it propagated arrogance, jealousy and naivety. 'If having enough land and resources was good, then having more was even better!' 'If my neighbouring country had greater wealth, it is better to deprive them of it and take it for myself' were some of the sentiments that arose in a form of twisted, perverted Darwinian survival.

Nationalism was in full swing and the royal heads of Europe did nothing to dissuade either their neighbours or themselves of nationalistic ego and chest beating. The honour of a country was paramount, as it directly reflected on the monarch and a monarch could not publically afford to be humiliated by another country, no matter how slight the offence or the particular perceived offence.

Finally, with the prolific adoption of the international telegraph and news services, nothing remained secret or local for more than a few days at best as far as European news was concerned and this meant that there was less time for logical thought and back-channel communications to take effect. Once again, technology trumped old paradigms. Newspaper headline rhetoric and inflammatory news articles like the ones issued by the American Hearst newspaper chain, served as a harbinger, and sometimes unanointed instigators, of this impending deadly new reality of a brewing war and other worthy international scandals. News became big business and small incidents were inflated beyond all proportion to the original event and if no worthy story existed then creative journalistic minds ensured that something was made to happen by either deceit or even an outright lie. The masses of a country could be stirred up into riots on the mere publication of a news headline despite the validity of the story. Yet too few of those in power realized it and those who did were dumbfounded about any way around the problem. All these innovations and changes were making the world a smaller, yet more deadly place. Nationalism and the previously unknown ability to logistically supply almost limitless war matériel that an army could consume, resulted in a situation in which there was incurred an enormous loss of life on a scale unheard of in the history of mankind.

While Europe and the entire world were making dramatic advances in science, technology, manufacturing, communications and transportation, European diplomacy was mired in the Ice Age! European diplomacy was still conducted in 'old-boy' fashion in which cables and communiqués were the primary source of function and form for trafficking official state communications. It was most plebian and most un-gentlemanly to pick-up that new fangled device called the telephone and simply speak one's mind to another equal party! If one was a noble, the entire idea of speaking directly on the telephone to another head of state was just simply alien and it simply was not to be done! Until and unless the 'old ways' proved to be insufficient, the established protocols of using ministers and bureaucrats communicating via diplomatic pouch was to be maintained. Europe danced to a tune of sweet ignorance as to the realities that were set to interrupt the seemingly peaceful music, yet a simmering subterfuge of personal ego, jealousy, ignorance, nationalism and lethargy of the dated ruling system were about to be eclipsed by the conspiring elements of modernism.

* * * * * * * * * * *

It was in this simmering crucible of political, social and economic dynamism, that The Great War origins were fatefully forged. Although the institutional changes took decades to fully ferment, it took only an unexpected political catalyst to ignite the flames of war, as a match placed to gasoline. On a quiet Sunday, June 28, 1914 the Archduke Franz Ferdinand, next in line as Emperor of the Austro-Hungarian Empire, and his wife the Duchess Sophie of Austria, were assassinated in Sarajevo and Herzegovina, Bosnia by a group of poorly organized, yet determined anarchists known as the 'Black Hand'. Europe was fractionalized by ancient nationalistic rivalries and loosely cemented by mutual, interlocking national defence treaties into a jigsaw mosaic of potential warring states and confederations. Threats to national honour and demands to restore any perceived dishonour, soon followed with lightning speed. Newspapers, rumours and vested special interest groups whipped up frenzy among the various populations. Rational debate and crafted, sober analysis were phantoms to the unfolding affair. There was no time for careful deliberations; indeed, no country really wanted to talk – they were blinded by the perceived glory of war, and in their sterile minds any war was to be fast and relatively bloodless.

As the senseless rhetoric and newspapers inflamed the public faster than the ability of diplomats to discuss and negotiate any reasonable compromises, the political system broke down and became a pawn of popular agitations. Frail politicians became unable to calm the public outcries for war. To one side were arranged the Central Powers of the Habsburg Empire: Germany, Austria, Bulgaria and Turkey. The Allied or 'Entente' Powers were composed of England, France, Italy and Russia. Europe, which had been largely at peace since the Napoleon wars, was once again at war on a more massive and terrible scale. The lights of peace were indeed being extinguished in Europe and it would be many years and millions of wasted lives before Europe would see the lights of peace again re-lit.

Germany, although technically a monarchy, was ruled increasingly as an authoritative and belligerent military autocracy, led by the Prussian leveraged German General Staff and its Junker Baron military nobles. Like an adolescent on steroids, it grew quickly and mightily without the benefit of maturity which only time can bestow. Germany sat as the new, anxious nation state in Austro-Hungary's empire crown of nations. The young German upstart nation should have been better mentored by its older neighbour Austria, but the Habsburg blood line had become old and lethargic in its leadership, so the young Teutonic nation took the initiative in statecraft and then military strategy. For the past two decades, it had slowly forged a great capital ship Navy, the German Imperial High Seas Fleet, this to rival the premier and indisputable British Royal Navy's Grand Fleet, a feat that was initiated out of the ego of the 55 year old Kaiser Wilhelm II to equally compete with and demonstrate to his friendly cousins the Tsar Nicholas II of Russia and King George V of the United Kingdom. Germany had come of age and it needed to be treated on equal terms with the other great nations of Europe. With efficiency and skill Deutschland also built a modern railway system, the main arteries that mainly transverse an east-west direction, the planning and logic for which was both industrial and military in scope. A latitudinal leveraged rail line system provided equal efficient access for heavy industrial goods among Germany's cities, while concurrently providing a world-class military transportation system that could move many tens of thousands of troops and massive tons of war material from one border of the Fatherland to the other in a matter of only a few days. This meant that Germany could theoretically fight a two-front war by transferring its troops to either its east or western borders, but only if there arose no anomalies.

Through the month of July 1914, any attempts to maintain peace had failed, most continental nations did not want peace, but to restore their national honour and abide to their interlocking treaties. Some nations like Germany even relished the idea and practice of war if only to test out long planned strategic war plans and battle tactics. There was still a chance for peace if only the Sovereigns and their ministers had the courage to react with their minds instead of their emotions, yet the royal blood of Europe was not up to this task. Weak kings and emperors listened to advisors and generals who had their own self-interests and institutions at stake, instead of their country and citizens. Any attempts at negotiations failed and by August 5, 1914, the great empires were hopelessly at war: Austria-Hungry was at war with Serbia in the Balkans; the newly minted German 'Empire' went to war with France, Britain and Russia; the Russian Empire went to war against Germany. Germany having crossed the neutral country of Belgium to which Great Britain had a treaty meant that Great Britain was obligated to act to preserve its national treaty obligations, despite having no vested continental desires or interests. With the greatest of hesitation, the British Empire declared war on Germany and de facto against Austro-Hungary.

The Ottoman Empire declared war on Britain and de facto Russia and France. The only countries to stay out of the insanity were the Nordic countries and Switzerland. As this was envisioned to be a quick war to be completed by Christmas 1914 or Easter 1915 at the latest, huge army reserve forces of all nations were brought into mobilization to make a quick end to the war. Few realized how long the war was to last and when it finally ended, few could remember or cared as to the original origins of the conflict. Ironically, the huge European armies of Reservists and later draftees ensured not a limited war, but a long and bloody one.

* * * * * * * * * * * *

The German army was most ably prepared and greatly enthusiastic for a quick, decisive war. Since the Napoleonic wars a hundred years earlier, the Prussian officer class had dominated society; when the new German state was formed, the Prussians formed the nucleus of the military upper ranks and for noble Junkers landed class, it was natural for at least one son, usually the elder one in the family, to enter lifelong military service and to carry on the lineage of the family august name which usually contained the 'von' so as to denote the geographic area of the family similar to the English landed nobles. Considerable effort of the finest German minds was devoted to the art of war and the preparation for it. The most famous Prussian and one of the greatest military theorists of all times was Major General Carl von Clausewitz, who, in the early 19th Century, codified the principles of land warfare in a series of writings that became mandatory reading for all German officers and military soldiers worldwide.

German military influence began to be felt across all social levels and institutions in Germany and it became a high mark of social status to be affiliated with the German army, if only even for service in the Army Reserves. As industry and technology progressed, these advances were immediately applied into the German military to include rapid firing machine guns, long range artillery, new explosives and propellants, modern deadly accurate long range Mauser rifles, submarines, poison gas, airplanes and zeppelins. Most efficient of all was the German military discipline and organization, the epitome of which was manifested in the elite German General Staff, which planned with mathematical precision the calculus for the future modern war. So efficient was their planning that they provided for the conduct of a two-phase war, the first part to be fought with France on the western front and the second part to be fought with Russia on the eastern front after the immediate and rapid defeat of France.

This two-front war was contingent on a precisely synchronized, rapid conquest of France in a mathematically synchronized and calculated

time-space sequence during which the German army was to invade
France through neutral Belgium and the Ardennes forest and then attack
rapidly through the northern plains of France in a large pincer movement
that moved across the northern coast and ended with a large encircling
movement behind Paris and its expected quick capitulation. This plan was
devised in 1905 and named after its chief architect General Alfred von
Schlieffen, who was Chief of the German General Staff, thus the coined
name of the Schlieffen Plan. The allowed timetable for complete execution
from the first-shot to an Armistice was carefully calculated to be a mere six
weeks. After the peaceful German occupation of Paris, the bulk of German
military forces were planned to be transported rapidly in a matter of days,
or a few weeks at most, to attack the very large and grossly inferior Russian
peasant-conscripted army, which was envisioned to fold like a house of
cards. Germany was to be the leader of Europe, a 'second Napoleonic order'
with a distinct German flavour.

Yet all hope to avoid war was not yet lost. In early August 1914, the
German Foreign Minister to Britain cabled the Kaiser to state that back-
channel discussion with Great Britain's Foreign Office and War Office
indicated that neutrality with both Britain and France could be maintained
and war avoided in the west if only Kaiser Wilhelm II provided a guarantee
to Great Britain that he would only attack Russia and not France. This was
surprising and pleasant news; Kaiser Wilhelm II had a natural penchant
toward the western powers, especially for Britain. The Kaiser welcomed this
diplomatic back-channel news – it meant that only a one front war could
be fought and this was against a very weak army: the peasant Russians. The
Kaiser's authority and monarchy was not, however, absolute in any sense
of the word and by both personality and circumstances, he was obliged to
seek the advice of his top military advisor – the head of the German General
Staff, General Helmuth von Moltke. General von Moltke was the successor to
General von Schlieffen and he knew every detail of the war plans, to include
'what could be done' and 'what could not be done'.

Kaiser Wilhelm II discussed the proposal that Germany only attack
Russia yet the old general turned cold and stoic; he pointed out to the
Kaiser that the war plans in place were so complicated and at an advanced
stage that the plan to invade Belgium and attack France was militarily and
logistically impossible to change – for the senior German Generals literally
impossible! This was an outright lie. The folly instead lay in the strategies
and perceptions of long laid plans and to change a war plan was to tempt the
Gods according to German military thinking. The stoic German Generals

were intransigent in their war plans and they could not be moved at this late date to any other viable planning alternative. So the tepid Kaiser bended to the will of his Field Marshal instead of his own judgment and he let the Schlieffen Plan continue to be implemented. The middle-aged Kaiser had not the moral courage or intellectual candour to defy the generals and Field Marshals who had devoted their entire lives to their profession of arms. The Kaiser himself had never heard a shot fired in anger and he was loath to question their 'expert' military decisions. Thus the big grey German war machine continued forward with irrepressible inertia and the war with the West was on. Oh how different history might have been if some men were made of sterner fortitude and grit. Germany now had to fight a two-front war for which it possessed insufficient military forces.

* * * * * * * * * * * *

From August through September 1914, the armies of the Central Powers carefully and quickly manoeuvred long grey-clad military troop lines of seemingly endless German and Austrian infantry units toward France; the complementary old world cavalry and modern artillery units marched westward across Europe through neutral Belgium and then into the eastern part of the French border. Their power and numbers seemed invincible to all those witness to this modern movement of an industrialized army, which could easily be kept provisioned with endless food and ammunition in no small part due to the excellent east-west railway links and the development of modern road systems. Problems, however, arose when the Central Power armies needed to cross the relatively heavy rural and agriculture areas in the northern part of France, the exact same critical ground that was outlined to be crossed and utilized by the Germans to rapidly move and outflank the Allied Forces and the capital city of Paris. The German von Schlieffen Plan overly relied upon a perfect mix of military forces, time and space for successful execution and with a two-front war, the Germans lacked sufficient soldiers to heavily weigh the offensive in their favour and any marginal disruption or halting of the offensive would doom its further advancement.

Geography, time and space cruelly colluded to place a sudden brake on the German army advances that were moving in the area northeast of Paris, a location that was well short of the desired distance outlined in the massive flanking manoeuvre directed within the von Schlieffen Plan. The German army was supposed to encircle and make a wide left flank encirclement at a great distance to the rear of the great city, however not before the city itself.

Yet the unexpected strong defence of both French and British soldiers drawn from the far corners of the British Empire known officially as the 80,000 plus strong British Expeditionary Force (BEF) and known unofficially as the 'Old Contemptibles', had stopped the German juggernaut and forced it to fight at a time and place not of its own choosing. The strong and unexpected Allied defence not only stopped the German army short of its objective of Paris, it also helped to produce the deadly defence strategy that was to become known as 'trench warfare', a military phenomena that was largely missing from the war being waged on the vast steppe and areas of eastern Europe and Russia. The German forces advanced so far and fast that their existing courier and landline communications proved woefully inadequate and the German commanders lost the command and control of their forces at all levels of echelon. Decisions were being made in complete ignorance of the true situation of both their own and that of the enemy forces; they did not know nor did they fully appreciate the exact location of their troops, nor the resistance that their forces were meeting.

No new orders could be received in time nor could new manoeuvres be properly prepared in enough time for successful execution. Outdistancing the lines of communications rendered the Germans dumb and blind. Information and events were happening faster than the information could be transmitted, received, processed and analyzed. Decisions were made at the lowest level possible and with fragmentary, incomplete and sometimes inaccurate information; this was known as the 'fog of war' and all armies experienced it to one degree or another. The front-line soldiers at the 'tip-of-the spear' of each warring nation acted exactly as they had been trained to do, namely 'when meeting enemy resistance and being outnumbered and without any higher orders' they 'dug-in' the ground which they occupied. Initially individual soldiers merely prepared small foxholes with their hands and shovels, which over time led to deeper, more elaborate 'trenches' which when connected onto other fighting positions formed a de facto elongated trench system. Any attempt to move forward by either warring side was met with the terrible slaughter of the new rapid firing and inexhaustibly ammunition-supplied machine guns and the complementary artillery ensemble of mortars, medium howitzers and heavy guns. A great mass of dead horses lay prostrated and eviscerated amid the initial battlefields in Belgium and France, as both cavalry and transport horses were efficiently slaughtered in the countless thousands, in an utter testament to immediate destruction of the 'old military' by the 'modern military'.

The reaction to these new deadly and well-supplied array of weapons resulted in even deeper and more elaborate trenches. The more extensive and elaborate the trench system became, the more offensive troops were required to overcome such a defence. With simple trenches, a two-to-one advantage in attacking or offensive troop strength was required for an attacker's success; however, with the elaborate in-depth trench preparation, a four-to-one attacking force was required; and finally with an inexhaustible trench system of many miles in depth, an attacking advantage of ten-to-one or greater was required. This level of mathematical extrapolation in modern defensive war could not be overcome by sheer force alone! Battle after battle and campaign after campaign resulted in no successful offensive operations or significant territory being gained by any warring fraction. The death toll rose into the thousands, then tens of thousands and finally millions of dead soldiers without any hint of a victory. Yet no one had the courage to halt the insanity.

It was here in eastern France, that the Allied and Central Power armies came to a stationary point of inertia; while the soldiers of each side fought with tenacious bravery and the generals planned with dull, unimaginative strategy and tactics, no amount of offensive élan or even sheer numbers could produce any sort of battlefield advantage or victory that consisted of a few hundred yards or sometimes a few kilometres or several miles of advance. Over time, failure reinforced failure and the only answer that was suggested was to throw even greater numbers of infantry at the trenches, to which the response was an overwhelming amount of machine guns and artillery fires. The more human sacrifices that were made, the more human sacrifice was being demanded by politician and general alike. Yet the general public of all nations involved supported the sacrifice of their young sons and husbands without great question or hesitation – patriotism and nationalism were stubborn things to displace without great effort and sacrifices. So these things had become in October 1914 and so these things were to remain relatively speaking for the next four years. Fixed perceptions, it seemed, could be as intractable and stubbornly unmovable as the fixed defences of the trenches.

With the generosity of the passage of time to better clarify past events, it can be seen that The Great War was not to be limited to the destruction of military forces alone, however. There was an unprecedented level of human and property destruction, which had previously been unknown in past modern European conflicts. The German Army seemed to be taking the practice of the American Civil War General William Sherman's philosophy of conducting the 'total war' concept to unheard of heights. Damage and destruction to civilian property not only seemed to be the rule, but it was greatly encouraged by the German officers as a matter of accepted German military policy! Nor was the average, often innocent citizen safe from the ravages of the war. Increasingly, civilians were being killed as a result of wayward exploding shells, disease and hunger, and by the decree of occupation force reprisals. If danger and possible death was always the lot which befell that of soldiers, it also became so for the innocent civilians of German occupied countries during World War I. As the war progressed and victory became more distant and elusive for the Germans, so also did increase their contempt and reprisals on the citizens of their occupied territories. In the year 1914 alone, there were over 6,000 Belgian civilians murdered by the German army – and this war was still in its infancy.

\* \* \* \* \* \* \* \* \* \* \*

# Chapter 3:
# The Eclipse of War

*"I realize now that merely being a neutral country was no insurance against being invaded by the Germans; we were so confidently naïve"*

Having been given his unofficial, secret mission from his Commander-in-Chief, William Donovan and his superior Herbert Hoover carefully deliberated on their plans and travel itinerary. Bill had to fabricate a phony, plausible 'cover story' for both his wife Ruth and his law partner Bradley Goodyear to believe. He took the easy and most plausible option: he told a half-lie that he had been engaged by the Rockefeller Foundation to assist in the War Relief Program to ascertain the best plan to supply food stuffs to the starving civilians in neutral and occupied countries of Europe and that he needed to make humanitarian aid coordination contacts in the countries of Great Britain, Holland, Belgium, Denmark, Germany, Austria, Turkey, Bulgaria, Norway and Sweden.

The two men received their official passports in expedited time and travelled first to Great Britain aboard the luxury liner RMS Olympic, the sister ship of the infamous, ill-fated Titanic. During the five-day Atlantic crossing, Donovan and Hoover became good friends despite their initial icy meeting at the White House. Upon docking at Southampton, the two men travelled to London and registered at the Vine Street Police Station as neutral aliens on official business of war relief with the Rockefeller Foundation. The two men gave the British military and government officials their passport and letters of appointment from the Rockefeller Foundation along with their personal data and place of residence in London, which was the fashionable Brown Hotel. During their stay in London, the two men met with the US Ambassador Walter Hines Page to get an update on the current state of affairs for both Great Britain and the overall war conditions that currently existed in Europe. None of the news was encouraging as the British blockade was slowly and efficiently starving many innocent civilians in Europe; the fighting was going badly for everyone as the killing machine of war was taking its toll on the young manhood of Europe. The fighting lines in April 1916 were almost the same as in October 1914 – nothing had changed except the death toll. Unbeknownst to anyone, the British were planning a major offensive for July 1916 in the Somme River in eastern France – on the first day of the battle alone there were 60,000 British casualties, as the modern war machine chewed up ever increasing amounts of young men as meat into a huge mincing grinder.

At the US Embassy in London, Hoover and Donovan met daily and made the final coordination details with the main European managers of the Rockefeller Foundation War Relief Commission – Messers Warwick Greene, Reginald Foster and Henry Topping. The Rockefeller Foundation men provided a dire warning about the millions of starving citizens across Europe as the British blockade had so efficiently stopped the natural flow of commerce and the agriculture industry was ravaged by the war's impact on young men to work the fields and the land taken out of use by war damage. The problems involved in getting stranded Americans out of Europe was also a major task; there were an estimated 120,000 to 160,000 US citizens scattered across Europe when the war erupted and most of them had no way home or sufficient funds to get transportation. Yet the Rockefeller Foundation was powerful, influential and very wealthy – it was also a neutral organization that was able to negotiate favourable terms for various nations receiving food and grains from the United States if assurances for civilian use could be guaranteed and assured means of continental transportation implemented. Hoover directed a multi-pronged European country inspection and Bill Donovan's first location of assignment was Brussels, Belgium. An official embassy cable was sent from Ambassador Page to the US Consulate in Brussels, informing the US Consulate Minister Brand Whitlock of Mr Donovan's impending arrival and to make all assistance possible for his mission.

With enthusiasm and purposefulness, Donovan made his way through France and Holland, ensuring to stop at The Hague in the Netherlands, also the centre for the Allied High Command for the British forces. He witnessed the massive physical destruction of the numerous buildings and farmlands across eastern France; the landscape appeared as the cratered moon. He made his normal liaison with the US Embassy and also checked-in with the various Allied High Commands for the purposes of both his mission and personal curiosity. After all, he had been ordered to investigate the military situation of both Allied and Central Powers, to specifically include the existing military and political postures of all nations involved. To his satisfaction and evaluation, he confirmed the fact that the Allies were planning yet another massive land offensive, yet he noted nothing in the Allied strategy, tactics or weaponry that was going to provide a positive or different result in this senseless frontal attack as to other proceeding fruitless campaigns. The only difference Donovan noted was the scale of the British attack preparations, which were more massive than any to date. Unbeknownst to the British, the Germans were preparing equally massive defensive measures to counter any attack. Most military planners were not cognitive to the reality that their enemies had a 'military veto' over their plans in the genesis of elaborate counter-plans. War was akin to a chess game in which the outcome depended equally on the placement of clever moves and foolish mistakes alike.

In hand he carried with him the safe letters of transit in several different languages, a valid visa and a letter in German signed by the German Foreign Minister Zimmerman granting permission for all members of the Rockefeller Foundation to travel to and transit through all Central Power countries for the purpose of conducting war relief work – they were all in proper order and presented without dispute or confrontation, such was the prestige and power of the John D Rockefeller Foundation and the US War Relief Commission. As arrogant and belligerent as the German military autocracy was, they were wise enough to recognize the great financial and military power of a still sleeping giant and they deeply wanted this sleeping giant to remain asleep. Belgium was the first neutral country to be militarily violated and now harshly occupied by the German military.

Donovan took a taxi from the Brussels train station to the US Consulate – a mere fifteen-minute ride. Brussels was a beautiful and quaint European city with well-maintained boulevard street arteries accented with precisely abbreviated spaced lush green oak trees, while masonry and varying shades of brick facade shops and homes three and four storeys in height, graced the sterile streets and carefully laid hand-cut cobblestone sidewalks. Periodically spaced alleyways divided the city blocks and quaint outdoor cafes with colourful awnings innocently adorned every city block. A city that should be alive with happy citizens seemed in inexplicitly reserved; the life had somehow seemed to be exorcised from the spirit of the people. He saw no smiles of those sipping drinks at the café tables, an odd social expression for such places of relaxation.

Donovan knew that the taxi drivers were most likely in the employ of the German secret police and military, thus he said nothing other than his destination to the taxi driver. He thought it best to check-in with the US Consulate officials before performing any other task. In short order he had arrived at his destination, a picturesque, visually impressive light brown and contrasting white coloured brick structure onto which was affixed the distinctive red and white striped American flag. The Great Seal of the United States was affixed directly above and outside of the US Consulate building. A warm feeling came over Bill as he saw the regalia of his country and it provided emotional reinforcement for him to know that he was soon to be among friends again. How natural and strange it was that once a native is overseas, their first instinct is to seek out and co-mingle with their fellow countrymen, no matter how great the differences may be in personal status, age or backgrounds.

"Hello, my name is Mr William Donovan, Esquire. I'm here to see the US Consulate-General; I believe that I am expected!" Bill showed his official passport to the United States Marine Corps guard and gently set down his suitcase at the entrance to the consulate entrance, which was erected with a tall wrought-iron black enamel eight foot high gate and small covered visitors' reception area. A serious and discerning look appeared on the guard's face; he scrutinized the document and it appeared correct, as did the stranger's eastern American accent. It was not unusual for an American to show-up at the US Consulate and request assistance. The US Consulates and larger US Embassies were like islands of safety in a sea of foreign despair; these were, and still are to this day, the hubs for all foreign US citizenry business and assistance.

"Yes, Mr Donovan, please let me make a phone call and someone will be here to assist you," the guard replied as the two men waited in an outside covered vestibule area. The weather was mild and pleasant. Donovan looked about the streets and these seemed to be a bit spartan in the numbers of people that he had expected to see in a bustling city like Brussels. He also noted the almost guarded and stoic looks on the faces of the men and women! Not one of them was adorned with a smile or friendliness for which the Belgians were famous. 'It must be the war and strictness of the German military occupation,' he correctly guessed.

Suddenly an unexpected voice echoed out to him from the US Consulate compound. "Well hello there, Mr Donovan, I hope that you had a pleasant trip from Antwerp. We received a cable from the US Embassy in London informing us of your visit. My name is Hugh Gibson; I'm the First Secretary of the US Legation in Brussels or unofficially the Number 2 man here after the US Minister Brand Whitlock," the mid-thirties, tall brown-haired man exclaimed with a sincere gentle white smile.

Gibson took note of Mr Donovan's single suitcase. "Please leave your suitcase here, I'll have it sent for and delivered by one of my aides to your room! Naturally, you will be staying with us here at the Consulate of course. We have a modest room for you and this will allow for you to conduct your work and converse with us here with total privacy and security. There's no need to let the Germans know more than they need to these days! There are German spies or 'agent provocateurs' everywhere in Brussels and their job is to ensnare innocent Belgians and perhaps the terrible bogyman himself," Mr Gibson snapped out a very demonstrative, half-joking manner. The two men talked casually about the weather and news until there was a proper sit-down with the US Consular General. They continued to talk socially, as they walked into the inner lobby of the US Consulate main building.

"Oh if you're not too tired from your jaunt from Amsterdam, I have you pencilled in for an hour to be introduced to the Consul-General Brand Whitlock, if that meets with your approval, Mr Donovan?", the Number 2 man of the US Consulate casually announced with clear forethought.

Bill was flattered by the quick-thinking Mr Gibson to act in such a forthright manner. "Of course I will be available – you just name the time and place," Bill replied in a Yankee 'can-do' informal fashion.

"I have a time of 3 o'clock pm; this will allow you a few hours to get settled in and it will be a fine opportunity for you to meet before our dinner this evening," Hugh Gibson replied and obviously not thinking of Bill Donovan's personal circumstances or plans. A fine reader of people's emotions, Gibson noticed a frown of uneasiness on Donovan's face. "What's the matter sir, did I happen to offend you? My sincerest apologies if I have, please sir what is the matter?" Gibson gently implored to the US President's designated VIP.

"Absolutely not, Mr Gibson! No, I'm the one who should apologize, Mr Gibson. I am travelling light, I have no evening clothes and I'd be under-dressed – an insult to the Consul-General, his wife and the rest of the Consulate staff."

Hugh Gibson smiled and gently touched Bill Donovan on the shoulder and dispelled Donovan's anxiety. "Bill, the war has made a mockery of the pre-war social etiquette of foreign Embassies and Consulates. Except for official functions, we no longer dress for dinner and since the war, there have been no official state parties, at least none that the USA has been invited to these days. We are unofficially on the German's black list since 1915." Gibson smiled as the two men walked up through the second storey hallway of the US Consulate. "Here's your room sir; it is clean, small, quiet and safe! I'll be up in three hours to fetch you for your meeting with the Consular-General, all right then?" Gibson remarked as he held out his hand as a sign of friendship.

Also at that moment, Donovan's single suitcase was being carried up to his room as well. Bill reviewed the room: it was simple and ample. He was relieved that he was on a tiny part of US soil. He hung up his hat and coat and laid his suitcase on a closet stand. He took out his other suit, shirts and underwear as well. He removed his shoes, threw off his shirt and pants and slid under the most inviting bedspread for a quick nap. In just a few scant seconds he lay dead asleep; he was more tired than he wanted to admit to himself.

In what seemed to be just a fleeting period of elapsed time, a sound awoke the slumbering Presidential emissary. He was awoken unceremoniously from his nap by the hard knocking of a heavy hand on his bedroom door. Quickly he threw on his pants and answered the knocking from behind a half-opened cracked door opening. It was Secretary Hugh Gibson wearing his warm smile once again. "Hello there, Mr Rip Van Winkle I presume? Well someone sure was tired, you must have had an exhausting trip and my apologies for not taking that into consideration! I'm sorry, Bill, if you need more time I can come back later and ..." Hugh Gibson remarked was cut-off in mid-sentence.

"No please, my apologies, Mr Gibson, it seems that my body was more tired than my ego; please grant me five minutes and I'll be ready!"

"Sure sir, no problem at all, take the time that you need. Do not hurry, I'll be waiting at the end of the hall for you," Gibson replied with a quick wink.

Showering was out of the equation, he hadn't the time; Bill had to settle for a quick shave, a face-wash and brushing of his teeth. The brief bodily revitalizing was enough for him. True to his personal decorum of promptness, the hygiene ritual took all but ten minutes.

"Ok I'm ready to go, Mr Gibson. Once again I'm embarrassed to have fallen dead asleep like that!"

"Forget it, Mr Donovan. Right this way please, the Counsul-General wants for me to give you some background information, diplomatic cables and reports, before he comes in to see you," Hugh Gibson announced in an inviting tone.

"That is fine and please call me Bill; I may be here on the President's orders, but I'm still an average American citizen," Donovan replied modestly.

"Sure thing, Mr Donovan, I mean Bill, and no one who the President of the United States charges as his special envoy is anything but an average citizen!" Gibson retorted again with his famous smile. "Here we are Bill, the Consul-General's very own private library and den; it's where all the real discussions and high-level work gets done too. I've prepared a set of reading materials and a pot of coffee and some light cakes for your pleasure – just a few snacks to get you through until dinner, Bill." Hugh Gibson opened up the massive oak doors to an oak panelled wall-to-wall fully stocked library complete with fire place, several sofas and numerous winged chairs. Off to the side of the rich, masculine styled enclave, there sat an eight foot long reading table adorned with twin Tiffany reading lamps, a foot-high pile of documents and a writing pad of paper sat neatly attired next to a sterling silver pot of hot, rich coffee and a set of Edgewood china. The aroma of the coffee was almost sensuous to the expatriate American.

"Wow, now this is what I call real living, Hugh and thank you for the coffee – I really need a wake-me up!" Bill exclaimed as he rushed over and poured himself a cup of coffee, adding a dash of cream and some sugar. "May I pour you a cup, Hugh?"

"No thank you, Bill, I have had my ration for the day. Please sit and read the materials before you; the Consul-General will be with you shortly," Hugh Gibson exclaimed as he smiled, turned and shut the Consulate library/den door carefully behind him.

Donovan was left alone in this quiet solitude to await the arrival of US Minister Brand Whitlock. He took a comfortable seat and a sip of the golden, hot caffeine laced nectar. It was just the stimulus that his body craved. From top-to-bottom he started to leaf through the stack of neatly piled documents. His cursory and preliminary review of the cables, reports and photographs of the war was very revealing. His eyes were drawn to the photographs and reports on the German atrocities such as the shooting of prisoner soldiers and civilians, looting of property, large scale destruction of property including the levelling of the town of Louvain and the curtailment of all levels of civil liberties, freedoms and movement. He read with awe Consul-General Whitlock's diplomatic cables to Washington DC and he now knew why President Wilson wanted 'eyes-on' information – if these cables and reports were even half-true, then Germany was to be a cruel master in their war victory. The minutes and the pages passed by without any reverence or memorial to time. He read and carefully studied photographs of the German employment of the horrific battlefield usage of poison gas, the use of submarines to sink civilian vessels including the Lusitania, the Zeppelin air raids on London and other cities for the sole purpose of instilling sheer terror on civilians. The pictures of the war dead and the horrific mutilated wounded soldiers turned Bill's mood to sombre; he did not think that modern war could be so horrible, efficient and indiscriminate.

He took another cup of coffee, then another and still yet another. About half the way down into the pile of documents, he came to a carefully bundled set of documents that were wrapped in a special red cover with the prominent, bold words 'SECRET EYES ONLY US CONSUL-GENERAL – BELGIUM'. The pile of documents were tied carefully with binding of white silk ribbon, which he carefully unwound. He read the type-written and hand-written documents, some of these in Consul Brand Whitlock's own handwriting and signature. His eyes became mesmerized by the bold words, spying, espionage and 'agent provocateur' – which he was later to learn was a French word used to describe a spy or agent used to ferret out information in an undercover operation. He had heard that word used before, but now its true meaning became more clear.

His fingers raced through the documents faster, deeper and with greater intensity. He was oblivious and senseless to the environment around him. He saw the haunting picture of a grey-haired, gentle-looking, middle-aged woman, who appeared to be in her early fifties. Her pale, sad, mysterious grey eyes seemed to look directly through him; he felt sad and uncomfortable for some unknown reason. Another picture was that of a dark, handsome man in his early thirties sporting a gentlemanly moustache and carefully groomed goatee. It was as though he was thunderstruck by the pictures. Scribbled neatly onto each photo was a name; the woman was Edith Cavell and the man Philippe Baucq. The names seemed familiar to him somehow; he thought that he had heard these names before, but he could not precisely remember when or in what context. He stared at the two photos for a few minutes and tried to guess at the lives of these people and their relevance to the US Consulate in Brussels, Belgium within the context of a secret diplomatic correspondence.

"Well hello, Mr Donovan, I see that you have met two of the most infamous personages in Brussels and maybe even the war itself to this point!" came a voice from seeming oblivion. Bill's investigative trance had been suddenly interrupted by the verbal pronunciation. Startled, he turned around and stared at the source of the voice. "Sorry to startle you, I am Consul-General Brand Whitlock, although the Europeans often refer to me as the US Minister. I'd be delighted if you simply call me Brand." The handsome man was tall, thin, almost lanky, with wire-rim spectacles and a pleasant smile, and he extended his hand in obvious friendship.

Bill arose and returned both the smile and the handshake. "It's my great pleasure to meet you Brand; may I offer you a cup of coffee?"

"No, thank you, Bill. I see that you have been whittling-away at the stack of confidential and secret files that I have amassed for your perusal, to include the diplomatic cables and orders from the Secretary of State, Mr Robert Lansing. Lansing directed that all materials be made available to you on the war activities by order of the President, especially political and military issues," Brand Whitlock exclaimed as he noticed the special restricted folder and photographs of Edith Cavell and Philippe Baucq staring eerily back at him from atop the table. Upon prolonged gazing, the US Consul's face immediately turned from genial to sad upon further recollections of these two photographs and Bill obviously noted Brand Whitlock's sudden facial transformation.

"Just who are these two people? How do they relate to the situation in Brussels and the German occupation?" Donovan asked eagerly.

"Please let's sit down on a comfortable sofa over here, Bill. This story is complicated and intriguing; it's going to take some time and it has everything to do with the war, Belgium and the German military occupation." The two men took a few steps over to the plush and comfortable red, gold and blue striped silk lounge sofa and became relaxed. Brand Whitlock did all of the talking and Bill Donovan listened most intensely and gathered up the information like a dry sponge to water. Over the course of the next two hours, Donovan received an abbreviated, but most detailed account of the war as Consul Whitlock could best remember it from the very beginning to the present day. The tutorial made short work of that which constituted the stack of faceless, emotionless official papers and photographs that had been laid before him. Bill's eyes, ears and mind were singularly devoted to every word that Brand Whitlock uttered and he was forever changed by this personal account, which had no rival.

\* \* \* \* \* \* \* \* \* \* \*

For the tiny and quaint storybook country of neutral Belgium, the Great War had begun with great trepidation, as the young and handsome regent King Albert I tried heroically to keep his country neutral and out of the war. He and the Belgium Parliament had sought to engineer neutrality akin to that of neutral Switzerland and make no treaty alignment or favour any particular country or Empire. Yet neither a King's nor a Parliament's best intentions could negotiate or abridge the reality of the impending war. Geography was a insurmountable mistress that could not be denied and tiny Belgium, unlike its southern neighbour Switzerland, was not blessed with the natural defence of high mountains, narrow passes and valleys by which a much larger enemy could be rebuffed and thwarted. A double insult was that Belgium lay as the singular channel through which the von Schlieffen Plan and the Austro-Hungarian armies had to pass through to get to Paris, France. For the German army to make their attack on France, there was no viable option except to pass rapidly through tiny, neutral Belgium. The young King and his loyal Parliament boldly refused the German diplomatic request for 'neutral and unfettered transit' for the military forces' passage through neutral Belgium to attack the French. This request was both unethical and unpatriotic from both a Belgian perspective as well as a diplomatic one; France was a close and friendly neighbour and Belgium was not going to acquiesce to foreign demands and threats merely to make a temporary peace with the belligerent Germans only to create forever an enemy of France. Temporary expedience made for permanent enemies. Every home and commercial establishment flew the red, black and gold flag of Belgium in support of their government and in defiance of the Germans. It was against this Belgian resolution that Germany invaded the peaceful, lush green country on 3 August 1914; the German army crossed into Belgium at Liege. King Albert I took to the field with his army and parliament took an indefinite hiatus; there was no more urgent government business than being invaded – if Belgium was victorious the government was to be shortly restored; if the German invasion succeeded, there was to be no form of Belgium government any longer. Events portended the latter outcome. England had a mid-nineteenth century treaty obligation to aid Belgium in the event of Belgian invasion or territorial trespass and now it was obliged to fulfill that agreement.

In city after city across Belgium, a seemingly endless column of grey clad German infantry marched through the conquered city streets. In a seemingly mocking atmosphere, the weather was warm and sunny, while a dark gloom of despair dwelled in the heart of every Belgian citizen. Smoke ruffled from the smoldering buildings and farm houses, casting an insulting black cloak of film over the clear blue sky, while volleys of thunderous barrage artillery whizzed overhead and then gave way to massive explosions of red, yellow and finally black plumes of acrid smelling smoke. Both human corpses and farm animal carcasses lay insultingly strewn about fields and country roads. Anything and any object that even seemed to pose a threat to the German military was shelled and shot to pieces – 'better to be safe than sorry' was the German military axiom and this principle was enforced from the German General Staff down to the lowest private and no one dared violate it; some even took sheer delight in it. The decaying bodies gave off a stomach-turning putrid sweet smell that soon turned to that of a foul rotten sulphur smell after having lain out unburied in the warm August sun for many days. Innumerable armies of flies gorged on the decayed flesh that harboured multiple diseases and soon the flies infected many Belgians. The reality and horror of war became too much for many Belgian citizens; countless of them hastily fled the carnage, leaving all possessions abandoned, and flooded onto the small country roads westward in hope of finding refuge in other towns or perhaps in France.

The hellish realities of modern war gave one the characterized impression of a monster-breathing dragon spewing fire and death from its nostrils or something akin to Dante's Inferno. The streets of every Belgian town were thick with the debris of war, the twisted and fallen buildings being a testament to the destruction wrecked by the modern implements of the 20th Century war machine. 'How could such primitive and terrible things be happening to us?' was a prevailing thought in many a Belgian mind, whose entire orderly world was suddenly dashed into chaos in just a matter of days. On some of these hot August days, there befell a warm, constant summer rain, making an already insidious scene even more so, as the calamity of mud added a dirty insult to the already sinful landscape. War had an inherent genius for the making of destruction and filth, yet it possessed no equal corollary to negate these tenets, so the children of this destruction and death lay unto nameless others and to another day for final disposition.

A myriad of horses and heavily laden wagons loaded with all the implements of war and war supplies filled the streets of Brussels, as the Imperial German army marched steadily forward. Immediately behind the German army, there trudged seemingly endless long lines of civilian refugees – the rural dwellers suddenly upended by war, now competed for urban sheltered sanctuary amid the modern forests made of pressurized formed brick and concrete masonry structures amidst a canyon floor of indestructible hand-carved Belgium cobblestones. Ever slowly the German logistical columns marched through the town on their vital mission of supplying the perpetually hungry war machine of the Imperial German Army. This modern war was waged by a ruthless aggressor who knew not the reverence of class, age, occupation or sex, for all were equal before the eyes of the German war machine. The options were simple: fight and die or surrender and die slower! Belgium and the Allies fought bravely and with bravado, yet the German mathematical model of war gave scant respect to these chivalrous acts of a bygone era. The knights and warriors of yore, the exalted cavalry now lay vulgarly vanquished across the fields of Belgium;

both man and horse were no equal to the rapid deadly spray of fast flying metal projectiles fired from bolt action rifles and water-cooled machine guns fed by an endless amount of ammunition. As if depicted in a tragic demonstrative illustration, the old warriors lay prostrated and vanquished to the new victorious icons of the modern battlefield, the machine gun and artillery howitzer.

On August 23, 1914 in the western Belgium city of Mons, the epitaph of Belgium independence was consigned for the duration of the war. The British and Allied military forces fought valiantly and with prodigious skill before being overrun by a vastly superior sized German military force. While many surviving Allied soldiers retreated in orderly fashion with their affiliated units, many others were not as fortunate, their units having been decimated or destroyed, while others were cut-off from friendly forces due to the battlefield chaos and rapid movement of the German army. These lost souls became cut-off from friendly forces and were forced by circumstances to make their own way behind enemy lines as individuals, pairs or small groups. The lot of any Allied soldier was bleak – either a long and arduous imprisonment awaited them or else they confronted the real possibility of being shot on the spot by the unsympathetic German army, especially if caught in civilian clothing and out of uniform.

\* \* \* \* \* \* \* \* \* \* \* \*

"Get down, sir! Shhhh... please be quiet, Colonel, the Germans are nearby, we must remain still, please be quiet! I don't want us to become Prisoners of War!" Corporal William Taylor whispered with great concern at his delirious superior officer Colonel Percy Chatsworth. It was pitch black; travelling at night was most dangerous, but preferable to being easily spotted in daylight by the Germans. The two British soldiers were among those unfortunate fighters from the Battle of Mons and now caught behind enemy lines. The Colonel had a concussion, a displaced injured shoulder and a foot injury, but no open wounds. His personal valet, Corporal William Taylor, or 'Billy' as his friends called him, was unhurt. Both soldiers were from the 8th Battalion of the Cheshire Infantry Regiment.

"I don't think that I can make it, Corporal Taylor. It's best that you make your way alone; I'm only slowing you down…go laddy and make a break for it! I'm old and you're young, go my boy!" the fiftyish Colonel pleaded with his dislodged shoulder aching with even the slightest movement.

"No sir…you can give me orders till kingdom come, but I'm staying,

Colonel. We both make it back alive or we end up in a prisoner of war camp, but we cannot stay here, sir, it's very dangerous!" the young battle-tested youth of eighteen replied to his senior officer. Colonel Percy Chatsworth was no mere career military officer; he was, in fact, the Earl of Derbyshire, the elder son of the Duke of Albemarle and holder of the succeeding lesser titles of the Marques of Exeter and the Earl of Derbyshire; the latter title being an 'honorary title' that the father requested to be bestowed upon his elder son as a courtesy-in-waiting title.

As a member of the English aristocracy, Colonel Chatsworth was the natural, eventual inheritor to his father's Dukedom, while brother James, eight years younger than Percy, was serving in the House of Commons and also being a member of the War Cabinet of the Prime Minister Herbert Henry Asquith, the 1st Earl of Oxford and Asquith, KG, PC, KC. Born out of the multiple reasons of patriotism, personal honour and family expectations, the Earl re-entered Army service shortly after Britain had declared war on Germany. Percy was not a mere untried Reserve Army officer, as he had served with great distinction in the Sudan and Boer War. He ended up his military career in India as a Deputy Colonial Administrator before returning to England. He was in gentle, sedate retirement from the active British army. His wife Constance and his three young teenage children were glad to be finally settled in their mother country and enjoying all that a privileged life had to offer. Upon hearing the call for volunteers, he requested immediate mobilization when there was announced an officer shortage. Corporal Billy Taylor had lived in a small village that was part of the Duke of Albemarle's estate holdings, where he worked in the livery service maintaining the Duke's equine stables. He joined the Earl's regiment and requested service as his aide as much out of loyalty as having the comfort to serve with a familiar leader whom he liked and admired both the Duke and his family. It was a most common practice for the aristocrats to have members of their estates serve in their units as aides.

"Ah…my damn shoulder is killing me! I think I've also got something wrong with my left leg too – it hurts like the devil every time I place force upon it," the Colonel cried out as both he and Corporal Billy Taylor crawled stealthily along the shallow furrows of a pasture that had been pot-marked with artillery shell craters. The entire earth had been disinterred with brown mud and dirt, which now had irreverently replaced the lush green grass that had previously graced the field. An alert German guard heard something from the field and immediately he fired off a white flare to ascertain the truth from the darkness.

"Quick Colonel – let's crawl into that shell hole and make no sound and especially make no movements…the flare betrays movement instantly," the scared, but battle-wise Corporal remarked in utter desperation, as the two men struggled to get into the safety of the shell hole. The German observation post looked for any movement but none was revealed. In a minute, the flare's eerie light had abated and the darkness quickly reclaimed the night. Slowly the two men moved westward, as to the west lay France and perhaps safety. Some miles more, they came to a barbed wire area and again more shell holes and German fortified lines. They had not eaten or drank for at least two days and they were dehydrated and physically exhausted. They were scared and not thinking properly either.

They carefully crawled under and through the deliberately tangled rolls of barbed wired called concertina, named after the small handheld musical accordion-like music box so popular across Europe for playing informal folk music. There was nothing, however, jovial about this new type of metal wire into which barbed, razor-like points had been manufactured to deliberately inflict skin wounds and impede the freedom of infantry movement in a given area. Soon both of their uniforms were in tatters from desperate negotiating through the thick twisted strands of dense concertina barbed wire.

Thinking that they were safe, the two English soldiers tried to make an upright sprint across an area of no-man's land, an area that was open to freedom of fires and for which random firing was both approved and encouraged. Regular British formation troops had vacated this area weeks previously, yet the German machine gunners had strict orders to fire upon anything and anyone not recognizable to them or for which a password was not yelled out. The German military was suspicious of stray enemy soldiers and perhaps the bold patriotic civilian. From a crouching position, the Colonel staggered under the weight of his injuries, wearily leading the way across a muddy shell-marked rural, pasture area. The smell from the churned-up farm fields that were amply fertilized with animal manure obnoxiously filled the nostrils of both soldiers; they each made concerted efforts not to gag or perform any other action that could possibly give away their position and alert the German machine gunners.

Suddenly he tripped and fell headfirst into a huge artillery impact shell hole. As he tumbled down he felt something soft and mushy as he pushed his hands away from the night-hidden object. As he knelt painfully down, Colonel Chatsworth struggled to get his metal trench lighter from his uniform breast pocket. Taking utmost care given their tactical circumstance, he carefully cupped his trench cigarette lighter with his left hand to safely cover any flame glow of the lighter and also to better focus the light of the flame. There before him was the rotted torso of a headless German soldier along with the rotting corpses of three other soldiers from the British and French armies. The grotesque sight and the smell from the putrid sweet-smelling decomposing corpses made him scream out instinctively in revulsion and he started to dry-heave the content of his now empty stomach. Corporal Taylor soon followed into the shell hole and both men screamed out in both primal horror and sheer anxiety release. The corpses looked something akin to a cheap horror motion picture show; the corpses were varying in shades of green, brown and blacked decay. Dead bodies were not a high priority for the German army – their interests were with military objectives and their own living soldiers. The battlefields lay with decay of man and animal alike for an indeterminate period of time, thus attributing to the profusion of nameless graves and missing dead throughout the conflict.

Instantly alerted from the distant reverberating sounds of horrific human screams, a series of German Maxim 7.92 mm water-cooled machine guns reacted instinctively to the muddled, primal sounds that echoed across the few hundred yards of open space with a continuous burst of grazing fires. The barrage of thousands of machine gun bullets lit up over their faces and produced an eerie, dull red glow from the overhead tracer bullets fired from the machine guns. In short order, a chorus of high angle firing mortars nicely complemented the stuttering cacophony of the machine guns. Large pieces of the bodily strewn battlefield were soon tossed up into the air by the mortar explosions and the debris rained liberally into the shallow shell hole that the terrified soldiers occupied. Still more pieces of decomposing and torn bodies and body parts from unburied soldiers flew into the air and into the shell hole. A decapitated head of a French soldier complete with attached helmet was hurled into the shell hole, this to be immediately followed by part of a torso and a body-less set of legs. Again both men dry-heaved in revulsion, their eyes bulging out in horror as witnesses to a scene of carnage that was happening to them; they screamed in horror at the charnel house of death that was exploding around them. If Almighty God was compassionate, the next shell should mercifully hit their shell hole and immediately bring an end to this horror; both of them prayed in desperation. Yet this divine mercy was not accorded unto them. From sheer nervousness and primitive terror, both soldiers' bodies instinctively relieved themselves of their bowels into their uniforms, sometime during the course of the German shelling. Neither man was aware of their bodily discharge; their thoughts and emotions lay elsewhere in the preserve of self-preservation.

The German Maxim machine guns continued to fire for the next thirty minutes just to make sure that nothing remained alive to threaten their gun positions and personal safety. Enemy sapper and reconnaissance patrols were the lore and bane of the German soldiers, many of whom had heard the unsubstantiated tales of German soldiers being found in the morning with their throats slit open. Like most war tales, this one lay mostly in the confines of the imagination than in proven reality and German officers did nothing to dispel the rumours as this kept their soldiers awake and alert. The Germans had more than enough ammunition to expend and it was not unusual for these water-cooled beastly guns to fire hours on end if so needed. Out of sheer boredom, gunners frequently felt the urge to let fly with a barrage of artillery or long bursts of machine guns just to relieve the boredom of manning a forward position. As the guns died down, the men made their way out of the firing fields and toward the forest of Wiheries, located in the southwestern portion of Belgium near to the French border.

"Look Colonel, there's a small hut over there; it's probably that of a local miner or farmer. Let's take shelter there, we'll be safe there, at least for a while and we can finally rest-up and maybe get some food in us, sir," Corporal Taylor pleaded with his superior officer, as the older burnt-out officer was now near delirium from pain and exhaustion. Neither man had slept in the last forty-eight hours – such deprivation played mischief with the soldier's psyche as their imaginations ran wild with an assortment of potential hazards and imaginary frights. At this point Colonel Chatsworth merely nodded his head wearily at anything that young Billy Taylor uttered. It was amazing how utterly malleable the human spirit became in the state of utter exhaustion and physiological affliction. The two men had indeed stumbled upon the field house of a local coal miner. Stumbling into the modest, smallish brick structure, the two men opened the door and nearly fell into the main living area, so desperate was their fatigue and dehydration. "Good, sir, the hut's not occupied; it must be a temporary abode for a few workers while they work the mines," Corporal Taylor whispered to the Colonel, not knowing who might be around or come suddenly bursting through the front door.

"Here now, come over on this small sofa, sir. Lie down, get some rest; I'll snuggle up in the corner! We'll rest, sir, we need to sleep, we can't do anything if we're exhausted….things will be better after we're rested!" Billy muttered to the Colonel, who had collapsed immediately upon touching the old sofa and getting comfortably horizontal. Likewise, the Corporal took an old dirty blanket lying on the back of the sofa and nestled himself up in a foetal position in a corner of the room. Both men collapsed in utter physical exhaustion. He and his Colonel slept like babies, their bodies desperately needed the respite and it recharged their spirits immensely. The 'Indian Summer' of late September and early October, a beautiful sunny and warm time of the year when summer had simply refused to 'give up the ghost to autumn, was most convenient for the Colonel and Corporal – this very fine warm weather served to allow their very survival and continued evasion from the German patrols. Their bodies needed to consume fewer precious calories and their very inadequate and torn clothing still served to provide barely minimum protection against the exposure to nature.

"What day is it? How long have I been asleep?" Corporal Billy Taylor muttered to himself as he awoke from his slumber. It was pitch black both inside and outside of the miner's small hut. Unbeknownst to the Corporal, he and the Colonel had slept twenty-four hours, yet their bodies had been starved of rest and even now both men were still exhausted. Now fully awake, Billy struggled to provide light into the pitch black darkness of the small cold room; it was a risk, but being in war meant taking calculated risks and this was a desolate area of the forest. He fumbled his fingers into his worn jacket pockets and retrieved a wooden friction match. 'Glad that I'm a smoker. I fancied that I had me a pack of fags just now, even a single one would suffice me!' Billy muttered to himself and referring to the English common slang name for cigarettes. He struck the match on a wooden table and cupped his hand around the lit match as he gazed eagerly about the modest room. He spied an oil lamp, which he lit with care, ensuring that the wick was drawn down to produce the lowest glow possible. 'The Colonel was twice his age and desperately hurt,' Billy thought to himself and he let his Commanding officer get all the rest that was possible. He placed the lamp back atop the crude wooden table from which he had taken it and looked over to his Colonel who was still sound asleep. He needed to wake the old gentleman, if only to check on the Earl's physical condition, which was more desperate than his own.

"Colonel! Colonel Chatsworth! Get up, sir! How are you feeling, sir?" Corporal Taylor pleaded quietly as he shrugged the greying haired officer hoping to awaken him and determine his state of fitness. Corporal Billy Taylor saw no immediate or heavy bleeding – a very good thing indeed; however, the Colonel had suffered soft tissue injuries to his right shoulder and to the left leg. The aged Colonel had also some level of dizziness suffered from a bursting German artillery shell. Billy knew that the Earl needed medical help and for a moment he thought it crazy for a fifty-plus year old man to be leading troops on the battlefield, yet this act was not unusual, as everyone in Britain and Europe was doing their part for the war – including old men, matronly women, teenagers, factory workers and even the aristocrats and Royals.

"Ah…ah…where…where are we…what time is it?" Colonel Chatsworth muttered as he slowly regained consciousness from his long slumber. The pain and hunger he had previously felt immediately returned to his physical constitution. "Ah…damn it all, Billy, the sleep did not take away any of the pain, my lad!" he cried out in despair. The young Corporal could do nothing for the aged officer; he knew that he needed expert medical assistance and quick. There was no way for the two men to continue to evade the Germans or even to survive without help.

Suddenly there was a distinct sound outside the miner's hut door; it sounded initially like a few twigs broken by the heavy weight of a body. "Ssssuuhhhh, quiet, sir, I heard something!" Billy warned as he pressed his finger up to his lips. It was too late to extinguish the oil lamp without alerting immediate suspicions. Billy suspected there was someone outside the front door, which was immediately confirmed by another sound – this one was that of a definite footstep bearing its weight upon the wooden door mat. Both the Colonel and his young aide's eyes met, their eyes bulged out in utter horror at the prospect of being discovered by the enemy. Adrenalin suddenly pulsed through both of their bodies and their military training and animal-like instinct took over from their fears. Billy rushed immediately and quietly behind the hut door, drawing his trench knife to kill any German intruder. Yet this position left Corporal Taylor blind as to the nature of the unwelcome intruder and the Colonel could not move off of the sofa and there he lay exposed to any hostile visitor. Both men's hearts were thudding. The door opened slowly and a slight cool breeze blew into the miner's hut. The figure betrayed a man of medium build; nothing more could be ascertained by the frightened Corporal. He had never killed a man before and killing a man, even an enemy soldier, with a knife was most personal and terrifying. His heart was pounding and his senses heightened. 'Was he up to this killing,' he thought silently to himself, as all thoughts of God, duty and country evaporated from his psyche; only the primal beast in him remained as he had become as a beast in nature. He sweated profusely, his eyes dilated, his blood pressure jumped and his heart pounded like a kettledrum.

"Monsieur l'Anglais, de soldats d'Angleterre, êtes vous ici?" a male voice whispered in a soft French tone.

Immediately relieved, the Corporal was only too glad not to hear German being uttered, yet he took no chances! He grabbed the silhouetted figure and threw the man to the floor and the falling of the body made a very audible sound as it contacted with the hard floor.

"Je suis Belge, s'il vous plâit ne me pas blesser!" pleaded the voice from the rumpled-up man lying upon the floor with utmost fear in his voice. A bewildered look came upon the Corporal, whose fearful body was acting on adrenalin alone.

"It's all right, Billy, he says that he's Belgian and to not hurt him! I think he's a local Corporal, some local worker or farmer I should suspect," Colonel Chatsworth accurately translated and surmised, French being the second language of the English elite and professional military officers. The young and uneducated Corporal took immediate relief and confidence in the Earl's words.

"Not to worry, Corporal, I'll ask for food and help, we have few options left, we have to trust him or become POWs," the Colonel wisely surmised, as the Corporal's physical state returned back to normal and he knew that the Earl had spoken correctly. Escape was their one true option; life in a German POW camp might kill the Colonel and internment did not suit the Corporal either. "Nous sommes les soldates anglais, nous avons besoin de la nourriture, de l'eau et d'une cachette…pouvez-vous nous aider?" the Colonel uttered in fluent high-French and asking the middle-aged Belgian field worker for food, water and help. The Corporal went over to the oil lamp and raised the wick stem in order to brighten the flame and the light's glow to that of a medium radiance. The lamp instantly revealed the face of a middle-aged man complete with black-greying-hair, weathered face and attired in crumpled, dirty work garments. It was indeed a Belgian worker.

The look of fear immediately deserted the field worker's face and a genuine smile abbreviated itself across the man's face; teeth were missing from various portions of his mouth, a sure testament to a hard and poor life. "Please get us help, sir, before we perish!" the Corporal replied back to his Colonel in obvious desperation.

"Oui Monsieur, naturellement, vous restent ici sont sur, je reviendrai, juste les soldats anglais d'attendez ici, mon nom est….oh mon nom est Pierre!", the Belgian field hand replied as he took his cap off the floor and hurried out of the door with utmost haste.

"What was that all about sir? Is that old Belgian bastard going to the Germans to betray us?" The agitated and suspicious Corporal showed his anxiety in his voice.

"No, no Corporal, I think not! He says that he's going to get us help and that we are to stay here and that his name is Peter," the Colonel remarked as he sat wearily up on the sofa.

"How do you know that, sir? I mean he could be in the pay of the Germans," Billy replied nervously.

"Well, Corporal, I don't know anything for certain, but I do know that we are in a desperate situation, behind the German lines and we have to trust someone. I've lived a good deal of years, I've seen a lot of human nature, both the good and the bad, and I think that old man will be back with help for us; he seems to be of a good spirit to me and his actions betrayed no hostility or nervousness! If not, we're none the worse for trying. We have no support presently, we're in God's hands and at the mercy and good-heartedness of others," the Colonel wisely summarized. The young Corporal weighed the Colonel's sage words and he had no better plan of his own. The two men waited in the small miner's hut for hours; their anxiety was now as great as their need for nourishment.

Although the two men waited patiently for a period of time measured in hours, the anxious waiting seemed to them an eternity. Periodically, Corporal Taylor looked out of the small miner's hut to make an observation, yet there was nothing to see except lush, green densely populated forests of hardwood and pine trees. There was a narrow line of sight that allowed a limited field of view into a uncut meadow a few hundred yards into the distance, yet everything seemed to be devoid of any human activity.

"I don't see anything, Colonel sir, not a soul is in sight; that means no German soldiers nor any help either…you think sir that the old Belgian deserted us? Maybe he's selling us out to the Germans for a reward!" the young, frightened Corporal yelled out desperately, letting his fears and vivid imagination get the better of him.

Colonel Chatsworth possessed more maturity than his young, frightened aide; he had a calmer, reserved, almost fatalistic view of the situation as a result of his age and war experiences in the Middle East, South Africa and India.

"Let's be patient, Corporal Taylor. Peter is probably waiting to come back when he has the safety and anonymity of the night…he's a local and he knows these woods better than any German does – and as for being a traitor to us, I see too many Belgians who despise the German army and its occupation of Belgium!" the wise Colonel concluded. The Colonel was in a more rational frame of mind now that the pain had subsided somewhat.

He rummaged through his numerous Army uniform pockets as a matter of daily routine and much to his delight he felt out a crumpled box-like item – it was cigarettes, fine top-end English blended cigarettes at that! He smiled with delight, his first smile of the day. There were still several cigarettes, some crumpled up, in the well-weathered red box complete with the British Royal Warrant which indicated that the King of England himself endorsed this brand of tobacco product. "How about a cigarette, Corporal, my last few at that? I think there are at least two that are fully intact!" Colonel 'Slim' Chatsworth offered his nervous young aide, hoping that the fine English Dunhill cigarette would help calm both of their nerves.

"Why yes, of course and many thanks, sir! I'm glad that you stumbled onto these treats! I developed the tobacco habit when I volunteered for the army. I figured if I'm gonna be a man, I might as well act like one too!" the young corporal replied and taking the kindly offered cigarette. While temporarily relaxing and puffing away on their cherished cigarettes, both men suddenly noticed their own most foul body odours and waste. For the sake of hygiene they had to at least get rid of their soiled underwear. Both men stripped down and threw off their cotton undershirts and soiled underpants, using their cotton undershirts as expedient toilet paper. They tossed their unsanitary clothes into a near-by rusted bucket for the time being. Now only clothed in the tattered remnants of their outer uniform garments, both men felt better, but they knew that they still stunk like skunks, they needed a bath and food desperately. Body filth was very unsanitary and it attracted, bred and ultimately became a host for body vermin and it contributed undesirable skin rashes and sores, which could become infected.

"Suuuusssshhh, what was that? Did you hear that, sir? Ah, I thought I heard a sound, just like before!" the agitated Corporal quickly whispered out to his superior officer. Both men froze in their place, not wanting to make a betraying noise and to better aid in discerning the next sound. They both detected the sound of footsteps a few feet from the door. It was now pitch dark outside and nothing could be seen. They heard the unmistakable audible sounds of footsteps – multiple sets of footsteps it seemed. There was a sudden knock on the door, then the slow manipulation of the creaky door handle and next the entrance of three individuals holding kerosene lanterns and two metal pales and a shapeless bundle.

True to his word, it was Peter the coal miner and field labourer! As promised, he had brought along with him another man and also a most unusual and surprising guest – a Belgian Catholic nun dressed in contrasting white and grey coloured habit that covered the nun from head-to-toe. She appeared to be a gentle and kind looking woman in her early forties. She had pale blue eyes and a fair complexion free of age lines or other physical afflictions. Her convent was located in the nearby village of Wasmes, in the province of Hainaut, of which the city of Mons was the capital.

"Blimey, never thought I'd be so thankful to see a Papist and a Catholic nun at that!" the Corporal replied, instantly betraying his traditional Anglican English upbringing of having enmity toward the Church of Rome.

Colonel Chatsworth slowly raised himself from the sofa, his eyes greeting the strangers with initial ambivalence, then a soft smile painted his face; he wanted to make friends, not enemies. For a few brief moments, no one said anything; both parties carefully eyed-up the other. Just as the Colonel was about to initiate a greeting in French, he was pleasantly interrupted by the strange man who uttered in perfect English, "Please English soldier, be not afraid, we are here to help you! My name is Monsieur Herman Capiau. I am a local man and I'm from the Borinage district – just a short distance from here! My companions here are Sister Josephine and you have already met Peter, who is a local farmer and part-time coal miner… we are friends and we will help you hide from the Germans." The thin man, aged around 30, spoke in fluent English accented with the slightest kiss of a French-Belgian accent. "I'm a mining engineer and Belgian patriot…we hate the Germans and we want to spare you becoming prisoners or worse – being shot! We have some food, water and some field labour clothes for you to wear. Please let us help you!"

Corporal Taylor was suspicious and his manner was guarded; however Colonel Chatsworth was more affable to the offer, as he knew that their situation was desperate and that no other options existed. He smiled and extended his hands in friendly appreciation. "Thank you, Monsieur Capiau, we accept your offer and we are at your mercy!"

Herman Capiau clasped the Colonel's hand and shook it in a friendly manner. The initial tension was broken.

"Please help these men!" Capiau remarked softly in French, gesturing with his hand as he addressed his remarks to Sister Josephine and Peter. With this encouragement, the pair rushed forward to assist the two deprived English soldiers. Peter unbundled some well-worn miner and field clothing, as he helped both soldiers out of their filthy and foul smelling uniforms that were now mere tattered rags from the weeks of abuse. The Colonel and Corporal quickly douched themselves with some water-soaked rags to remove the filth from their bodies. The desperate situation of the two soldiers was such that no modesty was betrayed by their brief temporary nakedness in the dimly lit miner's cottage to include that of the celibate Sister Josephine; war had made all men and women equal in their personal distresses. The old work clothes felt divine and served as a perfect disguise to dissuade any further inquiry by the wandering German patrols and by the local Belgian citizens as well. One could not be too careful even among the vastly loyal and anti-German Belgian citizenry, for every country harboured potential traitors and opportunists – it took only one traitor to betray many other citizens. The clothing fit the two soldiers adequately; the loose fitting clothing made their appearances even more natural, as such decorum was most common among the local miners and farm labourers.

"Now, please eat. I have hearty soup and bread!" Sister Josephine stated in a soft French voice as she opened a small bucket-shaped metal container which contained some delicious smelling vegetable and beef soup. It was thick, dark and rich! Two wooden bowls and spoons were also provided along with three loaves of hearty rich grain impregnated brown bread. The two famished English soldiers devoured their meal with great glee; it was their first real meal in three days and the food tasted as heavenly as it had smelled. In less than thirty minutes, the two men had consumed all the food that their friendly pilgrims had brought to them. The Belgians smiled with delight at having helped their Allied soldiers and were immediately reassured that their actions had been true and good, despite any personal risks.

"Thank you very much for your humanity; you are all great patriots and Christians!" Colonel Chatsworth exclaimed with extreme gratitude.

"That goes double for me too!" Corporal Taylor added.

"No, no…it's our pleasure and honour to assist the brave soldiers fighting the brutal Boche that we Belgians must give thanks! Our immediate task is to get you better, safer lodging, get you healthy and then, well we shall see about that next step later! I see that you are limping, sir – are you hurt, monsieur?" Herman Capiau inquired as the Catholic Sister and Peter remained silent. Herman Capiau was obviously the more extrovert and prominent member among the trio.

"Thank you, Monsieur Capiau and forgive my manners. I am Colonel Percy Chatsworth, but you can simply call me 'Slim', my regimental nickname, and this is my aide Corporal Billy Taylor. We were part of the BEF and we got cut-off in the fighting around Mons. The fighting there was horrific, never saw anything like it before in all my military service; the German artillery and machine guns are deadly and we suffered many dead. I tore or broke something in my left leg and I badly bruised my right shoulder – that kind of balances my old body out!" The Colonel laughed with a grimace as a mild streak of pain oozed through his body.

"Are you healthy, Corporal?" Herman inquired in turn.

"You bet I am, sir, I'm fit as a fiddle. It appears like I must have gotten lucky you might say!" the youthful, dark-haired Corporal replied with a boyish smile.

"Can you both travel now?" Capiau inquired further of the two now refreshed soldiers. "You bet! Yes, Monsieur Capiau," Corporal Taylor and Colonel Chatsworth uttered in immediate succession. Like a keen engineer, Herman Capiau thought quickly and logically for about a minute. He was carefully calculating a systematic method to lodge and transport the two refugee British soldiers in discrete stages that would best defeat any German detection or patrols. Like lightning, his plan was fully conceived; it was more complex than a simple, direct course of action, yet it was vastly safer and safety was the key factor in this highly dangerous harbouring and transportation of Allied soldiers.

"I am going to move you at night in discrete phases to places of safety first. The main priority is to get you both well rested and fed. The next step is to get Colonel Chatsworth healthy. The final step…is to get you back to the Allied lines and England!" the mining engineer boldly proclaimed to the two stunned soldiers. The Englishmen could scarcely think of where they would be sleeping this very night and here was this Belgian stranger speaking to them about escaping from German occupied Belgium and back to friendly lines and England. Exactly what was this crazy man telling them, the two bewildered soldiers thought to themselves.

"England, merry old England! Are you serious my friend? Can you really do that? I mean…getting us back to England?" Colonel Chatsworth couldn't contain his excitement at the very suggestion of a possible escape.

"Well, I do not see why it cannot be tried! I see no advantage to you staying in Belgium indefinitely and I think it best to try and get out of Belgium before the Germans become too settled and comfortable in this country. It is best to try and escape while the Germans are unfamiliar with the country and the people," Herman Capiau wisely calculated.

The two English soldiers looked at one another and simply nodded their heads in affirmation and agreement. They knew that Capiau's words and logic were spot-on correct. "We're at your mercy and charity sir!" the Colonel sparked back as he held out his sore right arm to extend a light handshake to Herman.

"Good then, this night and despite the German curfew, I take you to a friend's house that is safe from the Germans, then I'll take you to an even safer place. If that goes well I'll try and get medical help for the Colonel, but I'm deliberately vague in my details because if either of you get caught by the Germans, you will have fewer facts to betray and fewer lies to tell. Do not underestimate the cleverness of the Boche – they can get information out of a person without you realizing it! So knowing less is saying less and thus betraying less!" the astute Capiau noted in English to the two soldiers, even now cloaking his conversation from his two Belgian friends. Capiau's stealth was most wise and more of his countrymen could benefit from similar practised discretion.

"Quickly then and get ready! Put on these old coats and hat. You there, Corporal Billy, here is a small cloth sack filled with hay – you need to place it on your back under your coat…move slowly and stay bent over…everyone will think you are old and a hunch-back! A perfect disguise for a young man who should be in the army or out working in the fields!" Capiau carefully explained, taking the details of the subterfuge and deception to the zenith.

A small hand-cart filled generously with straw and some farm utensils provided the perfect canard to smuggle the two soldiers in addition to providing a most practical means of transport for the mobility infirmed Colonel. As an added bonus, the small wooden handcart was most ubiquitous, light, quiet and very manoeuvrable. Billy and Herman Capiau easily pulled the cart down the smooth country dirt road, while Colonel Chatsworth sat lazily and curled up in the cart bed atop a gentle and generous mound of fresh cut hay, and Sister Josephine and Peter walked to the side of the hand-drawn cart. Aside from being out after the German imposed curfew, the scene was both idyllic and non-suspicious. If challenged by the Germans, Sister Josephine could provide a false and tearful story of needing to have the men bring her hay to the nearby convent. Few, if any German soldiers refused the pleading of a middle-aged woman dressed in her religious order regalia. The rural farm areas were unofficially given more leniency in the German curfew enforcement; however, large cities like Brussels received far greater scrutiny in this policy.

The night was both clear and warm; there was a partial moon that made travelling the pitch-black back-country roads possible, but slow. The night was most temperate and the road was superbly level; the journey was a most pleasant one save for the anxiety that they all possessed from this most unlawful act and the draconian punishment they all would incur if caught by the Germans or betrayed by a disloyal Belgian. After about ninety nervous minutes, they had arrived at a non-descript red brick cottage with accompanying terracotta burgundy coloured roof. In front of the cottage doors, there were small kerosene exterior door lamps encased with amber-coloured glass that provided the barest of lighting conditions, yet in the darkness these seemed as radiant beacons to any dilated-eyed visitor. They gently pulled the handcart to the side of the residence; this was more unobtrusive and secure even though there was not another neighbouring house for another two miles.

"Stay here and please be quiet! I'll be back soon!" Capiau whispered to his co-conspirators. They needed no additional encouragement – all of their lives depended upon their being alert and following the orders of the leader, in this case Herman Capiau. He knocked three times firmly on the thick oak wood side door of the small cottage. A middle-aged man with a slightly receding hairline was seen to peer from a small opening in the door to preview the identity of the unannounced mid-night visitor. Cautiously and slowly the massive oak door creaked and opened slowly... a middle-aged man in a sleeping shirt and slippers appeared.

"Hello Albert, it's Herman! Quick, I need your help!" Capiau spoke out softly in French into the recess of the open door.

"Capiau, you must be crazy, it's past midnight and there's a curfew! What the hell is so important that you need to see me at this late hour!" demanded the middle-aged man who was seen holding a kerosene lamp in his left hand.

"We have some unexpected friends! English soldiers stranded and who need refuge before the Germans get them! Remember that we spoke about helping our country when the war started? Well the war has come to us in an unexpected way!" Capiau answered as his friend Albert suddenly recalled the conversation that the two men had had in a Brussels café after the Germans invaded their neutral country some weeks earlier. The two men had spoken of Belgian patriotism and resisting the German occupation.

"Who and how many Englishmen do you have, Capiau?" the inquisitive house-keeper muttered. "Only two, a Colonel and a Corporal. The Colonel speaks fluent French, but he is injured in the arm and leg. They both need rest, food and medical help for the Colonel – now, can you assist or do I go seek help elsewhere?" Capiau pleaded, anxious and nervous. There was a fleeting second of hesitation, but Albert saw the desperate look on his friend's face and he remembered his patriotic promise he had made to help out his country.

"Sure, bring them in. My wife is not here, I am alone, the soldiers will be safe here for a few days!" Albert replied.

Herman made a quick wave movement of his arm and also clicked his right thumb and middle finger. Everyone around the cart moved and assisted Colonel Chatsworth to carefully exit the hand-cart and they all entered the cottage with stealthy haste. The two English soldiers looked as ragged and dishevelled as ever. The Colonel and the Corporal looked like dirty Belgian work hands, they both sported unkept beards that had a growth of at least two or three weeks. This was a good thing too, Herman Capiau thought to himself – the beards could easily help disguise these refugee soldiers as simply Belgian workhands or farmers.

"Hello, English soldiers, I am Albert Libiez. I am a lawyer and you will be safe here for a few days. Monsieur Capiau and I will work to get you to your next place of refuge very soon. The Germans do not come here yet; you rest and eat, then you will be better!" Albert pronounced proudly in his broken English. The two soldiers sat themselves on a comfortable couch and soon were fast asleep. This time they rested soundly and without any trepidation. Peter and Sister Josephine also slept in comfortable reading chairs that were in Albert Libiez's small reading room. It was best for them to travel during the following day; it was best not to tempt fate and be discovered by either the Germans or wandering Belgian eyes. Libiez and Capiau took a drink of brandy and spoke for a few hours of the plan to remit the refugee soldiers to their next point of assistance. The details were carefully vetted by the agitated and agile minds of the engineer and lawyer, yet nothing was of a preplanned nature. It was a very productive night for both men. They were somewhat scared, but also energized with enthusiasm and patriotism.

\* \* \* \* \* \* \* \* \* \* \* \*

"I am glad, my dear brother, that the terrible German artillery has ceased. It means that Belgium is no longer the centre of war focus for the Germans; they have moved on westward and may the Lord pity our dear French neighbours…they shall be in for a horrific terror," the mild voiced, pretty, auburn-haired, early middle-aged lady spoke with a soft feminine French accent to her brother, as the two gazed out of their large front window looking for signs of war and the German army – yet none was to be found.

"Yes, my dear sister, the German front has moved westward into eastern France. It will be a bad thing for them, I fear and I hope our relatives are safe there!" the middle-aged man replied. He had a thin drawn face, flamboyant black moustache and receding hairline.

"The German advance has moved on, so that is good for us all?" the elegant lady replied, hoping for a positive, reassuring response from her more worldly, but younger brother.

"I do indeed pray that your hope becomes true, dear sister, yet I'm afraid that while the battles in our dear country are over, the dreaded German occupation has only just begun! Yes, the German army advances, while the Germans will still remain. I've seen posters all over the villages and towns across Belgium warning and instructing our citizens on 'what to do' and instructing us what is 'verboten'; there are warnings about severe punishments for breaking curfews, espionage, the restriction of possession of firearms, mass assembly, harbouring enemy soldiers and even negative public discussions about the German occupation and our reduced living standards. It's all legal too under international law! This is what happens when a bully neighbour becomes victorious – he crushes you!" the brother replied back in an embittered tone to his sister.

"I realize now that merely being a neutral country was no insurance against being invaded by the Germans; we were so confidently naive. Good Lord, I do hope and pray that our brother Leopold is safe – he's joined the Belgian army and he's serving under our King Albert probably in France somewhere – do you think he's safe?", the sister replied back with anxiety in her voice and a concerned look on her face, her pretty pale blue eyes moistening up over concern for her other, younger brother named Leopold.

"Safe, my dearest sister? I think in this new type of war that no one is safe, be they soldier or civilian, man or woman, old or young, innocent or complacent, citizen or nobility...smart or dumb! This modern war is an equal killer I believe. I have heard terrible stories of the Germans wantonly destroying and looting shops, homes and estates across Belgium; there are reliable stories from multiple sources of on-the-spot executions of Allied soldiers and Belgian civilians as well. I'm afraid this leads to two possibilities, either the German army is undisciplined or there is a brutal, deliberate war policy being enforced from the highest levels of Army Command. I fear that the latter possibility is the likeliest one as the German people and their army are a most disciplined lot!" the brother concluded with disgust as he placed down his cup of dark, rich coffee. He wondered how much longer such luxuries as coffee, tea, sugar, butter, cheese and other food items previously taken for granted were going to be available under the harsh German military occupation.

The conversation between this brother and sister could have been one of countless others being conducted across occupied Belgium in private houses, modest farm cottages and sidewalk cafes; however, these siblings and their family were not ordinary in any sense of the word. They were the infamous Prince Reginald Charles Alfred de Croy and his sister Princess Marie Elizabeth de Croy of the ancient royal family of Belgium dating back to the Middle Ages. The imposing four-storey family estate of Bellignies Chateau was located a few scant miles from the intersection of the Franco-Belgian frontiers. The Bellignies estate was a large feudal complex that was characterized by successive architectural additions onto the original Gothic-styled massive tower or 'Fortress Keep', which was later complemented by a more modern adjourning stone wall building that completed the estate compound that had been constructed about one hundred and fifty years earlier in the eighteenth century. The estate also included a massive forest area, which consisted of several thousand acres of lush, dense forests. All three of the de Croy siblings were in their latter thirties and presently unmarried, although the elder brother, Prince Leopold Marie Charles de Croy was now serving as an Infantry battalion commander with the Belgian First Guides Battalion, serving under the leadership of King Albert's Belgian army in France. Leopold was engaged to be married just as the Germans invaded Belgium. Like many others, he would have to wait until this war was over to fulfill this obligation – that is, if he still lived! With both of their parents being deceased, Prince Reginald de Croy was obliged to tender to the family estate at Bellignies, located near Mons, Belgium. The only other family member in residence was their maternal, English-born grandmother of eighty-five years, Mrs Parnell, who was largely bound to the confines of her large private bedroom.

Despite its noble lineage, the de Croy family was not of the laissez-faire landed nobles, who simply laid back on their fortunes and attended royal parties. To the de Croys, privilege imposed a sense of responsibility and duty. Their late father, Prince Alfred Emmanuel de Croy-Solre was a Belgian Ambassador, who was posted to London for many years and Prince Reginald de Croy was the Belgium Secretary or Consul for the last ten years at the Belgium Embassy in London. All of the de Croy siblings spoke fluent French, English and German. Princess Marie had also just finished up her certification as an auxiliary nurse, this to assist in helping the war wounded. She had no idea of the trials to be placed upon her and her brother.

"This war is becoming a terrible strain on our people, dearest brother. I see the worry and unhappiness in the people's faces and it is as if the joyful spirit of the country has been exiled along with our monarchy and Parliament!

"Yes, we Belgians of all ranks and social strata must do that which we can to help our country and her Allies. I am most glad that we offered up the Chateau Bellignies to serve as a International Red Cross Hospital and that I was certified with a diploma as a nurse to serve our wounded and those of the other nations at war to also include that of our enemies!" Princess Marie de Croy was proud of being able to help in some little way in this war.

"Yes Marie, you did a wise and courageous thing and I too am very proud to have the white and red international Red Cross flag wave prominently from atop our ancient home for this humanitarian purpose," Prince Reginald de Croy replied to his innocent looking sister. There were only a score of slightly wounded Belgian and some French wounded soldiers occupying the large ballroom, which had been sectioned into neat partitions by the Belgian Red Cross organization. Beds and white curtains were moved into the hall, which served as a short-term hospital ward for the wounded soldiers who were recuperating from the recent Battle of Mons. The German army was careful to keep a keen eye on the wounded soldiers and make proper note of their names and location for both identity and control purposes. As soon as wounded Allied soldiers were deemed healthy by the daily visiting German army medical officer, he was immediately fetched by a German ambulance and transported to Germany into a POW compound. Most of the remaining soldiers were British, the 'Old Contemptibles' of the regular colonial army that had been rapidly ordered back to the continent from exotic British colonies and who had contracted malaria in the tropical zones. Malaria was not well understood or treated in Europe at the time, so these soldiers were the last to be treated. Soon there were to be no more wounded Allied soldiers as the Germans policed-up the battlefields with ever increasing efficiency. Still, the Germans were not as efficient as they had thought, as desperate Allied soldiers continued with skill and cunning to evade their countryside patrols.

Unlike some of their aristocratic friends who fled to the safety of England, the de Croys thought it best to stay in Belgium and maintain their ancestral estate and render any help to their fellow citizens and fellow allies. During the early months of the war, the de Croys had the unfortunate displeasure of having to entertain some high ranking German generals, who took noted and vocal protest at staying in a residence that also housed wounded Allied soldiers. It seemed that the German generals, like their lonely privates, also had childish-like nightmares of having their throats also cut in the middle of the night by the British bogyman. Reggie and Marie gave out a great relief when these obnoxious uninvited guests left the Bellignies Chateau after having consumed their food, drunk their fine wines, abused their servants and insulted their hosts. To say that the German Generals were rude would be a gross understatement.

"I wish that we had more news about the war and the world! Ever since the German occupation, there's been nothing published from the Belgian newspapers. We are totally censored by German military proclamations, most of which are threatening, or which list all the things that we are no longer free to do! I hate the German military occupation! We are like captive birds in a cage and our cage is getting smaller each day!" Princess Marie railed bitterly as she sipped some coffee from her fine Wedgewood china that she had bought while in England some few years earlier.

"Yes Marie, I too hate this German occupation. I think it best that I plan for another visit back to England. I have my old diplomatic credentials and I have connections to get me through the enemy lines to either France or Holland and from there it's a short jaunt across the channel. I think that we need to be prudent too! Start to hide, bury and disguise any of our valuables such as china, silverware, family heirlooms, fine clothing, pictures, whiskey and wine! Over time, I fear that these items will be confiscated by unscrupulous Germans and as the war and occupation drags on, the German morale will ebb and their desperation will grow ever stronger," Reginald wisely calculated.

"Do you think that travelling to England is safe or wise, Reginald?" Marie inquired softly, as the conversation they were having was most private and now very dangerous. This was a matter now between family members only; both the brother and sister had a very close relationship.

Reginald thought for a few seconds then answered in an equally muffled voice. "Yes, I think we must take some risks – our country is at war. While we are occupied, we Belgians still are not defeated! I will make trips back and forth to England until it becomes impractical and I can make periodic visits to the US Consulate to get and receive correspondence from our friends in England. The Germans will not get too suspicious if I only make infrequent visits there!" the Prince replied as he tried to rationalize his plans to both his sister and himself, of the serious risks he was taking.

The Princess thought carefully about his logical words and for an instant she felt ashamed of herself. "How correct you are, Reginald. We are both adults in our prime of life and we are both unmarried – and our parents are deceased. If we do not take risks, then we are cowards compared to our countrymen who have wives and children in their care. We have no right to be selfish and try to just ride-out this war in the safety of our chateau!" Marie smiled and patted her brother gently on the hand.

There was a sudden interruption to the sibling discussion, as a firm, hard knock sounded on the solid oak door. "Please excuse the interruption, Prince and Princess; however you have an unannounced visitor: it's the Countess de Belleville and she insists on seeing you at once, she merely stated that it is a private issue that cannot be deferred!" the head housemaid Florine interjected in a very professional and cultivated formal-French accent.

"Of course, Florine, show her in at once and bring her here to us!" the Princess replied as Reginald nodded in agreement.

"Funny, I wonder what on earth Jeanne wants – it's a several-hour journey from her estate in Lille! This must be important indeed if she did not even telephone us!" Reginald remarked almost innocently.

"May I announce the Countess Marie de Belleville," Florine voiced in a most audible and formal annunciation to the royal siblings, as she discreetly closed the doors to the Chateau's drawing room behind her and went about her daily business chores.

"Why Jeanne, you look well and what a pleasant surprise! We were not expecting you!" Marie rushed up and kissed her friend on the cheek.

Reginald arose as well and also gave his regal neighbour a modest and proper kiss on the cheek. The de Croys had known the Countess for years and they were close friends. "I was just telling Marie that you should have called us – the phones are still working even in this war!" Reginald remarked innocently again. This time the Countess's face gave an obvious glance of disapproval to his last remark.

"Yes I'm afraid, Reginald, that the phones are working all too well!" Jeanne remarked with a tone of dread. Without warning the Countess quickly went to the door and opened it, she glanced around, saw nothing and then quickly closed the massive oak door again with a deft touch. She placed her white kid gloved index finger up to her lips in an obvious sign for the de Croys to be silent. The Prince and Princess stared with amazement at each other – the Countess had never acted like this before with them and her behaviour was quite strange.

"Please let us be very quiet and speak only in English. I do not trust using either our native French or the German languages – too many local people understand these languages!" the Countess warned in a hushed tone. For the first time that day, the Prince and Princess became very serious and a bit scared.

"You do not have to say anything, just listen to me please as you are both my lifelong friends and nobles; you are also loyal Belgians," the Countess de Belleville announced with a deadly serious soft tone. The Countess took a seat on the sofa and motioned with her hand for her two friends to gather close to her side to within whisper distance. The three now looked almost as a huddled football team conducting game strategy.

"I have been approached by some friends of mine, an engineer from Borinage named Capiau and a lawyer named Libiez who have arranged for the hiding of two escaped English soldiers from the Mons battle….a Colonel and a Corporal. They are now being hidden by Sister Josephine in a cloistered convent located near Witheries. The English Colonel is named Chatsworth; he needs medical attention as his right shoulder and left leg are injured and he has slight concussion. Can you get them medical attention and maybe even an escape out of Belgium?"

"Oh my, oh my God!' Marie exclaimed in amazement. She had no idea that the war and her principles were even now being put to the test. She and her brother had been discussing this very issue, but only vicariously! Now they were both faced with the true test of patriotism – that of action and risking their very lives.

"Colonel Chatsworth did you say? 'Slim' Chatsworth, the Earl of Derbyshire, the son of the Duke of Albemarle? My Lord, I cannot believe it! I know his family from my years in England; he is a very good man – we must help save him!" Reginald insisted emotionally and with a hurried air of urgency. Marie looked at her brother with an initial fear, which quickly turned to a faint smile – she too had met and known 'Slim' Chatsworth and she knew that he needed to be rescued from his desperate situation.

"Of course we'll help them!" the Princess remarked with no hesitation. This to reassure her brother that she fully endorsed his view. "He needs medical help and I am an active sponsor to a modern medical nursing clinique in Brussels – it's the Berkendael Institute and the Clinique rue de la Culture, founded by Doctor Depage, a leading Brussels surgeon and now operated by the head nurse, Directress Edith Cavell, a very competent, single English woman."

"The Earl can be treated there safely and recuperate before we send him and the Corporal off, probably through to Holland and then on to England," Reginald quickly and accurately articulated as the genesis of the escape plan and route brewed forth from his experienced mind. Even now, the French border was heavily fortified and arrayed with deadly covering fires from guns of both German and Allied armies alike and death was a very possible outcome should one foolishly attempt a border egress. Holland was much safer as a border crossing.

"I cannot thank you enough! I knew that I had come to the right friends for help!" Countess Jeanne de Belleville cried out softly as she burst forth into a wide smile and hugged her two friends. For better or worse the plan was etched and details were finalized. The Prince and Princess both agreed that Sister Josephine needed to act as an escort for the two English soldiers for the travel down to Brussels. A catholic sister in her long religious habit accompanied by two lowly looking Belgian peasant men would not attract the attention of the Germans. The English soldiers, however, needed official looking identification papers and accompanying photograph identification, without which they were liable to get into quick trouble.

"Jeanne you need to see if Libiez and Capiau can get some identity papers and a photograph of the two soldiers produced. I have a small camera if one is needed," Princess Marie de Croy eagerly volunteered.

"That's good thinking, Marie," Reginald sounded back with glee.

"Next Countess, you will need to request that Sister Josephine make herself available for the journey to Brussels in about a week's time. Meanwhile, I'll contact Dr Antoine Depage and Edith Cavell and tell them to expect the arrival of our two visitors and to prepare for their necessary medical treatment and recovery at the Clinique," Reginald announced with determination. "I know that Dr Depage is planning to leave Belgium very soon – he wants to join-up with the Belgium army as a surgeon – but we might be able to use his expert surgeon skills before he flees. Let's pray that he has not already left for the war. I cannot vouch for the integrity of an unknown Belgian surgeon for such a dangerous endeavour.

"That is perfect, Reginald! I guess you can now appreciate the reason for my not using the telephone – the Germans control everything, so I had to rely on seeing you both in person; it was the only secure way!" Jeanne gave a humble explanation of needing to see them in-person.

"No apologies please, Jeanne, you were very astute to do exactly as you have done. None of us can now or in the future depend upon the telephone for sensitive communications; everything we do must be done in person. We can only trust ourselves and our own devices," Princess Marie de Croy concurred.

"Jeanne, if there are any problems with these instructions, please contact either myself or my sister. We can make adjustments if necessary, but time is critical. We need to get Colonel Chatsworth medical help and out of Belgium quickly. The frontier becomes more stable and secure with each passing day and this makes the German ability to reinforce the border more feasible," Reginald replied as the Countess arose and hurried back to the Convent to inform Sister Josephine and the two Englishmen of the plan and preparations.

* * * * * * * * * * * *

All too quickly, the week passed without incident and as planned, Prince Reginald had contacted Dr Antoine Depage, the leading surgeon in Brussels and founder of the Berkendael Institute, or the more commonly named Clinique rue de la Culture, and Directress Edith Cavell had been contacted with a general request for assistance to help a wounded English officer, but no further details were furnished. Prince de Croy's conversation confirmed that Dr Depage was indeed planning to secretly leave Belgium to assist the Belgian army; however, he agreed to stay to help the wounded English Colonel. Secrecy and vagueness were paramount and needed to maintain the safe passage into Brussels of the two English refugee soldiers and only a minimum of information that was absolutely required was conveyed on a strict 'need-to-know' basis. Ignorance and innocence were two major advantages in conducting subversion in wartime.

The Princess Marie de Croy used a small pocket Kodak camera to take the identity photographs of Colonel 'Slim' Chatsworth and Corporal Billy Taylor. The camera had been conveniently rescued by the Princess when she was walking by the looted residence of a neighbour estate of the Chateau d Eth, whose owners had already fled to the safety of England. The film was furnished to Capiau and Libiez who then had the film developed by their trusted friend, a chemist named Georges Derveau. False identity card names were taken from real, but deceased local Belgian children who had died in their youth and whose age matched that of the English Colonel and Corporal. Together the three men prepared the forged paperwork and identity cards for the two English soldiers to get safe passage to Brussels. To maintain a solid cover story and to reduce suspicious 'eyes' among both the German authorities and Belgian paid informants, Reginald advised that Sisters Josephine, Sister Marie and Sister Madeline from the Belgian Catholic Convent at Witheries should accompany the two English soldiers down to Brussels. Although a train passage was the quickest travel method, it was also the most dangerous with nosey German police inspecting the identification of everyone aboard the train and it was an expensive means of conveyance, which also would generate suspicion as these were supposed to be peasant men not capable of affording a train passage. A better, but slower mode of transport was along the less travelled secondary roads. A horse team with a wagon could convey the entire party in a full day's journey. The sight of three catholic sisters was a very safe cover and the sisters could very easily obtain help from fellow Belgians whereas having male escorts would solicit more scrutiny and less sympathy.

The journey was on! The wagon and its precious human cargo slowly and carefully made its way from the rural dirt country roads through to the modern scenic streets of Brussels. Yet there was no molestation from either motor vehicles or humans; everyone in Brussels had become a pedestrian by decree of the German military, all citizen usage of motor vehicles and even bicycles was prohibited by the German Military-Governor as a means to exert control over the population, while the Germans were able to travel with speed and ease with confiscated civilian vehicles and bicycles. Even bicycles were sanctioned items that needed to be registered with the local police, lest these become confiscated. There were some inter-city trams that ran through the centre of Brussels, yet these were Spartan in numbers and duration. This limited transportation also meant that any Belgian was only as quick as his feet could carry him, save for those rural country dwellers who had the use of animal transportation.

The covered wagon stopped at a secondary street, the entire block of which consisted of neat, stone or brick façade three storey buildings. As expected, their wagon was one of the few vehicles of any type on the streets of Brussels; in these trying times most Belgians walked and this made for a lean and hungry populace – there was hardly any overweight person on the street, as food became scarce and fatty, rich foods disappeared for all save for that so afforded to the high ranking German officials and the back alley purveyors of the black marketer. Sister Josephine and her accompanying companions of Sisters Marie and Madeline carefully dismounted the wagon being mindful to maintain the decor of their clean white and grey religious habits, while hunch-backed Corporal Billy Taylor held the reins of the livery team firmly in his hands. Colonel 'Slim' Chatsworth was neatly and comfortably hidden in the back of the wagon bed; his leg wound was still in disrepair.

A hard knock was vigorously applied to the front door, atop which was posted a simple bronze plaque with gold painted lettering: 'Berkendael Institute: Clinique rue de la Culture'. In short order, a tall, thin-faced, middle-aged woman complete with greying brown hair and clear grey eyes opened the door and greeted the three sisters without emotion or expression. "Hello, may I help you?" the matronly woman queried them in high-class French that also hinted at a definitive cultivated upper English accent.

"Remember me, Directress Cavell? I'm Sister Josephine of the Convent at Witheries…we understand that you are expecting us!" Sister Josephine kept a low tone, ever mindful that her mission was one of absolute secrecy, otherwise they were all subject to death by the Germans.

"Why yes Sister, of course, I was informed of your visit and please take the wagon around to the back of the Clinique; there are fewer prying eyes than from the main front street," Edith Cavell remarked with street-wise acumen. A mature woman nearing fifty years of age, she was self-disciplined and regimented to the point of obsession, this due to her strict Anglican nature and her innate individual demeanour.

"Yes, Directress," Sister Josephine responded and dutifully obeyed the direction given to her.

Edith hurried to the rear alleyway of the Berkendael Institute, which consisted of a series of four town-houses that were adjoined through a series of basement corridors and upper hallways, at the rear of which there was located a small alleyway that bisected the entire block of buildings into two symmetrical sections. It was through the back alley corridor that wagons and carts delivered various items to all the block dwellings, as pedestrian entrances was restricted to the more proper front street door entrances. The on and off-loading of normal household and business supplies from the front street of any residence was a universal social 'faux pas', that instantly denoted redress and an obvious lack of upbringing. City ordnances and the police also frowned upon using the front street entrances for anything but normal pedestrian business and that all other deliveries and such be transacted at the rear alleyway corridor. Maintaining the veneer of social norms in the early twentieth century was paramount, as it was viewed as a means of collectively regulating and correcting the individual manners of the person, while imposing a modicum of civility on the collective whole, despite the proclivity of any private violations thereto. Discretion was a virtue that was not to be violated at the cost of social disapproval and even outright ostracism in severe cases of violation.

"Are the English soldiers well?" Edith quietly inquired of Sister Josephine, as she greeted her and the horse drawn wagon entourage assembled orderly at the rear of the Clinique.

"Oh yes, they are in a better condition than when they first arrived here, but there are some problems, Directress Cavell. The Colonel seemingly has a badly bruised left leg – it may even be broken – and he has concussion too! His right shoulder was also bruised, but it has mended well over the past week. The Corporal is well and in good spirits – he's young and resilient!"

She knew that expert medical evaluations were needed despite the 'good faith' medical speculations from these fine patriotic souls. As a trained nurse Edith experienced many cases where rather innocent-looking ailments became major medical complications from either the incorrect diagnosis or utter neglect. Still, these men looked relatively healthy and this was a good medical indicator of corresponding good vitality. Neither of these disastrous medical possibilities, however, was going to occur on her watch if she had anything to say about this issue, especially for a member of her country's armed forces and an exalted English officer at that, Edith secretly resolved to herself.

Edith nodded her head and quickly Corporal Taylor and Sister Josephine each took an arm around Colonel 'Slim' Chatsworth's upper torso and slowly walked him through the back door of the Clinique, up some stairs and into Edith's private office. Sister Marie and Madeline took charge of the wagon and horses, while also acting as look-outs for any German military presence. This same-type of patient conveyance was not at all novel – there had been other similar instances where a patient needed to be taken into the rear of the Clinique, where those on crutches or in stretchers were more easily transported into the large back alleyway doors than the very modestly narrow front street door entrances. If any nosey-neighbour or observer saw this scene, they would not notice anything odd at the occurrence.

"How do you feel, Colonel? My name is Nurse Edith Cavell. I'm the Directress of this Institute, which is the first Belgian institution to train professional nurses. I'm going to do some preliminary checks on your left leg and also a general examination, then I'll send my diagnosis to Dr Antoine Depage, head surgeon and founder of this Institute and the best surgeon in Belgium," Edith remarked professionally in perfect English as she took the Colonel's pulse, temperature and performed a quick 'hand and eye' coordination test – this being used to quickly judge the initial physical state of the patient and which served to detect more serious underlying medical issues, if any.

"Can it really be so! Why you are indeed an English lady. I am quite surprised as the Germans ordered the repatriation of all English citizens out of the country upon the opening of hostilities. The Prince mentioned your status and nationality to me of course, but just hearing my native tongue and accent again brings a tear to my soul. Why are you still here in this dreaded occupied country, my dear lady? Your presence here is simply amazing, almost miraculous I dare say!" Colonel Chatsworth remarked in utter wonder at hearing and seeing a refined English lady who by all rights should not be in Belgium in a time of war.

Edith was equally harkened to see and hear another of her countrymen, as she gave a gentle smile; it was quite nice to hear one's mother tongue and from a man of such obvious upper-class refinement.

"Well Colonel, you stayed because you had a duty to your battalion and regiment; I stayed at my post too! I am the Directress of this Nurse Training Institute and I am determined to serve in my post as well, during both good and bad times. It seems that we both have loyally and stubbornly served our respective obligations," Edith replied with a reserved sense of pride.

Colonel Chatsworth gently smiled at Edith – she was obviously a woman of strong English stock and she was possessed with a resolute inner personality.

"I just hope that we both made the correct decisions, my dear lady. I've been known to possess a stubborn streak, a curse of the Chatsworth family lineage I might add – my ancestors were frequently accused of possessing more tenacity than brains!" the Colonel volunteered in a strained, but very audible upper-class English accent that betrayed a lavish private tutoring and public schooling at Eton and later Oxford.

"Don't be offset by any of your foibles, Colonel. You see I too possess a stubborn streak; I am independent and I do not turn from trouble or suffering," Edith replied back with equal candour. The Colonel quietly smiled at Edith's personal grit and determination.

"Ouch that hurts a bit, nasty Nurse Cavell!" the Colonel remarked as she touched and prodded his discoloured left foot.

"Yes, Colonel and it should hurt too! It seems to be either a bad bruise or perhaps even a small chipped bone, but nothing more I suspect. The bone is not broken, but a doctor's diagnosis and treatment is definitely mandated. Now, how is your balance, eyesight and hearing?"

"There's still some ringing in the ears periodically, the eyesight is good for a fifty year old man and my balance is fine except for that pounding, swollen left leg," the Colonel replied.

"Sister Josephine, what level of improvement has he had over the past week at the convent?" Edith inquired of the on-looking sister.

"Oh a very great improvement in appetite, sleeping and movement; even his pain has decreased too, Directress."

"Right then, your right shoulder appears to be healing along well, probably just a soft tissue trauma, it still needs slow healing. Your senses seem fine, but that left foot does indeed concern me, Colonel. Supervised convalescence is needed, maybe an operation too!" Edith surmised accurately.

"I do not want any operation and I don't need any more resting, do you hear me, nurse?" the proud Colonel righteously protested, but to no avail.

"Look, my dear Colonel Chatsworth, you're in my outfit now and you will obey my medical orders. Life and war is not about one's personal desires, it is about doing the right thing and one's duty! I am placing you in a room located in a section of the Clinique previously used for nurse instruction – since the war our classes have ceased. Dr Depage will be here tomorrow, so rest easy and be assured that only I and my assistant Nurse Wilkins or Nurse White will know of your presence," Edith replied, as Sister Josephine escorted the Colonel and Corporal to their new lodging rooms within the Clinique. Colonel Chatsworth knew that further protest was to no avail. The day passed and the men rested in a deep sleep, secure in the confidence that they were in the most able hands of Nurse Cavell.

"That was an excellent diagnosis, Nurse Cavell. I'm suspecting a minor chipped ankle bone in the Colonel's left foot – it's a minor operation; I can have it done with luck in an hour's time if the chip is not too large and there are no other complications. Recovery will be a few weeks so long as the patient stays off his left foot," Dr Depage noted softly as he carefully and gently examined 'Slim' Chatsworth's swollen lower appendage. The handsome fortyish Belgian surgeon sported a moustache and goatee, while his hair was worn in a medium-short manner; his hair was dark and thick, his eyes were light caramel brown. He spoke perfect English with a velvet soft French-Belgian accent. He continued without any interruptions, "I also thought that it might be a bad bruise or even a soft tissue injury; however, it has been many weeks since the injury has occurred and his bruising, pain and mobility levels are all indicative of a bone fragment being splintered. It must be removed or I fear that gangrene will ultimately develop."

The greying English Colonel was disturbed by the need for an operation. "Can't I just hobble along with a stick or a crutch, Doctor? I mean…I do feel a lot better than a few weeks ago! Maybe I can make a go of it without an operation?" 'Slim' Chatsworth spoke with a typical English stiff-upper-lip bravado.

Dr Depage and Edith looked at one another, both of them expressing immediate facial disapproval of the Colonel's ridiculous suggestion. "Absolutely not! You either get the operation for the chipped bone now or later you will get the entire left foot amputated. For some ailments like yours, dear Colonel, surgery is the only viable option," Dr Depage remarked plainly as Edith Cavell also chimed into the unwelcome diagnosis.

"Dr Depage is absolutely correct! There is not the slightest chance, dear Colonel, of your travelling any distance without surgery. You would not make it even half a mile in your present condition before your foot would again start to distress you and journeying cross-country into the Allied frontier is much more physically demanding than anything you have experienced since you had this injury. No, Colonel, you are going to have this operation or else you are going nowhere! I am not going to allow you to place your life and that of Corporal Taylor in jeopardy because of your stubbornness and foolish pride! If it eases your anxiety, I will assist Dr Depage during the operation, if he so permits it."

There was a sudden absolute silence in the room. The Colonel was taken aback by being spoken to by a matronly woman and by someone not even in his social class, yet he was wise enough to know that she was honest and correct. Additionally, this woman knew her business: she was no pushover and the Colonel admired this. She was insisting, but not bullying. Dr Depage said nothing to distract from her assessment either, so Colonel Chatsworth knew that the decision to operate was a foregone conclusion. He realized that he had indeed been wrong and he hated to admit it publicly. "By golly, Miss Cavell, I wish that I had a few more like you in the British Army Non-Commissioned Corps, I'd have a lot less nonsense from the ranks, that's for sure. So, when is the operation?" the grey haired Colonel asked of his medical experts.

"Tomorrow morning! This operation needs to happen sooner rather than later. No medical injury of this nature repairs itself!" Dr Depage announced as he looked over to Edith and he saw that she nodded her head in agreement. "Rest assured, you shall be in good hands; both Nurse Cavell and I will be the operating team, with Nurse Wilkins as a third set of hands if so needed. The fewer people that know about this operation and your personage, the better I should think!" Dr Depage nodded as he eyed both Edith and Colonel Chatsworth. They all silently nodded to the plan and knew that their lives were in great danger should there be any discovery of this operation and the things to come.

"That's it then, 8:00 am tomorrow. Edith, please ensure that you and Nurse Wilkins are ready and place one of your other trusted English nurses as a temporary Clinique supervisor until the operation is completed. We need to ensure that all the other Clinique nurses and staff stay clear of the Clinique operating room for the morning hours. Also, immediately place the patient on a fast from solid foods, only liquid from now on – in fact, restrict him to water if you can. We're using general anaesthesia and I want him to be on an empty stomach in case there is any reaction to the anaesthesia!", Dr

Depage ordered as he took his classic black medical bag and departed down the stairs and out of the Clinique.

Dr Antoine Depage and his wife were totally trustworthy Belgians, devoted to their country and the Allied cause. Dr Depage was a free-thinking man of high repute in the Brussels social circles and intellectual sect, and his wife Marie was a highly cultured and refined lady who introduced her husband to the higher social graces and valuable social contacts throughout Belgium society. Their younger son Lucian was the 'apple of their eyes'; he was now serving as a infantryman in the Belgian army somewhere in the trenches of France, while his older brother Pierre had been serving in the Belgian army since before the war. Both parents worried about the fates of both of their sons, yet they were consoled with the reality that many other Belgian, French and British families were making the same sacrifices with their male offspring. For the Depages, patriotism was something that was expressed through action, not social armchair chitchat.

As planned, the operation was executed without a hitch and the Colonel was recuperating quite nicely at the Clinique; a small splinter of bone on the lower left fibula, the size of a small toothpick was found to be detached from the main bone, yet still minimally attached to the Colonel's left main foot bone. This was causing excruciating pain as the bone splinter was irritating the surrounding muscle and tissue. The bone splinter was gently removed and the wound was dressed with fresh, clean bandages and antiseptic; the bandages were changed with strict routine daily. The left fibula bone was left to heal on its own and a schedule of light exercise and movements around the cloistered area of the Clinique was instituted and enforced. The other nurses became aware of the two male strangers; they were only told that the men were Belgian rural farm workers being treated for a communicable disease and that Nurse Cavell wanted to maintain a quarantine of their care area so to avoid undue exposure to the other nurses in training and in residence. Many thought this odd, as the Clinique was a training institute for young nurses and those admitted had previously only been of a physiological ailment or war wounds, not communicable diseases. Still, aside from the handful of supervising English nurses, the trainees were young and they acted and believed as they were told until practical experiences were to prove otherwise.

The Indian summer had all but disappeared from Belgium, as the cool refreshing winds of early October swept into the land; as the days were increasingly getting shorter, so too was the convalescence stay of Colonel Chatsworth. His leg had mended magnificently and it was now time for both himself and Corporal Taylor to depart the Clinique. Edith was more than happy to have helped the two English soldiers escape from the brutal treatment of the Germans and she wished only that she could do more. She adored the conversations with Colonel Chatsworth about the latest happenings in England, which unfortunately were all related to the war. At times his talk was a bore, but it was a delightful, refreshing English bore for which she was absent for over five years and his rambling discussions on any matter was refreshing. The Colonel also spoke of upper-class, aristocratic subjects to which Edith was never exposed and to which now she became most fascinated; it was an entire new world that the Colonel's tales had opened to her imagination and she yearned to learn more about these things after the end of this terrible war. She speculated that perhaps one day she might have in her professional care some of the Dukes, Marquis, Earls, Countesses and Barons on one of those magnificent country estates to which the Colonel had so fondly spoken; this type of private exclusive health care position was a worthy way to wind down one's nursing career while also affording her the possibility of going back to her native England. Since the war and her appointment as Directress, dreams had become the things of luxury, as the realities of responsibility consumed all of her mental energies and her present involvement in helping these two English soldiers had merely added to her already full mental burden. Her days were sixteen hours long and Sundays with their obligatory Anglican Church services offered her sole weekly relief from the burdens of work.

The Clinique presently had fewer war wounded men than just a few weeks earlier, as German soldiers were now being treated by German army medical personnel and the Allied military wounded were being treated in central Belgian hospitals and even in German-run military facilities. Soon the Clinique would go back to treating impoverished Belgian civilians of which there were aplenty. The two English soldiers were getting edgy and so was Edith Cavell – she knew that it was time for them to be leaving. There were only two options open to Edith: stash the two soldiers into a rural, abandoned house or shelter of some type; or arrange for them to be transported back to Bellignies and to the more assured safety of the Prince and Princess de Croy. Always the pragmatist, she chose the latter option as the safest and best means to get the English soldiers across either the French or Holland frontiers to safety. As per Dr Depage's instructions, she sent word through his wife Marie that the soldiers were fit and ready to return to Bellignies and he would make arrangements for their transport back. Marie Depage journeyed up to Bellignies and made arrangements for Capiau and another man to assist in the effort. While the use of the religious was most preferred, it could not be a singular or guaranteed means of conveyance. In war chances were inevitable and needed to be taken.

"Well gentlemen, the time has finally arrived and now you must leave and I must sadly say farewell. I will miss you very much, my fellow and fine English soldiers," Edith uttered in a most emotional and tearful voice to Colonel 'Slim' Chatsworth and Corporal Billy Taylor. While Edith was a very professional and caring woman and nurse, she was a most introverted person who did not share her innermost feelings or emotions with others, not even with her Clinique English nurses. Seeing her two English countrymen fit and repaired, she knew that she had made the correct decision to stay in Brussels when the Germans came to occupy the city.

"Well this is a bitter-sweet moment for the two of us, Nurse Cavell! If it were not for you, Dr Depage and the Prince and Princess – well, frankly we'd be either dead or in a German POW camp in Germany. We owe you and all the patriotic Belgians our lives; we'll be forever grateful! What can we do for you now, Nurse Cavell?" Colonel Chatsworth was now graced by a six inch grey and brown coloured beard.

"That goes for me as well, Nurse Cavell – without the help of all the religious sisters, farmers, and even aristocrats, I'd be dead too! This really is a war for all of the Allied people, not just the rich, poor and working people – it's about everyone!" voiced Corporal Taylor as he unconsciously toyed with his now well groomed beard hairs. Tears formed in Edith's eyes, so consumed was she by this genuine gratitude from her countrymen, yet true to her personal constitution, she held back the tears and her emotions. She turned momentarily to shield her eyes from the two soldiers.

"Just keep yourselves safe and get back to England and win this war for those of us left here in Belgium and the other occupied countries! If you can, please get word to my family living in Norwich, especially to my aged mother and tell her I am both fine and safe. Tell her that I am doing that work for which I was trained to do, that I'm doing my bit here for God and England in this occupied land of our enemies!" Edith replied in a soft voice, as she stealthily wiped her eyes and turned around to face the two soldiers and to offer them her hand. In turn, both the Colonel and the Corporal took her hand and shook it gently; each of them then presented a soft hand-kiss. Edith was most flattered; no man had ever expressed such affection or gestures to her, aside from those of her parents and siblings.

"I promise that I shall do that favour for you, Nurse Cavell and if we make it safely back to England, I shall send you some letters through the

British Embassy channels back to you! If you ever need a reference from me, Nurse Cavell, consider it done as well – you are a most excellent nurse and English patriot," Colonel Chatsworth promised with a broad smile that accented and pierced his bearded face. An unexpected knock echoed through the wooden door and it opened slowly to reveal the Associate Directress's face, that of Nurse Elizabeth Wilkins.

"Please excuse the interruption, but there is a wagon from Bellignies staged in the rear of the Clinique alleyway. It's time for our two special guests to leave us!" Nurse Wilkins announced in a sad voice.

"We're ready. The sooner we start, the sooner we're back to mother England!" Colonel Chatsworth announced with both bravado and shielded sadness. He and the Corporal had grown most fond of this place, yet he was now healthy and walked now without either pain or a limp. For reassurance and aesthetic reasons, however, Colonel 'Slim' carried a carved wooden walking stick, just in case the weight gave out on his left foot or if he needed it to shoo away some wild animals.

"I brought both of you some bread and a few bottles of Belgian beer for your journey. Godspeed to you both. Tell the folks in England about the plight of the Belgians!" Nurse Wilkins announced as she handed the Colonel a small brown burlap sack.

"Thank you, Nurse Wilkins, thank you both for everything! Give our best to Dr Depage and his wife; I hope their sons remains safe in the service to his country!" Colonel Chatsworth took the sack of food and hugged both nurses one last time before being led downstairs to the back alley and the waiting horse drawn wagon.

Edith watched the bittersweet scene of departure from a rear second storey window which overlooked the back alleyway of the rear of the clinique, while Nurse Wilkins led the two soldiers slowly away. Two shabby-clothed men stood next to the wagon. Edith spotted the familiar face of the man from Bellignies, Herman Capiau, while the identity of the other man was unknown to her. Later she would know of his name and reputation. The stranger was named Philippe Baucq, a local Brussels man in his early thirties with dark hair, medium build and height, fair complexion and sporting a moustache and goatee. In a matter of a few minutes, the Colonel was safely hidden away in the back of the wagon along with the ever-vigilant Corporal. By nightfall they were back at the safety of Bellignies Chateau near Mons.

The Prince and Princess de Croy were thankful that the surgery on Colonel Chatsworth had proceeded without any complications and that the two English soldiers had made it safely back to Bellignies Chateau.

Colonel Chatsworth could walk very well, but still he could not risk a long endurance trek on foot at this early stage of recovery. Bellignies Chateau was closer to the French border than Holland, yet the French border was being heavily fortified by opposing armies and numerous minefields, trenches and stretches of 'no-man's land' presented formidable obstacles and great danger to their lives. Ironically, it would have been better for the two to have stayed in Brussels and try to sneak into Holland just to the north; it also offered fewer guards and there was a very porous border that was manned with old and lazy guards. Oddly, the de Croys had taken one step forward with the English prisoners and one step back. The Colonel was medically well, but the two English soldiers were no closer to escape and freedom than previously a few weeks earlier.

"Marie, I think that our English guests will need to be making another journey back north to Brussels again, then to Amsterdam and through to Holland. Furthermore I think that our friends are at great risk of capture, especially Colonel Chatsworth, if they try to make it across the numerous canals into Holland...it's too demanding a task in his recuperative condition," Reginald noted to his sister, as the two recuperating English soldiers looked innocently at the two siblings with obvious disapproval at the words being spoken about them.

"Now, see here, my good man. I am most grateful for everything that you and your sister the Princess have done for myself and Corporal Taylor. However, I feel great after that surgery, in fact I think that I'm good as new. Dr Depage did a splendid job of surgery on the old left leg and I barely have a limp now! Besides, we are closer to France than to Holland. This means another damn trip to Brussels and then all the way north to Antwerp and Holland, which makes no sense! We will be travelling farther and covering the same travelled ground over again! I feel like I am on a bloody Cook's Tour of Belgium here!" 'Slim' Chatsworth protested vigorously as the four adults mingled in a cozy private sitting room located on the secluded second floor of the Bellignies Chateau. Princess Marie thought it best to reservedly keep her counsel until her brother had fully vetted his reasoning with the visibly upset Colonel.

"Please do not be mad, Colonel – hear me out for a moment. Yes, the French border is closer, but it is also much more dangerous and fortified. If we use a series of discreet religious abbeys, monasteries and convents located throughout northern Belgium, there's a very good chance that we can get you up to the northern waterways and transport you into Holland as a stow-away on a coal or food barge – this means no walking, swimming or jumping! An added advantage is that it is much safer too! There are fewer inspections of barges and less risk of being sighted by roaming eyes, you and the Corporal will just be another set of barge hands with few, if any, questions being asked of you," Reginald responded with perfect rational decorum.

The Princess knew that this was her time to chime in and seal the argument. "My brother Reginald is quite right. Few Germans will be expecting stranded British soldiers to possess the wherewithal to be able to engineer a safe passage by water barge up through to Holland. He has not failed you yet and we will not this time either. We can arrange maritime seamen identity cards for you as barge merchants and, let's be practical, river barges are the best means of travel – the flow of the river does all the hard work for you! Why walk when you can take a leisurely cruise, gentlemen?" Marie concluded assuredly.

Colonel 'Slim' Chatsworth was silent and he stared forward, thinking critically without saying a word of immediate emotional dissention. He was open-minded at the suggestion of being ferried in a barge up to Amsterdam and his left foot was still in the process of mending. He knew that he was not up to the demands of jumping into ditches and high impact running. Despite his soldierly pride, he was mature and wise enough to concede that in this situation discretion was the better part of valour.

"By Jove, you both make logical sense and aside from my foolish pride, I can find no faults in your proposal! You have both been spot-on with your planning to date and I have no cause or reservations to doubt you now. Your kindness and assistance to both Corporal Taylor and myself are above and beyond that to be expected from any citizen in this war. Yes, I agree to your plan, now exactly when can we get started?" Everyone broke into a cheerful mood and smiled.

"That's great, sir. To tell you the truth, despite being a ground soldier, I'd rather fancy a nice, soft river ride!" Corporal Billy Taylor remarked with a broad smile, as he casually enjoyed a cigarette that the Prince had been kind enough to offer him. All parties present smiled as they were thankfully relieved at not having to argue with the tenacious Colonel concerning the proposed water barge journey north to freedom.

"Well I can assure you that the barge will beat walking," Reginald de Croy announced with a smile, as he walked over and poured everyone a glass of red burgundy wine. In short order they all rose up and lifted their glasses to the newly conceived plan. "Here's to all of us, Belgians, Englishmen and French – may we rid ourselves of the Boche and may the repatriation of our two English friends meet with utter success and smoothness!" Reginald toasted in celebration, his small speech and powers of persuasion were a testament to his shrewdness and to the wealth of negotiating experience he had gained during the decade that he was posted in London. Reggie could keenly spot the nature of a person and deal with each individual according to their individual 'strengths and weaknesses', a very valuable and yet rare innate ability.

"I'll get the coordination of the personnel together and we'll have to get some updated identification for both the Colonel and the Corporal, yet I think that if all goes well, in a few weeks or maybe less, we'll have everything in order." Reginald sounded positive.

"That would be great, your Highness. I promised that English Directress, Nurse Edith Cavell, that I would contact her mother and family once we get back to England. She is quite a remarkable woman – independent, yet shy; intelligent but very humble; very religious and also patriotic! When I get back to England I shall keep that promise and I'll try and transmit a letter to her through the United Kingdom Foreign Office via diplomatic pouch to the US Consulate in Brussels. If that woman ever needs a personal reference for anything, she'll have no issue obtaining one from me. She'd make a fine private nurse-Governess, which she once was before the war began and prior to her Directress posting in Belgium," Colonel Chatsworth announced with stalwart resolve in his voice, as he repeated the promise that he had made to Edith on this same topic a few days earlier. Edith had related much of her prior professional life to Colonel 'Slim' and he keenly remembered her fond talk of working in England.

"Yes, Edith is a very remarkable, yet mysterious woman. The Princess and I met her at a Brussels white-tie fund-raising event that Dr and Mrs Depage were hosting for prominent, deep-pocketed guests to start the new Nurse training Clinique in 1909 and Dr Depage personally recruited Edith to be the Directress of the Clinique due to her twenty years of professional nursing experience in England and on the continent. Miss Cavell is, however, a bit of an enigma – while her professional nursing credentials and character are beyond reproach, there is nothing known of her personal life: no close friends, no socializing, no gentlemen or lady friends, nothing except her two faithful dogs and her nursing work! I suppose we all make the best efforts with those things to which the good Lord has given to each of us." Reginald spoke candidly and softly. He knew through experience that each person in life was given various crosses to bear in this very finite life and it was not his place to judge the lot given unto others; he had his own affairs to manage and a vast war was raging all around him. It seemed that the personal life and things thereto had to be abandoned until the end of this war.

"Yes, I too hardly know her except professionally and of course by her high reputation, yet she is not alone in her courage and patriotism – the Depages are another prime example of these same qualities, as are the religious orders in Belgium, also the men who assisted in your rescue and transportation to Brussels and even the common Belgian worker – they are all loyal, patriotic and hate the Germans!" Marie de Croy announced with a resolute and forthright utterance.

"Well that's a fine thing to note and I am forever in everyone's debt naturally; however, if this patriotism is so fervent, my dear Prince, perhaps it should be further explored and exploited!" Colonel Chatsworth remarked innocently without realizing the profoundness of his words. Marie and Reginald immediately stared at one another; their thoughts were perhaps even identical.

"Well that's a very interesting proposal, Colonel. Yes, perhaps someone should do exactly as you suggest!" the Prince remarked, as he quickly winked to his sister and poured everyone another full glass of burgundy wine. The four privately toasted the respective royal families of England and Belgium and the talk then detoured off into discussing the memories of mutual friends and families of the English aristocracy. All the while, however, the Prince and Princess were also thinking about the future, planning for the fate of other similarly stranded Allied soldiers.

True to his word, over the next two weeks both the Prince – and Princess – coordinated with their close aristocratic neighbour from across the border in France, the Countess Jeanne de Belleville for the details to be arranged for the smuggling of the Colonel and the Corporal back north and eventually into Holland via river barge. There was no question as to the Countess' inclination to participate with this bold plan; after all, she and Sister Josephine were the two women who had brought Colonel 'Slim' and Sergeant Taylor to the Chateau Bellignies initially. The plan was straightforward enough, but like a fine Swiss watch, every piece needed to be perfectly fitted for the operation to work out. The Prince and Princess knew that they could use the services of Albert Libiez and Herman Capiau to prepare the paperwork for worker identification cards for the Colonel and the Corporal, in addition to having the two soldiers stay at either Libiez's or Capiau's house – either man's house would provide a perfect staging point for the guide to pick them up and escort them ever northward to Brussels. From Brussels there was to be the hand-off to either Edith Cavell's Berkendael Institute or lodging at Philippe Baucq's residence.

Reginald contacted and received cooperation from a friend, a Belgian Baron, for the safe transport of the two soldiers on a river barge company owned by the Baron. For a guide, the Prince and Princess knew of a local man in Brussels who was familiar with the entire northern part of the country and he could be relied upon to assist the two soldiers both from Bellignies to Brussels and from Brussels north to a small tributary of the Scheldt river – his name was Henri Beyns. Henri was well known to the de Croys and Herman Capiau for many years. Henri was to escort the two English soldiers from Mons to Brussels and then from Brussels to Molenbeck, which was a northern Brussels tributary that fed into the Scheldt river that ran north to Antwerp and then to the coast of the North Sea.

All the parties were contacted by known and trusted personal exchange communications. Everyone wanted to help these two English soldiers escape Belgium. By early December 1914, the plan was placed into execution mode. The Englishmen were ready, as were the entire escape plan members. Before the two soldiers departed, the Prince and Princess bade their guests farewell, with Reginald verbally giving the two soldiers the final instructions of reporting into the Allied Headquarters located at the Hague in the Netherlands and to give the senior Allied intelligence there a summary of the resistance activities in Belgium, as well as their personal experiences with the German military and its brutal occupation of the entire country. The Colonel and Corporal left with feelings of both sadness and eager anticipation – they both longed to see England again. With that, the two men disappeared from the Prince and Princess's lives, as the thirtyish Henri Beyns arrived at Bellignies to take the two men to the railway station and the short fifty mile journey to Brussels. From Brussels it was a very short walk to the Molenbeck tributary and then to their river journey north to freedom. The train was judged to be an acceptable risk, as the Colonel was now quite healthy. He possessed seamen identity cards which were in order and the border was stable.

\* \* \* \* \* \* \* \* \* \* \*

# Chapter 4:
# A Network Emerges

*"Yes, you heard me correctly, gentlemen, there are many, perhaps hundreds of other British and Allied soldiers being hidden across the countryside of Belgium and they risk being shot as spies for being in civilian clothing..."*

The cool weeks of November 1914 quickly morphed into a bone-chilling, cold December, as the Prince and Princess de Croy welcomed the holidays and a new year. No communication was received from Colonel Chatsworth or Corporal Taylor, not even a rumour was heard. Given the lack of news, they both wondered and worried about the fate of their newly found compatriots.

"Do you think they're all right? Did they even make it to England? I can't help thinking that they are not the only ones, that there are others like them still in hiding!" Marie confessed to her brother, as the two were out on a short walk about the grounds of the Bellignies estate. The Prince did not immediately reply to his sister's utterance, although he clearly heard her; however, he was also thinking patriotic thoughts of his own.

"Well Marie, remember that particular evening when we were planning the escape of the Colonel and the Corporal? Remember when I winked at you after hearing the Colonel's flippant suggestion that we should 'do more'? Well, I knew right then and there that a course was being chartered for us. We do need to do more for Belgium and these other Allied stranded soldiers!"

The Princess was flabbergasted and a bit put-off by the sudden remarks. "You mean that you have had this matter on your mind all these weeks and you have said nothing to me!" she retorted back in an obviously angered and hurtful tone.

The Prince stayed silent for a few pregnant seconds before finally answering. "Yes, but some things are best not said until the idea is fully hatched! I needed to ponder all the details, which takes time; also if we get involved in this, Marie, we are in it until this war is ended one way or another. Remember, we were lucky once and helping two English soldiers is vastly different to the multiple risks associated with helping maybe countless dozens or even hundreds of Allied soldiers – we risk our very lives, position and fortune if we take on this voluntary endeavour. Are you in for this level of commitment? Please think before answering!" Reginald asked and counselled, as the brother and sister stopped and faced one another.

Now it was Marie's turn to be silent. She thought a few seconds, then finally answered, "Yes Reginald, I place my life and fortune in this endeavour. I want to help other stranded Allied soldiers and do anything else to rid Belgium of the horrible German army! I am still young and unmarried, I have the luxury of risking only my material possessions and that of my own life. Too many other Belgians have wives, husbands and children to care about to take on any additional risks. Yes, I really want to do this!" Marie replied with the devotion of a zealot.

Reginald smiled and hugged his sister; he knew that they were both equal co-conspirators in the endeavour that they were about to embrace. "Well, now that we have that settled, we are going to need a more formal and complex support system and a standard operating plan. The next order of business will be to hand-pick our fellow 'helpers'; loyalty is a top consideration and everyone must feel as we do! No one can be in this group who is self-centred or insincere to Belgium and the Allied cause; each person must be a volunteer and totally committed to place their life on the line for this cause!" Reginald remarked with the greatest of seriousness.

"How can I but fully agree with you, my brother, we need to avoid traitors and infiltrators too!" Marie remarked and then added, "We should only work with those whom we have personally known for many years – this is the best form of security that we can have, the help and devotion of our close friends."

Reginald knew the strength of friendships, as well as the weakness of these bonds. He knew that friendship was a great facilitating asset, yet friends could also intentionally or unintentionally be compromised by the enemy, especially a cunning foe who stopped at nothing in getting their way. "You are right in that, my dear sister, yet the vulnerability is that if one of our members should become compromised, the risk to everyone associated by friendship or social bond is also greater. Loyalty is paramount, yet so too is intelligence and war treats badly and unmercifully the person who is a fool," Reginald added in retrospective analysis.

"Yet there is no other way, is there?" Marie de Croy was secretly hoping that her wise brother had an alternative solution. He did not.

"No, I guess there's no alternative, at least none that I can fathom; we shall just have to keep especially vigilant in selecting our network friends and instilling in them the urgency for stealth and discretion," Reggie confessed to his sister with a slight resigned sigh in his voice.

"All successful organizations require good people, trusted communications, funding and sound planning! After we select our hand-picked group of key members, we need to ensure and maintain safe communication from the nosey Germans and that means absolutely no telephone or telegraph communications; everything will need to be by private written cryptic messages or better yet, by personal courier using verbal messages," Reginald declared in a clear quiet voice. Marie looked on and listened very attentively, mentally noting the details of his conversation and trying to find any weaknesses in the logic; she could find none. Reginald's reasoning and planning was perfectly composed and expressed.

The Prince continued speaking. "To get funding and external support, I will need to go to London and contact the Allied sources there. I have friends in Parliament and the other government offices there who can further assist us in advice, funding and providing secure communications through the British Embassy diplomatic courier system. I also want to stop at The Hague and contact the Allied High Command staff to both obtain and render information concerning the war. They need to know of the atrocities being committed here by the Germans and the desperate state that the Belgian citizens are living under," Reginald summarized to his sister. Marie merely nodded her head in both acknowledgment and support.

"Marie, do you think that you can manage affairs here at Bellignies while I periodically go on these foreign excursions every several months? Can you take care of Grandmother Parnell while I am abroad? Will you independently handle any of the Allied soldier transfers to Brussels? All that you reply will be voluntary on your part, sister. I'll understand if you decide to decline," Reginald's concern showed on his face. His family meant everything to him and he did not want to overly engage his only sister into issues for which she was not mentally and morally prepared to fully and independently assume.

"These are not obstacles for me brother; as long as Grandma's health holds up, I shall be fine. After all Grandmother Parnell is eighty-five years old, God Bless her gentle soul, yet at that age we have to prepare for any health issues or circumstances that will arise and I think that if I can successfully manage the Chateau staff here since our parents died, I can comfortably handle the issue of any Allied soldiers," Marie replied with a confident, passing smile. Reginald patted his sister on the shoulder as the two siblings made their way back to Bellignies in the brisk wintery air. Upon entering the Chateau's main entrance grand foyer area, they noticed three unexpected guests: their dear neighbour and friend the Countess Jeanne de Belleville and two other ladies in their late thirties or early forties, whose modest and practical dresses betrayed an ordinary middle class or working background.

"Pardon this unannounced visit, Prince and Princess de Croy. However, there has arisen an issue of gravest concern of which I need to urgently speak with you about! It is most private – can we all go somewhere where we will be in total privacy?" the Countess Jeanne de Belleville conveyed in a soft whisper. She wore an expression of obvious distress upon her pale white face.

"Yes, of course, please come at once to my private sitting room just down the main hallway," the Prince announced in an equally quiet voice. Both he and the Princess said nothing more to their mysterious guests until they were in the audio seclusion of the Chateau's sitting room that he used for smoking and drinking with a handful of his most intimate guests.

"Here we are, ladies. Please let me take your coats and I'll get you some brandy to take the chill off your bones." Reginald took several finely crafted lead crystal brandy glasses from under a fine oak liquor cabinet and poured his guests an ample double shot of the amber coloured distilled sweet smelling brandy. "I'm sorry Countess, but we did not have the pleasure of meeting your two friends!" Princess Marie deliberately hinted so as to solicit an introduction to the strangers, who apparently played some vital part in this unknown melodrama visitation.

"Oh, please forgive me my manners, I'm afraid that circumstances have temporarily abbreviated my sense of social decorum and responsibilities," the Countess replied quite embarrassingly.

"My two friends here are Mesdemoiselles Louise Thuliez and Marie Moriame – they are from Lille and well, they walk and travel a great deal and so do many of their friends and well, they have discovered and taken responsibility for about twenty-five British refugee soldiers in hiding. The soldiers need help desperately – food, clothing, shelter and, most of all, passage to Allied territory!" the Countess uttered in one long breath.

The Prince and Princess both looked at one another in utter astonishment; they had both just agreed to start helping the Allied refugee soldiers, but neither of them had thought that their assistance was to be so immediate; they were unprepared for such a sudden request.

"Well, that's quite a lot to ingest so quickly, my dear Countess! Did you say twenty-five British soldiers? Where exactly are they now?" Reginald curiously inquired.

"All over the countryside of Mons – they are being housed in miner cottages, farmers' barns, abandoned houses, religious institutions and with help from ordinary Belgian citizens. Please help us. I had no one else to turn to and I cannot bear to hand these poor souls over to the cruel Germans, especially in this cold, harsh winter! The de Croys are a noble and powerful family. I know that you can assist us!" the Countess pleaded with a tearful response.

"Yes of course, both my brother and I will assist you, but that is a large number of British soldiers. We will need time to help them and naturally we will have to stage the men in small groups," Marie de Croy replied without waiting for her brother's response.

Reginald was not offended by his sister's response and her initiative was proof that she was up to the task of taking on this new responsibility; however, this sudden news did mean that he needed to delay his visit to London for a few weeks. He needed some time to plan out a strategy to get these men to the frontier of Holland, yet their number was too numerous for any water barge escape – these men needed to go through the forests, meadows and canals of northern Belgium and this journey was going to take many days. He needed more immediate information before he could speak intelligently.

"Are all the men healthy? I mean, are any of them seriously wounded and can they walk and move about quite freely? Can they swim if necessary?" he asked the three ladies in quick succession.

"Oh yes – I can firmly attest that they are healthy, save for a few scratches and bruises, although they have been through quite an ordeal and they are tired and worn down, but they are in good spirits, none are wounded and they can walk and swim!" Louise Thuliez spoke out in a manner that was very definitive and without hesitation. "Any Allied soldiers who are badly wounded have given themselves up to the Germans, so only healthy soldiers are remaining," Marie Moriame added as a matter of further explanation.

"Good! Well now, we'll just have to provide for them, just as we did before!" Reginald announced as he slowly sipped his cordial drink. "They will, of course, need to be processed with proper Belgian names, photographs and supporting identification. The next step is transport to Brussels, as this is the main transportation artery north into the northern frontier and Holland. Finally, we need a guide, or better yet several guides, men who are reliable and know the lay of the land into Holland! Safe lodging in and around Brussels will be the most challenging aspect to this plan – we need several reliable, discreet locations that the suspicious Germans and their informants will not suspect!" Reginald concluded in a single, brilliant summary of the draft plan that he had just extemporaneously outlined to the visiting ladies.

"My brother is absolutely right! This number of Allied soldiers increases the level of risk, logistics and possibility of German detection. The men will need to be taken to Brussels in small groups. We need several safe lodging places in and around Brussels, so come back here in a week and give us the location of the hiding places that you have personally investigated and gained permission to use. You must, I repeat, you must be absolutely confident of the reliability of the residences and the occupants thereof, to be totally patriotic and trustworthy, there will be no be no weak links in this regard or we all will be executed or sent to German prisons for our folly. Is this quite clear?" Marie de Croy was uncharacteristically stern. All the ladies sitting around her knew the profoundness of her words and they were profusely quiet as the seconds passed.

"Yes, I do!" the Countess remarked with a determined clear tone.

"I do too! So do I!" replied the two previously reserved Mesdemoiselles Louise Thuliez and Marie Moriame.

"I have a spacious townhouse in Brussels – some of the soldiers can stay there!" Countess Jeanne de Belleville volunteered immediately.

"I know of other safe houses in Brussels and on the outskirts of the city!" Madame Thuliez added quickly.

"There are abbeys, convents and monasteries where I have religious friends who can shelter some of the men as well!" Madame Moriame concluded the last of the positive responses from among the trio.

Both Reginald and Marie sat there in both amazement and admiration at these fine women, who were placing their very lives and way of living in jeopardy. This was exactly the type of courage and spirit that their rescue organization needed. It mattered not that these were women possessed of absolutely zero experience in the art or practice of subversion and deception – what really mattered was their character and these ladies had plenty of that ingredient. They were smart too and this meant a much greater chance of successfully conveying the group of Allied soldiers undetected into Brussels.

Stupidity could be as deadly a folly as stepping onto a landmine. Ignorance was a most deadly trait that had sunk many a noble plan and the de Croys needed clever people working for them, if they were to be successful and not get caught by the German secret police or intelligence network. The journey overland from Brussels northward was to be a literal learning experience for everyone, as none of them had accomplished such

AGENT PROVOCATEUR

a feat using a land route into Holland. Marie and Reginald were soon
smiling back at their extraordinary guests; these were kindred spirits just
like themselves and they had somehow found each other in the maze of the
German occupation of their tiny country. Neither brother or sister had ever
dreamed that there existed so many loyal and daring Belgian patriots willing
to assist stranded Allied soldiers. All that these normal people needed was
some organization and direction to make their assistance a more polished
and professional endeavour.

"That is very heroic and patriotic of you, ladies. I'd say that we have
ourselves an agreement and a plan then. My sister and I will need to have
the names, ages, military affiliation and physical measurements of the
Allied soldiers; we'll need this data for the purpose of procuring civilian
clothing, identity cards and, if possible sometime later, to inform the British
Government and the Hague as to the fate of these soldiers. They are most
likely listed as Missing In Action (MIA) and their families need to know of
their status. The photographs will be taken at a time that Marie and I will
coordinate with each of you. Until that time, you'll have to do your best to
continue to hide and feed these soldiers in-place until it is safe to move them
onward," Reginald carefully counselled to the three ladies. The three women
all smiled and nodded in affirmation to Reginald's instructions.

"A final issue which I think bears saying, even if you already know
it, which is the matter of security! Do not trust anyone who is unknown
to you personally; the Germans are no fools and in an occupied country
like ours, the German occupation forces and secret police will find things
to busy themselves and I fear that means discovering saboteurs, traitors,
spies, protestors and any other sort of trouble-makers, be these either real
or imagined. Try to write nothing down and, if you must, do not write
plainly for all to see; do not use the telephones to convey information and
speak softly in both your homes and in public places in any conversations
concerning anything to do with our 'business'. Finally once again, be mindful
of strangers – if something does not seem or feel right, it most probably
means trouble!" Marie de Croy added, as her brother sat and smiled in
admiration at his sister's sage advice. The brother and sister made a very
complete pair of budding underground masterminds.

"We all understand and thank you for those reinforcing words," Countess
Jeanne de Belleville remarked politely. Any doubts that Reginald had about
his sister running this Allied soldier escape network were now utterly
diffused and eliminated. Marie was an independent-minded and totally
capable decision-maker and she was to need all her wits in operating this

operation that combined the talents of manager, actress, and sometimes the innocent fool.

"Fine then everyone, let's plan to meet again…next Friday, unless that is too inconvenient for any of you? My sister and I will be working the 'other' details and please bring along the data that I requested on the soldiers." Prince de Croy rose to signal the conclusion of the meeting.

"Thank you for taking us into your confidences. We all need to work together as one family now!" Princess Marie de Croy announced as a sign of support and unity with the kindred group, as she clasped each of the visitors' hands and kissed them gently on the cheek, a social sign from a woman of her class that indeed she had formally bonded with all three of these ladies despite the fact that two of them were most ordinary women of a lower social class. The Great War was breaking many old bonds of senseless tradition, while conversely forging new links of friendship.

"We'll have to act quickly and contact everyone who had assisted us with the escape of the two English soldiers. This operation is going to be larger, more complex and very dangerous! The number of variables has increased and so has the number of 'packages'. The Holland land border is more dangerous than a barge merrily floating on a river!" Reginald muttered to his sister, as they waved farewell to the three ladies who mounted the Countess's fancy four horse drawn carriage.

"How right you are, brother. I'm going to Brussels and visit Directress Edith Cavell. She was so very helpful to us and her Clinique might be able to shelter some soldiers for a day or two while they await a guide to escort them north to Holland," Marie exclaimed with determined zeal. "That's a fine idea and, if possible, please inquire about the availability of any possible frontier guides that we can employ!" Reginald added as an afterthought.

Marie merely nodded to her brother's request. "I'll contact Henri Beyns to see if he has any trusted friends who can be recruited as frontier guides as well. I think that we'll have to have many more guides if this is to become a going concern," Reginald added as Marie smiled back and patted him gently on the shoulder.

Over the next week, Reginald, Marie and the growing number of associates informally involved in the Allied soldier rescue and repatriate organization drew upon all of their energies, expertise and patriotism to weave together a rudimentary system for processing the twenty-five odd Allied soldiers, most of whom were from Great Britain, but also a few from Belgium and France. As every detail and item had to be physically conveyed or communicated, everything took two or three times the normal time that was ordinarily required through more modern communications and transportation means. It also did not help hasten events along when everyone was nervous and suspicious of every action; this was something new for all of them. At first everyone thought that there was a German bogeyman behind every corner, window or tree. However, over time, these fears abated, as individual confidence grew. Yet everyone involved had a legitimate right to be scared. There appeared more dire posters warning of collaboration with or for the Allies – the penalties, which were prolifically advertised to be death or hard labour. These were not idle German threats either. Every week or so, there were trustworthy reports from fellow Belgians of reliable repute of someone being executed, taken off to jail, having their house ransacked or business looted. Executions of Belgian civilians convicted under a German military kangaroo tribunal were not uncommon. The citizens of Belgium were de facto German prisoners under 'house-arrest' and this brutal occupation led to hatred and belligerence by the Belgian population against the German occupiers, even the young children hated the Germans. Hatred needed a healthy outlet and helping Allied soldiers was a most appropriate means of venting this pent-up energy and it also served a very pragmatic and humane objective.

Ever so carefully, Marie and Reginald planned out the details of processing the twenty-five Allied soldiers for their organized evasion and escape from occupied Belgium up north through the forests and canals of Holland and then on to freedom, back to the Allied lines or their native country. The Princess busied herself in assisting with taking photographs with her Kodak camera of the fugitive soldiers, along with the assistance of Herman Capiau. Herman recruited a pharmacist in Mons that was very well known to him over the years; the man was Maurice Derveau. Derveau was a very patriotic and knowledgeable Belgian citizen, who wanted to directly assist in helping Allied soldiers escape. He assisted in the document preparation for the two English soldiers and he was enthusiastic to assist in any other efforts as well. Capiau thought that Derveau could be a trusted guide, along with the trusted and proven Henri Beyns. Derveau being a chemist was able to get his hands on the chemicals used to process the soldiers' photographs and he could also obtain vital medicines for those who became sick.

Meanwhile Reginald and Marie visited the nearby Mons retail shops, 'second-hand' stores and tailor shops, to scurry-up old clothing in which to dress the varying shaped and sized Allied soldiers. The Prince and Princess used the believable excuse to the various merchants that the old clothing was needed to outfit their estate male workers and that they were doing this act themselves in order to be frugal and patriotic. No questions or second-looks were made to them. They could use this shopping excuse only once. However, for the future, others were going to have to perform the same type of rummaging for used men's clothing; a predictable routine was to be avoided to lessen suspicion and make less impact on the merchants' memory. The Prince was mindful to ensure that the clothing was well worn, but not tattered and it needed to be warm as well. Reginald contacted Sister Josephine to get the old clothing washed at a local convent, as he lacked the facilities and resources to wash and repair a large amount of old clothing without observation or suspicion from the Chateau's servant staff. Marie and Reginald introduced Sister Josephine to Henri Beyns one Sunday afternoon at Bellignies Chateau; however, much to their surprise, Sister Josephine and Henri Beyns were acquainted with each other already, as Henri had been in active collaborations with Sister Josephine in assisting other Allied soldiers since the war had begun. Neither Henri Beyns nor Sister Josephine confided all of their secret activities to the de Croys or even wholly to one another, this to cleverly ensure compartmentalized restriction to their personal activities to only an essential few. Secrets were best maintained to a select few. It seemed that many Belgians were wisely practising good covert action operational security without ever being instructed on the intelligence operating principle of 'need-to-know'. Neither Reginald or Marie were offended by this secrecy; in fact, they admired and encouraged it.

The escape components finally came together. In early December 1914 all the personal identity documents and preparations had been made and rehearsed over and over among the key players until the details were memorized. Beyns and Derveau each guided separate groups of five Allied soldiers east and then northward towards Brussels using foot, wagon and finally rail transportation into Brussels, where they were taken at dusk to the townhouse of either Countess Jeanne de Belleville or Directress Nurse Edith Cavell's Clinique rue de la Culture. The Allied soldiers were each given twenty francs by the two guides; this money was provided through the good graces of the Prince and Princess de Croy. The soldiers were to be staying in Brussels only a few days, then they were ferried off northward again by the guides, again by walking, wagon cart or train. Before they reached Antwerp, they proceeded off the main road, which was guarded as one approached the city, and then they proceeded to travel on foot to the northwest of Antwerp and toward the forests and shallow canals that became increasingly de rigueur as the marshy border with Holland was approached. Nightly refuge was taken in barns and the humble dirt-floor huts of the local farmers, who were all too eager to offer refuge without betraying a word to the Germans. In a week's time, all ten Allied refugee soldiers were successfully passed across the frontier with Holland and they were headed toward the Hague Allied military headquarters as so instructed by Prince Reginald de Croy. In another week, the second group was on the same route northward and they too safely passed into Holland without detection, loss of life or any other dispute. By the middle of December 1914, all twenty-five Allied soldiers had escaped Belgium into Holland in large thanks to the efforts of many brave Belgian citizens like the de Croy's and English Nurse Edith Cavell. It was a feat worthy of pride, jubilation and new found confidence.

"By golly, we have done it! All of us have done it! Who would ever have thought that this could be done! What a great victory for us and the Allied cause!" Reginald de Croy announced in wild jubilation as he emotionally hugged and kissed his sister on hearing from the two guides that the final lot of prisoners had been smuggled through to Holland.

"I have no hesitation about our instigation of this organization, Reginald. It was dangerous, but it was the right thing to do!" Marie exclaimed in equal jubilation.

"So what do we do next, Reginald? Is this all there is? Can we go back and live like ostriches? Do we blissfully continue to do this same thing in the future or do we stop while our luck is still with us?" Marie asked rapidly and with a tone of urgency in her voice. She was both scared and anxious, having no idea as to what next step they should take. She knew that they had been lucky so far and that they had done well, yet would their luck run out someday? Reginald's face immediately transformed from childhood excitement to that of adult seriousness, as he drew back from his sister. He too realized that they had all been foolishly lucky and that they all could just as easily have been very unlucky and caught by the Germans and shot. She wondered if she had said something wrong or if there was another issue at work that produced her brother's sudden change of mood. She had not long to await the answer to her riddle.

"Stop or quit that which we have just successfully demonstrated can be done by determined civilian men and women? Can we stop now, my dearest sister, while this crazy war beats ever closer to our ancestral home each day? Do we pull back because to do more is to invite disaster? Can any full life really be lived in squandered recluse and personal safety?" Reginald chided back, revulsed at the mere suggestion of stopping their opposition of the German occupation and brutal occupation boot that was kicking his beloved

Belgium daily! It was unthinkable to him and he could not turn back now –
there was so much more to be done, he reasoned to himself.

"Marie, I thank you for your concern, which is only natural, even
instinctive! We have done something good and worthy of both ourselves, our
noble position and we have made a positive contribution to the Allied war
effort. There are probably many more Allied soldiers out there who will not
last out the year in Belgium without our assistance and I wager that there are
even healthy Belgian young men who want to flee and join our Belgian army
now valiantly fighting in France! You may quit this organization effort and
I will think none the less of you, but I am going abroad as I originally had
planned to London and coordinate with the British authorities concerning
this humble patriotic group of citizens that we have here!" Reginald
confessed with determination and emotion as his pale blue eyes fell upon
the concerned face of his pretty sister. Marie suddenly felt ashamed of
her feelings of self-preservation – she knew that Reginald was right in his
argument and she wanted also to be in this fight.

"I'm with you, Reginald, I want to be in this struggle too! Belgium is my
country and my life. I want to fight for her. I want to help out in this war in
any way that I can!" Marie confessed as she rushed toward her brother and
gave him an emotional hug. She finally realized that her actions and those
around her could very possibly take her young life, yet living under brutal
and increasingly harsh German military occupation was also a form of slow
death too. "How long will you be in London?" Marie asked in a sad, tearful
voice.

"A few weeks at most; there is too much for me to do here in Belgium for
me to stay any longer than that... I'll try and get back again to London in late
Spring if Providence permits!" Reginald hugged his sister and brushed the
tears from her eyes.

"What can I do while you are in London?" Marie inquired with
resounding spirit in her voice. She knew that time was of the essence in
helping more soldiers to escape; the winter was taking a toll on the soldiers
and the ability of those brave souls who sheltered these refugee soldiers at
great risk.

"Marie, you already know what to do! Just keep performing the same
actions, which we have already enacted for those twenty-five soldiers we
assisted to escape Belgium! Ask our friends to look out for straggler British
and Allied soldiers, give them food, lodging and medical care, manufacture
them new identity cards and move them in very small groups using only
trusted guides to Brussels and then into Holland!" Reginald remarked rather

nonchalantly to his beloved sister.

"That's it? That's all the guidance that you have for me, my dear brother?" Marie smiled back to Reginald. It all sounded so simple and in a way it was a very modest plan; however, the devil was in the details and these were many.

"Yes, Marie, that's about it, sister! You know as much about the operation as I do and I cannot think of doing anything else until I think this thing through in greater detail or unless I get better guidance from London. Do not do anything different or take on any new helpers until I get back, use your fine wits and judgment to be your best guide and you also have the counsel of our mutual friends as well. Take chances, but make sure these are calculated and reasonable, and not outlandish! You have superior instinct and judgment, so if something does not sound or feel right, defer to your inner feelings – you are a Royal Princess of Belgium. You have learned much in life and now you can make great practical use of this knowledge," Reginald added. There was nothing more to say and both brother and sister suddenly realized that fact.

"When do you depart?" Marie inquired of her brother. She knew that Reginald needed to do the tasks he had set for himself and she was going to miss his presence. Independence was such a fine and yet lonely thing that she accepted as a necessity, but she did not fondly embrace it in her heart.

"A week's time should complete my journey. I still have my diplomatic credentials, official passport and German letters of safe-travel for my authorized passage through to Antwerp and beyond. If the Holland frontier ever closes-up, I know enough people to get safely through, although I might get a wee bit dirty," Reginald smiled back as he deftly hinted of his intention to investigate the actual procedures to 'sneak-across' the Holland border in order to discover the 'realities' of crossing the border on foot like the other refugee Allied soldiers had done. He desperately wanted the knowledge of 'crossing-over' on foot into Holland – this would provide him with first-hand experiences of the procedures and challenges facing Allied refugee soldiers in the future border crossing operations. This being winter and the risk of hypothermia through body immersion in cold water needing to be avoided, escape through water was to be avoided and thus extensive use was made of small row boats or very shallow marshland routes.

Reginald contacted Henri Beyns to assist him in his 'first-crossing' north of Antwerp, so that his land travel was to be very minimal, as was any risk of detection. Henri was also to bring along another frontier guide, Victor Gille, a young man who had assisted other soldiers and civilians with crossing into Holland, but until the Prince's crossing, he had not worked directly with the de Croys or Henri Beyns. Victor Gille was to become one of the best guides in the network.

"Be careful brother, I need you to come back to me alive. Remember we have our brother's wedding to attend after this damn war is over!" Marie smiled back with a well-camouflaged, worried concern.

Both brother and sister knew the risks to which they were now fully engaged – they were underground Belgian resistance leaders now. Yet they both knew that they had few options available to them, given their upbringing and exalted position in Belgian society; a Royal position meant and bred an inherent corresponding responsibility. They could not shirk off their heritage or their responsibilities. They knew what they were doing was dangerous, but also it was most morally correct. The two continued to discuss the organization and its operations over the next several days to ensure that all issues and items were fully vetted to their mutual satisfaction.

\* \* \* \* \* \* \* \* \* \* \* \*

A most perfect island-child nestled within the bosomy embrace of its northern Atlantic ocean parent, Great Britain and her sister neighbours had obstinately endured the perpetual damp, misty, unwelcoming climate that chilled every being to its bone, to produced a people possessed of a bold, indomitable and noble character chiselled from the harsh environment of the North Sea, yet defiantly resolute and hardy in mind and spirit. The maritime weather in London was quite normal and non-descript for that of a typical January day: it was cold, damp, and filled with an over-abundance of low-level, onerous looking, grey nimbostratus precipitation clouds that effortlessly hid the rescue of the sun's warming beams. Within the repose of this dreary weather caldron, Prince de Croy had landed after his one-week journey to the Holland frontier via the canal system and then it took another week to get passage from Holland to Portsmouth, England. The entire escape was strenuous, but not overly dangerous, as only old or infirmed German guards resourced the border area and they were none too keen in either their duty or attitude – for them the war had disrupted their settled civilian lives. For old conscripted soldiers, the war was a most inconvenient part of their life, while the young soldier viewed it as his entire life. Carefully wrapped oilskin wrappings preserved all of his important documents from the water and weather elements. Reginald was now personally assured that this Holland land passage was quite reasonable and undemanding if even he as a thirty-six year old pampered gentleman could easily perform this escape feat and he was glad that he had made the decision to perform the illegal crossing of the border.

Reginald's trip was made even more possible through the benefit of his previous diplomatic credentials and he had wisely maintained a generous bank account with the Bank of England, which amounted to over £50,000, much of which had wisely been transferred by the de Croy family in the summer of 1914 when it was obvious that war clouds were forming over Europe. Having been a long-term member of Belgium's diplomatic corps, he decided to stay in the London townhouse of an old friend, an aristocratic English Viceroy who was retired from a Foreign Office posting in India. Having landed quite literally with the clothing on his back, his immediate order of business was to promptly acquire some men's wear and a few adequate suits, a topcoat and bowler hat from one of the fine English tailors located along the fashionable Bond Street.

As he walked briskly along the streets that were filled with uniformed men of all ages and ranks, his pace came to a slow trod and he stopped to glare at the scene before him. Like a majestic sculptured carving, before him stood a massive neo-Baroque white marble, 7-storey structure that occupied an entire city block. The impressive building was complemented with turret-like edifices and pillowing spiral-like towers. There along the House Guards Avenue, directly across from the governmental offices at Whitehall, stood the powerfully looking British War Office building. Within the huge labyrinth operated the nerve centre and human beings numbering into the hundreds that ran the massive British war machine from the creation of grand military strategy to the mundane ordering of munitions and uniforms. Built in 1906, it took five years to complete, it housed a thousand rooms of varying sizes and shapes, there were 2.5 miles of corridors and it cost £1.2 million to construct. Until the US Pentagon was completed some thirty plus years later, the British War Office was the largest military building in the world. Throughout his stroll along the crowded London streets, Reginald periodically looked carefully behind himself so as to possibly detect any unwelcome strangers or German agents and he saw none, yet in the affairs of spy craft, he was a mere neophyte and even a German spy trainee could have escaped his conspicuous attempts to turn about and look for the ever-present German bogeyman. Still, Reginald had an odd premonition that he was being watched.

Through his high level government contacts formed while he had served as a Belgian diplomatic official in London, he had made a late morning appointment through a high-ranking War Office administrative official in the intelligence and operations branch to later become known as Secret Intelligence Service (SIS)/MI6. He presented the credentials of his Belgian diplomatic service corps, as well as a passport that was still valid, unto a stern-looking British Army Sergeant Major attired in a sharply-pressed olive-drab military uniform, as he verbally presented the name of the office to which he had an appointment to visit. The Sergeant Major looked up his name on a clipboard to which was attached an appointment list and located Reginald's name, to which he checked-off and annotated the date and time. Reginald then autographed his full name next to a blank line that was immediately adjacent to his neatly printed name, annotating his signature in elegant Spencer-styled cursive script. He was directed to proceed up the main staircase up to the third floor and proceed down the corridor until he came to room #356. Without any further deliberations, he followed the precise instructions to the mark.

"Pardon me, sir, my name is Reginald de Croy, I have a 10:00 am appointment!" Reginald spoke politely to the dapper looking older sergeant, who sat attired in the same coloured olive drab uniform that he had seen numerous times within the interior of the War Office building. The older sergeant had only three prominent large stripes on both of his arm sleeves, attesting to the rank of a regular sergeant. The man had greying hair and a pudgy, middle-aged frame. Reginald rightly concluded that this soldier was in the auxiliary or reserve part of the British army and from the colourful rows of ribbons on his uniform, he must have seen much service in the regular army during his youth. Obviously and wisely, the British Army was using older soldiers to backfill administrative and non-combat jobs, leaving the younger and more able-bodied young men to perform the horrendous, hand-to-hand trench fighting.

"Oh yes, sir, please have yourself a seat; could I offer you a nice cup of tea, sir?" the old sergeant asked with a refined voice that also hinted of a slight east-end London accent that had obviously been culturally refined through extensive travel and postings with the British Army. "No thank you, I'll just take a seat in the corner," Reginald announced as he took off his coat and hat, placing these onto a naked coat rack that stood aback from the office door. Much to his astonishment, or perhaps not so seemingly upon reflection, he was alone in the waiting room – this was after all the secret administrative office of the British Army secret service operations, so caution was probably being exercised that precluded one party's business with the secret service apart from any other person having business there. A strict 'need-to-know' environment was being stealthily enforced with carefully crafted sedate appearing decorum.

Reginald waited patiently and picked up some newspapers and magazines that were lying about on an empty chair, the obvious reading refuge of a previous visitor. About ten minutes passed before the loud ringing tone of the black phone that graced the sergeant's desk suddenly interrupted the quietness of the main office waiting room. "Yes sir…yes sir, I understand…very good sir," the older sergeant spoke definitively. "Mr de Croy, sir, your appointment is ready, please follow me." The sergeant arose and smartly walked over to the solitary office visitor. Reginald arose and obediently followed the sergeant down an inner hallway and stopped after walking about fifty paces down a dimly lit corridor, which was symmetrically aligned with nondescript un-numbered and unarticulated office doors. They stopped suddenly and the sergeant simply knocked three short, firm taps on the door and awaited the salutatory response of permission to proceed.

"Come in please!" a faceless, middle-toned male voice announced from behind the closed door. The sergeant merely opened the door in polite accord, but he dared not enter or even peer inside, as he knew his place and position within this secret organization, thus down the corridor the aged sergeant returned back to the front office. In addition to the 'need-to-know' axiom, there was also the corollary of 'need-to-enter' rule that dare not be abridged upon the penalty of personal reprimand or peril of transfer. It was all about the intelligence chaps needing to be stealthy and covert in all their mannerisms and daily routine, 'practice in the office and barracks equated to perfection on the battle front' was one of their sayings.

"Please come in, Mr de Croy, or is it preferred protocol to address you as Prince de Croy?" announced a mid-fiftyish aged man with a thin face, pencil thin moustache and black hair that was accented around the temple area with greying strands that attested to either high stress or premature aging. The man was dressed in the line officer uniform of a Royal Navy full Commander, this visibly attested by three prominent gold bullion lace stripes affixed on each of his coat jacket sleeves. The Royal Navy officer extended his right hand and with a polite smile, clearly introduced himself. "My name is Commander George Smith-Cummings of His Majesty's Royal Navy, currently on loan to the War Office so to speak. Actually I'm one of the few officers in the British military balmy enough to have volunteered for this new branch called the Secret Intelligence Service, which some are calling us by some strange initials as well, but that's about all I can say about the matter…it's all so hush-hush," Commander Smith-Cummings announced as he gestured with his hand for the Prince to have a seat.

"Yes, well, you may simply call me Reginald or Mr de Croy. I did not think it proper either to reveal too much to the War Office when making this appointment as I too respect security. I understand that there are German spies among the masses in London and that Whitehall and the British War Office are their prime collection targets!" Reginald noted with a reply of most accurate summarization. The Commander smiled at the cunningness of his aristocratic visitor and he was deeply intrigued by this man's fine tailored appearance as well as his sage words.

"Well now, Mr de Croy, before we get down to more serious business, I'd like to extend my manners and offer you a proper drink. Is whisky straight-up, 10 year old single malt acceptable, sir?" the Commander inquired as he rose and stepped over to a plain oak, fine linen-draped table upon which lay several multi-coloured and one clear array of bottles containing various distilled and fermented brews. The tradition of the times dictated that a social drink be offered to visitors; to do otherwise was considered most rude and quite ungentlemanly. He poured two generous portions of fine aged malt scotch into the lead crystal glasses and handed one to his visitor.

"Thank you very much, but is it permitted to drink in uniform during duty hours, Commander?" Reginald inquired more as a matter of personal curiosity than one of social concern. "This is all for King and country. Besides a drink before afternoon never killed anyone sir!" the Commander announced as he raised his glass in a light hearted salute. "Here's to God, country, our Kings and victory over the Germans!" he proclaimed as the two gentlemen's glasses made a most audible mellow-rick clink sound that only fine crystal ware conferred. The two men sipped the amber distillation, the aroma and taste of which was slightly peaty with an after-taste of fruity, oak and spice – as evident from the aged barrels that were probably used to store either brandy or port wine.

"So I'm to understand that you made a journey from Belgium to Holland. How was your journey accomplished, if I may ask? Did you use any of your diplomatic connections or passport through Antwerp or France?" the Commander coyly inquired. He guessed that the Prince was a mere want-a-be spy dilettante, a type that so many other exalted personages so imagined themselves to be in times of war.

Reginald paused for a moment and took another sip of malt whisky before answering the inquiry. "No, that would have been the easy way; such a passage would also invite the immediate observation and recording of my travel by the German authorities and I could not risk that for this preliminary visit. I can use my diplomatic and German travel passes when it so suits my purposes and when I do not mind the Germans knowing my travel destination. I elected to come across the forest and canals of northern Belgium and southern Holland in order to avoid any sort of detection and I wanted to personally experience the escape routes that I ask others to use!" Reginald remarked with a straight emotionless facial expression.

Commander Smith-Cumming's attention was now keenly aroused. 'What sort of man, especially a Belgian Prince, would risk their life in a border crossing at a time of war, especially when he possessed a German letter of passage and Belgian passport?' he thought quickly to himself. This was no ordinary 'walk-in' or dilettante volunteering to assist in the war effort. The Commander decided to be blunt and simply force the issue from the Belgian Prince.

"Right, now what is it all about, Reginald? You mentioned something of a serious nature happening in Belgium and I'd dearly love to hear your story and perhaps even assist, if it merits both of our mutual attention and interest that is!" the Commander hastily inquired as he came quickly to the point of inquiry. There was a great war waging and the last thing he needed was to have his valuable time taken up by a rural Belgian Prince with tales of woe and dreams of spycraft. The Commander and other SIS officers were focusing on German spies, espionage networks and saboteurs – they had little time or tolerance to waste on dilettante, Royal-type, 'walk-ins' offering their help in the war effort. Reginald knew that he was being tested by the Commander and he had to come-clean immediately to the British naval officer. He had only one chance to make a firm impression and that time was upon him.

"We, that is, my sister and I along with a small group of patriotic Belgians, have been assisting over twenty-five British and other Allied soldiers across the Holland frontier and back to the Allied lines. We have not heard if any of these soldiers made it across to safety. One was an English officer, a Colonel by the name of Percy Chatsworth of Derbyshire, the son of the Duke of Albemarle!" Reginald noted with perfect recollection concerning the Colonel's lineage. Commander Smith-Cumming's face was drawn into an obvious expression of disbelief and awe; his mouth momentarily dropped open upon hearing these fantastic words.

"Excuse me, did you say Colonel 'Slim' Chatsworth and other prisoners were assisted by you and your sister? All were harboured and transported to safety you say?" the Commander questioned softly, as he quickly got up from his desk and hurried and picked up his phone and placed a direct call to an unidentified number.

"Hello, Sir Basil, this is George here. I just heard a remarkable story that

I need for you to verify with our operations chaps: it concerns the status of English soldiers who escaped from behind the Belgian lines in the past few weeks. One of the chaps is a Colonel named Percy Chatsworth, son of the Duke of Albemarle – can you please check this, sir, with your contacts and get back to me? I have a fellow in my office, he claims to have directly assisted in his escape along with those of twenty-five other blokes as well! Thank you, sir, I'll be standing by in my office," the Commander replied in a very excited voice.

"Excuse me, Reginald, that was my superior. The intelligence people are a bit of an eccentric and informal lot, except when the Brigadier shows up, which is very rare and quite fortunate for us! Too much gold braid around here just muddles up the work here," Commander Smith-Cumming remarked in a tone of framed levity, as he tried to recover from the shock of hearing that this gentleman had just confessed to crossing the Holland frontier and helped to plan the successful crossing of over twenty-five Allied soldiers in Holland using an amateur, ad hoc escape organization under the very eyes of the German occupation forces.

"Can you tell me a little bit more about the people who assisted you? I know that you have mentioned your sister, but I take it that there are others who assisted as well?" Smith-Cumming inquired, now with greater depth and interest than in his initial opening inquiry.

"Yes, of course, my sister the Princess Marie de Croy was approached by the Countess Jeanne de Belleville to assist in initially helping the Colonel and Corporal Taylor. We were aided in lodging and document preparation by Herman Capiau and the lawyer Albert Libiez. In Brussels we have the support of Dr Depage and his wife Marie, along with the temporary lodging and staging point, which was the Berkendael Institute operated by the brave English Directress Nurse Edith Cavell and her assistant Nurse Wilkins. For guides, we used local men such as chemist Maurice Derveau, Victor Gille and Henri Beyns. Numerous other people helped to bring the hiding soldiers to us, such as Louise Thuliez, the priest Abbe de Longueville, Mademoiselle Moriame, and Sisters Josephine, Marie and Madeline from the Convent at Witheries, who helped to transfer soldiers to Berkendael Institute, Clinique rue de la Culture," Reginald uttered forth in a flawless verbal diagraming of the escape organization.

The Commander sipped the last of the scotch in utter silence. The story was fantastically simple, yet still unbelievable in that such a myriad of people joined together in an unorganized manner that had quite simply worked and remarkably so. 'Could such a feat be repeated again and even continued and expanded on a sustained basis?' wondered the amazed Commander.

A simple quick knock on the door interrupted the temporary silence and another fiftyish aged man dressed in a British Army uniform boldly entered the office, upon which Commander Smith-Cumming immediately arose and loudly uttered out the word "Sir" upon seeing the man's identity.

"Stand easy, George and please introduce me to your esteemed guest!", the senior officer subtly ordered. "Yes of course, Sir Colonel Basil Thomson, may I introduce Prince Reginald de Croy. He's had quite an adventure and a tale to tell me, sir!" Commander Smith-Cumming announced in an almost embarrassed tone, not being completely sure of the correctness of the Prince's story that he had just been told.

"It's my humble pleasure to meet you, Prince de Croy of Belgium and I'm happy to say that his assertions are not mere stories, these are cold facts! The Hague has been forwarding to me the numerous debriefings of refugee British soldiers who have been conveyed through to Holland by the de Croy organization and their work has been utterly extraordinary. I dare say, in fact, Colonel 'Slim' Chatsworth is recovering at his family's estate and he has invited the Prince to be his guest there as well! Pardon my manners, your Royal Highness, but my name and title is Colonel Basil Home Thomson, Deputy of the newly created British Intelligence Section and I'd like you to feel free to ask for any help or assistance that we can provide during your stay in London!" the Colonel announced with utmost politeness and social deference.

"Thank you, Colonel Thomson and please everyone, sit down. I am here informally and secretly, that's why I clandestinely fled out of Belgium, I do not want the Germans to know of my presence here in London. Please call me Reginald. You must understand that my sister, myself and all the others in the escapee network, we want, no let me rephrase that, we are committed to helping the other stranded British and Allied soldiers in Belgium! I mean to return back to Belgium to do exactly that!" Reginald spoke plainly to the two British officers who were temporarily dumbfounded by his resolute statement.

"I do not think that is a wise proposition, Reginald! After all, you were lucky once, but do not think that you will have such good fortune again to get across the border to Holland!" Commander Smith-Cumming noted in a discouraging tone. His superior, Colonel Thomson, however, preferred to keep a more open-mind on the possibilities for the future.

"Prince de Croy, did I hear you correctly when you stated that there were 'other stranded British and Allied soldiers' in Belgium requiring your assistance and services?" Colonel Thomson replied with audible concern.

"Yes, you heard me correctly, gentlemen; there are many, perhaps hundreds of other British and Allied soldiers being hidden across the countryside of Belgium and they risk being shot as spies for being in civilian clothing or being shipped off to German POW camps, where the conditions are horrendous. I cannot allow this to happen and if you will not assist me, damn it, then we shall do this alone with the resources available to us! I am so resolved in this matter and so is my sister, the Princess." Prince de Croy was defiant.

"Well I guess the British War Office and Secret Intelligence Service know where we now stand regarding your motives and intentions, Prince de Croy! Commander, break out another glass, I'd like the honour of having a drink with this good man. It's not every day that I get to meet a royal hero and I think we should chat more about your future, Prince de Croy. Perhaps we'll even drop by and visit Colonel Chatsworth at his family estate and have a nice chat too!" Colonel Thomson proclaimed as three glasses of malt whisky were poured and toasts rendered to the respective two nations, their two kings and their brave countrymen.

\* \* \* \* \* \* \* \* \* \* \*

During her brother's sojourn to England, Princess de Croy was not sitting idly by waiting for either his return or instructions – neither of these could be assured in this war and she needed to act on her own until his arrival back in Bellignies, that is, if he ever did come back. Idleness was not in Marie's nature, nor did circumstances favourably contribute to any degree of lethargy. Soldiers were being brought to her usually one or two at a time, but sometimes three or more, by the local inhabitants about Bellignies and Mons. The word, as it inevitably does, spread among the locals from coal miner and farmer to shop merchant and religious members, that the Prince and Princess were the people to see to assist the plight and passage of refugee Allied soldiers. Usually under the cover of darkness or in the wee hours of the morning, the soldiers came with a trusted known escort to either Bellignies Chateau or one of the safe houses being run by the loose network of soldier refugee confederates.

Women formed an equal and very prominent role in the de Croy network; not only were they brave and patriotic, but they garnered less suspicion from the traditionally paternalistic minded Germans. Among the country women, the catholic sisters and the nurses – they formed the backbone of the escapee network. The last, but certainly not least, among the fairer sex were the young girls whose stamina and innocence made them natural guides and couriers among the various members of the escapee organization; they often travelled seventeen miles over a two day period to deliver messages or assist in guiding soldiers from one safe location to another without the least suspicion – most observers making a logical conclusion that this was simply a father or uncle out for a walk with his little girl. However the journeys to a large city like Brussels, and the gateway city of Antwerp or the frontier crossings into Holland, required the accompaniment by adults. For these trips, the de Croys relied on the religious sisters, priests and monks or the services of Mademoiselle Moriame and the widowed schoolmistress Louise Thuliez. In some instances, the Princess and Prince even made the journey to personally escort some of the soldiers down to Brussels and to Edith's Clinique rue de la Culture. The de Croys, like most royals and aristocrats, were not imagined by the Germans to be involved in any nefarious activity, so they possessed a natural ability to travel without question throughout Belgium.

In Brussels, Directress Nurse Edith Cavell formed the linchpin for the collection, temporary lodging and rallying point for the frontier guides to discreetly arrange for the coordination and escort of the Allied soldiers northward. Edith stealthily and carefully kept the details of her involvement and the Clinique absolutely to herself. She kept Nurse Wilkins at a safe distance in these matters – it was enough that she knew and helped with the matter involving Colonel Chatsworth and Corporal Taylor, she didn't need to be involved with the growing number of escapee soldiers too. Edith kept Nurse Wilkins busy by involving her in more administrative issues in managing the Clinique's Nurse Trainees and this also freed up Edith's time to devote to the escape operations. A new Clinique site location was being planned for opening in a year's time and this was the perfect camouflage for Edith to use to disguise her escape support tasks. The grey haired, steely eyed woman of severe Victorian self-discipline and resolve was determined to not let anyone else under her charge be subject to the highly illegal deeds to which she was slowly becoming ensnared. Edith also knew that the more people who knew of something secret, the more likelihood there was of either intentional or unintentional compromise. If there was to be guilt found by the Germans, she wanted only herself to bear the responsibility and the blame; she reasoned to herself that her life had been largely lived and that she needed to protect the lives to which she was entrusted as Directress.

None of the other English nurses, to include Assistant Directress Nurse Wilkins, appreciated the expanding extent to which Edith was becoming involved with the Prince and Princess de Croy in operating a soldier escape organization. She had more frequent guests than in the previous six years, with the de Croys, Countess de Belleville, and George Hostelet visiting her several times each month. The nurses saw various men coming and leaving the Clinique, but this was not so unusual; however, Nurse Cavell made attempts to segregate the Allied soldiers from the regular civilian Belgian male patients and this seemed unusual to the nurses, but no one dared to question Edith's absolute authority over the conduct of her Clinique. Over time, Assistant Directress Wilkins correctly guessed the full nature of Edith's extra-curricular activities, yet she wisely kept such suspicions to herself. Through long association with her superior, Elizabeth Wilkins knew that Edith was a secretive soul and guarded her personal affairs with a passion and if Edith had wanted her to know something, then she would have informed her of this. To the naked unassuming eye, the visiting de Croys were merely social patrons who had assisted in the founding efforts and initial funding of the Berkendael Institute and nothing more. Edith was careful to coordinate as much lodging of the soldiers off-site from the Clinique as was practically and humanly possible, accepting only a stray soldier in an emergency situation. She knew that the younger nurses were most vulnerable to the amorous ways of young men and she also knew that young nurses had greater difficulty accepting discipline in a time of war in which rules and regulations seemed so often out-of-place. Gradually through experience and word-of-mouth, both the de Croys and Edith developed a reliable pool of frontier guides, men who knew the Belgium-Holland frontier and who had the moral fortitude and courage to get soldiers across the forests and dykes into the safety of Holland.

In December 1914, Directress Cavell had about a dozen nurses, most of whom were young nurse-trainees. She was the leader of the Berkendael Institute of the Clinique rue de la Culture, the first Belgium institution designed to expressly train young women in the art and practice of modern medical patient care instead of relying on the former rudimentary and often ad hoc, uneven training afforded unto the nursing profession up to that time. She had three senior British trained nurse supervisors on her staff, Nurse Wilkins chief among these, while the other nurses were trainees ranging in age from seventeen through to twenty-three years old, most of whom had never been away from their parents' home or having been exposed to the needs and care of the sick. Nursing was not the profession of 'nice girls and ladies'; instead the profession was the domain of Catholic nuns who possessed no formal modern medical instruction in the rapidly emerging scientific profession. This parochial medieval attitude of nursing was changing and Edith was a pioneer in championing the nursing field into scientific modernity on the continent, just as she had previously done while in practice in England.

As the war progressed and stabilized, the German and Belgian authorities decided to cross-level the medical staff among the various hospitals which had the greatest need of medical staff personnel. This fortunate decision left Edith with only three or four young trainees to supervise and, if possible, she had these young, impressionable nurse trainees also perform rotating shifts at the larger hospitals and wards, for the dual purpose of greater experience exposure and to also lesson the number of prying eyes that could infringe on her increasing assistance to the contraband English, French and Belgian refugee soldiers. By German mandate, starting in December 1914, soldiers of any nationality were to be cared for in military hospitals established by the German Army and this left Edith and her Clinique to deal solely with indigent and needy Belgian sick, mostly older men, as the Victorian era treatment of the sexes mandated separate wards, living facilities and staff – for which there was not adequate resources presently at the Berkendael Institute. This was another fortuitous event, as being a male-only Clinique made the task of treating any Allied refugee soldiers easier and less suspicious.

Yet all was not delightful for Directress Cavell. She was having problems with one of her young English nurses who, like Edith and the other full-fledged English nurses, had refused to flee Belgium when so afforded the opportunity by the Germans in September 1914. Miss Anne Shepardton was one such young lost soul under the supervision of Edith Cavell. Anne was an innocent, blue-eyed, blonde haired, strikingly pretty young lady of a working class family. Her father was a tailor, while her mother filled the traditional role of home keeper to a brood of four other competing siblings. Anne was a high-strung, vivacious young girl who lacked a natural outlet for her youth and growing sexual libido. Her Victorian-minded family were perplexed as to what remedy could be found for Anne's adventurous nature and she consistently rejected any of her mother's attempts at match-making. The family feared that Anne was going to fall prey to a never-do-well man and end up being unmarried and pregnant, a scandal that her family could not afford to bear. Anne's personality was ill suited to teaching, domestic duties or even working in a factory or merchant shop. She tired quickly of any routine or repetitive work tasks. She yearned for the frivolous, glamour lifestyle that she read about in cheap dime-store books and she dreamed of escaping the mundane lot of life that was lived by her parents.

The new field of nursing was being glamourized among many of the lady journal magazines of the day and Anne caught a glance of a few of these advertisements and the idea of being a nurse intrigued her eager, imaginative mind. Pretty, young and adventurous, Anne elected to go forth and try new things and being a nurse-trainee posted to a foreign Clinique sounded very romantic and adventurous. She took note of the advertisement of the Berkendael Institute Nurse Trainee Clinique in Brussels and she dreamed of adventure and continental romance, Paris and many European capital cities being only a short distance away from Brussels.

Nurse White was a friend of the Shepardton family and it was through this affiliation alone that the young, inexperienced Anne was able to even be posted to a nurse trainee institution that was mainly designed for young Belgian ladies. Nursing turned out to be quite a different and far more demanding profession than the cheap dime-store novels that broadly and inaccurately portrayed the difficult and demanding nursing work of Florence Nightingale in the Crimea War. Both Anne's innocence and bubbly-constitution were not the fabric of which modern nursing was made and to compound the strain, she was training and exposed to the horrific wartime wounded, whose horrific bullet and shell wounds made the scene from a butcher shop look most tame. The ever present screams of the wounded and the blood, urine, faeces ether, vomit and prolific wound discharges from the gravely wounded young soldiers, along with their constant screaming, took the pretty young Anne to the psychological breaking point. She drank alcohol whenever she could find it, smoked cigarettes prolifically and longed for the arms of a handsome man to unlock her internal feminine passions.

Edith was not blind to the plight of a beautiful young budding woman, yet Anne was hopelessly trapped in German-occupied Belgium and unless there was an amnesty to grant the deportation of Allied nationals, there Anne was to remain for the duration of the war along with her matronly nurse superiors. Being a keen observer of human nature, Edith tried to give encouragement and routine counsel to her young charge. She tried to keep Anne occupied with meaningful, but occupying tasks, abbreviated with monthly outings to the cafes and shops in Brussels under the ever-present escorts of another superior matron nurse. For the time being, Anne's attitude and work steadily progressed, although Edith and Nurse Elizabeth Wilkins were ever vigilant to keep young Anne under their watchful guise. In this regard, she and the other senior English nursing staff were to be unsuccessful.

* * * * * * * * * * *

# Chapter 5:
# Success Breeds Suspicion

*"We trust no strangers! Recruit only those known and proven
to us! Use those people who the Germans will suspect least: our
aristocratic peers, women, religious sisters and priests, professional
men and girls…young girls as our country guides!"*

"It's so wonderful to have you back again, Reginald! I'm so glad that
you're alive…and unhurt too!" Marie exclaimed as she rushed up to
her brother, who had arrived back into Belgium only a few days previously
through the city of Antwerp, this time using his now weathered, but not the
worse for wear, passport and German transport papers that were carefully
kept preserved by a small, watertight oil-skin pouch. It was nice to not have
to crawl through fields or cold canals, especially given the cold December
weather.

"Thank you, dearest sister and I made it back for the holidays too!"
Reginald explained as he hugged his sole sister. Neither sibling knew just
how much they took one another for granted, save for this past separation
which served to strengthen their sibling bonds even more.

"I hope that you were productive during my absence," Reginald winked
in a coded-signal, so as not to arouse any suspicions from any of the servants
lurking in the hallway recesses of the Chateau Bellignies.

"Come with me, Reginald, we can talk more in private. Do you need a
drink or some food?" Marie inquired anxiously, as she grabbed her brother's
hand and walked him into a small ladies parlour or sitting room that was
decorated in the soft feminine colours of white, gold, pink and yellow; a
white and gold leaf pattern of expensive silk wallpaper graced the walls,
while salmon coloured matching sofas and chairs were arrayed around a
petit white marble oval table. The room was further accented by a small bay
window that overlooked the Chateau's garden, now in quiet hibernation in
the cold presence of winter. Reginald wore one of the tailor made wool suits
that was made for him in London from a fashionable Bond Street tailor.

"Here's a brandy for you, Reginald, it will warm your bones and I shall
join you in a drink as well. Here's to us, brother and the future!" Marie

rejoiced as she handed her brother a double measure of amber coloured Napoleon brandy that was poured into the mandatory lead brandy snifters. The aroma was richly familiar, welcomed and overpowering. The two glasses made a slight 'clink'; the two took a sip, seated themselves comfortably, then spoke in soft, hushed tones so that no one could discern their conversations.

"Marie, they're safe! All of them! We did it!" Reginald uttered with great excitement. Marie's face burst into a huge smile.

"Colonel 'Slim', Billy and the other twenty-five British soldiers, all alive and safe!" Marie exclaimed exuberantly. Reginald said nothing. He did not have to, as his gesturing eyes and nodding head spoke better than mere words.

"We, that is to say, our little group, have sent others through to the frontier as well, maybe a dozen or more in small groups of several men at a time. Edith and everyone else are simply marvellous; it's like a modern factory assembly line process. I hope that everyone we send out makes it to safety, Reginald," Marie uttered with delight that was wrapped in tears of joy.

"Listen carefully, Marie and keep that which I now say only to yourself," Reginald sounded in a very serious low voice before continuing his discussion. "Everything we do is on a strict need-to-know basis. I cannot even safely tell you with whom I met in London or what organization to which they belong, as greater knowledge means greater danger in this thing that we are doing under the very noses of the Germans. I even suspect that there are numerous groups similar to ours in Belgium and other countries at war with Germany, maybe even in Germany itself! Our orders are to convey as many Allied soldiers across the frontier into Holland as is safely possible and to pass any significant information about the Germans that we may come across. Everything we do must be compartmentalized, so that no one knows everything about the network, only their own little piece of the puzzle. This minimization of knowledge will reduce risks and exposure in case one of our members is caught. Our network must operate with organization, secrecy, professionalism and loyalty – does all of this make sense to you?" Reginald inquired as his sister looked on with undivided interest.

"Yes it makes perfect sense, go on, brother. I am one with you on this!" Marie replied as she sipped her warming cognac.

"We trust no strangers! Recruit only those known and proven to us! Use those people who the Germans will suspect least: our aristocratic peers, women, religious sisters and priests, professional men and girls…young girls as our country guides!" Reginald quickly uttered off rapidly.

"That's just what we've been doing; we'll just do more of it!" Marie exclaimed as her brother spoke out once more.

"Exactly, Marie! We need to ensure the others are briefed on these procedures as well," Reginald sounded back quickly.

"As needed, we'll use code names! For our organization, we'll have everyone in our network employ the code name 'Yorc has sent me' – this is our name pronounced backwards of course, so our network will be the 'Yorc network', to be composed of three parts or organs: the Bellignies cell will be for control, information collection and gathering of refugee soldiers; the Borinage cell of Capiau and Libiez will concentrate on photography and false identification preparation, and finally the Brussels cell, which Edith Cavell will lead, is for the final step of coordinating guides to sending the soldiers off to Holland," the excited Prince summarized in one, long, continuous breath. It all seemed so simple and clear, yet they were all 'babes in the woods', mere amateurs playing in the world of adult subversion and espionage as the British War Office referred to them. Yet no other options, other than to flee Belgium, were available to patriotic citizens who wanted to be active, not passive bystanders. There was silence for a few seconds as the Prince's words seeped deeply into both of the siblings' consciences. Both brother and sister realized that, if caught, the Germans were going to shoot them, if only to make an example of them and to illustrate the fate of royals foolish enough to meddle in anti-German activity.

"I want to do this with you, Reginald, I want to help operate this network, I want to help get as many of the Allied soldiers as possible away from the Germans!" Marie whispered in subdued excitement. "We have the experience, resources, contacts, and dedication of many Belgians to support this network! When do we start?" Marie replied with a hushed soft smile.

Reginald clasped his sister's hands with his own and slightly smiled. "Why, my dear sister, don't you know? We are already in operation! I brought back some funds from the Bank of England in Belgian, French and British currency – we have to be able to deal with multiple payment methods to pay for food, clothing, bribes to border guards and to give the frontier guides some modest appreciation payment. The German-issued occupation script is not worth the wipe of one's fanny! I'll be travelling back to London in the spring and probably in the summer – I have to maintain my in-person liaison with the British authorities and I can use my relationship with the budding War Relief office that is just now being stood-up in the US Consulate in Brussels under Minister Whitlock. My visits to the US Consulate will provide a perfect cover for my travelling down to Brussels to escort Allied soldiers. I can also check for correspondence via the diplomatic pouch courier and it will furnish me a valid reason to travel to Amsterdam and Holland!" the Prince announced as his sister followed carefully his every word.

"I need for you to be my partner in this, Marie. I'll be travelling, so while I am away you are in full charge – is this acceptable to you?" Reginald inquired out of sibling politeness; he knew that his sister was his equal co-conspirator in this entire network formulation and operation, but still he needed to hear such devotion from her own lips.

"Of course, my dear brother, we have been in this together since the first two English soldiers came our way!" Marie courageously replied.

Marie instinctively knew the next step to be taken. "Reginald, we must get everyone together quickly and inform them of the procedures and safeguards to be followed for our network to flourish and assist more stranded soldiers before they are discovered by the German patrols! I think Brussels is the perfect gathering place – it is well served by transportation and it is a large public area that will not invite German suspicions, nor that of the locals or neighbours either. We can meet safely and discreetly in the town house of our friend Countess Jeanne de Belleville of Lille and no one will think the less of it either! We need only the key members, so a handful of people will not attract undo attention and what is more natural than a Prince and Princess to meet their friend the Countess in her Brussels city mansion!" Marie de Croy announced in a manner that was logical, well-composed and very practical.

Reginald never ceased to be amazed by the brilliance and independence of his sister. "Ah, you're a smart one, sister, you have great planning skills. A weekend may be the better day to meet as those paid-German agents are sometimes a bit lazy and don't like to work more for their thirty pieces of silver than necessary – a lazy Saturday or even a Sunday afternoon visit immediately following church services is perfect – we can have our little meeting accompanied by tea, coffee and cakes. Such a seemingly innocent social visit will not solicit any second looks from anyone including the normally suspicious Germans, I should think!"

"That's good thinking as well, Reginald," Marie smiled back. "Let's see if next Sunday morning is possible for everyone. I'll coordinate this with the Countess and Nurse Edith Cavell; can you contact Libiez and Capiau?" Marie inquired as she placed her empty brandy snifter down on the table.

"Most definitely, no problem at all. We'll lay out the details just as we have discussed, only leaving out the information of my liaison with the

British authorities in London and visits to the US Consulate in Brussels... remember Marie, everything is on a 'need-to-know' basis; London is keeping both of us in the dark too and it's for our own protection and that of others operating networks against the Germans, inflicting a hundred cuts at a time! We need to make sure that everyone knows of this secret operational necessity – our lives and those of everyone in the network is at severe risk should the Germans catch on to what is happening under their very noses!" Reginald reiterated again to Marie. He knew that he also needed to be constantly mindful of this necessity for secrecy as well.

\* \* \* \* \* \* \* \* \* \* \* \*

The Christmas holidays were in full celebration and newly fallen snow had covered the war remnants that were scattered throughout the countryside, with a soft new canvass of white snow. The city stores were adorned with the traditional holiday decorations with colours of vibrant red, green and yellow filling both the interior and exterior designs of the storefronts in Brussels. It was always proclaimed that no one in the world did Christmas better than the Europeans and after seeing the colourful pageantry of the decorations, few could dispute the claim. There were not presently any Allied soldiers in hiding within the dispersed cottages, barns, and private residences employed by the network members and to date about fifty soldiers, mostly British, had been safely ferreted out of Belgium into Holland. An older frontier guide named Louis Gille, no relation to the much younger Victor Gille who had assisted the Prince through to the Holland border, had been shot dead by German troops while attempting to cross into the French border assisting some French soldiers on a self-initiated, independent escape mission. The tragic news brought great distress to everyone in the de Croy network and it illustrated both the seriousness of their work, as well as the increased dangers rising in the border crossings, especially the French border.

All arrangements were made and ready for the Sunday afternoon meeting and the weather provided perfect accommodations: abundant sunshine and a soft, gentle, light breeze. Countess Jeanne de Belleville hosted the meeting in her Brussels townhouse, which some may call a city pocket-mansion, due to its luxurious construction and design. Located on the very fashionable and extremely exclusive 'Bois de la Cambre', which some referred to as Brussels' Central Park due to its scenic view of the city's meticulously manicured central park, it was in the heart of the most exclusive shops, residences and charming sidewalk cafes. The magnificent, eye-catching three storey, light beige coloured marble facade was modelled in the neo-classical design with ornately carved cartouches arrayed above each of the exterior window moldings fashioned with the de Belleville family coat of arms, which were visually complemented with the rich ebony wrought-iron balcony railings accenting each of the second storey windows. The residence rooms included six spacious bedrooms and five full baths, not to include two other half-bathrooms and a full basement. The interior was decorated in Louis XVI rich décor and furnishings with a full marble foyer and graceful spiral staircase. Silk wallpaper of various colours and patterns tastefully adorned each of the main rooms, which was colour-coordinated with the requisite furniture to provide a fully matched room décor. The entire space of this jewel-box pocket mansion was over 7,500 square feet.

The audience assembled was small, selective and most regal. Besides the Prince and Princess de Croy, those in attendance included the hostess Countess Jeanne de Belleville, Herman Capiau – the mining engineer, Albert Libiez – the Mons lawyer, Directress Nurse Edith Cavell, Abbe de Longueville – a strong patriotic priest from Mons, and a strange handsome man in his mid-thirties with thick black hair and whose handsome face was neatly framed in a coarse black moustache and matching goatee. The mysterious young man was a Brussels architect and a friend of the de Croys; his name was Philippe Baucq.

The French Countess Jeanne de Belleville of Lille, France welcomed each guest into her Brussels retreat home, taking their outerwear garments and items personally into a huge foyer clothing closet and directing them in-turn of arrival into a lush, light mint green- coloured intimate tea room located off the main hallway of the first floor. She personally announced each guest's name to the other guests who had arrived earlier. A fireplace was dutifully lit and it provided old world atmosphere to the intimate setting even as the entire mansion was centrally heated by a modern oil furnace located in the spacious basement. On huge silver serving trays, she had arrayed a neat compilation of hors d'oeuvres, sweets and two large sterling silver serving pots – one contained tea and the other one rich roasted French coffee. Out of character for her aristocratic position, Countess Jeanne herself had prepared the entire serving array, not wanting to have even the slightest detail of this meeting being suspected by her three-person household staff, to whom she had given a mandatory and generous week's holiday vacation of house duty. She gave the shielded excuse of taking-time with their families for Christmas as a cover story for the generous and unusual paid time off. She was wise as a fox in making sure that nothing she did was suspected or observed by

119

anyone. Her husband, like those of other Europeans, was absent due to war-related support efforts ever since the war had begun. The ladies were in an excused social situation shared by millions of other women across Europe, who also had absent husbands and boyfriends. It was just another sacrifice to be made for Belgium and the war effort. In a span of ten minutes from the appointed meeting hour of 12 o'clock noon, all the guests were present and Reginald and Marie de Croy aptly noted this fact, as their network rested on dependability and punctuality. They all sat about in a circular-array of strategically staged sofas and chairs. All parties dutifully took their cups and saucers and drank ever so awkwardly, as each person nervously gazed at one another or at other inanimate objects located throughout the room.

Finally Prince Reginald broke the ice and diplomatically so. "Well I'd first like to thank our gracious hostess Countess Jeanne de Belleville for the use of her marvellous home for this important meeting. We are all loyal and proven patriots and each of us has proven this recently by assisting Allied soldiers escape to friendly lines. I have it on most reliable evidence that all the soldiers who have been guided through to Holland are safe and back to their respective military units or country of origin; but, these are just the 'first steps', my dearest friends. There are hundreds more soldiers hiding throughout Belgium and they need our assistance…can I trust that everyone here wants to continue our efforts in this, but do it even better and bigger than before?" Reginald announced in a simple, yet clever lead-off introduction and individual solicitation of intention.

"Yes! Count me in! Of course! There's no turning back! What are we waiting for? Absolutely! Positively!" an immediate chorus of positive words showered back in quick succession and it was music to the Prince's ears. He really didn't expect to hear any dissent, yet he knew that a public proclamation from the network members was a necessary initiation rite for its key members.

"Very good and thank you everyone. These are dangerous things we are doing, yet these are dangerous times for all of Europe and our countrymen too! Ignoring an evil does not make it go away! Actions by good people are required. The Germans are no fools either. While we are not under their observant microscopes yet, a time will come when something will set them off and then the full fury of the German military and police will be upon us! If caught, well we might be killed or placed in a German prison performing hard labour!" the Prince accurately surmised, giving a stern warning as to what dangers they were all about to enter into. Not a word or body posture betrayed any hint of hesitation or second thoughts. Reginald smiled and he knew that they were all in this for the duration of the war or until they were discovered. He continued his informal instructive lecture without trying to appear too authoritative or condescending to the assembly – these were, after all, all women and men of achievement, status and intelligence and he could not afford to alienate any of them. Additionally, there was perfect equality in the risks that each member now personally bore.

"Thank you all once again for your patriotism. Our lives, positions and wealth are now in jeopardy. I have been in contact with 'higher authorities', to which I am not at liberty to divulge to you – in our work, knowing more is dangerous, so everything is on a need-to-know only basis and you need to exercise this procedure in all your dealings with anyone as well," Reginald emphasized to the attentive group.

"Although no one deliberately planned it, we have a remarkably sound and proven system to get soldiers and information out of Belgium and to the Allies through the system that is in-place presently – all we have to do is slightly improve and refine our operating procedures. Suspicion and inattention to detail will be our main enemies, as these are the culprits that will bring the Germans down on us! To our advantage, the Germans will least suspect aristocrats, mature women, nurses, professional men, religious men and women and even young children, especially young girls!' the Prince continued along in his monologue. All the faces were stoic; they hung on every word of the Prince's and they needed to, as their lives depended on being attentive.

"As with the existing structure, Bellignies will be the centre for gathering up all refugee soldiers in the Mons area of Belgium; Messers Capiau and Libiez will be our experts in preparing false identifications and photographs to get our soldiers north to Antwerp and then Holland; and finally Directress Nurse Edith Cavell will be the Brussels leader who arranges for the soldiers to be housed and handed-off to the frontier guides for the Holland journey. I have not forgotten Abbe de Longueville – he will work with Sister Josephine and the sisters at the various convents to locate Allied prisoners, courier messages and perform various travels on behalf of the network. The Germans still respect the religious, especially the cloistered monks and nuns. Now as to the strange man who most of you did not know before today, he is Philippe Baucq, a Brussels architect who assisted in getting our first two English soldiers north for the passage into Holland; he also has access to a safe house to shelter a few soldiers and he is a keen gatherer of information among the local populace. Philippe will work with Nurse Cavell in addition to performing other missions that I and my sister may have for him!" Reginald noted to Directress Cavell's sudden amazement – she was unsure if she could work with a stranger, but her hesitation melted when she remembered that this was the mysterious man who helped Colonel Chatsworth onto the horse-drawn wagon behind her Clinique many weeks ago. This favourable memory, and action, endeared Philippe to Edith as a trusted alley.

"Can we recruit new members to our network, Prince de Croy?" Edith inquired in a monotone non-emotional voice. Reginald smiled back with a slight grin, as he delighted in hearing an intelligent inquiry from among a group of very impressive people, each in their own capacity and talents.

"First, please call me Reginald – this war and our actions have made us friends, except where there are strangers present or to avoid undue suspicions, so in private let's use first names please and that is an excellent question, Edith. You may, if you are absolutely sure of the person in question, recruit new members, but do not inform them of anything greater than their mission or role! Remember that information is power and it is dangerous in the wrong hands. If at all possible, Edith, try and get people to do things for your mission without them knowing the purpose or cause behind it! Also, beware of anyone who asks too many probing questions for which they have no right to know; you must all be vague in dealing with anyone unknown to you. This guidance is for everyone else in the group as well: people who do things in innocence have the greatest chance of not acting suspicious or letting their actions betray them to the clever Germans if they are stopped or questioned! Remember, lying and being deceitful, even for noble reasons, cannot be easily hidden from the suspecting Germans and none of us are professional spies or agents! Remarkably, it takes skill and cunning to be an excellent liar," Reginald wisely noted and everyone knew that his words sounded true.

"Do we do everything the same, just as we did before?" Countess de Belleville inquired in a quiet voice.

"Another excellent question. We follow the same process, but we have to impose standard procedures in our tasks and actions. For instance we can use code words and phrases to ensure safety. As an example, when sending strangers to anyone in our network, use the code phrase 'Yorc sent me!' Do not use any telephones or telegraphs for any messages, use only couriers – speaking of which I recommend trusted people only, to include using young children. For the rural areas, I recommend the use of small and adolescent girls as they attact less suspicion and they can cover terrific distances. Also, do not write anything down which cannot be quickly destroyed and this destruction means burning, not tearing up papers. Vary your routines and make your actions unpredictable to any observer. Try to meet and coordinate in safe places, some of which are best done in plain sight, such as in cafes, but be mindful of loud discussions and do not mention names or places in your open conversations. If your cell or the network is discovered by the Germans, make your own way to safety in Holland and do this quickly! Do not feel guilty about leaving anyone behind; the Germans reward chivalry and loyalty with a rifle bullet. For those interrogated by the Germans, try to say as little as possible as the more you talk the more you can divulge – they are clever rascals, who use lies to get information from you and in many cases the Germans are merely guessing at pieces of facts!" Reginald concluded as everyone took stern notice of his words.

"I think that I can get a false Belgian, official-looking stamp made-up for the identification papers!" Herman Capiau noted with glee. "Yes, Maurice Derveau, a chemist that I know in Mons, can forge a very professional rubber seal of a fictitious Belgian town for use on the German mandated identification cards and I have stolen a nice inventory of blank German identity cards that we can easily fill out as we see fit," Capiau explained in more detail.

"That will be a great help: we need the most professional looking identification cards possible to get the soldiers out of Brussels through the frontier area," Reginald replied with a smile.

"I can procure basic food and medicines from my friends in Brussels, but food is getting expensive and rare. Still, I think I have enough goodwill capital in Brussels to get loaves of bread and vegetables for the soldiers' diet during their stay in Brussels. I have only limited facilities to cloister soldiers, just a few at a time, as young men at a nurse training Clinique draws unwarranted attention!" Edith Cavell spoke gently, but with sincerity of concern.

"I can assist you with that problem, Nurse Cavell. I have a modest, working class home at No 49 on the Avenue de Roodebeek, Brussels; it can easily be reached by the trams or by foot from either your Clinique or the Countess's mansion! I also know of several other safe-house residences in Brussels that can each cloister several soldiers for a few days before they go north…up to twenty-five soldiers can be discreetly lodged among all of the Brussels locations," Philippe Baucq followed up in a energetic voice.

Edith smiled and knew that Philippe was a man she could trust and rely upon in the future.

"I'll give you my address. You can come by anytime and just introduce yourself to my wife and you will be our welcomed guest!" Philippe remarked as he drew a pencil and pad from his suit jacket, upon which he wrote down his address and handed it to Edith.

"Abbe de Longueville: Father, I need for you to connect with Sister Josephine and Sisters Marie and Madeline at the Convent Witheries – they and all of their contacts are going to be our 'eyes and ears' for discovering the hidden Allied soldiers, most of whom have been in deep hiding since the Battle of Mons. I also need for the priests and monks to ferret out all information on hidden soldiers! We need to know precisely who and how many soldiers are in hiding so we can make for the proper processing and scheduling of the soldiers," Reginald pleaded gently with the middle-aged priest.

"This I can do. The religious of Belgium are horrified by the brutal German occupation. If we do not assist you now, later the Germans will come after us religious folks. We clergy in the Catholic church also have the silent seal of the confession box to gather up information discreetly from our flock of parishioners should they feel the urge to confess any critical information to the priests," the Abbe replied with his full support for being an active participant in the new de Croy network.

"The only thing left that I have to say is thank you all very much! Our country and all of Europe is in great danger and we all need to do our parts. Many of us here are single or widowed, so perhaps we can be a bit braver than those who risk their family's welfare as well as that of their own lives. I shall be travelling from time to time, the details of which are privileged, but my sister Marie is my co-agent in everything, so if you cannot contact me, please feel completely free to indulge in Marie's assistance," Reginald concluded. No one said anything more. Reginald had covered all the details and from now on most of their meetings were to be in much smaller intimate groups or even in pairs.

* * * * * * * * * * *

The de Croy network grew ever so slowly over the winter of 1915, yet it was slowly and consistently improving in its efficiency and confidence. Bellignies Chateau was the operational centre where the Allied soldiers were conveyed and housed until arrangements were made for the transportation to Brussels. Ever since November 1914, Bellignies Chateau had not been used as a Red Cross hospital and the distinctive white and red flag had long since been replaced by the traditional de Croy family coat of arms flag that flew high from the medieval tower Keep mast. The 'Royals' of the network consisted of Prince Reginald, Princess Marie and Countess Jeanne de Belleville – they were invaluable assets without which there could not have been a sustainable or organized soldier escape network. They provided key organizational support in getting the ever increasingly scarce food items, assured and safe lodging for groups of men and unique level of influence and cloistered support that was not available aside from that which was equally supplied by the Belgian religious member support system. The middle-class members provided the implementation means of getting practical work done, such as physically transporting the soldiers and getting their identity papers and photographs prepared. The lower class field workers, farmers, miners and girl guides provided the literal leg-work of finding the soldiers, escorting them to Bellignies Chateau and to the Countess Jeanne de Belleville for subsequent handling. Throughout the winter months only a trickle of several soldiers each week were processed through the de Croy network, as the harsh weather forced many Allied soldiers to stay in hiding except for the most desperate ones, who needed to be moved due to increasing German patrols or weakened physical conditions made worse by the cold and damp temperatures.

By March 1915 only about eighty-five Allied soldiers in total had been moved through to Holland, yet none had been detected, killed or foiled by the Germans. The de Croy (Yorc) network remained safely under the perusal of the German intelligence system; this was due to the fact that they had made no cardinal errors and, more importantly, the Germans were more focused in the intentions and resources upon the military activities of their enemies and not focusing on the egress activities of stranded Allied soldiers. The Prince provided the critical pocket-money funding for the network, which helped to pay a nominal fee to the frontier guides, food merchants, second-hand clothing purchases, medicines for any sick soldiers and small amounts of money to assist Edith Cavell's operating overhead expenses incurred in provisioning the soldiers. Reginald also established a vital contact link for the refugee soldiers to contact once they had crossed the border of Holland and then to The Hague and the Allied Military Headquarters. The frontier guides were told to inform the soldiers once they were a short distance from the Dutch border to proceed to the Allied Headquarters at the Hague and specifically request to personally see either General Dupre of the French army liaison office or Colonel Oppenheimer, the British Liaison staff officer, and to use the code-phrase 'Yorc has sent us!' In this manner, the refugee soldiers could be efficiently screened and debriefed by the proper military authorities who had been personally briefed by Reginald concerning their status.

The key network members became proficient at recruiting like-minded Belgian patriotic citizens well known and trusted by them personally. Network members also exhibited great initiative and imagination as well. Herman Capiau developed an ingenious system for conveying secret information to the Allied military at The Hague by hollowing out the heel of a special boot, in which was wrapped in double oil-skin water-resistant cloth short messages concerning the activity and location of high-value military information such as munitions trains, German units and airfields. The soldiers were unaware of what information they were couriering and it was only upon arrival at the Hague that their second-hand civilian clothing was thoroughly examined for the vital evidence by specifically trained British intelligence staff members.

Philippe Baucq personally recruited a widowed, highly patriotic woman named Ada Bodart. Ada was a middle-aged British widow, who Philippe had known and trusted for years and she was instrumental in aiding the refugee soldiers into Brussels and then handing them off to the frontier guides. She also acted as a message courier, assisted in preparing false identification and she sometimes concealed a few soldiers in her modest house in Brussels.

Edith Cavell decided to keep her section as small and intimate as possible. Aside from having Philippe Baucq the architect more or less 'involuntarily' placed into her charge and whom she now trusted after forming a good working relationship with him over the past several months, Edith recruited and involved a minimal number of people into her 'cell' or group. This was both by deliberate design and the fact that personally she was a minimalist by nature and by her personality, which was cloistered and independent. In short, Edith trusted herself more than strangers; however, once ingratiated into her confidence, her trust and friendship became absolute. So it was with the local Brussels chemist Louis Severin, a middle-aged, thin, balding man appointed with piercing blue eyes and a very prominent long brown-grey coloured beard. Louis was instrumental in providing medicines for her Clinique and for some of the refugee soldiers who came to her nursing school in ill health. He also became an intermediary with Philippe Baucq and Ada Bodart among others in the underground. Severin was a man to be trusted, as he had personally recommended Louis Gille, the frontier guide who was shot and killed by the Germans in eastern France while returning from a successful Allied soldier repatriation mission. Another 'helper' of Edith's was that of her select personal friends, Georges Hostelet, a prosperous and prominent 40-year-old doctor of physical and chemical sciences and he worked in the chemical industry in the employ of the multimillionaire manufacturer M. Solvay. He was very patriotic. He knew the risks that Edith and the other network workers took. He visited the Clinique often. He was very good friends with Edith. On his visits they could be heard shouting and laughing from Edith's private office located on the second floor of the Clinique. In a very short time, Georges Hostelet became Edith's #2 person assisting in the Allied prisoner escapee network.

Thus, akin to a spider's web, the de Croy network grew ad hoc through the spring by a series of inter-connected personal and trusted relationships. This arrangement was not the textbook model for the establishment of a professional underground movement, but it did work as long as there was no compromise by outsiders. The vulnerability of such an amateurish network was that, once compromised, it was highly fragile and subject to complete self-collapse like a house of cards. The Prince de Croy knew of and expressed this exact same sentiment to his sister Marie. The fragility of the network design was also confirmed to Reginald by the SIS in London, thus the foundation of the network and recruitment had to be based on individual trust, reliability and the absolute 'need-to-know' basis.

A long time mutual friend of the Prince and Princess de Croy, was a Mons dentist and English expatriate of many years named Dr James Bull, who had been visiting Bellignies for many years, usually on a Saturday or Sunday and sometimes dining with the de Croy family. He mingled with Reginald whenever the Prince was back from London, but he was more familiar with Leopold de Croy. He had been a widower for some years and the rest of his family was grown and back in England living out their lives, while he preferred to remain on the continent in Mons. A man in his mid-fifties, Dr Bull sported thick black hair and brown eyes framed within a slightly pudgy face gained over the years through a rich diet and a poor exercise regime. He was orthodox in his English attitudes and he expressed these quite openly with his friends the de Croys in unmistakable terms. A frequent traveller to Brussels and Antwerp, Dr Bull was a keen observer of the world around him and his observations of politics, technology and society all made for great social conversations with the de Croys. When the war began, Dr Bull became staunchly anti-German and he could accurately note with a high degree of fineness, the types of German military equipment being employed, as well as the war effects on the Belgian population. Reginald took mental note of this ability and, in March 1915, he and Marie recruited Dr Bull to be an 'information gatherer' of German military significance, to which this data was conveyed innocently through the refugee soldiers to General Dupre and Colonel Oppenheimer at the Allied Headquarters at The Hague.

Meetings were conducted as needed at Bellignies, the Countess Jeanne de Belleville's townhouse in Brussels or at one of the innocuous cafes operated by network sympathizers Oscar Mathieu and Maurice Pansaers – both men knew and were known by the de Croy Brussels cell members. The two café owners, like other Belgian citizens, merely offered peripheral aid and support, this consisting of food and shelter to refugee soldiers and a safe meeting place for the members to congregate. Yet in the German eyes, even this mere act of kindness was dangerous, as it was seen as direct collaboration and assistance to the enemy in a time of war. Yet such threats did not deter most Belgians and the de Croy network found profuse support from many Belgians whenever it was needed. No one in Belgium, not even the children, liked the German occupation forces and the Germans were keenly aware of the sentiment and thus they took no mercy upon the civilian population – the winning of Belgian hearts and minds was futile.

With the coming of spring and warmer weather, came the inevitable German patrols, which awoke from relatively placid winter hibernation to a fair weather awakening. The patrols ventured throughout the Belgian countryside and as the weather warmed, so too did the patrols. The patrols were instigated out of both sheer military necessity and desperation. From a military perspective, the young German troops needed to be kept gainfully employed and performing a useful mission – the searching of the Belgian countryside and homes was a marvellous way to keep the young soldiers in shape by walking many miles per day and it also became a sad necessity that the German army was not being adequately supplied with enough food to keep it satiated and thus the foraging of food from private farms, rural shops and residences became necessary, although not officially condoned by the Higher German Military command.

The German patrols were now posing a serious threat to the local hiding places, which had previously provided a secure, anonymous hiding place for the Allied soldiers. Luckily, the young Belgian children could easily travel faster than the heavily combat gear-laden German infantry soldiers and the children knew the countryside better than the foreign soldiers. In the Belgian countryside, in a time of war, regular schooling was a luxury and school attendance was not the norm, as all able bodies were needed for farm work – education was a luxury to be resumed upon the time of a future peace. When the Germans approached, the children easily sounded the alert to their parents and guardians; the young children could travel fast and long. The Allied soldiers were quickly spirited away without anyone being the wiser. Yet the de Croys knew that this 'cat and mouse' game could not succeed forever; a better, more permanent solution for hiding refugee soldiers needed to be found and quickly.

Marie and Reginald gave sombre thought to the problem but no immediate solution was self-evident. The monasteries, convents and abbeys offered some level of solution for several soldiers at any given time, yet the demand was for a sanctuary that was able to accommodate ten or twenty soldiers if so required. Reginald paced back and forth in his masculine decorated library seeking a solution. He nonchalantly gazed upon the old paintings on the walls that depicted his ancestors, which in some cases dated back to the Middle Ages and he marvelled back to postulate the possible remedies that his ancestors could inspire. "What would my ancestors do in a situation such as mine?' he asked himself incessantly. He knew that they too faced persecution, including the great Protestant-Catholic Inquisition that spanned the 12th through 14th centuries. He gazed at the old painting that depicted the old Bellignies Keep. In an epiphany moment, a mental lightning bolt jolted through his mind to inspire an ingenious 12th century solution to their 20th century sheltering problem.

Quickly he called his sister Marie and they recollected that many years earlier their father, Prince Alfred Emmanuel de Croy-Solre had an architectural engineer perform a structural forensic analysis on the old Bellignies Tower Keep and further examination revealed that within the recesses of the Keep's nine foot thick stone walls, there was hidden a secret stone-carved stairway that had been used since medieval times to hide various persons from both religious persecution and local unpopular wars. They looked at each other with hopeful stares like small children making a potential treasure-trove discovery. The Prince and Princess rushed to the far old wing of the chateau and then to the ancient Keep area, where they discovered that the entrance to the stairway was through a walled-up ground floor tower window. Yet this was just a canard to defeat the curiosity of over-zealous amateur explorers. The entrance to the stairway was hidden by a cleverly installed permanent wooden cupboard, the back panelling of which upon being deftly removed by hand, revealed the cavity to the stairway. The secret nook was pitch black and the Prince needed to strike a match to reveal the inner recess of the secret chamber, which smelled of old mildew and old hay. Against the wall they spotted a sturdy wooden ladder. The nine-foot ladder was needed to actually reach up to the level of the stone stairway and this necessity provided a secondary means of safety since anyone hiding in the Keep stairway could naturally pull up the ladder with them and thus making any innocent discovery of the hidden recess totally useless without an accompanying self-furnished ladder. It was the perfect hiding place!

The Princess ran and fetched a kerosene oil lamp, whereby the Prince manoeuvred the ladder so as to examine the size and extent of the secret stairway and he discovered that it was a huge stone recess that could hold many men in it all the way up to the roof level of the Keep's pointed top. The spiral stairs were about the length of a man's body and no sound from within the stairwell could be heard. Anyone coughing, sneezing or making other human outbursts were not heard unless one was directly a few feet away from the sound source. It was a fine example of a medieval 'safe or panic room'.

They carefully placed back the single false back panel to close-up the secret stairway entrance. With utmost diligence they also replaced the shelving and other rustic items as well – the two cupboard wooden shelves adorned with rustic bottles and cups made for a quite convincing camouflage of what secret actually lay beyond the back recess panelling of the cupboard. They were careful to ensure that the ample layering of cupboard dust and grime was not disturbed, as it too needed to look to any observer that this item was not recently attended to or disturbed. With all the careful re-arrangement of all the items concerned, it again appeared that no one had touched this rustic cupboard for many countless years. The massive stone staircase was perfect and it could stow away up to twenty-five or thirty soldiers if absolutely necessary and without anyone hearing or suspecting them. The issue of housing refugee soldiers safely and secretly at Bellignies had been solved.

★ ★ ★ ★ ★ ★ ★ ★ ★ ★ ★ ★

By April 1915, well over one hundred Allied soldiers had been smuggled out of Belgium to Holland. In addition to the British, French and Belgian refugee soldiers, the de Croy network was now assisting young Belgian and French men leave their occupied countries and reach Holland to volunteer for war duty on behalf of the Allies. The number of monthly escapees averaged 25-30 men a month being processed through the network and among the local Belgian citizens in both Mons and Brussels were the inevitable hushed whispers and rumours of there being a underground network. Despite the rumours, no Belgian citizen said anything to the German authorities, this in obvious rejection of the myriad posters and newspaper warnings that warned the Belgians not to harbour any soldiers or perform any acts of subversion. Yet the free Belgians in Brussels had their own propaganda cause. An anonymous underground source in Brussels was distributing an anti-German newspaper called the La Libre Belgique, which called on all Belgians to defy and defeat the illegal German occupying forces by all means possible. The illegal newspaper started to appear in cafes and shops shortly after the German occupation of Belgium and the German authorities had offered a 5,000 francs reward for any information leading up to the arrest and conviction of the publisher and distributor. There were no takers for the reward and no one knew how the newspaper was published and distributed.

Reginald travelled back again to London, this time travelling in the open and using his German issued travel pass that allowed his travel to Antwerp unimpeded. He also visited the US Consulate in Brussels and he spoke with Minister Whitlock. The two men discussed the impending war relief efforts that were to be directed to Belgium through the US Consulate, yet nothing of substance had originated other than mere general discussions and some preliminary planning. Reginald wisely confessed nothing to Consul Whitlock concerning his work with the British War Office, as the United States was a neutral country and it was unwise to involve neutral parties in the affairs of war and subversion. Reginald only informed Consul Whitlock that he had arranged for correspondence to be delivered to him at the US Consulate from un-named parties in London. The US Consulate decided it prudent not to insist on further divulgences that were obviously masked in secrecy, yet Brand Whitlock took careful note of any British diplomatic pouch correspondences that were addressed and left for Prince de Croy. Whitlock wisely suspected that Prince de Croy was involved in some secret dealings with the British authorities to include the Foreign Office and the War Department. Yet these affairs concerned him little at the present time.

In London, Reginald confirmed by-name the safe passage of all the Allied soldiers and Belgium and French civilians that had passed into Holland. Once again, not one person had been compromised; the network was operating like a fine Swiss watch. Reginald also passed along the names and status of various Allied soldiers who had either died or become POWs – this data was much appreciated and it brought comfort and closure to the families who theretofore had their loved ones listed as Missing In Action (MIA).

Commander George Smith-Cumming also personally thanked Reginald and the entire de Croy network for getting vital war information on the Germans' military activity in northern Belgium. The insightful Dr Bull had recently received information from some Belgian construction workers that a large area of forest near Evere, a hamlet in northern Brussels, had recently been cleared, gravel laid and large soccer-field sized buildings had been expediently constructed. He also received information that large cylindrical metal containers were also spotted. This assembled data clearly indicated one thing: the preparation for the operational use of German Zeppelins from a location approximately 15 miles to the northwest of the city of Brussels. These deadly new weapons, for which the British had no adequate defence, could be used to perform reconnaissance on the British blockade that was slowly starving Germany and the occupied countries of food and every other vital war item; conversely the German Zeppelins could also be used for the more nefarious purpose of terror-bombing British cities, to include London. This was exactly the type of actionable intelligence that the SIS needed to gain advantage over the Germans. Reginald stayed in London only a scant two days; he had nothing new to report, nor any new missions to perform. He was to proceed exactly as he had been doing since the network started several months earlier. His travel back to Belgium was exactly the reverse of his travel out of the country. If the Germans inquired of his travels, he would rightly state that he was coordinating war relief for Belgium – the worst that the Germans would do is to forbade any future travel and rescind his German issued travel pass.

Before returning to Bellignies Chateau, Reginald stopped at the US Consulate to check for any courier correspondence. This time he was fortunate in that there was a letter given to the US Embassy in London for transport by diplomatic pouch to the US Consulate in Brussels – this was the only means of communication that was secure without meddling or open-search by the German authorities. The plain white envelope was simply addressed to 'Edith' and Reginald knew immediately that it was for Edith Cavell, his network co-conspirator. Upon his visitation at the US Consulate in Brussels, Reginald simply signed for the letter from the US Consulate staff and then simply dropped the letter off at the Clinique rue de la Culture. Nurse Wilkins received Reginald, as Edith was away on an errand and Reginald just thought it best not to reveal any further information about himself to someone he did not know. The plain envelope was, in fact, a personal correspondence of thanks from her old friend, Colonel Percy Chatsworth. Later, Edith read the letter with great relish, as she was glad that both the English Colonel and the young Corporal Taylor had made it safely back to London. Edith kept the letter in her private office drawer and she read it periodically, as it provided her with inspiration to continue her work to assist Allied soldiers escape the clutch of the Germans.

Late April 1915 brought not only showers, but also a short re-visitation of war to Brussels. Based on the intelligence that the de Croy network had passed from its information gathering member Dr James Bull, the British launched a bold air raid of over a dozen planes in a very daring set of air raids against some railway marshalling yards that contained some fully-stocked high explosive ammunition box cars, but more importantly a successful raid against the newly completed German Zeppelin aerodrome hangars and air facilities at Evere was managed. The British used bombs and incendiary bullets to set afire the entire complex and all of Brussels was abuzz with the stories of this magnificent daring British airplane raid. The exploding huge quantities of concentrated high-pressure hydrogen gas exploding into huge fireballs of flames could be seen from every part of Brussels and it was rumoured that there had been a huge loss of German lives and much physical destruction; the windows of many houses even a few miles away from the Zeppelin airfield were all shattered. It was a magnificent sight to behold, like that of Dante's Inferno.

The German military surveillance of the British blockade fleet was severely hampered and the planned Zeppelin raids on London needed to be diverted for at least a month. This was a major military strategic setback for the Germans. The German General Staff was in an uproar over this brazen and brilliant British air attack that smacked of careful planning and very accurate targeting information. 'Yet where did this information originate from?' the Germans wondered, as such a carefully planned attack needed good intelligence and the only means of obtaining this information was by spying, that is spying from the ground – and this meant that there were British agents working in Belgium! Such a situation could not be tolerated or allowed to continue, the Germans accurately reasoned. They knew that success only breeds more success and that spying only begot more spying and this eventually led to greater rebellious acts such as sabotage, assassinations and outright rebellion. Such acts must be nipped in the bud and a very firm example made of all the culprits involved. Harsh treatment was going to deter other copycats to commit similar such acts or to shelter those who committed any such acts. An emergency staff meeting was called and fervent discussions followed; all of the German staff generals agreed to the conclusions. All acts of treason, espionage and rebellion must be quashed and quickly before the patriotic contagion spread like a commutable disease.

The Generals decided that they had been too kind to the civilian population of Belgium, especially Brussels, and that instead of using a 'velvet glove' to placate the population, an 'iron fist' was needed to be exerted to subdue any traitors and spies among the population. 'People tend to think and act less patriotically when they are scared and people are most scared when their lives are in jeopardy of being taken from them!' the German generals pragmatically reasoned, so they were going to recruit the hardest counter-intelligence personnel to the nest of Belgian saboteurs that they could find from within the ranks of the Imperial German army. The German General Staff under the new leadership of Field Marshal Erich von Falkenhayn was going to make a stern example of this incident and they were also going to appoint a more ruthless, no-nonsense German Military Governor for the Brussels district. The Germans figured if they could not be respected and loved, then at least they needed to be feared.

\* \* \* \* \* \* \* \* \* \* \*

# Chapter 6:
# A Plot is planned

*"I want to extensively use 'Agent Provocateurs', Belgian civilians in our paid employment, who will hide and infiltrate all aspects of Belgian society with the aim of uncovering secret information on the underground network and the people employed in it"*

"Bastards! Stinking, lousy, traitorous Belgian bastards! That is what the German Army is facing with these Belgian swine!" the grey-haired, lean, cropped fifty-three year old Field Marshal Erich von Falkenhayn screamed at his quiet and dumbfounded deputy chief of military operations. "Our Zeppelins have been bombed by the British and the only way they could know the exact location of our aerodrome field was by spying or a traitor! It might have been one of the construction workers or maybe an employed worker, but someone collected and transmitted this information to British intelligence and this person or persons must be stopped at once. The German Army has more operations and secrets to protect. I am going to make sure that the Military Governor-General of Belgium, Generalleutnant von Bissing, Political Minister Generalmajor von der Lancken and the Brussels Military-Governor Generalmajor Richard Kraewel are contacted immediately to be informed that by my order a special intelligence team is being sent to Belgium under the direction of the German General Staff to ferret out the den of spies and traitors that obviously exists somewhere in occupied Belgium," the head of the German General staff noted in a loud baritone voice.

"Yes sir! It will be done immediately!" the cardboard stiff Colonel Rudolph Mansfeld replied obediently.

"Well, what are you waiting for, Colonel Mansfeld? Or do you have something to add in this matter! If you have something of value to say to me, then spit it out, man and quit your silly throat clearing! It is not becoming of a German Army officer, especially one who is posted to my staff!" the middle-aged Field Marshal shouted as he was obviously aware that his trusted staff officer seemed to have something to say to him – the Colonel was audibly clearing his throat in his usual habit whenever he had something to tell his superior.

"Well yes, thank you, sir, if I am not speaking out of turn and if I may be so bold as to suggest a very capable and no-nonsense officer in this matter, may I offer the name of Captain Hans von Kirchenheim – he was the young, aggressive infantry officer who helped to rid the village of Louvain of those troublesome civilians who were sniping at our German forces in August of 1914; he ruthlessly helped to level that town and rid it of the meddlesome Belgian resistance forces. His methods are harsh, but he gets results and he is a hard task-master once he is given a mission to fulfill. We can assign him with two or three fine military police officers as well, men who have experience in criminal matters from their civilian careers," Colonel Mansfeld stated in a very cogent and logical fashion.

The Prussian sect that dominated the upper echelons of the German military was a small circle of highly trained and devoted military professionals where family affiliations were well-known and respected. To a land owning Prussian 'Junkers', soldiering and military honour was akin to taking a priestly vow. Field Marshal von Falkenhayn knew of the Von Kirchenheim family and he trusted that if this young, energetic officer was assigned the task of finding Belgian spies and traitors, he would be honour-bound to complete the mission lest the assignment be given to a mere middle-class Army officer.

"That is a fine suggestion, Colonel Mansfeld and that is one of the reasons that I keep you on the German General Staff despite your request for a field command – your sage advice and insight are too important for you to be elsewhere!" the top German general replied in a masked compliment.

"Yes, Herr Field Marshal, I will compose the order and have it ready for your signature within the hour!" Colonel Mansfeld replied loudly as he saluted his superior and quickly left the large oak panelled office. Falkenhayn knew that all of the occupied countries needed to be safely secured if there was to be a seamless military continuity of the Imperial German war machine in occupied countries. New, massive military operations were being planned for the upcoming year and he could ill afford to have precious war assets diverted to fighting amateur civilians, who were trying to be local or national heroes. Munitions trains needed to flow without disruption, airfields needed to be safe and anonymous and the new Zeppelin aerodromes needed to be operational for strategic reconnaissance of the North Sea and to bomb cities such as London. The Field Marshal knew that they could eventually capture the culprits; however, he was as not so certain as to the amount of time that this effort was going to take and as all professional soldiers knew well, time was never a factor to favour carefully planned military operations.

* * * * * * * * * * * *

"My greetings, gentlemen! I have brought all of you to Berlin so that you may all get an appreciation for the seriousness of the problem that faces the German Army. By way of introduction and authority, my name is Captain von Kirchenheim and I have been appointed by the German General Staff to personally weed-out the nest of traitors, spies and saboteurs that have been popping up sporadically over occupied France and especially Belgium. Before summer is out, I have vowed to eradicate by all means possible this cancer that has plagued our army and its war aim!" the lean and handsome young Army officer stated to the three assembled German field-grey uniformed officers seated stoically before him. A set of medals were proudly displayed upon the young bellicose officer's chest, to include the prestigious neck-draped Pour de Merit gold and blue enamel medal and the tunic-button affixed red and black Iron Cross First Class ribbon.

"What methods can we use?" one of the men, who was in his mid-thirties and dressed in the uniform of a German military police Lieutenant inquired in a loud, shrill voice that equally matched his stern, unpleasant, unemotional granite sculptured face.

"That is an excellent question, Lieutenant Bergan; I'm glad that we recruited you for this task," Captain von Kirchenheim replied back in complimentarily fashion to the grim-faced officer. "Belgium is under German occupation and under German military law, you may do everything permitted under the German military justice codes and provisions!" the young Prussian officer replied as military police Lieutenant Bergan nodded in visual acknowledgment and obvious satisfaction.

"How far do we go with our inquiries and how far can we go in our investigations? Is anyone to be privileged?" the other German military police Lieutenant with a thick black moustache and prominent purplish coloured facial birth mark inquired, as he sought to determine if there were any sensitive parties who were not to be investigated.

Captain von Kirchenheim looked sternly at Lieutenant Pinkhoff and responded immediately without pausing. "You are both to take this investigation to the lowest and highest level possible. No one is immune to a German military official investigation," was the no nonsense response. Lieutenant Pinkhoff was immediately satisfied with the answer as he merely nodded his head vertically in silent affirmation.

"The Belgians are a very brave, stubborn and clever lot, Captain von Kirchenheim. These people are not going to volunteer information to us freely. I have been in Belgium, as have you. The Belgians are a closed-mouth lot of people," the third officer, a German Army Captain, commented with some concern.

"That is quite correct, Captain Joel; we cannot expect any cooperation from these occupied people voluntarily, although we will gladly take any walk-in, voluntary information that comes our way, so we'll have to employ other methods to pry open their stubborn lips. Under the right environment and circumstances, anyone can be made to divulge information – all we have to do is to use the correct method!" von Kirchenheim remarked, knowing full well the plan and methods that he was going to use to trap these Belgian 5th columnists in occupied Belgium.

"You all here are members of the German military police and you have a great quiver of weapons to deal with these scoundrels. Money, food, special privileges, threats, fear, ego manipulation, jailing, sex, lies…these are weapons that you are to use. The German Army has plenty of money and people for you to utilize in this effort, so use these without hesitation – but we need results and we need these quickly. For this operation, I want to extensively use 'Agent Provocateurs', Belgian civilians in our paid employment who will hide and infiltrate all aspects of Belgian society with the aim of uncovering secret information on the underground network and the people employed in it. Use the 'Agent Provocateurs' extensively, but with as much pinpoint accuracy as possible, choose your agents who are trustworthy, intelligent, ambitious and anonymous," Captain von Kirchenheim coolly and concisely outlined the genesis of his plan to the trio. They were all intrigued at both the mission and the methods to be afforded them.

"Finally, let me establish the lines of control and responsibility for this task. I am in total command of this operation and you will all report to me weekly every Monday with a summary of your results to date. I am in charge of all investigations for the whole of Belgium and I will maintain a small office in Brussels, where I will occasionally be physically located there and this is where Captain Joel will have his permanent office in the German Military Governor's office building, while Lieutenants Bergan and Pinkhoff can establish their offices at a location most conducive to their operations. Captain Joel is one of the best German counter-intelligence officers and he will be my lead officer for the city of Brussels; he has my complete confidence, so he will be your daily supervisor. Both Lieutenant Bergan and Pinkhoff will work for and directly report to Captain Joel. As I am a professional German Army infantry officer assigned to this counter-intelligence task as a special duty assignment, I am relying on all three of you to provide and execute operational details that are of a counter-intelligence and police detective nature," Captain von Kirchenheim remarked succinctly, as he looked at his three hand-picked subordinates for any feedback.

"Do we happen to know if these 'acts of sabotage and espionage' are those of the British Army or War Office agents?" Captain Joel inquired to ascertain more information on their new found enemy.

There was only silence in the room, as Captain von Kirchenheim paced with a slight nervousness before finally answering Captain Joel's inquiry. "I'm afraid that there is very little information on these underground enemies of the German Army. They may be professional British or French intelligence agents or they may be amateurs…they could be man or woman…sinner or saint! We simply do not know and that's exactly what we are going to find out – and, gentlemen, we will find out who is reporting the status of our forces, logistical points and airfield information of our planes and Zeppelins. Unless there are other questions, I think that you have enough information and guidance to start your work. Advise me if you need anything. I know that you will be needing some seed and pay-out money – just keep accurate receipts of this information and forward it to me in your routine reports. Now are there any final comments, gentlemen?" von Kirchenheim concluded to the three silent men. There were no responses.

"Good luck then and we'll meet again in a week's time in Captain Joel's Brussels office for our next progress meeting…good day and good hunting!" Captain von Kirchenheim stated as he picked up his peaked visor hat and walked smartly out the office door to meet with another set of counter-intelligence agents that he was using for another operation in a separate Belgian city.

\* \* \* \* \* \* \* \* \* \* \*

The two German Lieutenant military police officers had been well chosen by Captain van Kirchenheim to perform the task of uncovering illegal underground activities – both men were experienced, dedicated, cunning and utterly ruthless. Lt Ernest Bergan had over a decade of practical, hands-on experience of tracking criminals and uncovering suspicious behaviour from his years of being a German policeman and detective in the city of

Dusseldorf before the war. He was ruby red skinned and with dangerous piercing black eyes, heavy-build; he was forty years old with a wife and two children. In his behaviour, he demonstrated attributes of being over-bearing, loud-mouthed and possessing an abrasive bullying attitude. Maybe such stereotypical street behaviour contributed to his eventual rise to the position of Kommissar of the Dusseldorf police. His negative demeanour drew the ire of the criminal underworld and he earned the moniker of the nickname 'Black Devil', a title that was to follow him to Brussels in his new position within the German military counter-intelligence and secret police department. He spoke no French at all, nor did he care to develop any aptitude for it. Lieutenant Bergan's arrogance led to a singular and self-righteous view of the world in which any means was justified by the German police goal of catching spies and traitors. This may have made him a very successful officer in closing many police investigations through bullying and dubious underhanded methods, but it conversely made traits for a very cruel and ruthless human being, a type of man who never made true friendships or possessing any other socially redeeming values.

The counter-balance to Lieutenant Bergan was that of his partner. Lieutenant Henri Pinkhoff was the perfect complement and foil to his partner Lieutenant Bergan. Whereas Lieutenant Bergan by nature and character was well suited to playing the 'bad cop', Lieutenant Pinkhoff was moulded to be the 'good cop' on the team. Despite his muscular and strong framed body, his face was coarse in texture, which was made the more sinister by the purplish birthmark on his right cheek; in personality and character he was a charming fellow who was able to engender himself with myriad characters by the sheer nature of his gentle, pleasant voice and personality. His manner was at once disarming and this led suspects to lower their defences when speaking with him, often resulting in a suspect volunteering information that they otherwise would not have divulged to someone like Lieutenant Bergan. Lieutenant Pinkhoff possessed a natural ability to 'read' a person's demeanour, as well as being able to accurately judge a person's weaknesses. He used these innate skills to become a very good police detective in Germany, he played upon a person's fear and he could extend contrived and convincing sympathy to many a suspect. When questioning multiple parties to a crime, he cleverly used practical psychology to play one person against the other, often using fear, conjecture and lies to get one party or another to 'break' and confess to turn against the other silent party to the crime. He was quiet, observant, soft spoken and smart. He spoke several languages and he had a great interest in the world and the things around him, he had even served one tour early in his life in the British Army. As needed, he knew he could even manipulate his technically superior partner, Lieutenant Bergan.

A week after their meeting with Captain von Kirchenheim in Berlin, Lieutenants Bergan and Pinkhoff, under the supervision and approval of Captain Joel, had selected and set-up their special office in Brussels at the rue de Berlaimont, which was also conveniently the Headquarters building for German military police, thus it was a perfect location in which to leverage the resources of the existing German military police staff and it allowed the two officers to instantly share their information with other members of the German military police corps. 'Section B' was the special staff of the German military police that dealt with secret matters, to include counter-intelligence, black market activities, smuggling and the like.

Having thus established a base of operations in Brussels, Lieutenants Bergan and Pinkhoff needed to establish a counter-intelligence collection network of their own, an independent organization and group of people that were capable of gathering information on Allied espionage activities. Yet how was this data to be gathered? Anyone capable of performing such a dangerous and secret activity as spying was unlikely to be very obvious or easy to detect. By its very nature, spying and sabotage were very covert acts to which the perpetrators were ever vigilant to remain vague and hidden from both the public and, more especially, the German counter-intelligence police. One proven, but timely, method was to look for unusual activity patterns among people, yet Brussels was a large city with hundreds of thousands of people who were acting strangely and defensively under the watchful eyes of the German occupying forces. Odd behaviour in war was not so unusual, as people were suspicious of the Germans and they were hiding personal items, usually family valuables, money, fine china and other items worthy of German 'confiscation'. Another method was to 'bait' or set the stage for an irresistible 'dummy' or bogus target in which the spy or saboteur was 'lured' with a valuable target too tempting to resist, such as a fake munitions train or unusual piece of military equipment.

Yet unless they were very lucky or their adversaries were careless and made a mistake, it was going to be near impossible to break into the underground network. Still, battles and wars were won not on tenet of flawless execution of design alone, but more often due to errors in judgment, careless procedures and sometimes deliberate betrayal.

Throughout April 1915, the de Croy network continued to extract Allied soldiers and increasingly more Belgian young men, from Bellignies to Brussels, then on to Holland. The monthly number of refugee Allied soldiers and Belgian young men was now averaging over fifty men a month. The warm weather allowed more men to be sheltered in the local woods, if for only a few days. A few miles distant from Bellignies Chateau there lay the great forest of Mormal, which consisted of over 30,000 acres of magnificent unspoiled, thick woods on which were populated the occasional keepers' houses and woodmen's cottages. The soldiers and young men found outdoor lodging in relative safety, until German patrols came and then a hurried refuge in the Chateau Keep became necessary. The only major issue was the continued need to procure more funding and supplies, especially the increasingly scarce food, to keep the men supplied with basic needs. Reginald, Edith Cavell and Georges Hostelet provided as much money as they had available, but it again became necessary for Reginald to make additional trips to London for supplemental funding.

The Germans meanwhile launched more countryside patrols and planted numerous Agent Provocateurs numbering into the hundreds within the city of Brussels to detect any suspicious activity, but to date there were no productive leads of any substance, aside from a few stray cases of black-marketing of some food stuffs. Captain von Kirchenheim was not yet overly nervous, he knew that intelligence took time to develop; still he saw no telltale evidence of any serious espionage or sabotage ring. As he waited for a lead, more German supply points and munitions trains were being bombed by the ever bolder British bombers around the outskirts of Belgium. As the bombing increased, the patience of the Berlin German General Staff became frayed and Captain von Kirchenheim gave the generals no reason for any future optimism. In silence, some of them wondered if he was the right officer for the job.

\* \* \* \* \* \* \* \* \* \* \* \*

"Well this Taverne Royal is a picturesque place envisioned on the front of the tourist postcards; it's a charming little café that is tucked away from the crowds, yet convenient enough for us to leisurely gaze down the entire avenue. How did you ever find it, Philippe?" Louise Thuliez innocently remarked, as she self-proclaimed the quaintness of their open-air café meeting rendezvous.

"Ah well, you know I have many friends in Brussels, Ada Bodart and George Hostelet being among my closest and I have known the café owner Maurice Pansaers for the last fifteen years, since my days of studying architecture at the university. Monsieur Pansaers is a fine old gentlemen, he's a loyal Belgian, but he knows nothing of our affairs, so please keep quiet around him. I don't want this innocent man to get wrapped up in our business; he's very neurotic and incapable of handling pressure of any kind," Philippe Baucq carefully explained to his collaborators of the Brussels cell. The typical seasonal sordid cloudy weather had suddenly ruptured into an early and pleasant spring, so an open-air, public meeting was both inviting and most secure.

"I understand that Reginald is away again on one of his 'sojourns'. I do worry every time that he travels – even innocent civilians these days can become the unwitting victim of random war violence. The borders are dangerous and the seas are treacherous. Foreign travel is even more dangerous than ever before; the Germans have promised to resume their horrible U-boat war and sink any Allied ships that are even remotely suspected of providing war support to the Allies. The Gemans think that if Britain can starve out Germany through a blockade, then Germany has a right to do this as well. The difference is that the British do not torpedo ships with innocent civilians onboard!" Countess Jeanne de Belleville spoke candidly in a hushed voice to her four companions, as she sat in a very fashionable white and canary-yellow chiffon dress and sporting an equally matched wide-brimmed hat.

"Yes, we're all playing with fire here, but we are adults, we know the risks and there are no other options. Our men need our help and we're doing exactly that – soon there will be none of them left!" Edith Cavell remarked as a sober reminder that time was quickly running out for any refugee soldiers still remaining in hiding behind the German lines – they were being caught or surrendering out of sheer desperation or starvation.

"I hope Reggie gets back soon. I need more money than my budget will allow; I never thought that helping these men was going to be so exhaustive or so expensive," Georges Hostelet remarked as he sipped on a cup of coffee and little pastry, as the small group huddled around the table whenever one of them ventured to speak about sensitive things. There were increasingly 'paid-ears' listening in every urban crevice in Brussels and discretion ruled over social decorum. The prosperous George Hostelet and the noble Prince de Croy were the 'de facto' financers of the de Croy network and although the sums needed to support their network operations was not obnoxiously expensive, pre-war currency had all but disappeared from commercial usage. The Germans had issued almost worthless military script and bartering had become a common medium of exchange. Foreign currency and precious old coinage was most desirable. Yet as things became more desperate, even money and precious metals lost usage, as bartering of goods and services became a more practical means of exchange. The market for commercial goods simply dried-up.

"It must be lonely for Marie living all alone in that big estate with Reggie and Leopold being away and her aged grandmother being an almost shut-in invalid," Philippe said in passing.

George Hostelet almost coughed on his hot strong coffee. "Lonely? Philippe, you must be joking! Marie has about twenty-five of our 'friends' that both Edith and yourself should be expecting within the next fortnight! Marie also has been entertaining the Countess Marie de Lichtervelde and the elderly neighbour Baron de la Grange as her routine guests to help 'assist' with any minor details concerning the 'guest lodging'," George Hostelet noted in a cryptic, talk-around language that the de Croy network had developed as a crude form of code to refer the smuggling of refugee soldiers and able young men.

"I did not think that Countess de Lichtervelde and Baron de la Grange were recruited into 'the cause'," Edith Cavell remarked in a hushed soft tone of inquiry.

"No Edith, I'm afraid that neither the Countess or the Baron are 'active members', but they are 'aware' and they are our friends. We cannot expect every Belgian to feel and act the same as we do, yet they are our friends and that which they see, they wisely keep to themselves!" Countess Jeanne de Belleville remarked in a passing defence of her aristocratic friends who had preferred to remain neutral in the activities of the de Croy network.

"Oh Edith, please excuse my forgetfulness – speaking of Reggie, he wanted for me to present these correspondences that came to him from some mutual 'British friends' that both of you have in common and he wanted to ensure that you received these in a timely manner. He also wanted me to ensure that you keep these letters in a very safe place." Countess Jeanne winked as she discreetly handed Edith a pile of envelopes that constituted letters of appreciation from some of the escaped soldiers, two of which included additional correspondences from Colonel 'Slim' Chatsworth and Corporal Billy Taylor.

"Thank you for this kind act, Jeanne. I'll eagerly read these in my private office and I'll ensure these are secured properly," Edith replied as she took the pile of envelopes and placed these into her handbag. Later she read these private letters and carefully placed these away along with the other letters that she had previously received. From time to time she would read these letters as a form of therapy, as these letters kept her spirits flowing and encouraged her to continue her soldier smuggling activities in spite of the high risks.

"Oh my Lord, look at that man over there smoking his cigar and shamelessly reading that infamous La Libre Belgique newspaper! That underground newspaper is a recipe for arrest, if the German secret police find him with it! They've been trying to close it down and arrest its ringleaders ever since it was published after the German occupation!" Countess Jeanne de Belleville remarked in amazement as to the brazenness that some ordinary Belgians exercised to defy the German decrees about reading the illegal paper, which served as the only foil to the German propaganda that proliferated throughout the city. It seemed that every person exercised defiance to the German occupation in varying personal forms.

"Oh I think he's quite bold to be reading that underground newspaper and I admire the people that publish the infamous La Libre Belgique – it's the only source of uncensored news there is and the citizens of Brussels take great pleasure in reading it. It's like ordinary Belgians are sticking a thumb in the Germans' eyes each time a person picks it up and reads it; it's the only source of news for knowing what occurs outside of Belgium," Edith Cavell noted with obvious glee in her remarks.

"I fully concur with Edith – each of us is part of this group, yet as individuals each one of us also have our individual ways of resisting and thwarting the Boche," Philippe Baucq added with a faint smile.

"On another topic, is Doctor Bull still performing his periodic 'dental visits' to your Clinique, Edith?" Countess Jeanne de Belleville inquired as both a matter of inquiry and curiosity, as she was serving as a periodic information conduit between the Brussels cell and the Bellignies operations centre.

"Why yes, of course. He makes a visit every week or two to my Clinique, he ensures that his 'prescriptions' are properly noted, packaged and dispatched to the proper patient – other than that, I try to stay to my own business, which is more than ample to fill both my time and curiosity!" Edith smiled as she sipped her tea, suspecting but never actually confronting Dr Bull over the conduct of his clandestine information couriering activities. She did not want to confirm that which she and the others merely suspected. If confronted by the Germans, she wanted to possess deniability of Dr Bull's suspected actions. It was enough for her to know that he was doing his duty as a dentist and ensuring that the soldiers had no dental hygiene issues that could interfere with their escape from Belgium. For his part, Dr Bull continued to visit and administer care to the Clinique civilian patients and Allied soldiers, in addition to covertly planting the cryptic messages of German military details hidden within the clothing and shoes of the select refugee soldiers smuggled into Holland.

"Well I think that everything is proceeding quite well and normally; let's meet again after Reggie's return, or maybe later depending on the circumstances," George Hostelet suggested as he tried to gently suggest a conclusion of discussions of the Brussels cell members. Everyone around the table simply smiled and nodded silently to one another; there were no words left to say and despite the social cajoling, everyone was deeply serious and focused on the details that governed their 'secret' lives of being spies in a brutally German occupied country.

"How is everyone here? Was everything to your order and satisfaction?" a kind, frail middle-aged man with a brown-grey moustache inquired with a gentle smile, as he patted a friendly fatherly hand on Philippe's shoulder. Monsieur Maurice Pansaers, the café owner, made an impromptu table visit to his long time client and friend, Philippe Baucq.

"You look well, my friend. It seems that the war and German occupation have not been too cruel to you! Business looks good too!" Philippe announced with a wide smile as he rose to shake hands with his own friend Maurice Pansaers. "I'd like you to meet my friends Jeanne, Louise, Ada, George and Edith." Philippe was mindful to use only the first names of the group for security purposes.

"Oh there's no need to introduce Directress Nurse Cavell – all of Brussels knows of her and her nursing Clinique! As for business, the damn Germans are lousy for my business, they pay me in worthless German marks or occupation script! Their mere presence drives away loyal Belgian customers who cannot bear to drink in the presence of Germans or to even look at another German soldier and finally, my food and alcohol supplies are drying up from the war embargo. Flour, sugar, spices – everything is in either short supply or overly priced. I am hard pressed to stay open, my friend; if this crazy war lasts much longer, all of Belgium and Europe will be broke!" Pansaers cried out bitterly. He was correct too: as the 'short' envisioned war had turned into a 'long' one, Europe was becoming bankrupt as the tenets of basic banking and commerce collapsed.

"Don't fret, my dear Maurice: the war cannot last forever and besides, we Belgians are a hearty, patient lot. Here's twenty-five Belgian francs; these are real, but as far as buying anything of value in Brussels, well I guess we'll all have to await for the armistice!" Philippe replied back as he handed over the devalued Belgian currency in a pleasant voice. Pansaers took the francs with a grin on his face. They all knew that they had to outlast the Germans and that this was turning out to be a very protracted war. Food was becoming a hoarded commodity, as was alcohol and other imported goods. Unless the war ended quickly, Europe was going to slowly starve to death. Money itself was becoming useless, even the gold and silver that some people had hoarded. Gold was useless if there was nothing to purchase.

\* \* \* \* \* \* \* \* \* \* \*

"Well Marie, is Reggie off to London again on one of his 'little missions' or is he again playing the part of the Scarlet Pimpernel rescuing English soldiers from the clutches of the Germans?" the aged 84 year old Baron boldly charged to Marie de Croy as they sat comfortably in the Bellignies Chateau stately library. Countess Marie de Lichtervelde sat quietly sipping on an afternoon Earl Grey tea, seated upon a comfortable green silk winged chair. She and the old Baron often came to visit Princess Marie ever since the war had begun and both were privy to knowing about, but not being active members of, the de Croy refugee escape network.

"That which my brother and I do is our own affair and my dear Baron it should in no case be a concern to you!" Marie de Croy scornfully chided her regal neighbour that was most uncharacteristically out of both her character and behaviour. The Baron who was twice her age was taken aback by such a direct response from someone whom he had known since her birth. The words stung because the Baron had cherished Marie as his own daughter.

"Marie, I'm sure that you did not mean to say such things to Baron de la Grange; he's only concerned for you and that of your brother's welfare!" Countess de Lichtervelde quickly interjected to help diffuse the tensions between her two close friends.

"I'll apologize for my tone only, not my words or my actions, nor those of my brother or any other patriotic Belgian who resists the Germans in any way possible! I may not be in a position such as my brother Leopold to take to the battlefield and fight in the trenches, but I am resolved as a loyal Belgian woman of a long and proud family lineage to offer any assistance to the Allied cause and to hinder in any way possible the occupation of the German Army for the country that I love," Marie spoke back sternly and without any feelings of guilt or attempted apology.

"Yes, I'm an old man now, Marie, but I have seen a lot of the world and I believe that the actions that you and Reggie are performing place both of you and that of your estate and grandmother at great risk and possibly grievous harm! I know, as many others around Mons also suspect too, that you are harbouring and helping British soldiers and young men escape to Holland. There are rumours that you are engaged in other activities as well! If I as an old man know these things, so too in time will the Germans, who have thousands of paid informants scattered across Belgium and in time someone will break or talk. Please quit now while the Germans do not yet suspect you!", the old Baron earnestly tried to reason with the Princess.

"Please Marie, listen to the Baron!" Countess de Lichtervelde chimed in as she too pleaded for Marie to listen to mature reason.

"The Boche! Germans! The Germans are coming! They're coming right toward Bellignies, Princess de Croy…help, we must help our soldiers!" a pre-adolescent girl named Denise screamed out in a near hysterical voice, as she came running into the Chateau past the house-maid and into the library room. Three faces were immediately frozen with fear upon hearing the shattering words. Marie de Croy quickly regained her senses in a few short seconds.

"Denise, how far away are the Germans and how many of them are there?" Marie knelt down to look directly into the young girl's pale eyes.

"I think about thirty or maybe forty soldiers on foot and with carts. They are about thirty minutes away, Princess!" Denise replied, panting after having run several miles to bring the urgent news.

"Soldiers! Only German soldiers? No dogs?" The Princess looked intensely into the small girl's clear blue eyes.

"No Princess, just the typical German soldiers and their carts," the small girl replied with childlike truth and without fear, the German raiding parties now being a familiar sight to the little girl and most rural Belgians.

"Go now quickly, Denise and find any British soldiers wandering about the estate and bring them to me without delay and bring them inside to the old wing portion of Bellignies…do you understand?" Princess de Croy directed quickly, calmly and with cold determination. "If you'll excuse me, Baron and Countess, but I have some 'business' to attend to before the Germans get here!" the Princess remarked to her two stunned guests, who could be charged as guilty co-conspirators on the discovery of any Allied soldiers found on the Bellignies premises. "Both of you are free to go and flee before the Germans arrive. I know that neither of you want to 'get involved' in my little sordid affairs," Princess Marie remarked tersely in obvious reference to their conversation.

"I have absolutely no intention of going anywhere except that ground on which I presently stand and which is called Bellignies Chateau! Now is there anything that we can do to help you, Princess?" Baron de la Grange replied with a direct and defiant voice as Countess de Lichtervelde also nodded in agreement and silent affirmation. Princess Marie was obviously shocked by their sudden decision to collaborate with her at this awkward moment; still, her two friends could help her visually stage a scene to psychologically disarm the Germans – three outraged citizens were more convincing than one, she thought.

"Well for someone who did not want to get involved, you chose a very peculiar time to change your mind! Very well then, I'm taking the soldiers to the Keep, the best that you both can do is to be my cover, play-up your innocence and outrage at the Germans invading a private Royal residence and be boisterous about your titles and positions – sometimes the Germans are disarmed by titles!" Marie de Croy quite calmly pleaded to her two friends, as she hurried about the lower first floor rooms and garden areas where the twenty plus Allied soldiers were casually mingling and smoking.

"Quick, Sergeant Preston, the Boche are coming on a raiding party. Quick, get your men to the ground floor of the old Keep. Pick up all the cigarette stubs too, I do not smoke and it will make the Germans suspicious, if only to try and find some hidden and very valuable tobacco...go quickly now!" the Princess urgently ordered one of the British soldiers who was milling about the Chateau's garden.

"Yes Princess, I'll get the lads together!" Sergeant Preston yelled back to Marie, as he stomped out his cigarette, picked up the debris and blew a loud, shrill mouth whistle several times in quick succession. Upon hearing the loud whistle, which all the soldiers knew to be a signal to assemble at the chateau, men came rushing from all directions. In several minutes, all twenty-five soldiers and young civilian men had gathered on the back lawn of Bellignies.

"Hey everyone! The Germans are coming, men, about thirty-to-forty of them and they'll be here in twenty minutes or less. They are a raiding party with carts, which means they want booty and whatever they can legally steal! The old Keep can keep all of you safe until the Germans leave. It may be a few hours, so please be patient and quiet," Marie de Croy pronounced calmly as if she was a veteran at doing this, which she was, but never on this scale. "Follow me, this way!" Marie forcefully commanded, as they went into the old wing of the Bellignies Chateau and toward the old first floor Keep tower area that now served as a make-shift workman's shop used to repair various tools and carriage wheels used for maintaining the Bellignies estate property. The Princess went to a wall and carefully removed an aged wooden cupboard panel, which cleverly hid the entrance to the Tower Keep's medieval stairway.

"Sergeant, here's a lantern to light the way and here is a ladder to gain access up to the hidden stone stairway. Be careful climbing up and take care to pull up the ladder after the last man has made his way up, that way no one without a ladder can access the stairway located ten feet above the hidden opening!" Marie directed like a company-level army officer.

"Sure thing, Princess, we'll never forget this…never, Ma'am!" young Sergeant Preston announced as he supervised one of the last men up the ladder before making the short journey himself and then carefully lifting up the sturdy ladder into the upper recess of the stone staircase. The stairway entrance was now secure and, without a ladder, quite impossible to access even should one know of its hidden location.

"Remember, I will personally return for you as soon as I am able. Please be patient and quiet," Marie reiterated in assurance to both the soldiers and her own psyche. 'Well I'm glad the Germans are not bringing along their sniffing dogs, then we'd have real trouble!' Marie thought to herself and quickly dismissed the idea before she induced more fear in herself as the Germans were keen at detecting fear.

The Princess was lucky this day: she and the English soldiers had ample time in which to prepare their recluse preparation. The Princess even had time to ensure that nothing incriminating or too valuable was in visible evidence and thus be an invitation for immediate confiscation. The Germans had looted many estates across Belgium and France, stripping bare the treasures that had been amassed over generations by their owners with the most tender loving care. Everyone in Belgium soon learned to hide things in the most cunning of ways. All was in order and she was ready. She hoped that today she was going to make a very fine actress.

"Open up in there! Open-up! German army…official business!" shouted a brash, middle-aged and over-weight German Sergeant in a very crude French jargon. He pounded the door a few more times with his long, heavy Mauser Gewehr 98 rifle butt. The grey-haired sixty-year-old housekeeper named Florine hurried as best she could to open the massive wooden oak front door, the integrity of which provided a physical immunity from the stout pounding of the German's rifle butt battering. The Princess nodded to the housekeeper who dutifully opened the massive four-inch thick door. Immediately there rushed-in six grey clad German soldiers, who looked anxiously at the visibly astounded Princess, Baron and Countess.

"My name is Major Vollmer and this is Sergeant Koller. We're here to do a 'courtesy inspection' and to make sure that all German military laws are being obeyed and that any contraband are seized!" the tall, lean, fortyish German major pronounced matter-of-factly in perfect French, as he arrogantly placed both of his hands on his hips, resting his right hand onto the holster of his Luger P.08 pistol.

"Sergeant, have three squads disperse to the outer property and buildings, while one squad will remain with me in the Chateau proper," Major Vollmer shouted loudly, as Sergeant Koller saluted and took about thirty German enlisted soldiers with him to explore the outlying woods and ancillary small houses that composed the Bellignies Chateau compound. It was a common practice for mid-grade German officers to reserve the right for themselves to inspect and confiscate the residences of the upper echelon dwellings in Belgium, as these residences naturally contained more exalted and exquisite goods to 'confiscate' or just admire. It also provided them a rare chance to mingle with non-military personages and people who were possessed of higher educatation and social refinement. Both German officers and enlisted soldiers relished these 'booty raids', as these offered a means to leave their barracks and it broke the drudgery of military garrison life and military routines.

The Princess was not one bit disturbed or intimidated by this brash upstart person invading her family home and in a most crude manner too. "Of course you are going to issue us with the requisite German military voucher for any property confiscated?" Baron de la Grange boldly inquired of the German Major, as he was keen to exercise his visible outrages as previously encouraged by his hostess.

"Are you the master of this estate, Monsieur?" Major Vollmer asked directly and with a skewed sour look upon his face.

"No he is not! But I am the Mistress of this estate! My name is Princess de Croy and these are my dear guests, the Baron de la Grange and that is Countess Marie de Lichtervelde. They are both close friends of my family. My brothers and I are the owners of Bellignies Chateau and I demand to know the answer to the Baron's inquiry concerning the property voucher!" Princess Marie responded in a stark conjured reply that was aptly worthy to this most 'unwelcomed and uninvited guest'.

"It is my pleasure to meet you, Madame, but be advised, Your Highness, that a voucher is given only for legitimate property taken in use for the German army; for contraband no vouchers are given for illegal property, Your Highness! So let us pray for your sake that we find nothing illegal here!" Major Vollmer snapped back in a terse reply. All three of the regal personages remained quiet; they knew that further protest against a blatant, arrogant individual was folly and counter-productive. They had to feint the posture of being civil, but undue friendliness to a German looting party would breed undue suspicions. They deftly played their subtle roles without being overly melodramatic. In essence they portrayed their innate personalities, but with a slight flare of theatre.

"Corporal…komm hier!" the Major barked out and immediately a corporal accompanied by three other privates with long metal rods in hand appeared in the main hallway of the Bellignies Chateau. The Major shouted out a few more orders in German and the men with the long metal rods began to bang their steel rods along the floor and the walls of the chateau. "Looking for something in particular, Major?" the Princess injected with obvious concern and masked outrage.

"I am not accountable to answer Belgian civilians. I am an officer in the German Imperial Army and I am doing my sworn duty," Major Vollmer arrogantly replied without a pause or hesitation.

"Does the Imperial German Army not respect private property, Herr Major? I'll have you know that these floors are the finest granite and flat stone in all of Europe and your crude metal rods are doing the polished surface irreparable damage, Herr Major," Princess Marie sternly noted and making known her obvious displeasure.

"What are you looking for and doing with those nasty metal rods?" Marie inquired further with indignation in her voice.

"Echoes, hollow sounds, Your Highness; the sounds from the metal rods vibrate through material and return back either a solid or hollow sound – if hollow then there is a cavity or false space being indicated," the Major replied unemotionally with utter directness.

The Princess's heart sunk on this declaration. She could only hope that the massive stone walls could structurally defeat the echoes from the metal rod soundings. The German soldiers apparently found nothing in the main corridor, so their prodding proceeded down the other first floor rooms. The scene was repeated over and over again in each room with the metal rod prodding, and after about an hour the work seemed to be finished and without any serious damage to the chateau structure, although cosmetic blemishes in the polished stonework were inevitable, but repairable. The Major then ordered his men to search the other rooms of the mansion to include the basement.

Another small group of German soldiers searched the library. The Major, seeing a crystal decanter of brandy on a nearby table, directly poured himself an ample glass of the amber coloured aged liquor into a crystal snifter and watched his team do their work of searching – searching for anything of either value or incrimination. This Major appeared and acted as the master of the house himself, whereas he was just a mere interloper and messenger boy sent out on a military errand by his superiors. Any power and authority he possessed originated from others and that of his present bestowed, temporal military status, not that of self-made achieved accomplishment. Such men exalted by their offices in war made the most of this fact and they abused their bestowed power to the extreme – they were more dangerous than those who had inherited and grown up with power and wealth.

"Be thorough men, we do not want to miss anything! Libaries are known to hide secrets of their own kind!" Major Vollmer arrogantly shouted as he stood back and watched his soldiers climb the library affixed book-shelf ladders, as numerous books of all descriptions were barbarically cast down carelessly onto the library's wooden, rich oak parquet floor. The physically molested literary works consisted of numerous collections of old and carefully crafted leather bound books – the collection had taken decades and a small fortune to assemble and maintain.

"Be sure to get all of the books from the upper shelves. The owners often keep hidden documents, valuables and money in the books that are the most difficult to reach and this is where valuables are often stashed – examine every book and page. I know all the tricks of these clever aristocrats!" the rude major added to his conceited instructions, as the three helpless aristocrats looked on in horror as old and valued texts were carelessly tossed down onto the hard floor with many binding spines of books becoming broken and other books were crudely opened, resulting in torn pages in a frivolous attempt to reveal hidden items. None were to be found. The Major looked like an overseer of a press gang and he appeared as master of all that he perceived – such was the manner and character of the arrogant German occupying force. It was no wonder that so many Belgians hated the Germans. Soon hundreds of valuable old books, some first editions, lay scattered across the massive, thick, red Persian carpet that graced the honey-coloured oak floors of the chateau's library floor. As so ordered, each book was opened, but nothing other than various book mark slips of paper fell to the floor. This search lasted two hours during which Major Vollmer consumed about half of the brandy in the lead decanter; he was starting to feel his drink and he became less animated and more talkative. Distilled spirits had an unfortunate and uncanny ability to liberate the nature of a person's soul as well as their tongue.

"In civilian life I was a professional architect and, Princess, I must say that this is a remarkable chateau – it is a mixture of Roman, Gothic, Classical and neo-classical all contained in a single mansion; it is simply remarkable, Madam. The structure was obviously built in separate segments over many centuries. At the University of Heidelberg I also studied history and art. I seem to recall that some of these older structures sometimes contained hidden or secret rooms or passages for clandestine reasons, isn't that true Princess?" the Major inquired as his face turned into a faint smile.

"Well there are a lot of rumours about these old structures – some of these are even true, I dare say! My brothers and I as children searched in vain for such marvellous places to explore and hide, but we never found any, I must confess," Princess de Croy responded as she tried to lie about the secret stairway that now hid twenty-five refugee soldiers and young men. The Princess became scared as she fiddled with her hands. The Baron and Countess also changed their facial appearances into those of grave concern and the Major noted these bodily changes too. He became intrigued.

"Let us see what secrets may await us! I am very interested in that Keep Tower – shall we not go have a peak at it, Princess!" Major Vollmer gestured for the Princess to lead the way toward the old forbidding structure. Step-by-step, they neared closer to the hidden twenty-five contraband men. Marie's mind raced with anxious thoughts of being discovered by the Germans or maybe the British soldiers would kill the Major and a melee would erupt, she anxiously imagined.

"Is the Keep Roman or medieval Gothic?" he asked as Marie had no choice but to accompany the Major along for the short walk down to the old part of the chateau.

"I'm not sure about that, Major Vollmer. My brother is the history expert in the family and he's away right now. My brother the Prince de Croy is working with the War Relief Commission to get aid for the Belgian civilians," Marie volunteered in hope of distracting the nosey German officer. Her hands were sweating profusely despite the cool temperature.

"I seem to recall some reading of mine about there being a secret passage in the Keep or was my research in error, Princess?" Major Vollmer persevered.

Marie stared straight ahead and said nothing; she was dumbfounded. 'How in the hell did this damn German discover the existence of this secret stairway? What the hell kind of books was he reading?' she pondered angrily to herself. Her heart was pounding and her blood pressure was elevated. The gig was up, she thought with great despair. She had to think of something quick and accurate to deter further inquiry of this half-drunken German Major who knew far too much to suit Marie de Croy.

"Ah so here it is, but I do not see any opening from the ground floor, Princess?" Major Vollmer asked with keen acuity, as he noted the disturbed look in the Princess's face and countenance.

"You are quite observant, Major, but there is no open entrance to the old Keep from the ground floor, at least not any longer. It was walled up decades ago due to wild animals entering the Keep and the structure was falling into disrepair with rotting wood and loose stonework appearing, so it was decided that it was best to merely wall-up the entrance and simply abandon the structure for all practical purposes. It now serves as a fond architectural remnant to the family estate and that's all that it is now! I think my father once referred to the term attractive nuisance to describe this old Keep and the stories surrounding it," Marie replied in a half-truth response that did not make any additional mention of the secret stairway.

"Well that might be so, Princess, but I think maybe there is a concealed chamber to the Keep. It has massive walls that must be ten feet thick! Such thick walls need to serve a purpose for all the energy and expense in added construction," Major Vollmer accurately concluded.

'Doesn't this damn man ever stop in his nosey inquiry?' Marie thought contemptuously to herself, whilst her heart raced with adrenaline. "As a military man you know that thick walls make for a good defence – I suppose that was a good enough reason for my ancestors!" the Princess deflected back in her reply.

"Maybe so, maybe not so!" The Major possessed a short, two foot steel metal rod in his hand and he pounded it mightily on multiple Keep walls, floor and ceiling areas; there were no hollow sound returns from his vigorous strikes. The walls seemed rock solid.

"Princess, you seem a little nervous; I noticed that common anxiety in the faces of both you and your friends. Why should that be so, Princess? What secrets do you have to hide?" Major Vollmer inquired as his hands ran across the rough, chisel worked massive stones that formed the Keep's outer walls.

"To be truthful, Major, we Belgians are frightened by you Germans. We have been through raids before, to include some prominent field generals of the German Army during the Battle of Mons. No one likes to have uninvited guests, Major, I'm sure that you can understand our feelings," Marie honestly replied this time without any hidden verbal or bodily subterfuge.

"Major! Major! Major Vollmer, come quick, sir! We have found it! What a find!" Sergeant Koller yelled out like a street merchant from down the massive main hallway. Marie's face was alight with obvious fear, while Major Vollmer's was sprinkled with sheer delight.

"I knew it! I knew that you and your friends were hiding something! I've got you rascals now!" Major Vollmer shouted in zeal to Princess Marie, as he firmly took hold of her hand and pulled her ungentlemanly down the chateau's main hallway to the scene of the yelling sergeant.

"Let's have it! What have you discovered, Sergeant Koller? What is afoot?" Major Vollmer demanded as all three of the aristocrats now anxiously surrounded the team of German soldiers. "In the cellar we found it! It was carefully hidden, but we prodded with the metal rods and we discovered a well-concealed, hidden room, Herr Major!" Sergeant Koller replied back almost hysterically.

"What was discovered in hiding, Sergeant? Answer me at once!" Major Vollmer demanded in a raised voice.

"It's in the cellar, sir! Wine, many wonderful wines! Many bottles of wine and some champagne too, Herr Major!" Sergeant Koller replied back with enthusiasm.

The Major was delighted – he had finally found the contraband that he was searching for and his hunch to continue the search had paid off well!

"Well, are we not the coy ones? All three of you knew about this secret and you tried to hide it from us! No wonder you were so nervous and acting strange when we started to probe the walls and floors of the chateau. Did you think that you could hide such a valuable cache from the German Army without its discovery?" Major Vollmer was victorious at the find.

The Princess, Baron and Countess breathed a sigh of inner relief, yet they wisely posed looks of guilt so as not to betray any additional human contraband that was hiding just a short distance away.

"How many bottles are there?" Major Vollmer demanded as he hurriedly walked down toward a rustic door located near the butler's pantry that led to the main chateau basement and not ironically to a cavernous wine cellar that was located in a thirty foot deep separate room from off the main cellar area.

"I think a thousand bottles, but this is private property if I may remind you, Herr Major," the Princess meekly replied. The dark recess was cool, dark and damp- – a perfect location in which to store wine. The de Croys had wisely hidden their vast reservoir of fermented and distilled spirits in a series of small, discreet basement locations off of the main wine cellar anteroom and this was one of three large caches the de Croys had hidden.

Out of the three secret wine caches, the Germans had only discovered one of the caches. If their luck persisted, this was to be the only wine cache that the Germans would discover, leaving the estate with a still sizeable hidden supply of vintage wine and other rare liquor and whiskeys intact. All other aristocratic and middle class families had also taken similar careful measures to either bury or hide their liquor and other valuables soon after the German occupation, as stories quickly spread of the German Army looting parties taking all before them. Experience soon proved the stories to be unfortunately the norm among the rural Belgian citizenry.

"What are you planning to do, Major Vollmer?" Marie inquired in a hesitant voice. The Major looked about the vast array of wine bottles lying in a neat horizontal position that were covered with an old canvas tarp used to disguise the vintage wine cache.

"Why confiscate it of course! We are not fools, my dear Princess. The German Army needs its fair share of goods liberated from the greedy hoarding Belgians!" the Major replied with delight, as he descended the basement stone stairway to personally inspect his prized trophies. "There must be a thousand bottles here, Princess, just as you correctly stated!" the Major announced with glee. Marie de Croy was still cherishing her relief at the Germans discovering one of the chateau's hidden wine supplies and not that of the twenty-five refugee soldiers hidden in the old Keep stairway. Still, she needed to act the part of the bereaved and outraged 'Mistress of the Manor', lest the observant German major become suspicious again.

"Confiscation is just a convenient word that you Germans use for stealing! You cannot take the entire supply of spirits, Monsieur Vollmer! Please! It remains all that my brother and I have to entertain guests, to include high-ranking German officer guests! You must leave me something for entertaining, given my social position and rank! If I am left nothing Monsieur, I'll have to file a protest with the Belgian Military Governor-General Lt General Baron Moritz von Bissing – he was once my house guest here along with other high ranking German generals soon after the Battle of Mons. He said that I could contact him at any time!" Princess Marie lied very skillfully and with a tone of conviction. The German major was no fool! He was not going to leave such a prize to either the Princess or, worse, another German raiding party. This wine was his and he was going to impress his superiors with it as a gift, but then he thought perhaps he did not have to take *all* the wine; some could be left to placate the Princess and there was more than enough for him not to be too greedy. He lacked the means to cart and carry away all 1,000 bottles, yet he enjoyed kibitzing with the Princess –

she was a worthy opponent, he thought.

"How many bottles are here officially, Sergeant Koller?" Major Vollmer demanded of his overweight, over-aged draftee Non-Commissioned Officer.

"Sir, we count 1,075 bottles, Herr Major!" was the immediate reply.

"How about I leave you 75 bottles, Princess?" the Major shrewdly proposed. The Princess, having regained her wits, made a counter-proposal, as she did not want to appear too gullible or eager to appease the Germans. She knew from the Major's conversation that he was a keen observer and no fool, despite his semi-intoxicated state. Additionally, she did not want to give the arrogant German any more wine than was absolutely necessary.

"I have important people to entertain, Major…I am a Belgian Royal and this war may last a long time and I have no source to get any more wine as France has become one huge battlefield. No, I need 350 bottles!" the Princess counter-offered.

The Major knew that this was a good deal and that he was going to have a task to even transport even half of the inventory of wine; still, he was not about to let a woman, even if she was a Princess, get the better of a German officer.

"No, Madame…250 bottles or I take it all and you can go and protest to General von Bissing," Major Vollmer replied back as both the Princess and the German soldiers looked on nervously at the face of the Princess. Everyone hoped that she was going to agree as a phone call to Baron von Bissing may result in their getting no wine at all.

"You win, Major! Yes, I will agree to that and you drive a hard bargain. It is 'reasonable' given the circumstances, Major Vollmer! However, I insist upon a signed receipt too! I want personal reparations after this war is over!" Marie replied as everyone in the basement smiled at the final bargain level. The Major directed all forty of the soldiers to immediately form-up for a bucket-party to carry the 800 plus bottles of aged wine and champagne from the wine cellar up to the waiting carts in the backyard of the chateau. The German soldiers found a few wheelbarrows in addition to their wooden hand carts and some straw for cushioning the precious, fragile booty. It took over an hour for the task to be completed, yet it was soon accomplished and Major Vollmer handed Marie a worthless military voucher receipt to be claimed after the war for the cost of the wine.

"If I were feeling sociaable, Major, I would offer you a drink, but as I am not feeling sociable today and since you have taken a great deal of my wine inventory already and consumed a half bottle of my brandy, I shall not offer you one either," Princess Marie bade a sarcastic farewell to her unwelcome guest.

"Well good day and my best regards to you, dear Princess de Croy.....you have been most generous and accommodating hosts I must confess, we must all do this again some day and soon. Guten Tag!" the arrogant, ill-mannered and half-drunk Major proudly pronounced as he forcefully clicked together his hobnail boots and issued a smart, precisely executed proper German military hand salute.

Like most German promises, the voucher note was quite worthless, but after five long hours the Germans were gone along with the bulk of the wine, the library was in a state of distress and the rest of the chateau was a bit frayed with wear from the dirty and careless marauding German soldiers. Yet the Allied soldiers were safe! The de Croys had just dodged another bullet; the de Croy network was safe and still in operation.

"Thank you, Baron and Countess de Lichtervelde, you both played your parts without too much nervousness! My heart was beating like a kettledrum and my hands were sweating awfully...I cannot believe our good fortune. Major Vollmer was so very close to the truth and physical presence of that Keep's secret stairway that I was sure that I would be discovered! I guess that nine feet of ancient block stones are mightier than the modern German steel rods – not one echo was false!" Princess Marie remarked to her two guests who had skillfully played the innocent house companions for their friend and neighbour.

"If I may be so forward with your charge and your wine, but would it be out of line for me to suggest that we let all of those cramped-up, tired soldiers have a drink on you, Princess?" the elderly Baron de la Grange suggested boldly to his brave hostess. "That's a damn fine recommendation, Baron. In fact, let's make it a bottle per soldier; they damn well earned it! Will you please help me with the cupboard panelling removal, Baron?" Marie replied with a warm smile, as the three aristocrats strolled down the main hallway to the old Keep Tower to release the cramped up and by now exhausted Allied soldiers.

"Oh please accept my apologies, Princess, regarding that remark about your brother playing the role of the Scarlet Pimpernel. I now realize this is no game that is being pursued – your lives and others are in grave danger here and I greatly admire the actions and risks that both you and your brother are taking in aiding these refugee Allied soldiers...I still do not think that your actions should be continued, but as your friend and a loyal Belgian, I will assist you and your brother," the old Baron pledged in personal support, but without fully endorsing the spirit of the de Croy network. In war, each person plays the part which they are best able to resource, and sometimes this simply meant being a devoted friend.

\* \* \* \* \* \* \* \* \* \* \* \*

"Surface readings are as follows: Target bearing 030 degrees… speed 20 knots…range 1,000 metres…four funnels…no flag is seen…coordinates 51°37'0" North by 8°31'30" West…key landmark the 'Head of Kinsale' off the coast of southeastern Ireland…time is local of 13: 20 hours…mark," noted the German junior officer of the Imperial German Navy to the vessel's log keeper posted immediately next to him on the coning tower.

"Go below and immediately copy those record entries into the ship's log at once and ask the Captain to come up to the tower for an urgent observation!" the young Lieutenant sharply directed to the Navy seamen, who rushed below the deck to complete his orders. Seconds seemed like hours to the anxiously awaiting young naval officer getting ready to complete his first baptism of fire by completing his first cruise on the new deadly and dreaded German wonder weapon, the U-boat. Another young German Navy officer climbed up onto the small coning tower of the vessel that gently bobbed up and down in the calm greenish-grey water of the Atlantic Ocean like an over-sized black cork.

"What is this serious business which cannot seem to wait, Lieutenant Schneider?" the slightly older thirtyish bearded officer replied in a very monotone, almost weary voice of a captain who had seen his full share of sea duty in a time of war. In the recesses of his mind, especially while at night lying alone in his bunk, the scenes of burning ships and screaming men echoed in his mind. His vessel was unable to offer any rescue or assistance to distressed or sunk vessels, thus depriving him of any opportunity to offer redemptive mercy on those to which he had inflicted his military deadly duty. Kapitänleutnant Walther Schwieger was the highly successful Commander of submarine U-20. He was blessed with youth, handsome appearance and a calm introspective persona. He was a young German Naval officer on the rise and his was the sixth most successful U-Boat Command to date with a confirmed record of 150,000 gross Allied registered vessel tonnage being sunk.

"I see a large vessel at heading 030, Captain Schwieger, see just over there!" Lieutenant Schneider announced eagerly as he pointed in the northwestern direction where he had spotted the boat; as he excitedly handed over his binoculars to his Captain.

"Good Lord…it appears to be a passenger liner, a 'four stacker' with no flying flag, most likely British is my guess – they have taken down their national flags since we declared submarine warfare on merchant and commercial ships engaged in war support about three months ago…let's submerge, I don't want her to see us!" Captain Schwieger announced to his Number 2 officer.

"Dive to periscope depth of 11 metres…intercept course 030…. maximum submerged speed of 9 knots!" Captain Schwieger commanded to his Number 1 officer, who in turn relayed the commands to the dive plane operators, who in turn repeated back each command as they executed it. The procedures on a U-Boat were double-checked to ensure that no procedural mistake was made – they had great power at their hands and it needed to be exercised precisely and judiciously. As the U-20 submarine underwent its underwater manoeuvres, its periscope was retracted. Another twenty minutes passed and the periscope was raised again for target-to-shooter verification. The huge vessel moved again and U-20 again had to make counter-manoeuvres to compensate for that of the vastly faster ocean liner. The U-boat was slower underwater than a surface vessel, so the speed of both surface and sub-surface vessels had to be constantly checked and re-adjusted.

"Full speed… rudder right 6 degrees…mark," Captain Schwieger pronounced as his orders were repeated again in succession. He waited another ten minutes to ensure that the submarine was aligned correctly. "Periscope depth and up periscope!" he commanded slowly to ensure that the periscope was not raised prematurely and thus cause damage to their only sense while submerged with the outside world. The Captain waited patiently as the periscope was slowly raised to his eye level.

"There she is now, only about 700 yards in the distance." Daylight was receding, but still perfect for the task at hand. "I do not want to lose that enormous four funnel British passenger ship and it must be the RMS Lusitania…there's a report a few days ago of her making a New York-to-Liverpool crossing and I bet that this is it! Wow…she's turning away from us and she is more than twice our speed while we are submerged…we can't even catch her while on the surface, she's too fast…it's now or never! Load torpedo tubes numbers one and two… calculate range of 700 metres… torpedo depth of three metres…time is now 14:10 hours local. Fire tube number one….mark!" Captain Schwieger methodically commanded.

His crew reacted instantly and with keen professionalism. There was no loud sound heard in the control room, but an unmistakable sound of compressed air was heard in the forward torpedo room, indicating that a 'live fish' or torpedo had just been sent to destroy its unsuspecting vulnerable prey.

"Down periscope…dive to 30 metres and level off the diving planes!" Schwieger shouted as the elite crew instantly obeyed his commands like trained seals. All was quiet and every crewman perspired profusely, not from the humid internally confined temperatures, but from the sheer stress of the combat engagement. In war, and especially for the deadly and novel submarine weapon, any danger could occur from the deadly discovery by an unseen escort destroyer to a runaway torpedo that had become estranged and misdirected. The sound technician listened for any underwater reports of the explosion, as the Number 2 officer held a stopwatch and counted down the seconds to the calculated time of the torpedo hitting the vessel.

"She's hit!" the sound man yelled out, as a low rumble was heard throughout; the metal resonating skin gently vibrated from the underwater explosion wave returning to the boat. Everyone smiled including the Captain, as boisterous yelling echoed throughout the small metal boat.

"Quiet everyone! We're not finished yet! Continue on course and slow to half speed! Raise diving planes three degrees and take us to periscope depth," Schwieger commanded in a calm tone. Immediately, everyone dampened their enthusiasm; the Captain's orders were law aboard a naval vessel. Calm immediately returned to the crew as a hushed quiet again enveloped the entire control room. Slowly the periscope was raised and instantly another loud explosion was seen and heard, this one being much larger than the one just inflicted by the single fired torpedo.

"Explosion number two indicated, Captain," the sound technician voiced unemotionally in a monotone voice.

"What the hell was that? That was a distinct second explosion! Did someone fire torpedo tube number two?" the amazed Captain shouted out. "No sir…no…only one tube fired!" came three successive and independent responses from the Number 1 officer, firing officer and firing crew member. Indeed, torpedo-firing tube number two was still loaded in the firing tube and on standby condition only. Firing a precious torpedo was the sole decision of the boat's Captain or Officer in Charge should the Captain be so indisposed. The second explosion baffled everyone aboard U-20. Was this indeed proof that the RMS Lusitania was not neutral in the true meaning of the word and that she was carrying war cargo like munitions and high explosives from the United States or could it have been a secondary detonation caused by the explosion of fine air mixed with coal dust? No one knew.

Captain Schwieger slowly looked into the periscope eyepiece and he witnessed a dreadful scene. He gave the courtesy of letting his Number 1 officer also view the horrific sight. In a few scant minutes all power aboard the RMS Lusitania became unavailable for anything other than a separate electrical source that powered the wireless telegraph system, which frantically tapped out the now standard SOS for immediate assistance and distress. The doomed vessel soon went into blackness and distress. After just five minutes, the Lusitania was listing dangerously close to capsizing on its starboard side. Ten minutes after the torpedo hit, lifeboats were launched, but many of these could not safely reach the water. There were lifeboats aplenty for all passengers and crew – a total of 48 – but the problem lay in that with a sideward list of the vessel, the lifeboats on the starboard side were of no use and the lifeboats on the port side of the ship encountered a lowering problem into the water due to the severe angle of the ship's listing to one side. Further technical insult was added to the lifeboat issue launching in that the ship's plate rivets damaged some of the lifeboats' hulls as these were being lowered over the rough metal rivets.

Other lifeboats overturned while in the process of being lowered, while some lifeboats overturned while in the water when lifeboats hit up against the ship in the moving waters. Only a handful of lifeboats were launched and panic and disorder reigned supreme on the decks. In just eighteen minutes, the RMS Lusitania lay beneath the waves of the Irish Sea and with her 1,195 lost souls out of the boarding list of 1,959. Bodies floated like helpless corks in the ocean, which was only 11 miles from the Irish coast. Most victims died from drowning or exposure. In comparison it took the RMS Titanic two hours to sink in a leisurely and orderly fashion. In disgust and helplessness, Captain Schwieger allowed his control room officers to witness the horrific scene. They were helpless to assist and the 'laws of war' and the universal 'law of the sea' to assist stranded or floundering personnel did not apply to U-Boats for reasons of practicality and limited space. Only fifteen minutes after the launch of a single torpedo by U-20, Captain Schwieger ordered his vessel back to a base in northern Germany and to a warm welcome by his superior officers and countrymen.

In the days that followed, the Allied authorities recovered 289 bodies, one of which was recognized as being that of Mrs Marie Depage, aged 43, a Belgian-nurse, socialite and Belgian war relief fundraiser. She and her husband Dr Antoine Depage were the precursors to the visiting international medical workers programmes assisting people in war torn lands. While her husband was busy with running Allied war hospitals, Marie found an

equal task in obtaining funding for the Allied cause in Europe, especially
for the wounded soldiers. Yet this was not nearly enough of a challenge
for this energetic Belgian patriot woman. With the support of Belgian
Queen Elizabeth, Marie toured the United States for two months from
coast-to-coast and raised over $100,000 in cash alone for badly needed
medical supplies for the war wounded. Marie Depage wanted to get Edith
Cavell to work with her at a hospital in La Panne, located near Le Havre
in northwestern France, but this meant that Edith was going to have to
abandon the Clinique and travel as a network refugee to get into France.
Marie Depage's death, by drowning, made any such plans moot. Everyone in
the entire de Croy network knew and loved Marie Depage, especially Edith,
as both of the Depages were instrumental in establishing her Belgian nurse
training Clinique and for lobbying to get her selected as its first Directress.
The de Croy network had suffered its first 'family-member' casualty. Spring
had turned suddenly sombre, as the reality of war reverberated throughout
the de Croy network.

The German military's use of the deadly new terror weapons such as
poison gas, submarine warfare against civilian passenger liners and Zeppelin
bombing raids against British cities were fracturing points with the Allies,
making the Germans appear as new barbarians among the civilized nations.
From a military perspective these unchivalrous weapons christened Imperial
Germany as a military pariah, unworthy of either respect or esteem.
Germany's continued existence needed to be extinguished before its power
became intractable.

* * * * * * * * * * *

# Chapter 7:
# Spies Among Us!

*"I hate being a junior to a bunch of old matrons...they don't seem interested in men, alcohol, smoking, laughing or anything else pleasurable in life...all they think about is that bloody nursing business and changing bedpans and the such!"*

"Damn it! We are not making enough progress and it is already the beginning of May! I promised results to the General Staff by the end of summer and I mean to keep it! Do you understand me, gentlemen? I demand information! I want some leading evidence of this underground network...names, dates, places...We have nothing except some petty black market arrests! What sort of counter-intelligence work is this shit?" the irate Prussian Captain von Kirchenheim shouted in anger as he pounded his fist on the table of the modest office room within the bland inner recess of the German Secret Police HQ Section 'B' that was located in Brussels along the rue de Berlaimont.

"Do you know what it is like to send these shitty reports to Berlin week-after-week? My reputation is on the line, my family honour is at stake! These types of results are embarrassing to me, my family and the entire German intelligence profession! This incompetence must end, do you hear me?" the furious captain shouted as he banged the hard oak desktop with his fist in utter frustration. The three other men were humbly silent in their individual and collective embarrassment.

"Captain, we have hundreds of paid agents on the streets and we have come up with nothing. These things take time to cultivate, like fine grapes!" Captain Joel spoke with a very defensive tone, as Lieutenants Bergan and Pinkhoff sat quietly around the massive oak table.

"We are not making wine here and time is something we do not have, Captain Joel and I am thinking about a new set of counter-intelligence agents unless I start getting results in a week, gentlemen!" Captain von Kirchenheim shouted aloud again before being interrupted by a sudden knock on the office door. "Come in!" he yelled, as a young nervous corporal entered the room with hesitant gestures.

"Excuse me, Herr Captain, a call for you from Berlin, a Colonel from the General Staff office, sir," the young soldier conveyed with a declarative, but meek tone.

"Alright I'll be there in a minute. Meanwhile you three gentlemen had better come up with something of substance on identifying and capturing these traitors and saboteurs!" the visibly irate captain yelled out as he exited the office to take the phone call.

"Well, I'm fresh out of ideas! We've spread money about the city, we planted agents, we leaned on the various street urchins and stoolpigeons – what else is to be done?" Captain Joel remarked to Lieutenants Bergan and Pinkhoff. No immediate response was made to Captain Joel's comment. Everyone sat uneasy in their chairs. The tension in the room was palpable. Every one of them was an experienced professional and yet none of them could uncover any suspects or methods that were being used to convey secret German military information to the Allies. There were no native British agents caught in the country. There were no leads of any consequence among the hundreds of paid agents in their employ.

"Maybe pay out more money and increase the number of Agent Provocateurs in Brussels?" Bergan suggested.

"No, doing merely 'more' is like putting gasoline on a fire! We should not reinforce failure, instead we need a better lead, a better approach. We need to discover the key to this network! The culprits must be not only someone who hates Germans, but who has the means, opportunity and especially the nerve to commit espionage. People like this are rare birds...sure plenty of Belgians hate the German occupation, but over 99% will do nothing other than a prank like defacing our posters, spitting in our coffee drinks or trying to cheat us on a transaction," Captain Joel wisely concluded.

"Pinkhoff, you sit there like a bump on a log and have nothing to say? That is remarkable for a man of so many words and opinions!" Captain Joel voiced out in mere observation, as Lieutenant Pinkhoff was mired in deep concentration of a recent German newspaper.

Captain von Kirchenheim suddenly re-entered the room and, from his facial appearance, the phone call from Berlin had not relieved any of his professional frustrations about his espionage network discovery efforts. "What the hell is this, Pinkhoff? We have not one clue about this espionage network and here you are sitting on your ass and reading a worthless newspaper! What's the matter with you – not enough to do with your time? Perhaps re-assignment as a police officer to Russia will perk up your interests?" von Kirchenheim remarked in a tone and intention that was only half-mocking.

"Newspapers tell us much if we are careful and take the time to ferret through the news stories! Well you might be interested, sir in knowing that I have been digesting a story about the sinking of the RMS Lusitania about a week ago and it seems that it has made quite a ruckus with everyone, especially the English and the neutral Americans. There were some prominent people aboard the ship that our U-boat sank!" Lieutenant Pinkhoff smartly remarked as he slowly placed down the folded paper onto the oak table. He seemed very pleased with himself too, given the bawling out that he and his colleagues had just received from their arrogant Prussian leader.

Captain von Kirchenheim was livid at Pinkhoff's candid, seemingly stupid reply. "You must be going nuts, Lieutenant, the Lusitania is an issue for the Imperial Navy and General Staff issue. We are in the employ of the Imperial German Army and our business is not the Lusitania, but espionage and sabotage being committed against German munitions trains, logistic depots, airfield and Zeppelin aerodrome hangars around Brussels!" von Kirchenheim yelled back in a incredulous tone and bewildered Captain Joel and Lieutenant Bergan sat dazed and perplexed at Lieutenant Pinkhoff's reply as well.

"Exactly, Herr Captain and that may in fact be the missing key that we have been searching for these past few weeks," Pinkhoff retorted back immediately and obviously prepared for a full justification of his cryptic reply.

"You obviously have something on your mind, so let's hear your hair-brained theory, Pinkhoff; you deliberately spoke those mysterious words with a purpose...what is it and I mean now!" Captain von Kirchenheim demanded as he seated himself once again at the table and lit-up an English Dunhill cigarette, insultingly blowing the blue-grey acrid smoke toward Pinkhoff's direction.

"Yes sir, well I happen to have noticed that the passenger list dead included Marie Depage, wife of the noted Brussels surgeon Dr Antoine Depage, both husband, wife and the entire family are staunchly anti-German and very pro-Belgian. In fact, Marie Depage was so patriotic that she was on a fund raising tour in America to assist in the Allied cause in Belgium and she raised over $100,000 US in cash. She also had the full endorsement of exiled Queen Elizabeth as well. I submit to you, Captain that Doctor and Mrs Depage have links to anti-German sympathizers right here in Belgium and that by identifying and placing agents on these members, we could very well uncover our sabotage network," Lieutenant Pinkhoff replied dryly and calmly.

Pinkhoff's argument sounded fantastic, yet somehow slightly plausible to everyone listening; there were no immediate objections shouted out.

"A sabotage and espionage Brussels network that was organized and operated by the social elite and not from the peasant, unwashed masses?" Captain von Kirchenheim muttered out in a low, introspective voice as he slowly puffed on his half-consumed cigarette.

"Maybe, just maybe, I think that Pinkhoff could be on to something interesting here!" Captain Joel interjected in a reinforcing manner.

"What better place to hide than that of being in plain sight than among the elite of Brussels – it's the perfect cover that no one would immediately suspect!" Lieutenant Bergan chimed in to remark.

"Yes, yes I think you may be on to something here, Pinkhoff. At least it is a theory to which we can apply some resources against. Here are my orders, gentlemen, I want you all to do a node-association analysis of all of the Depage friends, acquaintances and benefactors from a social, business and personal perspective and I mean everyone, regardless of age, sex, or social position. Take that Depage association list and identify all of those who are dead or out of the country. Then take the list of secondary characters and run down that list of people in the same manner as prescribed for the first tier of contacts. I want this information in three days and work nights if necessary. We meet again here at 10:30 am four days from now, this coming Friday. Any questions?" Captain von Kirchenheim remarked.

Not a soul uttered a word; his orders and intentions were crystal clear. The Captain got up and immediately left the room. Although slightly more optimistic than he had been at the start of the meeting, yet still he was not convinced. As far-fetched as Lieutenant Pinkhoff's idea sounded, it was still a viable lead, one which required immediate additional investigation. Captain von Kirchenheim had just the right police officers to do the job. Von Kirchenheim was going to reserve his opinion until he has seen some more information and analysis before placing more assets into this investigation – if nothing promising came out of it, then other options would be pursued. There was already proof of other networks existing in northern France and Belgium for him to apply his resources.

"Pinkhoff, do you really believe that fantastic theory that you just uttered a few minutes ago?" Captain Joel inquired in seriousness, as he too took a cigarette from his tunic pocket and quickly inhaled the strong, distinctive French-made Gitanes cigarette.

"Well it's the only idea that I have now; it is possible that the Depages are involved in a spy ring, but somehow I do not think Mrs Depage was an Allied agent – although some of her friends and associates may well be!" Pinkhoff replied honestly.

"Well, let's get to work. We have nothing to lose by running down those nobles who the Depages were famous for associating with before the war. They were a very prominent Brussels couple and they helped to subsidize a lot of charity work and causes – we might find a lead in these associations too," Lieutenant Bergan admitted in a low voice that wrought of some slight despair. If anyone was looking for the immediate evidence or association of a 'smoking gun', none was to be immediately found within the content of this superficial discussion. Still the embryo of an idea had been conceived and this gave everyone a new, focused area in which to concentrate their efforts. Both good intelligence and police work usually hinge on detailed street-level, detective gum-shoe questioning of various people or the very mundane task of searching files and newspaper archives. So it was to be here as well, along with an added bit of luck.

* * * * * * * * * * * *

"Well, my dear Reggie, I'm afraid that you unfortunately missed a lot of excitement around Bellignies a few weeks ago," Baron de la Grange chuckled with a light mood of laughter, as both the aged Baron and his visiting companion and longtime friend the Countess de Lichtervelde smiled at the suddenly bewildered Prince de Croy.

"What are you two muttering about? What has transpired in my absence? Is something wrong?" Reginald queried rapidly with a disturbed look upon his face.

"Just ask your sister here about the German raiding party that came around here a fortnight ago! That damn German officer was a damn student of architecture and he was poking around looking for a secret passage in the chateau and the bumbling fool almost discovered the Keep's secret stairway!" the old Baron half-joked as he quickly confessed the ordeal that the three had encountered with the German raiding party.

"No, my dear Baron, I'm afraid that this is the first that I heard of this dreadful incident. Obviously my sister did not wish to worry me about her safety while I was away on my excursion abroad," Reginald replied, as he gave a quick glancing look of nervous disapproval back to his sister, who merely sipped her tea and looked quickly away from her brother and to the nervous eyes of Countess de Lichtervelde.

"Maybe this 'rescue business' of yours is getting too dangerous, Reggie. Sooner or later the Germans will get wise – but forgive me, this is not of my affair; however, I am your friend and I fear for both of your safety. I think you should get out now before the Germans get lucky or someone makes a mortal mistake and unintentionally alerts the Germans…how much longer can your luck last?" the Countess added in genuine elevated concern.

The Prince said nothing for a few seconds, he looked at his sister Marie and he saw that she too was concerned about the safety of the network operations.

"Thank you for the concern from the two of you! I know that neither of you support the 'work' that my sister and I established and that your words are out of both love and loyalty to us. I also want to thank you for staying with Marie for all the times that I am away and you must have been a great deal of help during that surprise German raid, of which we can only expect more of as the Germans become more desperate. My 'friends' in London have 'unofficially' discussed with me some of the information on the Germans and the war is not going well for them in Germany, as the British blockade has drastically cut grains and food supply from the nation and there are not enough men to work the farms since the war began. Many Germans are starving and starving brings about desperation, desperation further breeds violence and revenge," Reginald sadly concluded.

"Then the Allies are winning the war!" the Countess sparked out in temporary gleeful exclamation. No one else shared in her temporary emotional outburst.

"Well surely then, we cannot be losing!" the Baron echoed the obvious alternate outcome possibility with an incredulous tone.

"I'm afraid that neither side is either winning or losing; it appears that we are in the worst situation possible – we are at a military stalemate and unless there is a miracle of some sort that happens, it may well stay that way for an indefinite duration," the Prince concluded with sad resignation in his voice.

"What are we to do then if neither side is either winning or losing?" the Countess erupted back in a bewildered, flabbergasted inquiry outcry.

"We simply soldier on and do that which we have been doing! You have heard from my brother about the food shortages and starvation conditions in Germany and these are only going to continue unless either side achieves a major military knock-out punch and we cannot wait for this to occur," Marie vocally announced her intentions about the continued operation of the de Croy network.

"If we allow these soldiers to become German POWs, their fate is not very good, especially in a prolonged war environment. Any soldier that gets out of German occupied territory is much better than the one who stays. We can only operate until the autumn to get any remaining Allied soldiers out of Belgium; after that, the harsh winters, raiding parties and our own diminishing resources will make sheltering and helping refugee soldiers escape a most impossible venture to continue," Reginald concluded with a very logical estimate of the state of affairs, as he outlined the limited shelf-life that remained for the de Croy network in helping Allied soldiers escape Belgium.

"What about the War Commission relief operations – won't this help alleviate the food shortage conditions?" the Baron interjected, offering a possible better outcome for his country.

"Well yes, it will help us, but these efforts are starting up slowly and the United States has offered huge shipments of grain for those civilians in the German occupied territories; however, this is going to take time and coordination, getting valuable grain from a neutral country in time of war through battle lines to starving civilians is not so easy. The United States needs to ensure that its humanitarian support goes only to needy, non-aligned civilians and not to feed the Imperial German Army or German civilians, so the food distribution guidelines will be strict and this too will mean delays in the food distribution," Reginald explained most fully and well to his older neighbour.

"Our future seems a bit bleak, my friend. I'm afraid that every time I speak with you, Reggie, I am getting bad news," Countess Marie sighed with a tearful voice.

Her friend the Baron immediately added his sage comments to those of his friend the Countess: "I for one am very glad that I am now old and I have lived my life and it's been a good one. I feel most sorry for the young people and children in this horrible war."

"I'm sorry, Countess Marie, but there's no way to 'sugar coat' the present situation and as the war goes on longer, the worse things will become for everyone here in Belgium, including the Germans. We have to help one another now. We cannot await the arrival of the United States like a knight on a horse to save us! I have heard reports that in Lille several inhabitants were shot at the Citadel for having hidden an English aviator. In Fourmies, four French soldiers, of whom one was a coloured man, a Senegalese, were shot – all four of them on the spot. At Hiron, nearly a dozen Allied soldiers along with the miller who had hidden them, were all condemned and swiftly executed by German Military Court Martial," Reginald boldly pronounced.

"Just look at what our friends the Depages and others have sacrificed in this war. Dr Depage fled his thriving practice and position in Brussels to aid the war wounded under our brave King Albert; Queen Elizabeth and all the government has fled and are trying their best to beat back the Germans; the two Depage male children have volunteered for the Belgian Army; and finally our dear friend Marie Depage was tragically drowned on the civilian passenger liner RMS Lusitania – she was bravely collecting aid for medical supplies for our wounded soldiers. The network has helped about one hundred and fifty soldiers and young men to date escape Belgium and I am committed to assist even more until it becomes too dangerous. The Germans know nothing thus far and until we get a hint of German snooping we should continue to see the operation through until the winter season, then we can stop!" Princess Marie recounted with the perfection of detail and resolution.

"Are the Countess and I cowards then?" the old Baron cajoled in an almost embarrassed voice.

"Not at all, my dear Baron. You are supporting us with your friendship and visits to Bellignies to speak with some of the stranded soldiers. They greatly enjoy your company. Everyone in this war does that which is in his nature to do! If your heart tells you not to be an active participant, then you should not be one! It will only bring danger to yourself and everyone else involved. The Germans can sense fake characters and I'd rather have you and the Countess be our innocent friends than less than genuine co-conspirators. Besides the Princess and I will need to have innocent friends to visit us in our prison cells someday!" Reginald remarked, as he playfully patted the old Baron's knee with his hand and everyone burst out into a chorus of light laughter. Yet the laughter was merely a comic mask and physical relief for the very real tensions that now gripped this small party of friends. Their meeting seemed more of a conclusion to events and not merely a routine social visit. Unbeknownst to anyone at Bellignies, the magnifying glass of German inquiry was soon to descend upon their actions, associations and lives.

\* \* \* \* \* \* \* \* \* \* \*

"Well now everyone, you've had a few days to gather the required information as per my instruction and now I want to hear what items you have found concerning the possible leads associated to the late Marie Depage and her associations with any possible underground network operating in

Brussels," Captain von Kirchenheim authoritatively addressed to Captain Joel, Lieutenant Bergan and Lieutenant Pinkhoff. They all looked at each other nervously, but Captain Joel was the senior intelligence officer and he spoke up for the group.

"Yes, well, as suspected, Marie Depage, along with her prominent surgeon husband Antoine, was a member of high-society Brussels. The couple were 'social-climbers' as the expression goes and about a decade ago the couple became fully engaged in grooming ties to high-status Belgian citizens such as industrialists and bankers; however, her main focus of association was with the Belgian Royal family and aristocratic class. To gain social favour and notoriety, she and her husband became involved in philanthropic work, especially of a medical nature. In 1908, the couple were instrumental, with the generous, added financial support of the Royal family and aristocrats, in establishing the Berkendael Institute, the first Belgian nursing training Clinique rue de la Culture, appointing English nurse Edith Cavell as its Directress. Mrs Depage also made numerous associations with various middle class professional people to include lawyers, architects, industry managers and religious leaders. Both wife and husband are extremely nationalistic and anti-German, as witnessed by the recent pro-Allied actions of the couple," Captain Joel concluded in his opening remarks before being interrupted by his superior.

"Stop, Captain Joel! You are not telling me anything that is amazingly new or which leads me to believe that this woman or anyone she associated with is even remotely connected with anti-German espionage and sabotage. I cannot use any of this to placate my superiors in Berlin! I need more information, better leads and a motive!" Captain von Kirchenheim remarked nervously.

"Yes, well of course there is no direct evidence per se, otherwise these people would have been exposed and arrested a long time ago. These are clever people that we are dealing with and they will not be readily identifiable; that is the genius of their network design – these are people who no one suspects on first glance, thus they are automatically overlooked by our intelligence and police," Captain Joel sounded off logically.

"You are right, Joel, yet how can we discover the underground members if they are so clever and covert?" Captain von Kirchenheim remarked with pragmatic puzzlement.

"We examine those people who associated most often with Mrs Depage. She became a nurse, so devoted was she to the cause of helping the Belgian sick and then later the Allied wounded, she was on a fund raising tour in

America for that express purpose," Lieutenant Bergan announced as an afterthought.

"Wait, wait there just a minute, will you please, Bergan. Did you say that Mrs Depage was a nurse and that she had a devotion to helping the Allied wounded soldiers?" Captain von Kirchenheim uttered as his face clearly showed that he was making a mental connection on Bergan's recent uttering. "You mentioned the name of some English woman, a nurse Edith something or other?" von Kirchenheim muttered out and gasping for a recently heard name that he could not immediately recall.

"Yes, that is English Nurse Edith Cavell, the Directress of the Berkendael Institute at the Clinique Rue de la Culture in downtown Brussels," Captain Joel replied back quickly.

"Cavell the English nurse...she stayed here in Belgium...why? Why did she not leave as directed, gentlemen? She is English, a native of the country which is one of Germany's prime enemies," Captain von Kirchenheim questioned to both himself and the three others present. No one yet had a ready answer.

"Who among the royals and aristocrats that Mrs Depage mingled with are still left in Brussels or even Belgium?" von Kirchenheim demanded urgently. There was a rumbling of papers as all three men tried to correlate the Captain's inquiry request.

"There is no one that I can see still in Brussels, but there are some friends in Mons, the Prince and Princess de Croy and there is a French Countess in Lille and an eighty-four year old Baron – all major donors to the Berkendael Institute and other causes," Lieutenant Pinkhoff concluded smartly.

"There it is again, the same threads of continuity...the Berkendael Institute, the royals...women...nursing...professional people and anti-German. All these people have a funny, eclectic theme...I think that what we have here is a network composed of and headed by the elite members of Belgian society assisted by professional people and a large number of women!" Captain von Kirchenheim stated to his stunned audience. "Tell me more about these de Croys of Mons," the captain ordered, as he looked directly at Pinkhoff.

"Yes, Herr Captain, the de Croys are a most ancient Belgian family dating back to the early Middle Ages. There are two unmarried brothers and one unmarried sister and a great English Grandmother – all residing at the family chateau known as 'Bellignies'. One brother Leopold is serving with King Alfred and Prince Reginald served over ten years in London as Secretary to the Belgian Embassy in London and he has many friends there among the politicians, aristocrats and British Royal family. Reginald has a valid German travel pass and he is working with the US Consulate in Brussels to get food relief for Belgian civilians through the War Relief programme," Pinkhoff again expertly summarized in exquisite detail to everyone's amazement.

"Ah gentlemen, yet another thread...that of England! Mrs Depage was on an English vessel and she travelled to London; there is an English nurse named Cavell leading a Belgian medical Clinique in German-occupied Brussels; and finally we have a Belgian royal who has very close ties to the power brokers in London and who may be in direct contact with them through all of his acquaintances – there may even be a United States connection in this somewhere, but I think that we may have just stumbled onto something here, gentlemen There are either threads of continuity or threads of coincidence and I for one, gentlemen, do not subscribe to the phenomena of coincidences!" Captain von Kirchenheim smiled.

"Excuse me, sir, but why would the British employ people such as these? I mean Belgian Royals, aristocrats, an English nurse and ordinary women? These people are neophytes, they are not trained in any intelligence crafts!" Lieutenant Bergan asked, in bewilderment, of his superior.

"Ah, my dear Lieutenant Bergan, I think that we have all simply over-looked the obvious, just as the British had so carefully planned! Professional operatives were going to stick out like a sore thumb, so use regular, professional-class and aristocratic people; give the members limited, yet adequate support; employ only the most loyal people possible, preferably with strong English sympathies; and finally recruit the most unlikely people possible. That is the genius of the British intelligence services and they have been doing this with similar networks throughout northern France, Belgium, Germany and even Russia. Such 'normal' people are less suspect and they are wonderfully expendable; besides the British Government can simply disavow any knowledge of their existence or having made any official sponsorship to them," von Kirchenheim stated in a low voice. His analysis and conclusion were quite correct.

"Do we develop the situation then?" Captain Joel asked.

"Most definitely! Identify the most vulnerable people first, then place in our Agent Provocateurs, gain their trust, gather intelligence and evidence, then we will swoop down on them!" von Kirchenheim clapped his hands together and laughed heartily, the first time any of them had seen this stoic man ever smile.

"If these traitors know anything upon their sudden arrest, they will spill their guts to us at that time when we interrogate them; none of them know the bleakness of being arrested or being placed into a cold jail cell," Lt Bergan added with a zesty tone.

"If they are innocent of anything, their arrests and subsequent sordid tales of jail will serve to be a deterrent to the population as well," Captain Joel correctly concluded.

"Good, I think that we have a game-plan, gentlemen. Lieutenants Bergan and Pinkhoff have vast police and field work experiences, so I'll not tell you how to do the particulars of your jobs, but you do get my intentions of placing agents among those whom we can extract the most information using positive persuasion and means," von Kirchenheim commanded in a subtle manner.

"Do we meet again next week, Captain von Kirchenheim?" Lieutenant Bergan inquired in closing.

"Yes, weekly until events escalate, then more frequently, maybe even daily. Captain Joel will be your information conduit to me and I want your weekly reports prepared and distributed through him. If there is an urgent matter Captain Joel will contact me immediately. Remember we need hard intelligence and information – presently we have a theory that fits some of the pieces to a puzzle but this is far from factual and there is zero evidence for any sort of a trial, so work along the lines of establishing a hard motive, the means employed and the people involved. Any questions from anyone?" von Kirchenheim asked. There were no takers to his offer. The meeting dissolved and the real work of gathering information had just begun. This was a hair-thin theory, but it was the only one that the German intelligence staff possessed. Pinkhoff and Bergan knew the type of persons necessary to exploit any potential opportunity and they soon engaged these people with ruthless efficiency and cunning.

\* \* \* \* \* \* \* \* \* \* \*

"Hello and good day, is Directress Cavell here? We have been sent here by a Mlle Thuliez from Lille and we have a reference from Mr Libiez. They told us to say that 'Yorc has sent us'!", the two dishevelled and unescorted young men, both in their early thirties, so informed Edith Cavell, as she opened the door to a sunny mid-June day, she being attired in her official Red Cross blue and white blouse affixed with a prominent red cross and upon a white full apron dress. "Did you say that 'Yorc sent you and that Mlle Thuliez of Lille and Albert Libiez were known to both of you', is that correct?" Edith carefully repeated to confirm the words meant that these men were either refugee Allied soldiers or Belgian young men seeking to escape Belgium and join up with the Allied forces through Holland. The two men simply nodded in the affirmative to Edith's inquiry.

"Come in then and please accompany me to my private office on the second floor, gentlemen," Edith remarked as the two scrappy men, one of whom was quite handsome, entered the small vestibule area that was situated immediately behind the door entrance to the Berkendael Institute, Clinique rue de la Culture. They both quietly followed Edith along the small dark stairway and up into her quaint office, the door to which she quickly closed behind her. She was ever mindful of the threat posed by German spies – Brussels was filled with such vermin and she and everyone else in Brussels had heard many stories about strangers luring innocent citizens into police traps through both careless words and actions.

"Sit down please. Right then, now first some questions gentlemen, you have me at a disadvantage in that obviously you both know of me, but I know absolutely nothing of either of you. Would you please care to tell me about yourselves and how you came by my name and this Clinique and for which purpose I still remain blissfully ignorant?" Edith coldly inquired of the two suspicious strangers who had appeared out of the blue to show up at her clinique with only the names of two people that she had known. Edith was no fool and she was ever being mindful of the need for security for both her own safety and that of the de Croy network. For some unknown reason, these men did not seem 'quite right' to her; she had an initial, uneasy feeling about them that could not be logically quantified by rational argument; her uneasiness was of an inner, predisposed nature. Her feeling was of the type that one experienced upon meeting a stranger and instantly disliking him for no rational reason. Always a most logical person, Edith tried to dismiss her feelings as being un-Christian and that of an unknown personal prejudice. To counter-balance such thoughts, she overly compensated and perhaps deferred too greatly toward accepting the two strangers on their words alone.

"My name is Armand Jacoby Jeannes and I'm an escaped soldier from the Belgian army; I am a sergeant of infantry and I have been on the run since Mons. Everyone simply calls me Jacoby,, the short, blue beady-eyed man replied with a nervous voice and manner.

The other man immediately chimed into his personal introduction. "My name is George Quien, but I use Gaston as my nickname and I too was a Belgian soldier, a Lieutenant and I was both assisted and recommended by your friends and acquaintances of Prince de Croy, Mlle Louise Thuliez and

Albert Libiez," the six foot tall, handsome man replied as he removed his hat and scratched his coarse, close-cropped black hair. This man Gaston had a devilish, Romeo-type smile that Edith immediately found too contrived and playful. Edith also keenly noticed that both men looked rather too well groomed and too well-fed to have been on the run since the Battle of Mons, despite any food that the de Croy Mons cell had provided to them. Yet both men knew the secret de Coy password and their references were sound. She could find no immediate fault against them; still her uneasy feelings lingered. She vowed to herself to be most careful around these two men; inner feelings were to be tempered but never ignored.

"The Battle of Mons was over six months ago. It must have been difficult for you to hide and avoid the Germans for all that time – how on earth did you do it?" Edith probed a bit more deeply.

"Oh we hid here and there; it was not too bad," Armand Jacoby Jeannes replied back with a most vague and inarticulate response that seemed bordering on the ludicrous.

"Madame, my friend means to say that we stayed with farmers, miners and anyone else who was kind enough to show pity on us, as I hope you now will also extend to us," the smooth-talking Quien quickly replied with a contrived, doe-eyed innocent expression.

Quien's words struck a soft spot in Edith's heart, although she still had her own reservations about the two men. A sudden knock interrupted their conversation.

"Pardon me, Directress Cavell, but there's a telephone call for you in the main office. It is from the Brussels hospital; there is a urgent inquiry concerning the status of the Clinique's nurses…can you take the call?" the young pretty nurse-trainee Anne Shepardton interrupted the conversation, as her pale blue eyes instantly met and locked attractively with Quien's sleepy-appearing 'bedroom' grey eyes. Anne was wearing the distinctive outfit that was standard for the nurse probationers: a full-length blue dress with a white apron and white collar coupled with a light blue starched hat that was bonnet-like in appearance and which hid all of her beautiful blonde hair, yet which also accented and framed Anne's stunning white porcelain flaw-free skin.

"Please wait here with these men, nurse, I'll be back in a few minutes and do not go anywhere, Nurse Shepardton," Edith commanded with the slight compliment of not addressing her young novice as a Nurse-Trainee.

"Well you are indeed a pretty one!" Quien immediately started to flirt with the obviously pretty young nurse. Anne strangely was not at all embarrassed by the forwardness of the handsome Quien – she was usually quiet and reserved with men, but that was before the war had begun and she had grown out of her shy shell since then.

"Sir, where are you from and what are you doing here?" Anne inquired back, as she looked intensely at Quien and directed her words only to him, ignoring the rather ugly looking man calling himself Jacoby.

"What is your name, pretty nurse?" Quien immediately inquired as he stepped forward and clasped Anne's hand, then kissed it gently.

"I think, Monsieur, that you heard Directress Cavell address me as Nurse Shepardton, did you not?" Anne replied back immediately, hoping to further engage this handsome man in further verbal flirtation. Quien knew that this young nurse was interested in him; he could detect it in her eyes and nervous body language when she first gazed at him. Anne was not only attracted by this stranger, she was flattered that he had taken an obvious likening to her and he seemed like a gentleman. She had had no contact or relations with any man since she came to the Clinique, which she now considered to be equivalent to a convent or woman's prison.

She blushed at the handsome young man's flattery. "I did not get your names, gentlemen," Anne inquired softly and with some embarrassment.

"Yes my apologies, Madame, I am George Quien, but you can call me Gaston and my travelling friend here is Armand Jacoby Jeanne. We were recommended for medical treatment to the Clinique by the de Croys and Mlle Thuliez, but again I did not get your first name, Nurse Shepardton?"

"I am Anne, that is Nurse-Trainee Anne Shepardton," the young nurse responded in workable French, as her hands sweated and betrayed the unconscious nervousness of her own attractiveness to the young handsome stranger. Young English women of the day were not supposed to have any carnal feelings for a man and a desire for sex, yet these things she both felt on seeing Quien.

"Ah Anne, a beautiful name and from your accent I see that like Directress Cavell you are also English, and very far away from home and in a time of war too!" Quien replied, digging for some leading information.

"Yes, we are both English women and proud of it, our country and that of our brave fighting men!" Edith replied as she suddenly re-entered back into the Clinique foyer area after having completed her phone call with the Brussels hospital. "Are you gentlemen in any pain or need of medical treatment? This is a medical Clinique and we do take on a small number of Belgian civilian men in need of medical care," Edith inquired both as a matter of professional inquiry and to defer the conversation away from

Nurse-Trainee Shepardton's personal chit-chat.

"You are dismissed, Nurse-Trainee Shepardton, you may continue with your duties," Edith announced to her young charge in a very cold manner and this time verbally invoking Anne's inferior trainee status, much to Anne's embarrassment and increasing embitterment.

"We're tired and hungry, but that is about the extent of our ailments," Quien brashly responded for both himself and his companion, Armand Jacoby Jeannes.

"Is that all you want of me is food and shelter? Nothing more?" Edith inquired as she tried to get more information out of these two new strangers seeking her assistance. She was not going to eagerly volunteer services for men of whom she was suspicious.

"Well, maybe we were hoping for something more, to get out of German occupied Belgium," Quien replied without any further clarification or amplifications.

"So I am to understand that you both also want to 'travel' out of Brussels too?" Edith Cavell further queried of her new guests; she inquired as much for their individual verbalized commitment to escape, as well as to 'flush out' any misunderstandings that inhabit the minds of some of the soldiers and young men sent to her. She wanted no lingering doubts from the men and she wanted to hear their intentions to escape Belgium personally.

"Yes, Directress, we are soldiers and we want to leave Brussels; we want to escape – can you assist us?" Quien smartly declared without hesitation or evasion.

"Good then, I always try to assist those in need, especially the brave Belgians who have to leave the country and continue the fight elsewhere," Edith replied in a supportive reply that actually confessed nothing too incriminating. She continued her welcoming speech: "I can place you both in the basement of the Clinique; there are some fold-down beds there and you will be apart from the 'other' Belgian indigent male patients. You will most likely be here a week…maybe two; however you must obey my Clinique rules: no contacts with anyone except myself, no drinking, no swearing, smoke only in the basement or in the back alleyway, no leaving the Clinique and absolutely no relations with any of the nursing staff!"

Quien nodded in silent acknowledgment with Jacoby following his lead.

"Follow me and I'll take you down into your basement temporary quarters!" Edith commanded and the two men eagerly followed.

"You never explained how you came to be found and steered into safety, Monsieur Quien," Edith continued her subtle probing inquiry, as she took an old fashioned oil lamp and descended the old dark stairs leading down to the cavernous-like basement area that nested various heating and plumbing fixtures and numerous storage bins and racks for laundry, beddings, and some foodstuffs. The furnace was coal fired and a vast array of anthracite coal occupied one complete side of the basement.

"Well, we were in hiding at a farm and the farmer must have informed Mlle Louise Thuliez and she in turn helped to hide us on a small miller's lodge near the de Croy estate. We also stayed with Mr Libiez – he provided us with travel papers and we were told to make our way to Brussels and contact you. I was surprised to discover that a royal like the Prince and his sister were engaged in such activities… do you do anything more for soldiers like us?" Quien answered and inquired in a single statement and Edith became disturbed by this handsome young man's curiosity – none of the other soldiers and young men had been so inquisitive. Most Allied soldiers did not ask this many questions, if any at all, save for the impending escape out of Belgium to Holland, yet all this man wanted to discuss were the people and details of the network. Edith began to distrust both men, most especially Quien, but it was already too late to turn him back and he had been passed along by Louise, Albert and the de Croys – and besides, he had already seen much of the network.

"We all do what we can in this terrible war! The Prince and Princess's affairs are their own, as so are my own actions; I shall not speak of others. I am surprised that you two were not provided an escort from our other 'Mons friends' – this is the first time that two unescorted men have shown up at my clinique doorstep and quite unannounced! Strange isn't it, gentlemen?" Edith cajoled at her two new guests.

"No, not at all strange, Nurse Cavell. We are Belgian soldiers, we are not like the British soldiers who are unfamiliar with the country and language; after all we are natives and Belgian soldiers within our own country. If mature Belgian men cannot make their way from Mons to Brussels then we are indeed poor specimens of Belgian men," Quien quickly and succinctly explained with a flawless and logical explanation to Edith's inquiry. It seemed to Edith that Quien had a quick ready answer for each inquiry that she posed to him; he seemed like a real smooth operator.

Edith still had her inner feelings of uneasiness, yet she believed that the best course of action was to quickly send these men along their way as soon as possible. For her own sake and that of the de Croy network, Edith refused to furnish any more details in response to the two strange men's inquiries. "Here you are, gentlemen, it's not the Savoy, but it is safe and clean. There are three meals a day and I shall personally bring your meals down to you, so that you do not mingle with the regular male patients. If you need anything, come looking for me – no one else at the Clinique is directly involved in my private affairs, is this understood?" Edith concluded with both a directive and a closing question.

"Yes, Directress Cavell, we understand," Quien replied for both himself and the quiet Armand Jacoby Jeannes. The two men were left alone for the rest of the day and night, yet they whispered secrets to one another in hushed tones in the dark and solitary abode of the darkened basement.

* * * * * * * * * * * *

"Beautiful…simply radiating! Your skin is flawless…beautiful in fact! I've never been with a woman like you…so young, innocent and so gentle…a true English rose! I think you are wasting your life here at the Clinique. You are in the bud of life; the sick and wounded are not for one such as you. You belong in a Parisian salon or on the arm of one of those titled European barons!" Quien softly whispered the sweet becoming lies into his new lover's ear, as he kissed her breasts and stroked her beautiful long blonde hair. Anne and Quien lay naked on the bed of Quien's basement fold-out bed; the sheets were damp with the sweat and secretions of the post-orgasmic exhausted lovers. It was Anne's first love and sexual encounter; for Gaston Quien it was another woman in a long nameless list, to which he could barely recount.

"What! Are you trying to get rid of me so soon, Gaston!" Anne giggled as her long slender fingers brushed carelessly through her lover's thick black hair.

"Not at all, Anne. I want you in my life forever! A young beautiful woman should not waste her youth away in a charnel house like this. It is amply supplied with sick old, indigent men and matronly women who have never known love," Gaston whispered the soft welcomed words of deceit and dissent into his inviting lover's ears, softly caressing and kissing her fingers and erect nipples.

"Who exactly are you, Anne? What drew you to Belgium? What are your dreams?" Gaston Quien whispered softly into young Anne's ears and slowly rubbed his muscular, inviting hands up and down her slender soft body. The mere touch of a man alone was almost enough to sexually climax the young, love-starved nurse. Quien manipulated Anne's sexual libido such as a violin virtuoso to a finely crafted Stradivarius violin, as he expertly drew the innocent Anne into his deviously contrived confidence. He whispered to her lies that she was only too eager to accept.

"There's not a lot to say really. I was an ordinary English girl trying to make her way in the world. I was drawn to nursing out of sheer boredom at home and I was tired of living with the parents. I wanted more out of life, I wanted fun and excitement…all I got was being stranded in this boring old nursing school and attending sickly old Belgian men! I dreamed of travel and I haven't even been to Paris and now this God-awful war has spoiled that dream as well!" Anne wept gently as Quien caressed her warm, smooth, naked body. He said nothing, he knew that Anne was telling a long-delayed confession of dashed hopes and dreams. "I hate being a junior to a bunch of old matrons…these old biddies, they don't seem interested in men, alcohol, smoking, laughing or anything else pleasurable in life – all they think about is that bloody nursing business and changing bedpans and the such!" Anne lashed out in a bitter verbal denunciation of her superiors, the nursing profession and her captive plight. Gaston encouraged Anne's outrage; he knew that her strong stored up emotions and bitterness could easily betray Edith's secrets.

"Edith is the worst of the lot, followed by Nurse Wilkins, two old maids fit for nothing but nursing and caring for sick old people. I think that God made a mistake with those two bitches," Anne verbally abused her superiors in a bitterness that had been resonating for many months. "Directress Cavell makes us sit in her office and she lectures us about the nobility of nursing, the need to remain chaste and to maintain our womanly character as examples to other women! Hah, she is an example of how not to be a modern woman! Well I don't want to be an example to anyone and I sure as hell don't want Edith to be my example either. She is one of those perfect Victorian woman who lives her life in a shallow, closed, little box and I'll have none of that for myself. I'm young and I want to have fun before I too become an old maid like everyone else around this damn Clinique. Often I hate her, I hate this Clinique and I hate this damn war. I want to escape… can't we go away somewhere, Gaston? Let's escape to Paris! Take me with you please! I don't care about the danger, I cannot stay in this place with these women much longer, I'm young and I don't belong here with these old women, sick old men and living in a city where the spirit has been killed!" Anne continued to vent her personal detestation with utmost abandon with her newfound lover. She confessed her repressed hatred that had no other outlet.

Gaston carefully cultivated Anne's poisoned verbal wrath. "Oh I'm sure these nurses mean well, Anne. Ah, you are so young and maybe a little impatient, Anne. Tell me more about the things around the Clinique and Directress Cavell – these things cannot be that severe?" Quien cajoled as he kissed Anne's neck, cheeks and ears.

Anne was ever so eager to decry the Directress. "She's a strange bird and getting stranger, more mysterious too! She goes out more frequently and meets strangers in cafes, yet she always goes out alone, she meets strangers at early and late hours, young men come here for a day or two then disappear and her only friends are out of her social class like the architect Philippe Baucq, Countess Jeanne de Belleville of Lille, engineer Capiau, industrialist George Hostelet and the Prince and Princess de Croys – they have their own little clique. I can't see what they all have in common! We have only a handful of older male patients, yet Directress Cavell always seems very engaged and busy, she keeps her office locked at all times and this is where she receives all of her 'special' visitors. She is a strange, cloistered woman! She'd be right at home in a nunnery, she is always on my bloody back and I don't get a chance to enjoy myself...damn this Clinique!" Anne voiced softly. She had had enough of talking about her matronly mistress, she wanted to continue love making with Gaston and he was all too eager to oblige the young woman's desires. The two continued their sexual liaisons for over a week. Quien had enough information for now. He now patiently waited for Edith to reveal more of her hand.

While George 'Gaston' Quien was busy bedding Nurse-Trainee Anne Shepardton, the quiet, short and ugly Armand Jacoby Jeannes was busy at his own type of subterfuge. He carefully observed the comings and goings of the Clinique nurses, especially the movement of Edith Cavell and Nurse Elizabeth Wilkins. When the Clinique leaders were away or busy, Jacoby secretly picked the lock of Edith's office and rummaged through her locked desk drawers and filing cabinet. He happened to find receipts for food, second-hand men's clothing and medicine prescriptions from the local chemists. There was a long listing of men's names and addresses, many of these of a British origin, carefully noted in Edith's writing that were located on carefully folded sheets of Edith's personal stationery paper at the bottom of one of the desk drawers. All these items were in amounts that far exceeded the needs of the small handful of Belgian civilian older male patients. Something seemed odd with these receipts and records.

Additional snooping over several days also revealed many handwritten letters addressed entirely in the English language and addressed both to and from people in Great Britain. He observed that one letter had a fancy English Coat of Arms engraved at the top of the paper stationery and that it was signed with the name 'Percy' in fancy Spencer script styled writing. He also discovered some blank identity cards and photographs of young men dressed in rumpled civilian clothing. The names on some of the identity cards were filled-in, all with Belgian names and addresses, along with an official looking stamp and official signature, which could not be legibly read with any ease. All these things indicated a smuggling operation of some considerable size; however, nothing was yet discovered that was of a direct espionage or sabotage nature. Maybe time would reveal this as well, Jacoby secretly hoped to himself.

* * * * * * * * * * *

"Well I have a nice surprise for both of you! Mister Quien and Mister Jacoby, you are both going on a little visit this evening…your time here is finished and you are moving on!" Edith Cavell remarked to the two men as they sat on their beds in the basement of the Berkendael Institute.

"What do you mean? We're leaving tonight! Why now?" the usually stoic and meekest Jacoby echoed out in a stunned voice. Quien wisely remained quiet with a subdued demeanour – he did not want anyone to suspect that he was not anxious to leave Edith's clinique and besides, he had had his romantic fling with the deflowered English nurse Anne and he had strict orders from Captain Joel to check out the complete litany of any details that he was able to discover. The two men had to see their roles through to completion. Knowing the details of how the de Croy network smuggled Allied soldiers up through to the Belgium-Holland frontier and observing the details of the actual escape routes was the culmination of the data gathering plan without which the German authorities could not bring about a complete prosecution of their case in a military court of law.

"Well that is a very odd reaction I must say! What is the matter, gentleman? You have been here over a week now and I would have thought that any Allied soldier would be more than eager to hear this news! You seem a bit disturbed about this happy news – is there anything wrong?" Edith inquired. They look startled, while every other Allied soldier previously had broad grins that travelled from ear-to-ear upon hearing such delightful news. Again Edith was suspicious about these two soldiers, but they were leaving her Clinique and they would soon be across the Holland border in a week's time if they were lucky.

"No, no, that will be very fine, Miss Cavell, we're just slightly stunned by the suddenness of this announcement. What time are we to leave and who is our contact?" Quien inquired with a contrived innocent sounding voice, as he tried to deflect any further suspicions and thereby reduce their opportunity to discover the workings of the frontier passing procedures.

Edith did not respond immediately to Quien's inquiry; she was in charge of this Brussels section of the de Croy network and she wanted to ensure that her two Clinique 'guests' were properly prepared before she answered any of their inquiries. "Yes, well, these journeys happen in a unscheduled manner and you just happen to be lucky that a frontier guide was available to escort you at the present time and not later. Now, you both have your false IDs and travel papers prepared by Libiez and Capiau, correct?" she coldly inquired.

"Yes, Directress Cavell," Quien and Jacobs both responded in-kind.

"Each of you will be given some modest food to take along for your journey; be sure not to lose it as food is as precious a commodity as silver is in Belgium. Be ready to leave after dinner and you will be accompanied by a group of four other men," Edith remarked succinctly. Edith portrayed the cold and unapproachable persona of a woman and neither man had ever felt completely at ease or comfortable enough for either of them to address her by her first name. Edith was an introvert and she made friends slowly and at her own discretion; these soldiers were merely passers-through in her life, but she accorded them a correct and polite civility, but nothing more.

"We'll be available whenever you need us, Directress Cavell," Jacoby replied softly.

She nodded in affirmation and walked back up from the dark recesses of the Clinique's basement, as both agent provocateurs gathered-up their meagre belongings and made ready for the last leg of their journey, for which both men were most relieved. Neither of them felt comfortable around the Clinique or any of the people in it; they were content that this mission was almost completed.

The evening came more quickly than they had anticipated as a firm knock was heard on the Clinique's back alleyway door. "Are they ready Edith? I do not want to miss the last tram and the curfew is going into effect soon!" Philippe inquired anxiously in a soft voice. He was dressed in modest, pleasant looking, urban wear of a suit jacket and tie, as too many men dressed in rural, second-hand clothing might attract suspicion; he wanted to ensure that he was the well-dressed member of the trio and thus he could better provide for the explanation that he was merely hiring workers to do day-labour on one of his building projects.

Edith smiled and simply nodded her head in positive affirmation that all was ready.

"I have the four others waiting at my safe-house along with the two guides to take them over the Holland frontier," Philippe stated as he saw something he had not noticed in Edith's clear grey eyes before – nervousness. In the past, Edith had always met Philippe with a smile, a warm welcome and an offer of some tea, but not on this particular visit.

"Yes I have them; they are called George Quien and Armand Jacoby and God forgive me in my suspicions, but I do not trust them – and worse, I do not like them!" Edith confessed quietly to Philippe.

"Do you think they are not genuine, maybe in the pay of the German secret police?" Philippe responded with great concern in his voice.

"I cannot be sure, but I do know that the faster that they are gone the better we all will be. They ask a lot of questions that no other soldiers dreamed of asking before and I do not trust that handsome Quien around my young nurses, especially Trainee Anne Shepardton," Edith remarked in a hushed voice to avoid being overheard.

"Yes, Edith, they'll soon be on their way to the frontier tonight and in a week or less, they should be crossing the Holland frontier," Philippe responded. "It is too late to cancel this crossing; there are other soldiers waiting to cross the border and the longer they stay in Brussels, the more likely it is for them to be discovered by the Germans. It is best that we simply and quickly move along these two suspicious strangers. I have arranged for Henri Beyns and Victor Gille to assist in this passage; they are our best and most experienced guides. Did you know that Henri Beyns has over three-hundred and seventy-five successful crossings to date and these include some independent missions that he has been doing freelance?" Philippe Baucq noted with a hint of admiration.

"Yes he is quite the frontier guide and we are lucky to have him in our group. I'll get our two 'guests' and remember Philippe, don't show or tell them anything!" Edith warned Philippe as she lightly patted him on the forearm. Edith and Philippe walked down the rear stairway that led down to the darkened basement to fetch their guests.

"Quien and Jacoby, come up here you two! It is time, your escort has arrived," Edith announced in an unemotional clear tone as she also held a kerosene oil lamp in her right hand. The two men slowly walked up the steps to greet the Directress and her companion. "This man will take you to meet your guide; listen to him and do what you are told!" Edith announced in a very no-nonsense tone and without revealing Philippe's identity any further. Edith was going to leave the rest of the passage details to Philippe to disclose to the two men; it was common practice for each segment of the de Croy network to operate on delegated and sometimes fragmented procedures. This meant that various network members could, and did, weave their own cover identities, to include false names and personal history. All this served to create confusion if ever one segment of the network became compromised and thus allow the network to quickly fold-up and its members escape or go into deep hiding among the sympathetic Belgian population and religious community. The three men walked out the Clinique back door into a gentle blood red setting sun.

"We will take a tram just down the street to a place three stops away and then we go down a side street to a 'safe house', where we will meet our other guests and guides," Philippe announced in a rumbled low voice. "You are both Belgians, but still I want for you both to keep your mouths shut and remember say nothing in public and do nothing suspicious. There are German eyes watching everything and everyone," Philippe counselled quietly and obviously ignorant that two sets of German eyes were even now carefully observing him for future reference.

"Thank you, but who the hell are you and what is your name? After all we are placing our lives in your hands, Monsieur. We have a right to know some things, do you not think so?" Quien inquired of the stranger of whom he had not been formally introduced.

"Now get this straight, soldiers, it is my ass that is the one that is on the line, along with Edith and every other person who has assisted you to date. If you get caught, our entire operation and very lives are in great jeopardy; the Germans kill people like us! You really have a right to know nothing! You came to us, so you have to trust us. I'm sorry for being so blunt, but that is the way things work here. As for a name, you can both call me simply 'Fromage'. Remember that the less you know and remember, the better it is for everyone concerned," Philippe quipped without any trace of levity. Like Edith, he did not feel comfortable around these two men.

Humbled by Baucq's verbal reprimand, there was no further argument or discussions. The three boarded the inter-city tram and within about fifteen minutes they had arrived at their required stop. Philippe à la 'Fromage' escorted his two charges down a small street where a nondescript, quaint three-storey townhouse was situated. He knocked three times and was greeted by the youthful Victor Gille. No names of the frontier guides was ever mentioned, nor did it need to be; this security measure kept the guides' identity safe. In the small living room, they met Henri Beyns and four other soldiers – two British and two French. They drank some tea and discussed the details of the passage procedures to be followed in the strictest detail.

Each guide was going to take three men apiece in separate groups so as to avoid a massing of personnel, which increased the odds of border detection. Small groups of men were also easier to manage. Philippe took careful note of each man's true identity and unit; this information he forwarded to Reginald de Croy for conveyance to The Hague and the British War Office for accountability purposes. All the soldiers' families became greatly relieved upon hearing that their loved ones were no longer being carried as POWs or MIAs; the families were overjoyed that the soldiers were soon to be back home to rejoin their families, even if for only a short duration, before returning back to the war again. After a good night's rest, they were off! Philippe returned back to his own house and family just a few blocks away. The gentle warmth of a Brussels June was blossoming into the full heat and humidity of summer with the advent of July 1915.

Unbeknownst to Captain Joel and his team, another Allied spy network located in northern France was also providing data on German military operations, to include information on the new German wonder weapon, the Zeppelin. This network was known as the 'Alice network' and it was being run by a very patriotic and daring French woman from northern France; her name was Louise de Bettignies. These other Allied agents were passing information to the British via the courier system that the de Croys and Dr Bull had established and this was a secret that Dr Bull kept compartmented to just himself. Neither the Prince or Princess de Croy ever knew the sources or agents to which Dr Bull had obtained his German military information, nor did they ever have an interest in knowing such things either. Secrecy and 'need to know' was the over arching dogma of the de Croy network and everyone abided by this cardinal rule.

A low-level disgruntled German soldier named Rammlere was working at the newly constructed German Zeppelin aerodrome at Evere just outside Brussels. This German soldier was conveying secret data to Allied secret agents about the new weapons and its operational status, to include the critical date and time of departure of these giant lighter than air behemoths of death that were to rain death down upon many English cities. This fact was kept compartmented by the German Secret Service organization operating in Belgium in hope that leaving the leaker of the information intact for a short while, could possibly lead to other members of the network being revealed. Captain Hans von Kirchenheim knew of these other secret operations and the suspected German soldier traitor, yet he had conveniently stumbled upon an equally and perhaps more rewarding type of treasonous operation – that of Allied soldiers being smuggled out of Belgium. The

Germans referred to this illegal activity as 'enemy soldier recruitment'. This was a capital crime in the German military regulations and equally as serious as the charge and crime of espionage, sabotage or sedition.

* * * * * * * * * * *

# Chapter 8:
# Betrayal and Arrest

*"...you see neither a tiger nor a scoundrel can change its stripes
or his nature, a man can lay down and sleep with a woman,
yet still not be brushed by the wings of her passions"*

"I've seen that our efforts over the past several weeks have revealed some very interesting facts and incriminating evidence! Do you not agree, gentlemen?" Captain Hans von Kirchenheim spouted off in jubilation to the now familiar trio of men that sat before him during this all too frequent ritual that had begun only a few months previously. Captain Joel, Lieutenant Bergan and Lieutenant Pinkhoff sat quietly without much outward emotion, yet each man now possessed an inner confidence that they had indeed discovered something amiss in Brussels – that of an underground Allied soldier escape and support network.

"Well, I think it is fair to say that we did discover a conspiracy, a loose network of Allied sympathizers," Captain Joel stated in a less than enthusiastic rebuttal that Captain von Kirchenheim found to be quite unexpected.

"What's wrong, Captain Joel, you sound unimpressed about your team's remarkable discovery of this band of traitors? You should be ecstatic about this. We shall all probably be awarded medals and promotions if we can destroy the network and bring the culprits to German military justice," von Kirchenheim announced, as both Lieutenants Bergan and Pinkhoff smiled upon hearing about the possibility of rewards for their sullied actions.

"Naturally I am pleased with discovering this band of amateurs obviously involved in ferrying Allied soldiers across the border, but I thought that our main objective was to discover the party or parties engaged in passing German military data to the Allies or finding those agents involved in acts of sabotage. These people, excuse my expression, are like second-rate amateurs. I feel somewhat deflated and cheated!" Captain Joel confessed in utter professional truthfulness. Captain Hans von Kirchenheim, however, was not to be denied his victory and he wanted to hear no dissent from within his team; he needed his men focused and dedicated to breaking this underground network.

"So this den of rascals is not prestigious enough for your ego, Captain Joel! Well, my dear Captain Joel, Germany's enemies consist of those scoundrels wherever they are located and whatever illegal activities in which we may so discover them doing! Your problem is that you want to arrest the glamorous, headline type of criminals, but do not despair as we have all done very well in detecting these soldier smugglers. Do not be too disappointed in the type of crimes that you have uncovered; just be glad that we have discovered the illegal activities! Remember that just a short time ago, we had absolutely nothing on this network, we did not even suspect its existence and where there is one rat discovered, there are others lurking as well. These clever scoundrels may be professional saboteurs or amateurs assisting Allied soldiers escape to safety – it matters not to me, nor should it to you either. Consider that from the 'little fish, the big fish eat' and there's no telling what we shall uncover when we rupture their network, which is very soon now," Captain von Kirchenheim boldly proclaimed to the small assemblage.

"Do you think, sir, that enough evidence exists presently or should we wait longer before we arrest them?" Lieutenant Pinkhoff inquired intelligently.

Captain von Kirchenheim smiled and he was pleased by the professionalism that the young Lieutenant was exhibiting. "That is a very good question, Pinkhoff. I think that we have some very promising leads for arrests, but not enough for a courtroom trial and I do not want any frivolous case that will not result in convictions. I want everything rock-solid and that means outlining the entire network and laying out the various roles and responsibilities of those involved. After we as a team do this, then we make the arrests and after the arrests, both you and Lieutenant Bergan will perform the interrogations playing 'good and bad' policemen roles, we get various bits and pieces of information from one suspect and we use it against the successive prisoners. In the end, all the pieces are put together to form the complete picture and from there we get their confessions. I don't want the German Prosecutor to have to 'go fishing for answers' among these people in the court room; he will need to know every answer to every question that is posed to them and I want the Prosecutor to know as much information about this case and network as we do and I want to publically portray these people as fools!" von Kirchenheim stated with confident resolution. It was obvious that he had a wealth of experience in conducting such matters.

"Did our agent provocateurs perform to your personal satisfaction,

Captain von Kirchenheim?" Captain Joel asked, as he lit up a cigarette and stood up to exercise his circulation and take a leisurely gaze out of the window upon the beautiful warm summer day.

"Oh yes, even more than satisfactory, they were excellent! I hoped that you paid those rascals a bonus because without them, this entire underground network would have gone on undetected and indefinitely so. I want to commend both Quien and Jacoby, especially that Quien fellow – without his bedding that young nurse at the Berkendael Institute, we'd never have any idea about that sweet, innocent and matronly Edith Cavell running an underground railroad right under our very eyes in the centre of Brussels. Those two agent provocateurs even made it all the way up through to Holland with their guides before getting conveniently 'lost', while swimming across one of the dykes up there – they must think that they both drowned or something else disastrous!" Captain von Kirchenheim belted out one of his rare comments of praise.

"Do you think that Quien is still reliable enough and not emotionally involved with that young woman? We still need him for the trial and he seemed to be very involved with that young English nurse at Cavell's Clinique, that girl named Anne Shepardton," Captain von Kirchenheim inquired of his three colleagues as they sat around the plain wooden office table, draped with a simple, plain white cotton table cloth, atop which were placed four table settings of simple plain white ceramic coffee cups and saucers, along with several dainty spoons. Lieutenant Pinkoff personally selected and hired Quien, so he thought it best to respond to the Captain's inquiry. "Yes sir, I do think that he will continue to be depended upon, you see neither a tiger nor a scoundrel can change its stripes or his nature, a man can lay down and sleep with a woman, yet still not be brushed by the wings of her passions."

"Quien will make for a fine gigolo after the war," Bergan added. Pinkhoff and the other men laughed heartedly; they realized that Quien was a low-level rogue of a man – if he could not cheat or steal to make a living, he would swoon down and live off the good nature and fortune of many a woman, be they young or old, married or single, the woman's status mattered not to the unscrupulous womanizing Quien.

"Those arrogant amateurs never thought to make sure that the soldiers that they were assisting might have a 'jackal' within the ranks. How stupid can they be to take everyone who came their way to be that which was merely verbally proclaimed! A real 'confidence man' could have a profitable time with these gullible people, especially those arrogant royal de Croys!

They thought nothing of Gaston Quien's or Armand Jacoby Jeannes' sudden appearance and fanciful story, which was the stuff of theatrics. The height of stupidity was using the family name spelled backward as a code word! I'm going to be chuckling all the way to the military court and Tri National firing range on that silly little ploy they used!" Lieutenant Bergan noted with hostile scorn of the leaders of the underground network that they had uncovered.

"Well let's not be too harsh on amateurs, my dear fellow Lieutenant Bergan, if this network had been operating since November 1914, then perhaps we should have been more alert to their activities over such a long duration. After all, gentlemen, it was only after the bombing of the Zeppelin airdromes that the High Command became interested in this Brussels backwater," Captain von Kirchenheim retorted back to temper the over zealousness of the young Lieutenant.

The Captain shrewdly appreciated that personal anger and contempt for an adversary often tended to cloud the mind and lead one to make inappropriate and often exaggerated judgment. 'Better to keep one's head than one's heart,' von Kirchenheim mused silently to himself. Von Kirchenheim realized that this small group of Belgian patriots and an old English nurse had outwitted their paid agents and that it was mere luck and a careless young nurse, which had led to its discovery and downfall; he was glad, but not overly proud. He knew what the others in the room did not, that other similar Allied soldier smuggling cells, espionage networks and saboteur cells had successfully infiltrated into other occupied cities in Belgium and northern France and that this discovered cell was only a single victory in fighting the more prevalent danger of active resistance against German occupation and that, like a deadly cancer, it would never die. Still von Kirchenheim was a professional soldier and despite the futility of eliminating every German resistance cell, he was obligated to perform his duty and to install in his subordinates the spirit to continue the fight. He needed to inspire an atmosphere of optimism in his team, so that they would not become discouraged and cynical.

"Well now, let us get to work identifying the key and minor players in the network. We don't want to miss anyone; we want to cast as large a net as possible. If we are very lucky, we may even get some leads or even agents from complementary networks. We are lucky in that these amateurs are easier to detect, compromise and destroy, as opposed to highly trained government agents," von Kirchenheim accurately attested with a keen knowledge of these civilian spy networks.

"So sir, are we really sure that the British are behind these people and this network?" Lieutenant Bergan asked earnestly.

"We're not absolutely sure of anything until these people confess and we make our raids and gather up incriminating information, but from experience we know that the British support these cell networks at least passively. We do have confirmed information that the Prince Reginald de Croy has been travelling a good deal and our agents in London have seen him on the streets near Whitehall and the British War Office. Given his anti-German sentiments and his Anglophile background, it is only logical that he and the others are in league with the British Government in some shape or manner," von Kirchenheim again correctly deduced. "If the British are involved, they are very 'hands-off' in controlling the de Croy network and this works to their advantage too – they can simply deny everything and there's no strong trail that leads directly back to their involvement; it's a 'win-win' for the Brits," Kirchenheim added.

"This is the information that we have, Captain von Kirchenheim: the de Croys appear to be the brains of the operation. From all indications both brother and sister are very pro-British, anti-German and their ties to the English aristocracy and London power elite are deep to be sure. The de Croys may also be enlisting either consciously or innocently, some of their aristocratic friends like that French Countess from Lille; then there are the 'professional men' from the Borinag – the lawyer, engineer and chemist – these are the identity and documentation piece of the network. Finally then there's the innocent, little English matron nurse Edith Cavell and her band of very respectable men like industrialist Georges Hostelet and the architect Philippe Baucq – this is the last and most critical component of the network – it coordinated and sheltered the soldiers in Brussels and they arranged for the frontier guides. You know, it's kind of funny, it was the Depages who were the initial catalysts in all of this! After all, they brought this entire network into being, even if they did not realize it at the time! Dr Depage personally hired Edith Cavell and he also enlisted the Prince and Princess de Croy and even the King and Queen, to authorize the foundation of the Berkendael Nurse Training Institute and this action conversely brought Nurse Cavell to Brussels along with the nurses and in a most quaint, convenient location of the clinique in the heart of downtown Brussels. Like a spider web, these people spread their influences and recruited the others, the lesser network players. The network was a random combination of the confluence of people and events that could not possibly happen under any other circumstances; it was all fate, not deliberate design!" Captain Joel noted stoically.

"Enough philosophy, now let's name the key characters and the smaller fish too. We need a prioritized listing here," von Kirchenheim commanded to his trio.

"There's no doubt that the de Croys, both Reginald and Marie, are the primary culprits! Even if they refuse to talk after arrest, the confessions of the other 'weaker' members and the contributory evidence will make their guilt self-evident to the court," Lieutenant Bergan spoke out bluntly and with no dissention given. His words were self-evident to say the least and no one was impressed by these self-evident details.

"Let's add in here that guilt of the French Countess, Jeanne de Belleville – her hand is all over this as well!" Captain Joel noted in his concern to address all the members of the aristocratic players involved.

"She's guilty and she's a primary player too," Lieutenant Pinkhoff retorted with his other two colleagues nodding their heads in obvious agreement.

"Yes, I too think that the Countess de Belleville is one of the top instigators in this operation," Captain von Kirchenheim concluded equally.

"What does everyone think of the Countess de Lichtervelde and that old Baron de la Grange? These two are always hanging about the Bellignies Chateau," Lieutenant Bergan pointed out to his colleagues.

"There's no evidence, absolutely none, that identifies them as being anything more than mere neighbors and semi-house guests of the de Croys. My opinion is that unless any confessions flush-out their network involvement, we let these two alone. They appear to be only social friends of the de Croys and nothing more!" Captain Joel noted with perfect reasoning.

"I agree to that," Lieutenant Pinkhoff added.

"So do I. Let's wait and see about those two; we can always grab them later anyway. Besides we cannot arrest every aristocrat in Belgium!" Captain von Kirchenheim concluded smugly.

"We cannot forget that woman! Edith Cavell is a prime participant and she's English too! Her confederates Philippe Baucq, Georges Hostelet, Ada Bodart and Maurice Severin – are all primary network players," Lieutenant Pinkoff added from his keen analytical memory.

"Let's not forget Capiau and Libiez either, nor any of the guides, café owners, chemists, bakers and farmers!" Captain Bergan chimed in again in chorus-like fashion to add to the lengthy suspect list.

"Good, this is all very good, gentlemen! We can always modify the list as we get new facts, yet for now I think that you have a good working list of the capital members. Also include anyone who was peripherally involved and, more importantly, those from whom we can pressure under interrogation and thereby incriminate others. Even if it is only a small piece of evidence, it will be enough to help us catch the major players. We are looking at capital crimes here and that means executions and long prison terms," Captain von Kirchenheim noted with obvious satisfaction as he smiled and puffed on a strong Gauloises French made cigarette.

"Do you think that we make a single, massive police round-up or do we arrest the underground network partners separately?" Lieutenant Bergan inquired as a matter of procedure for the impending arrests.

The young arrogant Prussian Captain thought for a few seconds. He knew that rashness bred mistakes and that thoughtful deliberation needed the grace of time. The hot, smoke-filled room was quiet as they waited for their superior's decision.

"Let's go after the worker bees first, those professional people, who were recruited by the de Croys first. Word will spread, as it always does, throughout Brussels and about the arrests being made against this network. We keep constant surveillance on those not immediately arrested and see where these scared rats flee. Then when we go after the leadership, as the network middle and lower members talk, they will incriminate more and more information on the leaders. Who knows, there may be elements of society that we haven't even touched yet!" Captain Hans von Kirchenheim noted boldly and brilliantly. Everyone knew that this was a masterful analysis and its logic had no flaws. The royals and aristocrats had few options to flee; all of their roots, power and prestige lay in their cloistered chateaus, castles, villas and townhomes. The total abandonment of relatives and property was not a task to be taken lightly without deep contemplation. Country abandonment was an easier act of verbal proclamation than physical action. These material things to which they were heavily invested, they were most reluctant to abandon and by the time they discovered the danger to themselves, it was going to be too late.

"When should we initiate the arrests, Captain von Kirchenheim?" Captain Joel remarked as the meeting discussions were drawing to a close.

"Let's not be premature, I want all resources assembled, to include extra police, cars, and jail cells. Make sure your offices are ready for a flood of interrogations and that the St Gilles warden is alerted and has the required amount of cells. The royals will be kept at a local officer's barracks; the Prince and Princess may be spies, but they are royals both of them! I want to go over the details of the surveillance and arrest plan too...I want no one to get away. Let's do this no later than the first week of August. Any objections, comments or concerns?" Captain von Kirchenheim concluded. There was only silence among the three other military intelligence officers.

The preliminary plan was in place. Little did anyone in the de Croy network know just how short his or her unfettered existence was to remain untouched by the Germans' discovery of their little secret. There was covert surveillance on the de Croy chateau, on Capiau's and Baucq's residences, the familiar gathering watering hole of the Taverne Royale and naturally Edith's Berkendael Institute nursing Clinique. The summer was indeed getting much hotter.

✱ ✱ ✱ ✱ ✱ ✱ ✱ ✱ ✱ ✱ ✱ ✱

'Where on earth are those men? It's been over thirty minutes since the rendezvous time and they're late! What could have happened to them?' Louise Thuliez muttered anxiously to herself as she sat alone at the café Taverne Royale as the evening grew late. Mr Pansaers had discreetly darkened all the main lights of the cafe, only keeping on a faint lighting at the rear interior part of the cafe for minimal lighting; he needed to forestall any curfew inquisitions from the German secret police.

"The men may still come, Louise, do you not think so?" the visually nervous Maurice Pansaers stuttered, as he nervously puffed on a cigarette to help calm his frazzled nerves. He was visually agitated, he had risked the ownership of his café so that Louise and the other de Croy network members could meet discreetly in Brussels without undue suspicions being generated. Pansaers had violated the curfew by allowing select clients to stay past the appointed hour by taking a quiet, discreet table on the inside of the shop. The police had never bothered him before and he had no reason for any future police harassment; he often gave patrolling police a late night cup of coffee or drink to keep on their good side. Louise had waited patiently to make contact and direct a small party of Belgian miners from Maubeuge to assist the French military construct underground tunnels on the battlefields. The request had come through Reginald de Croy via a diplomatic pouch letter that was given to him during one of his routine visits to the US Consulate in Brussels.

It was now 10:15 pm and Louise Thuliez had wisely concluded that the men were not showing up for one reason or another. Sometimes there were delays or errors in understanding the prescribed meeting time. No matter the reason, it was not wise for an unescorted woman to stay alone at a Brussels café at night after the curfew, it invited unwelcome attention and suspicions if anyone noticed her, which the German police so accurately did. Louise wanted to take the short tram ride to Philippe Baucq's house to report to him that the appointment with the miners had not materialized; yet since the German imposed a curfew of 7:00 pm, the trams had ceased to operate past that hour. Walking remained her sole option. It was a rather warm evening, so she decided to take the fifteen-minute walk to Philippe's townhouse. Her large bag was filled with letters, maps and even coded sheets of paper, a coded notebook of network member addresses and names and blank false identity cards.

"It's no good, Maurice, something has happened to those Belgian miners, it is far past curfew and I need to leave here and discreetly make it over to Baucq's house without being stopped by the German police. I'll try to sort out this missed meeting tomorrow. Have a great night and good night." Louise made her evening farewell to the friend who had been introduced to her by Prince de Croy and Philippe Baucq some months earlier.

Louise carefully negotiated her way to No. 49 Avenue de Rodebeek, the modest, if not stylish, four storey, maroon coloured brick townhouse of her close network confederate Philippe Baucq. Louise often used the Baucqs' home as her temporary Brussels resting stop, along with alternatively using the town mansion of the Countess Jeanne de Belleville. One needed to always alter one's routes and residences if at all possible. She looked over her right shoulder to ensure that no one had followed her and she saw no one noticeable, then she stealthily knocked on the door, in hope of avoiding the unwanted stares from any of the neighbours. It was a hot summer night and most people in downtown Brussels had their full-sized windows wide-open on each level of their town homes; few things remained un-noticed by the Belgian urban dwellers.

Mrs Baucq possessed superior auditory acumen; she keenly heard Louise's muffled knock on her front door quite distinctly over the other house sounds. "Just one minute please!" Marie Baucq voiced out loudly as she hurried down from the second storey front room to open the front door of the multi-storey townhouse. Upstairs there remained the two Baucq daughters; the older one was named Yvonne who was thirteen, while Madeleine was an energetic nine years old. Both girls were with their father Philippe. They were all busily engaged in folding large sheets of papers from a pile of six large stacks of flat paper; each pile must have contained several thousand sheets, each of bold, black printed news type.

"Oh hello Louise, good evening and please come in, Philippe and I had expected you much earlier and to be accompanied by several 'friends'! You're looking tired tonight; how about a cup of tea? Philippe, the girls and a few friends are upstairs folding up and preparing the papers, so just go right on up, I'll be with you shortly!" Marie Baucq spoke rapidly as she warmly greeted her all too familiar houseguest with a pleasant smile.

"There were some problems. My 'friends' never showed up and yes, some tea would be most appreciated, Marie. I must tell Philippe of the bad news immediately," Louise Thuliez replied quickly, as she smiled back at Mrs Baucq and quickly ran up to the third storey landing. Two flights up the Baucqs' townhouse, Louise found her close friend and compatriot Philippe, who was enjoying the delightful companionship of his two daughters, young Madeleine and the older Yvonne. Two of his young nieces were there as well.

"Is this good, Papa?", the innocent, blonde haired and blue-eyed doting Madeleine asked in natural inquisition of her father, as she dutifully folded the large paper neatly in half sections. Philippe turned and smiled with radiance at his adoring little girl. "Yes, that is perfect, Madeleine, you are the best paper folder in all of Brussels, maybe even all of Belgium!" the devoted father replied back to his daughter and picked her up high to almost the ceiling in fatherly play. The other three girls were oblivious to Philippe's fatherly play antics, as they engrossed themselves in folding and neatly stacking huge piles of paper in neat piles arrayed before each of them.

"Well this is the reason why La Libre Belgique is slow on distribution this month, huh!", Louise Thuliez lightly laughed and mocked at Philippe in sarcastic banter, as she smiled at her friend in play with his young daughter. The La Libre Belgique was an underground French language newspaper published in Belgium by various anonymous printing houses located throughout Belgium by the newspaper publishing brothers of Louis and Victor Jourdain and distributed in bulk by patriotic locals for collating and circulation by local nationalists such as Philippe and Louise. Like the de Croy network, no one in the La Libre Belgique distribution knew of the names or members of this publishing initiative. The newspaper gave great encouragement and inspiration about the war news to the average Belgian citizen while under Imperial German occupation.

She threw off her hat and carefully placed her bag into a dark corner of the room to remove it from the clutter of the present frenzied activities.

"Yes Louise, it's all my fault; the underground leader with a soul, that's my bane and I wear it proudly," Philippe half-jokingly confessed as he toyfully paraded around the hot room with his child on his shoulders.

"How did things go? Are the miners with you?" He suddenly remembered the reason for Louise's visit for the evening.

"I'm afraid not, they did not come at all! Pansaers was kind enough to leave the café open after curfew, but they never showed up. I do not know what could have happened, but Edith did not communicate any change in plans to me," Louise Thuliez remarked with a tone of curiosity in her voice.

Philippe looked perplexed initially, then the frown on his face quickly dissolved. "Ah, these things happen, maybe someone got spooked or perhaps some identification papers needed to be fixed, it could be any number of reasons," Philippe remarked with hapless resignation. He had no reason to suspect anything nefarious in the miners not showing up at the appointed hour.

Louise, however, was not as casual in this failed hook-up with the Belgian miners and she thought the worst of it. "I don't like it when the men do not show up on schedule. I always think the worst, that something has gone awfully astray or that we've been found out," Louise confessed, obviously nervous.

"I understand fully, Louise. We just have to continue to be careful and do our part; everything has gone fine so far, this has happened before and it will happen again, so rest assured. Now onto another matter, I have over four thousand copies of La Libre Belgique that will be ready for pick-up tomorrow morning by our young girl and boy couriers. I bet that no one in our network even suspects that we are the leading Brussels distributors of this underground newspaper. It is prudent that we kept this little enterprise to ourselves, this way we only incriminate ourselves and not the others."

Suddenly their conversation was interrupted by a shrill, loud barking voice, accompanied by a loud heavy banging on the sturdy front door. "Open-up! Open-up in there! German police...open-up or we'll break down the damn door!" came the loud and brutal shouts from behind the exterior of the Baucq's front door.

"What on Earth? What should I do, Philippe?" Marie Baucq cried out frantically as her calm face broke out into sheer terror and despair.

"Stall! Simply stall the bastards! Tell them you're looking for the key or something!" Philippe shouted out to his wife, as both he and Louise gazed frantically down from the staircase. Philippe had never planned for this possibility; there was absolutely no physical way to destroy four thousand copies of the illegal newspaper. Still, they had to try something. The shrill blowing of the high tone German police signal whistles could be heard throughout the neighbourhood and now everyone was alerted that the German police were making a raid and that trouble was afoot for some unfortunate soul. Brussels citizens had been hearing many such police actions for the past nine months.

"Quick girls, out with everything! Rip up everything! The Boche are here!" Philippe cried out to his two daughters and two nieces. They tore up every piece of newsprint in sight, yet it was useless – there was simply too much paper to destroy. Philippe panicked! He knew that the underground newspaper was the least of his problems; there were soldiers' letters to their families, correspondence from refugee soldiers, depot and munitions maps and papers with cryptic writing and numbers that outlined the grid coordinate of critical German logistic points. He was doomed and he knew it, so he decided to go out like a wild patriot. Also, Louise Thuliez possessed similar incriminating evidence in her handbag, not the least of which were the name of the Belgian miners. The incriminating evidence against both Philippe and Louise was indeed mortal.

"Bastard Boche! It is liberation day, my fellow Belgians! Long live La Libre Belgique Long live Freedom! Long live a free Belgium!" Philippe shouted as he threw hundreds of unfolded newspaper pages from his second storey balcony, as the street and pavement below were increasingly littered with pages of the illegal newspaper. The Belgian and German police looked helplessly onward at the surreal scene of hundreds of white sheets of paper flying down onto the street. No one in the neighbourhood could venture outside for fear of violating the curfew. Fellow neighbours could not help but hear the commotion, as they lit their gas and kerosene lights to peer stealthily from behind lace white Belgian curtains to ascertain the antics of a screaming wild yelling man atop of his balcony on the hot summer evening. Philippe's wild antics offered a form of perverted voyeuristic entertainment and diversion from the mundane routine of the average Brussels citizen. Some were even so bold as to venture onto their own balconies to better see the public display. The force of twenty-five German military police, accompanied by Lieutenants Bergan and Pinkhoff hastily entered Baucq's house and placed everyone in it into immediate arrest.

"Grab that woman there!" Lieutenant Bergan announced quickly as two burly police officers took Mrs Marie Baucq by the arms and ensured that she made no further movements. "Where is your traitorous husband?" Lieutenant Bergan shouted out to the hysterical woman. She said nothing, but rumbling sounds from above clearly indicated the probable answer. "Quickly, this way, up the staircase and go to every floor and room!" Lieutenant Bergan ordered loudly in German, as he and over a dozen officers ran up the Baucqs' staircase.

"You there – stop it! Stop right now, you swine, or I'll shoot!" Lieutenant

Bergan shouted as he pointed his German P.08 9mm calibre Luger pistol into the third storey room that was serving as a de facto newspaper assembly and distribution venue. There before them were assembled the entire troupe responsible for assembly and distribution of the anti-German La Libre Belgique newspaper. Philippe turned around and saw the pistols and rifles of the German soldiers and military police being pointed at both himself and his daughters and nieces. He immediately froze on the balcony. No one else in the room moved as well.

"Hands up high, everyone! That means little girls too!" Lieutenant Bergan shouted harshly in German, but whose words were plain as day for all to appreciate.

Lieutenant Pinkhoff entered the room and he too was armed with a German Luger pistol, yet he did not point it in a menacing manner, as did Lieutenant Bergan. Lieutenant Pinkhoff knew that his greatest weapon was his superior intellect. "You are all under arrest under German military occupation regulations for anti-German actions, conspiracy, espionage, sabotage and any other charge that we can see fit to apply against you traitors," Lieutenant Pinkhoff spouted forth in perfect French for all to understand. There was no confusion or argument with his charges, everyone present was 'dead-to-wrong' and the evidence of the underground newspaper alone was enough to convict them all, save for the children, to a sentence of possible execution or at least a long prison term.

"We know that this man here is Philippe Baucq and this is his wife, children and the other young are most likely relatives or family friends, but for you Madame, we do not have an actual name, would you like to give it to us now?" Bergan spoke with the voice of a well seasoned police officer, as he looked directly at Louise Thuliez.

Pinkoff quickly translated Lt Bergan's words for Louise to comprehend. With great nervousness she began to speak and finally uttered the words, "My name is Madame Martin." Both officers looked and then immediately smiled at one another; they suspected that this woman was Louise Thuliez and her role was as a soldier-escort and courier for the de Croy network. They decided to play along and humour her – for they knew the truth.

"Of course, Madame Martin, why and for whom were you waiting this evening at the café Taverne Royale? It was a bit late to be waiting for anyone especially past the official curfew," Pinkhoff asked as a leading question to which he did not expect to receive any response. As expected, Louise Thuliez wisely kept silent. She was wise enough to know that speaking at the wrong time and with the incorrect response had led many a suspect to conviction and execution. Being smart meant being quiet for the time being. "Well I see that Mlle Martin is as wise and silent as the cunning fox; let us hope that she has the wisdom to speak to us later," Pinkhoff remarked confidently.

"Now downstairs everyone at once! Do not touch or take anything, we're all taking a nice little trip to the Brussels German Police Headquarters building where identities will be checked, names taken and questions are going to be asked! Don't think that you are going home either, your beds tonight will be a cold, hard prison bunk," Lieutenant Pinkhoff shouted out loudly again in French as the soldiers and police officers took everyone down to the awaiting cars that had been staged for just such a purpose. The children were crying with great remorse, as was Marie Baucq. Philippe was shocked in disbelief; he could not fathom that his newspaper operation had been discovered and his entire family and Louise Thuliez were now in German military custody. This was bad and he knew it emphatically. He knew that the Germans made arrests of this size of scale only when they already had much evidence against those being arrested.

'Who could have betrayed the network? What mistakes had been made?' Philippe wondered all the way to the police station. There he and the others would spend incalculable hours in solitary detention cells, only to be suddenly interrupted by a jailer coming by and taking each one of them away for separate interrogations. Children were not to be spared either; in fact, the jailing of children in the cells along with their parents, made confessions and the breaking of a captive all the more easier. Few people could bear having their children scream with terror as their parents were taken away to uncertain places and at irregular times, usually under the duress of a deliberately rude shouting guard. Many a parent betrayed secrets on hearing the crying torments of their children.

"Well this is one hell of a mess here, Lieutenant Pinkhoff. We're going to have a long night sifting through this mess!" Bergan announced with a feeling of power and revenge in his voice.

"No problem my friend, we caught them with their pants down! Did you see that Baucq throwing those newspapers off of the balcony? We suspected him of ferreting refugee Allied soldiers to Holland, but running one of the premier underground newspapers is like finding a diamond in a coal mine! I am sure that when Captain von Kirchenheim makes his report to Berlin, the General Staff is going to be dancing with delight on this mere discovery alone!" Pinkhoff replied back with glee in his voice.

"Maybe there are other such treasonous gems yet to be discovered in this den of inequity," Bergan noted in obvious excitement.

"Yes, so let's carefully go through and examine each and every piece of paper in this house. I bet we will find just the type of prosecutorial evidence that will make their trial just a matter of form and format," Pinkhoff replied as the two men took off their jackets and proceeded to carefully scrutinize every piece of paper that came before them, consorting with one another each time they came upon an incriminating piece of evidence of which there was aplenty.

"My oh my…now what do we have here, Pinkhoff?" Bergan noticed a large woman's handbag that had been carefully placed in a visually unobtrusive corner of the room under the darkness of a small wooden table. The two officers looked inside and as they rummaged through its contents their eyes gleamed as if they had uncovered a trove of gold bullion. They quickly discovered the very incriminating frontier routes, escape maps, the coded names of the Belgian miners, messages and a secret address notebook.

"Well now my dear friend, why on earth would a mere smuggler of Allied soldiers use a cryptic secret cypher to encode ordinary, perishable information? I think that we have just uncovered supporting evidence of an espionage and sabotage ring!" Pinkoff remarked to Lieutenant Bergan. They found other incriminating items to include the letters written by Allied soldiers to their families in England and France and a paper that contained the scribbled details of various German munitions trains and marshalling points in and around Brussels. The Germans had discovered the 'smoking gun' for the de Croy network.

Both men simply smiled at their good fortune of this discovery. It was more information than they could have ever hoped to have initially uncovered. Everything had proceeded remarkably well with the implementation of Phase I of the Germans' arrest plan having just been completed with wild success. Now the stage was set for Phase II as the German noose drew tighter on the de Croy network.

* * * * * * * * * * * *

"Edith! Edith! Did you hear? They've been caught! Philippe and Louise have been arrested," Nurse Elizabeth Wilkins shouted out as she ran unannounced into Edith's office at the Clinique. It was Sunday and Edith was in her modest church clothing; she had just attended a morning service at the Brussels Anglican church earlier that morning and she was totally unaware of the events that preceded the early morning hours, yet even now the Brussels gossip network had transmitted the news with almost electronic efficiency.

"My dear Lord, who was taken? What details do you have?" Edith replied in a soft hushed voice as she arose slowly in a stunned leaning posture.

"Philippe, Marie, Louise, the two girls and two of their nieces!" Nurse Wilkins responded with an obvious tone of resigned despair. Edith turned a pale shade of white, as her face drew into an elongated dejected form. "The rumours on the street are that Philippe and Louise were heavily involved in the underground newspaper La Libre Belgique. I never would have thought," Nurse Wilkins' voice trailed off as she saw a look of fear spread over the usually self-confident Directress's face.

"La Libre Belgique newspaper! No, I never suspected their involvement in such an enterprise. I suppose that each of us have secrets that need to be maintained and I think that Philippe thought that 'knowing less is being guilty less'. I fear now for the others and all that we have done!" Edith remarked with great candidness to her deputy Directress who had remained largely ignorant of the working of the de Croy network, save for providing tacit and obedient support to any of Edith's strange requests and orders over the past nine months.

"I hope you know, Nurse Wilkins, that it shall not be long before the Germans come for me too! It had to happen one of these days. It could not have gone on forever I imagine. I'm sure that you suspected what activities I had been secretly engaged in, yet you wisely kept silent," Edith announced softly and with pitch that seemed to imply inevitability or even fatalism.

"Edith you must try to flee now! Save yourself! You assisted others, now get out while you still can!" Nurse Wilkins cried out with a tearful plea.

Edith looked out onto the rue de la Culture street below. She seemed as if in a trance for a few seconds, so intense was her stare. "No, I'm afraid that my flight is most impossible now, Nurse Wilkins. There are two men posted not fifty feet down the street and their eyes have not left the front of our Clinique. We are being watched by the German secret police even now. Remember that you know nothing and that you only followed my instructions, is that clear?" Edith announced as a command rather than a suggestion. She immediately turned around and gave a faint smile to her dear friend and associate. Nurse Wilkins was devastated by Edith's announcement.

A look of fear and dread suddenly draped over Nurse Wilkins' face. "Yes, Directress Cavell, I understand and I'll do as you so order," Nurse Wilkins announced in bitter submission and frustrated that her dear good friend was in imminent danger from the Germans.

"Good then, remember that whatever happens to me, you are the

Assistant Directress and you will carry on the work at this Clinique with or without my presence, administer to those things as I have so taught you." Edith concluded her short discussion with her Assistant Directress.

"Nothing has been the same since Mrs Depage was drowned on the Lusitania! I don't know if we'll ever see England again!" Nurse Wilkins cried out as she ran sobbing from Edith's private office. For Edith, she was resigned to whatever fate Providence may have in store for her. She quietly composed letters to her aged mother and family and then resumed her daily Sunday routine of reading the Bible and her favourite book, 'The Imitation of Christ'. With a touch of fatalism and a pocketful of courage, Edith was resolved to live her days as she had lived her life, one day at a time in peace and existence with God, family, friends and duty. A mere few weeks earlier, she had sat blissfully at a café with Louise Thuliez and Herman Capiau, enjoying the late July sun and some light hearted banter over tea and biscuits. Edith thought to herself how ironic and fragile life was in that events could change so quickly and without any warning. She was determined to meet any threats or sentence that the Germans may have for her to include forced exile, imprisonment or even death. The surveillance of Edith was now constant.

Bergan and Pinkhoff started to arrest the other 'working members' of the de Croy network before anyone had the opportunity to flee. Over the next several days other arrests of prominent de Croy network members were made, to include Herman Capiau, Albert Libiez, Maurice Derveau, Louis Severin and Maurice Pansaers and Oscar Mathieu the two network café owners where the de Croy members often met – they were all arrested by the German secret military police. It was time too for the Germans to shut down the central nervous system of the de Croy Brussels cell – the Berkendael Institute nursing Clinique and its Directress Edith Cavell.

It was a sunny, hot, and humid Thursday in downtown Brussels on the day of August 5, 1915 and Lieutenants Bergan and Pinkhoff sweated profusely in their dark grey German wool military uniforms. The cool air of the open black automobiles provided a pleasant, if only temporary, respite from the torrid heat. They had come on a mission which they had been relishing for over a week now and the Clinique had been under vigilant observation. The four huge black vehicles stopped about thirty feet from the Berkendael Institute building. To the naked eye, everything appeared normal and the best intelligence indicated that Directress Cavell and Assistant Directress Wilkins were both physically present in the building, yet nothing could or would be taken for granted by the two seasoned military police officers. Both they and everyone else, after all, had been totally fooled by

Philippe Baucq using his family home as a clever disguise for the distribution centre of the La Libre Belgique underground newspaper that used small children to courier the malicious underground newspaper across the city and under the noses of the German military authorities. Looks were very deceiving and indeed using an International Red Cross sanctioned nursing Clinique supported by the Belgian nobles and aristocrats was pure genius in the eyes of von Kirchenheim, Bergan and Pinkhoff. These men may have been made fools of once, but definitely not a second time.

Bergan looked at his watch – the time was 4:00 pm – 'as good a time as any to make an arrest', the two policeman surmised as they and a dozen German policemen and soldiers exited the vehicles and deliberately walked toward the front of the Berkendael Institute along the rue de la Culture street. The hard leather hobnail boots of the group of determined, stern faced men upon the cobblestone bricks made a distinct, harsh noise that foretold gloom to all those witnessing the scene and wise citizens quickly made a wide path and even avoided the group of German soldiers and policemen walking hurriedly forward down the street. Suddenly, their short pedestrian journey had ceased. Before them lay the innocent and soon to be infamous Berkendael Institute for Belgian Nurse trainees founded a scant six years earlier by the Depages and Edith Cavell. It was amazing that such an innocuous looking urban structure could harbour the dangerous denizens and devious acts for which the German authorities had presently come to formally admonish and destroy.

"You soldiers go around to the back alley of the Berkendael Institute and make sure that no one gets away and do not be fooled by any of the words or actions of the fairer sex – these ladies have been behaving such as men and they will be treated accordingly. You uniformed police officers will come with us into the front of the building and make sure that no mischief is done and that no one runs out of this building!" the senior ranking Lieutenant Bergan barked out to the soldiers as he snapped his fingers and pointed to the rear of the building.

"Unless you object, Lieutenant Bergan, my command of the French and English languages will best serve our purposes if I am allowed to address the nurses, especially Nurse Cavell and Nurse Wilkins, both of whom are English women and who speak and comprehend both French and their native tongues," Lieutenant Pinkhoff spoke in a phrase that was more in line of suggestion rather than direction to his technically senior ranking fellow officer. Bergan merely nodded without any hint of personal offence, as he was a practical if not very intelligent man; however, he knew sound advice when he heard it. Lieutenant Bergan waited a few minutes for the German soldiers to make their way around to the back alley of the building and then he initiated a forceful knock on the door with his strong right hand. There was no immediate response, so he repeated the action a second time with even more offensive hand pounding.

A pretty, young blonde haired nurse with azure pale blue eyes and dressed in a blue and white blouse nursing outfit complete with a carefully starched white nursing bonnet answered the door. "We are the German authorities and my name is Lieutenant Pinkhoff and this is Lieutenant Bergan and we are here to perform an official investigation. Take us at once to see Directress Cavell and make sure that no one leaves this building!" Pinkhoff loudly announced as he and the other German military police officers rushed past the startled young nurse trainee and into the foyer of the building.

"What is your name, my dear? My, you are a pretty one!" Pinkhoff remarked in perfect French to the young nurse as they all walked up the narrow second storey staircase toward Edith's private office.

"My name is Anne, Anne Shepardton. I am a nurse trainee for about the past eighteen months," she replied in an obvious nervous and rudimentary level of the French language – her English accent was most apparent to Pinkhoff's trained ears. Instantly Bergan and Pinkhoff looked and smiled silently to one another; they knew that this pretty young nurse was the one who had betrayed the de Croy network to the Agent Provocateur Gaston Quien several weeks previously. Anne began to feel ill; for some unknown reason she felt guilty, although it would be some time before she was able to face the truth that she had, through her hatred and immaturity, betrayed Edith and the network to her lover Gaston Quien over several all too brief love-making sessions some few weeks earlier. She knocked on Edith's office door and softly spoke through the door, "Madame Directress, there are some visitors to see you, they are German officials!".

Edith gazed up from her ledger books in which she kept steadfast and accurate accounts of the personnel status, expended funds, patient logs and material inventory of every thing and person within her establishment. Her pen slipped a fraction of an inch when she heard Anne speak the words 'German officials'. Instantly she knew that they had come for her, ever since Philippe's family's arrest a week earlier, she had known of this impending moment and it came with a thud to her heart. Never a woman to shrug from difficulty or inevitability she calmly spoke the words, "Come in please".

"I am Lieutenant Pinkhoff and this is my superior Lieutenant Bergan, we're here from the German military and police authorities and I think you know why we are here, Madame Cavell?" Pinkhoff entered Edith's office without removing his hat, as was the regulation for personnel bearing weapons.

Edith looked stoically and without any visual emotion of either fear or guilt. She arose from the desk chair before answering, "You should know better than I your own business and to what it involves."

Pinkhoff disliked evasion of any sort and he was having none of Edith's 'stiff upper lip', cool English detachment from his official inquiries.

"If you want to play it this way, Directress Cavell, you are welcome to be my guest. We arrested Philippe Baucq, his wife Marie, his daughters Yvonne and Madeleine and some family members too," Pinkhoff stated matter-of-factly, as he initially led off his conversation and hoping to break Edith's emotions with each stunning detail that he had uncovered. Edith knew that she could not lie about her actions, but that did not mean that she had to confess everything either. She decided to say as little information as possible to the Germans and provide minimal details.

"Yes, Lieutenant Pinkoff, we heard rumours to that effect and the Baucqs were acquaintances to us here at the Clinique. That is very sad news and we are all very distressed to hear about a Belgian family being arrested in such a manner," Cavell remarked in earnest, but mindful not to volunteer details needlessly.

"Yes thank you for that acknowledgment, Nurse Cavell, yet I am a bit perplexed that both he and his collaborator Mademoiselle Louise Thuliez, the widowed Lille schoolmistress and the architect Philippe Baucq made quite the odd pair …no? Not only an odd pair, but they had unusual hobbies…no? Stranger still is that these two strange birds meet up with another strange lady who operates a nurse training Clinique that has very few Belgian nurses to train since the war, yet your little establishment has a regular clientele of 'sick men', many of whom are young…no?" Pinkhoff accused with both mild sarcasm and the devilish smile of one who knew all of Edith's secrets. Pinkhoff like a clever cat had not yet tired of playing with his struggling victim, not yet anyway.

Pinkoff continued to relish in his accusations; he had waited many weeks for such a confrontation and he was not going to be denied. "Yes, yes those poor people, it seems as if they like to play at writing and publishing things, untrue things, nasty things about their German occupiers…did you know those two were the distributors of the Brussels underground newspaper La Libre Belgique? A most terrible affair, Madame, with those young children crying and screaming as they were being led off to the Police Headquarters. I think they are crying still in those terrible criminally infected prison cells at St Gilles!" Pinkhoff added with sadistic satisfaction as Edith's face turned-away for a moment, her face crumpled into immediate sorrow. She could not imagine those innocent children crying in that terrible prison. Pinkhoff knew he was wearing Edith down emotionally; she was going to confess either now or later, it mattered not to him.

"Oh we also came across some very disturbing information in Philippe's newspaper room and from Madame Thuliez's generously sized handbag – there were some odd things for an architect and schoolmistress to possess – things like maps, coded messages, names of strange men, coded address book, maps of Holland containing passage points and some information on German military matters. Why would a man and woman possess such information?" Pinkhoff inquired with a supreme command of the facts that he had uncovered from the raid at Baucqs' home.

"Why do you require any information from me? I have no idea about these things," Edith responded tersely without any further elaboration.

"Of course, Madame Cavell, you are just a Directress Nurse and an Englishwoman caught up in a war in a country not her own. I understand fully. You knew Dr and Mrs Depage, yes? So tragic her death on the Lusitania, but they were all warned. She and her husband both helped to establish this Clinique and they hand-picked you as Directress – this is quite a compliment for an English woman," Pinkhoff stated very declaratively.

"Yes, they were both my dear friends, I have made many dear friends in this fine country over the years," Edith replied as a matter of proud acknowledgment and not that of a guilty personage.

"Yes, yes, friends are the things of which we value and the means by which others judge us; it is like the old saying, 'show me your friends and I'll tell you what you are'!" Pinkhoff remarked shrewdly leading up to his summary point. "You are quite right, Directress Cavell, you have made a very interesting set of friends over the years, friends like the Depages, the Baucqs, Louise Thuliez, Georges Hostelet, Louis Severin, Herman Capiau, Ada Bodart, George Derveau, Countess Jeanne de Belleville and lastly the Prince and Princess de Croy. This is quite a lot of friends and all of them spies, traitors and saboteurs. You are one of them too, Directress Cavell!" Pinkhoff stated plainly in his verbal indictment.

Edith knew that the Lieutenant had just cleverly informed her that the entire de Croy network was known and compromised by the German intelligence service. She didn't want to betray anyone intentionally even at this point, so she said nothing in self-defence, as all of the de Croy network members had agreed to some months earlier.

"Ah I see, you are still playing the quiet mouse in this game, Madame Edith. Well, that's your privilege of course, but in time you shall speak; the evidence and confessions will do all the work for us! Now, one last question before we rip apart this place, do you have any Allied soldiers or young men at the Clinique currently?" Pinkhoff asked with a smile.

This time Edith replied without trepidation: "Sir, we have no English soldiers here, nor are there any young men. I welcome you to check out every room of this institute please!" Edith was able to speak with candour, since the last group of men had been sent out with the frontier guides about a week earlier and she had refused to accept any more Allied soldiers as her suspicions increased about being watched by the Germans.

"Very good, Madame Cavell and now I must inform you that both yourself and your Assistant Directress Nurse Wilkins are under arrest under the charge of recruiting Allied soldiers in the war against Germany and other charges will be forthcoming. These soldiers will escort you to your bedrooms and you will both pack only one bag of clothing and necessary personal items as you may need. Your detention is indefinite!" Pinkhoff concluded as Nurse Wilkins watched teary eyed at the opening of Edith's office door. Both women were each escorted by two armed, grey uniformed German military policemen to their bedrooms.

Pinkhoff briefed Bergan on his little talk with Edith Cavell that had been conducted in French and in short order both women appeared back with one suitcase each filled with clothing and other overnight and personal items. Off into the awaiting black cars they went and then down to the German Secret Police HQ Section 'B' at the rue de Berlaimont, Brussels. Official interrogations and transcripts in German were prepared and dutifully recorded on each person and for every interrogation session, which usually began with the simple and innocent determination of the specific name, occupation, address and other related personal data. The Germans knew exactly who the primary and secondary members of the de Croy network were and so Nurse Wilkins being unassociated with the network activities, was quietly released and driven back to the rue de la Culture later that night. For precautions, however, both Nurse Wilkins and the Clinique remained under 24-hour surveillance. However, Edith Cavell, like her fellow network conspirators, was going nowhere except to St Gilles prison cells to await further interrogation and formal charges, which had no set limit of time. The waiting could be days, weeks or even months and it was during these times that a captive was subject to mental stress, suicide and eventual emotional breakdowns.

The other mid-tier of de Croy network prisoners were carefully being arrested, interrogated and jailed over the course of the next two weeks. Some few fortunate souls, however, were more lucky, such as the Abbe de Longueville and two other Belgian missionary priests received the news of Philippe Baucq's arrest and they managed to escape to Holland, being just one step ahead of the German police. The other religious 'helpers' of the de Croy network managed to escape the attention of the German's secret police and the indictment of any of the jailed network members. The Germans had enough work with the existing number of culprits, the initial arrested number of persons, which was about one hundred in number, out of which the Germans would carefully distill down into a more manageable number for formal prosecution. Phase II was being drawn to a close and the Germans were about to close the loop with the initiation of Phase III – the royals.

* * * * * * * * * * *

"Marie! Marie! Come quick!" Reginald de Croy shouted as he ran into the main entrance of the Chateau Bellignies in a most uncharacteristic manner that was more becoming of a vegetable merchant hawking produce than a member of one of Belgium's royal families. He was flushed with sweat, his face was red and his pulse was racing like a second-hand movement on a fine Swiss chronograph watch. "What in heavens is the matter? What is it, brother?" Marie shouted back in equal alarm, as she too momentarily forgot her manners and instinctively surrendered to the emotions of the moment. She rushed down the grand, long marble staircase and braced both of her hands onto those of her brothers.

"What on earth is wrong, Reginald?" Marie cried out softly as she saw the clear emotional signs of worriment upon her brother's distraught face.

"They are caught! Arrested! It's all over!" Reginald confessed in a short phrase that instantly drew equal concern of his sister.

"You mean our network? My Lord have mercy on us! Who? How? When?" Marie slowly uttered with great emotion, yet her inquisitive mind sought for more details.

"I'm not really sure of the 'how', but I can tell you that all our couriers and the people in Mons are whispering the names of Cavell, Baucq, Thuliez, Capiau, Libiez and Derveau. The Brussels and Borinage cells are gone! It all happened a few days ago! I fear that we are next Marie!" Reginald confessed in an excited breath as he rushed toward the study for a drink to help calm his nerves. Even rumours took some time to travel from Brussels to Mons.

"What can we do? What are we going to do?" Marie agitatedly inquired as she too took a small glass of brandy.

For once the clever Prince was without an immediate or helpful answer. "I'm not sure! I think I should warn the others or maybe just stay here with you!" the Prince spouted off quickly.

"No, you must be mad, my brother! Please follow your own advice and the orders that you gave to our other network friends – flee and go quickly without any hesitation or regret! Don't stay here, Reggie, that would be suicide and the others still remaining free need to be warned, to include the guides!" the Princess courageously counselled back.

"I don't want to leave you here alone, Marie!" The Prince showed his brotherly concern.

"What is destined to happen will happen! I will be all right and I have to take care of grandmother Parnell. She's 85 years old and an invalid; I cannot leave her at Bellignies alone and she's too old for travel," Marie cried out desperately. "I'm a middle-aged spinster with an ailing grandmother; maybe the Germans will have sympathy on my plight given these circumstances. In any event, you must leave at once or the Germans will surely arrest you; in this case, having them only arresting one of us is best!" the Princess rationalized passionately, hoping to convince herself of the Germans having sympathy on her.

"All right then, I'll go then. I'll pack an overnight bag and then I'll be ready. Do you think that you can manage everything here?" Reginald asked with a worried concern on his face.

Marie smiled back and hugged her brother for what might be one of the last times that she was to see him. "My silly brother, who do you think has been running things every time you have been off to Holland and England?" Marie replied tearfully as she hugged her brother tightly in emotional desperation; she realized that she may never see her brother again. All of their lives were now in mortal danger.

"Wait, Reggie, I'll contact Sister Josephine. She can arrange for you to hide tonight in the nunnery and then, in the morning, she can guide you safely to the Mons rail station!" Marie suggested. Sister Josephine had been of great aid when the first Allied soldiers needed the de Croy's assistance and now Sister Josephine was only too willing to return the favour for her friends.

Within 30 minutes, Reggie had packed his simple belongings and gave his sister a peck on the cheek and a farewell bearish hug. It was much harder to leave all his worldly belongings behind than he had calculated, yet this same act was being demanded of so many others during the war that he thought himself the worse for even contemplating such materialistic sentiments. The convent was but a short distance from Bellignies and Sister Josephine was glad to have him stay with the sister community this evening; even the nuns had heard of the arrest in Brussels and they all feared for their religious colleagues, who had also been assisting Allied soldiers across Belgium, it was the traditional respect for religious habits and the backlash of the Belgian population that gave the German authorities any second thoughts on conducting mass raids of the Belgian religious institutions, especially the cloistered religious orders. Even the Germans exercised constrained decorum in certain instances.

Boarding the train from Mons to Brussels, Reginald dutifully left behind Bellignies, his stalwart sister Marie, his grandmother and everything else that was dear to him in this world. He had to flee immediately before his personal description was posted across Belgium. He knew not if he would ever return alive to his birthplace and if he did, what was to be left of his family and the Bellignies Chateau? Yet such concerns were most venial on his part; he had started this dangerous underground venture and he was obligated to closing it down the best he could. He was obliged to warn the other network members of the German compromise of the de Croy network. Surely, some of the lower ranking members and guides were still free, he thought hopefully to himself. He was not sure if this was a fool's mission in which all his efforts were to be woefully inadequate and too late or if he had the slightest chance of warning anyone who was not already being detained or under German surveillance. His one chance to make a difference lay with the improvised lodging keepers and warning them to go into hiding. Fortunately, there were no Allied soldiers or civilian young men who were presently in the network system for a border crossing.

Arriving in Brussels, Reginald was able to warn the widow Ada Bodart about the German arrests and she, in turn, went forth to the other safe-houses to warn the others of the German menace and it was at one of these safe houses that upon knocking on the door, she was greeted by a German policeman and promptly arrested. The German net was being pulled ever tighter on the remaining de Croy members at large. Reggie had to go into deep hiding; however, he contacted the reliable frontier guide of Henri Beyns in Brussels and he hid out there for about two weeks. While being housed at Beyns townhouse, contact was made through the catholic religious community and Sister Josephine was able to make a visit with Reginald. Countess Marie de Lichtervelde was contacted in turn, she was a trusted friend and she knew associates who could assist in crossing the Holland border.

With the aid of a pretty network adolescent girl to act as his witness and a diversion to the German officiating personnel, Reginald also had the foresight to have had prepared for both himself and his sister Marie fake identity cards with accompanying photographs some months ago for just such an eventuality. He now made use of this fake identification card on which he was using the alias of Rene Desmet. All the bridges at Waechter, a town 20 miles northeast of Brussels, had increased guard security, making a crossing of these conveyances most dangerous and prohibitive, so Reginald and Henri made their way instead over open fields until they came to the cottage of a friend of Henri Beyns.

The next day, their journey northward on foot resumed through the green and peaceful woods of Merodes near the infamous town of Waterloo and then onward further another several miles until they came to the Abbey of Tongerloo where welcome sanctuary was afforded by the friendly and quiet monks. When at all possible, travel was done from dusk to dawn to avoid German patrols and inquisitive Belgian eyes. Aside from the religious monks, temporary lodging was afforded by the poor local farmers, who shared the little food that they had with the two famished men. Nourishment consisted largely of potatoes, black bread and some chicory that served as a poor substitute for coffee. Their daily beds consisted of haystacks or dirt floors. This travel routine went on for five days, yet this was tolerable as the August weather was warm and welcoming to the human spirit. As they neared the dykes of northern Belgium that would lead Reggie into the safety of Holland, they met local border Belgium sympathizers, who initially searched the men for safety purposes, then hid them in a small hut for the night.

Beyns had been through this routine many times before and he was mindful to have brought along a long rope and a canvas waterproof bag for their clothes, and he also carried two packets of letters and military documents. If caught by the Germans with these items, Reggie and Henri could have been shot on the spot for being spies or smugglers. With night came the 200-yard swim across the canal to Holland and with it freedom for Prince de Croy. The men stripped down and carefully placed their clothes into the waterproofed canvas bag attached with the long rope to Henri's body; they would need warm clothes once they reached Holland. Both the Prince and Beyns were in excellent health and strong swimmers; the swim was no great feat for them. However, a searchlight constantly dashed periodically across the water looking for an activity as an excuse for the trigger happy and greatly bored German guards to fire off their weapons. After about thirty tense minutes, the two men reached the safety of the shore of Holland. They spotted some Dutch guards and raised their hands high as they also spoke of their identity as refugees from German occupied Belgium. The Dutch guards were most accommodating and they took the two men to a humble guard shack, where the two men were offered strong black coffee and cigarettes. They gladly relished the coffee as if it were fine champagne.

It had been over three weeks since the Prince de Croy had fled Brussels and September was only a few days away. The next day the Prince de Croy boarded a train and headed toward The Hague and the Allied High Command. Henri Beyns however returned back to Belgium in the same manner as he had originated, by swimming through the canals. Unbeknownst to the Prince, a few days previously Henri had discovered through one of his underground contacts that Countess Jeanne de Belleville and Princess Marie de Croy had been arrested by the Germans on 24 August, yet Henri dare not utter anything of this to Reggie for fear that the Prince would immediately return to surrender himself in a futile attempt to free his sister Marie. Henri knew that having the Prince surrender himself to the Germans would only result in two of the de Croys being in prison instead of only one. The Prince was going to find out soon enough that his sister had been arrested and he was better able to serve the Allies in his freedom rather than sitting behind bars and possibly to be executed.

\* \* \* \* \* \* \* \* \* \* \*

While her brother Reggie was making his stealthy way through northern Belgium toward Holland, Marie was undergoing her own trials and tribulations at the Bellignies Chateau. Captain von Kirchenheim had designed the three tier arrests with cunning and skill. He knew that the royal and aristocratic leaders within the network were the most prominent and stable personages among the lot of network members – consequently they could be taken up last. He therefore wisely waited until all of the low and middle operatives were identified and arrested before he made his move against them, yet in this waiting time the Prince had escaped and was nowhere to be found despite the best efforts of the German military intelligence and police staff. The Germans were hoping that the Prince would show up after he had heard of the arrest of Edith Cavell and Philippe Baucq, but such hopes were dashed. So they waited longer still in hopes that this 'royal pigeon' was going to fly his way back home to the Chateau Bellignies to escape with his beloved sister Marie, yet this did not happen either. The Germans could afford to wait no longer for the 'missing Prince' to reappear; although they wanted the ringleader of the de Croy underground movement, they would settle for his co-conspirator sister and the Countess Jeanne de Belleville.

"Excuse me, Madame, but there are some men here to see you – German soldiers," Florine the house-keeper remarked to Princess Marie de Croy as she and her 85 year old grandmother sat peacefully on grand sized white painted wicker lawn chairs perched upon the lush overgrown green garden grass that was located at the immediate rear exterior of the Bellignies chateau. The carefully sculptured shrubbery and prudently manicured lawns of the pre-war Bellignies estate had long since fallen into ruin as money, manpower and resources had been sapped by the direct effects of the war. All the other royal estates across Belgium had suffered the same fate, as more urgent concerns of food shortages and survival took immediate precedence in everyone's lives.

"Please show them in and bring them here. I think I know what the reason is behind their visit." Marie spoke with a monotone voice. Wild thoughts began to race through the Princess's mind, yet from the conversations that she had had with her brother Reggie several weeks earlier, she knew that both fleeing and lying were not options in this deck of cards – she had to see the German game through despite the inevitable outcome.

"Good day, your Highness Princess Marie de Croy! My name is Captain Hans von Kirchenheim of the German Army, Special Operations section. I hope that I am not disturbing you, Madame!" the almost debonair Prussian announced as he stood at almost parade standing erection in front of the two women. The old grandmother was diminished in both her visual and auditory acuity, making this meeting a most one-on-one affair and perhaps this was for the better so as to spare the constitution of the aged woman who had seen so much of life thus far.

"Excuse me for being so blunt, but I'd like to inquire about your brother, Prince Reginald de Croy. Is he here or do you happen to know of his whereabouts, Princess?' von Kirchenheim noted in a dry serious voice. The Princess, however, was not to be denied the formality of either her position or manners by this arrogant Prussian officer.

"Oh please forgive my manners, my dear Captain, but my grandmother and I are going to have some tea. Would you care to please sit down and have some refreshments and then discuss this matter further?" Marie softly offered the German officer mockingly, but the most proper deference that was expected of a proper hostess even to the most vulgar of guests.

"I'm afraid that I do not have time for tea or any such refined 'niceties', Madame Princess and neither do you!" von Kirchenheim interjected with an obvious bitterness in his reply. He was an aristocrat too, but he was also a Prussian soldier on German state business and he was not going to be deflected in his duty by mere social protocols. "Now I ask you again, Princess, where is your brother?" he demanded in a harsher more indignant tone.

Marie arose from her lawn chair; she knew that the officer wanted answers, not social subterfuge. "I'm afraid that in all honesty, my dear Captain, I cannot say with any definitiveness exactly where my dear brother is presently; he travels a great deal. You see, he was a diplomat in London until just before the war and he's busy working with the Americans to try and get food through the War Relief effort to the starving Belgian civilians," Marie announced with a defiant tone of truth and satisfaction in her reply.

"I see all too well, Princess! Do not toy around with me, dear Princess, we Germans know exactly who your brother is and what nasty little actions your brother has been doing and we also know that you and your confederates are in league with him! Please tell me where he is now!" von Kirchenheim replied, this time with even greater anger in his voice. The Princess refused to answer the arrogant Captain's demands.

"Guards, search the estate at once, top-to-bottom, especially the personal rooms of the Prince and Princess. I am sure that we can find something of incriminating evidence there!" von Kirchenheim shouted out to the pack of over a dozen German soldiers accompanying him.

"What in heavens do you hope to find at Bellignies, dear Captain? Your German raiding parties over the past several months have stripped the estate and the countryside bare – there's nothing to be found!" Marie declared in a self-righteous indicting statement.

"Be quiet, Princess! Let us Germans be the judges of what is of value and that which is not! I suggest we all go inside and await the fruits of the soldiers' search of the Chateau premises," von Kirchenheim directed as the two women walked ever so slowly under the careful eyes of Captain von Kirchenheim and several other German soldiers armed with their long Mauser 98 Gewehr rifles replete with fixed eighteen inch long bayonets as if the soldiers needed to be attired for battle with Allied soldiers, instead of merely escorting two helpless Belgian women. The minutes passed ever so slowly.

"Captain look here, we found a camera, many photographs of young men, some blank identification cards and letters written to English families," an excited German military sergeant announced anxiously as he ran from atop the grand stairway and handed the items to the none too surprised German officer.

"Good work, sergeant, continue with your search! We will take these items into evidence. One can never tell what gems one will find in a search!" the Captain announced as the sergeant smartly saluted him and ran back upstairs to the other rooms of the chateau. "Well Princess do you have anything to say? Do you want to make an admission or full confession?" von Kirchenheim noted with a smug attitude in his voice.

"No I do not! These things prove nothing, my dear Captain! Photography is my hobby. It is not against the law to possess a camera and I have no idea about any sort of identity cards either. Neither my brother nor I are guilty of anything and that is all that I am going to confess to you!" Marie blurted out angrily in obvious defiance.

"What other things are your hobbies Princess? Spying? Treason? Sabotage? You silly, foolish, proud woman! You meddle in the affairs of men and war – both you and your friends will suffer accordingly. You are under arrest for espionage, treason and assisting the enemy. As for your obvious cowardly brother, who has apparently run away rather than be a man and allow women to take the blame, he will have a reward of 20,000 German marks placed on his head – dead or alive!" the Captain shouted out in one of his rare moments of visible anger. "Oh, my dear Princess, we have also just arrested your aristocratic friend Countess Jeanne de Belleville of Lille and Dr Bull this very morning, so you might have some high company in jail. Take her away to the automobile!" von Kirchenheim shouted to a pair of waiting German soldiers.

"You can't do this! I am the Princess de Croy! Who will take care of my aged grandmother?" Marie cried out as the guards immediately took her forcefully by the arms out to a waiting vehicle.

"Well Princess, you should have thought about the consequences of your actions before you began this stupid amateurish enterprise! Your grandmother will have to fend for herself!" Captain von Kirchenheim shouted back with a mocking self-righteous tone.

"Florine, Florine! Please get help from my friends the Countess Marie de

Lichtervelde and Baron de la Grange, tell them to take care of grandmother!" Marie screamed out to her loyal housekeeper as she was forcibly rushed from the chateau and into an awaiting black sedan.

Out of deference to her royal status, Princess de Croy was not taken to St Gilles prison in Brussels; instead she was taken to the Kommandantur, the residence of German military officers who were stationed in Brussels. There she was lodged in a modest small room with a private toilet and sitting area. For interrogations, however, she was transported to either the German Police HQ 'Section B' or St Gilles prison. Except for the Prince de Croy, the Germans had completed Phase III of their surveillance and arrest strategy and it had proved most successful.

The de Croy network had been operationally neutered from assisting any additional trapped Allied soldiers and young men escaping forth to Holland, but the arrests had also stopped the possibility of any additional German military information from reaching the Allies from any de Croy network operatives. Instantly the British War Office and The Hague had been curtailed of any additional information. The Germans now needed to make a public spectacle of these traitors, both for the sake of German justice, but also as an example to other foolish Belgians and more importantly, to the other Allied underground cells that were operating in both northern France and Belgium.

\* \* \* \* \* \* \* \* \* \* \* \*

# Chapter 9:
# Judgment in Brussels

*"Some of these accused must die! Germany cannot afford to be seen as weak or faltering, we have thousands of young German troops dying every day in France and Russia! Can the lives of nine civilians really matter so much in a world where tens of thousands are dying daily?"*

The primary and lesser players in the de Croy underground network, save for the Prince Reginald de Croy, the Abbe de Longueville and the frontier guides of Victor Gille and Henri Beyns, and a few others, were all now trapped by the wide net woven by the thorough Germans. The peripheral observers, like Nurse Wilkins, Baron de la Grange, Countess Marie de Lichtervelde and Sisters Josephine, Marie and Madeline from the Catholic convent at Witheries, had all escaped in-depth scrutiny and arrest. Nurse Wilkins was released only a few hours after her arrest and initial questioning by Lt Bergan and Lt Pinkhoff; she knew little of the de Croy network activities and the Germans released her to pursue Edith Cavell in greater depth. The Berlin bureaucracy and the German General Staff were ecstatic with Captain Hans von Kirchenheim's success. The Germans knew that anyone could be arrested; however, getting confessions and conducting a successful trial was quite another matter and they wanted an iron-tight case; the facts and confessions needed to be absolutely clear and concise to defer any post-trial arguments or appeals lodged by other countries.

Over 100 people were initially arrested in the de Croy network. This included farmers, merchants, seamstresses, market women, miners – anyone who could possess one piece of innocent observed fact to the network puzzle. Fear, threats and arrests were the main weapons and these tactics worked. Innocent mothers with young children were often placed into the prison cells, this to deliberately incite fear among the inmates, who grew fearful of howling women and crying babies; the innocent women and babies were released after a few hours' confinement. The added benefit was that the mothers also spread fear and stories among their friends and relatives – further increasing the effectiveness of the police through fear and obedient compliant behaviour. Fear was a policeman's best friend.

The trial, like the arrests, was to be conducted in secret, this to avoid external interference and possible delays. The Germans, like a neurotic movie director, wanted to control all aspects of this trial. The prisoners waited as all jailed men and women do – they waited in Spartan conditions and suffered mental despair in their cells, never knowing when the German officials were going to call on them. Some prisoners, like Edith Cavell and the Countess Jeanne de Belleville, were maintained in isolation in order to restrict their conversations and avoid a collusion of stories, while others like Baucq, Capiau, Bodart and Hostelet on occasions shared their cells with other prisoners and sometimes even German planted agent provocateurs. The interrogations were performed at either the Section 'B' at the German military secret police station or in a private room at the St Gilles prison. Along with the deliberating effects of being in a prison and deprived of all normal freedoms, the time-proven interrogation technique of the 'good cop/ bad cop' was employed to psychologically confuse the captive and produce a mental breakdown and complete confession and the process worked more than it failed. The prisoners never knew if the information that the police interrogators were releasing to them were outright lies, the truth or merely hunches.

"Your name, Monsieur, is Philippe Baucq, a citizen of Brussels, Belgium?" Lieutenant Bergan inquired through a French interpreter, as Lieutenant Pinkhoff sat observantly from a chair at the far end of the wooden table.

"Yes, I am Philippe Baucq," the dishevelled, unshaven man replied as he looked blankly at the grim grey painted wall before him. It was obvious that he had slept little.

"You live at No. 49 Avenue de Rodebeek, Brussels, correct?" came the next question posed by Bergan.

"Yes, I live there, that is, I used to live there," he replied in obvious acknowledgment of his present fate.

"You have a wife named Marie and two daughters named Yvonne age 13 and Madeleine age 9. They all also reside at No. 49 Avenue de Rodebeek, correct?" Bergan continued his inquiry.

"Yes, thank God for that and for releasing them too!" Philippe's relief of hearing his family's fate after they had been arrested with him that terrible night was obvious.

"Oh you thank the kindness of God before that of the German military and police for that decision, Baucq! I do not think you realize in whose hands your fate resides and it is not God! Now as to your profession, you are an architect, correct?' Bergan inquired mundanely, as Pinkhoff stared off in obvious frustration at the same questioning that had been going on for days now and without a confession.

"Yes, I am, or at least I was an architect and an under-employed architect at that, ever since the Germans invaded my country!" Philippe replied back with a faint, defiant smile.

"Just what the hell do you mean by that remark, you little Belgian traitorous bastard!" Bergan yelled out in German as he rose and lost his small level of self-control. Philippe knew enough German to understand Bergan's outburst.

"I mean that you bastard Boche are masters of destruction, but you cannot create anything constructive or beautiful! Building will come again after this wretched war's over!" Philippe elaborated in a manner that ostracized him from the pleasure of his captors. Baucq knew that it mattered not if he was either kind or rude to his German jailers – they were going to treat him as they damn well pleased and they were also going to find him guilty too. Pinkhoff rose as well and went over to reassure his partner to better control his emotions in front of a prisoner. Philippe began to exercise his speech in a totally unexpected manner that did not serve the purpose of the Germans. The two officers needed to regain control of the interrogation from the prisoner.

"Now about your friends and associates, Monsieur. Do you know Directress Edith Cavell, the Prince and Princess de Croy?" Bergan inquired, yet only silence met his inquiry. "Then do you know the Countess Jeanne de Belleville of Lille, Herman Capiau, George Hostelet, Albert Libiez, Louis Severin, Maurice Derveau, Maurice Pansaers and Oscar Mathieu?"

"I know a lot of people in Brussels, Lieutenant! I've met all those people you mentioned. The fact that I know those people proves nothing; in fact, Maurice Pansaers and Oscar Mathieu are just café owners – even the Germans cannot be so naive to think that every café and shop owner in Brussels is their enemy!" Baucq countered back with sarcastic contempt of his captors. He was determined to deny his interrogators any satisfaction of success.

"We Germans are not fools, nor do we think that you are either, Monsieur Baucq, yet you keep unusual friends and one judges a man or woman by the company that they keep. One will seldom see an honest man make friendship with a thief or liar," Captain Joel added in a rare act of interrogation injection.

"Then am I judged guilty already?" Philippe sounded forth in a hostile verbal banter.

The Germans were not amused by his outburst and the questioning continued. "We ask the questions here! We do not answer the questions placed by an arrogant prisoner!" Lieutenant Bergan angrily snapped back.

"What was Mlle Louise Thuliez doing in your house the night of 31 July? What was she doing in that café past curfew? Who was she waiting for? What items was she carrying in that large handbag?" Captain Joel again interrupted for a second time.

"Mlle Thuliez is a friend and a school mistress; she was helping my daughters with their studies!" Philippe replied with an obvious rather flippant lie.

Lieutenant Bergan continued his interrogation. "When we raided your home, we found that you were engaged in some non-architecture duties, like underground newspaper distribution. Tell us now who is the author of La Libre Belgique? Where is that lying rag of a newspaper being printed?" Bergan demanded through the interpreter as he pounded the sturdy plain oak table.

Philippe did not respond to Bergan's frustration. Philippe merely sat in his chair and smiled without saying a word. No one, especially the stern, proud Germans, liked to be made a fool of and this was Baucq's intention.

"Very well, you can play the Belgian mime, you are still guilty and we both know it!" Bergan shouted as he read off another charge against Philippe.

"There was also found in your house letters from English soldiers to their relatives in England. Can you explain your courier system to transmit these correspondences?" Bergan barked out angrily like a junkyard dog. Philippe simply shrugged his shoulders and rendered a disgusted look, but no verbal response. Bergan desperately wanted to smack the insolence off Baucq's tongue, yet he restrained his anger. This was a man who could not be beaten into making a confession.

"We discovered ciphers, coded address books maps to Holland and detailed information on German munitions sites, railway coordinates and staging points! These are not the mere items of an escape network, these are the things of espionage, spies, saboteurs and traitors!" Bergan yelled out in his most boisterous voice of the interrogation session.

"Now you wait there just one moment, Lieutenant. I am a Belgian patriot, I am no spy or saboteur; you cops and the Germans are just too lazy or stupid to locate any real saboteurs of German assets and Zeppelin aerodromes! I am guilty for only one thing: publishing a torrid little harmless pamphlet and a newspaper, that's all!" Philippe spat back furiously.

"Well now, Philippe, you sing well like a canary when you are angry, such is the outrage of a passionate man! Now where in the course of any of our questioning was there any mention pronounced about German Zeppelins or aerodromes? What do you know about these things if you are only an innocent under-employed architect, huh?" Monsieur Henri Pinkhoff smilingly toyed as he implicated Philippe into another unsubstantiated charge.

"I admit nothing about these things! We Belgians are not stupid! We hear news all the time through word-of-mouth despite your German censorship rules. Everyone in Brussels including the blind men on the street corners knew about those Zeppelin aerodrome sheds being bombed – you could see and smell the fires from the explosions many miles away! You German police make up whatever fiction and charges that suit your ends. Everyone in Brussels knows about these German activities; these are not secrets in themselves. Go fishing elsewhere for more grandiose charges, you will not find any more satisfaction from me. Good day, Monsieur Henri, I am done talking to you," Philippe disgustingly remarked as he threw his arm over his eyes and attempted to get some sleep.

The short interrogation was interrupted by a firm loud knock on the interrogation room door. It was Captain von Kirchenheim. He had come down from his fourth storey office to observe the progress of the questioning of one of the prime de Croy network agents and he was not pleased. He saw and heard Lieutenant Bergan's outburst from the recess of a small observation door portal and he knew that Lieutenant Bergan possessed neither the talent nor personality to break this proud Belgian patriot. Another point of leverage needed to be applied and he knew just the technique to break this proud, stubborn man. He snapped his fingers and pointed to both of the Lieutenants and Captain Joel. All three men came out from the interrogation room along with the interpreter. A German private soldier quickly entered the room and acted as a guard over Baucq to ensure that he did not try to escape or injure himself.

"What in the hell is going on in there? I see you are making absolutely no progress whatsoever with this intelligent, proud and obviously very stubborn man. It has been three weeks since his arrest and we need confessions to take with us to the trial. He talks rubbish and says nothing of importance. I want to take direct charge of breaking this man down!" von Kirchenheim announced as the two Lieutenants and Captain Joel silently acquiesced to the desires of their superior officer. The four military men and the interpreter entered the hot, stuffy room to resume the interrogation of Philippe.

"Well, good day Monsieur Baucq. You are quite an interesting fellow around our Police Headquarters and at St Gilles prison as well. You and Miss Cavell are celebrities among the other prisoners too. I understand that you have been our guest for over three weeks and still you do not have the good sense to make a confession. Do you not know that we know everything anyway?" von Kirchenheim politely pointed out to the downtrodden Baucq, whose red eyes and drooping eyelids betrayed a severe lack of sleep. "Under German law, we can keep you for months or even years without making formal charges and conduct a trial, so your defiance is quite without merit or purpose," von Kirchenheim added to remind the prisoner of his hopeless situation.

"Well then, what in the hell am I doing here being interrogated for all this time? You Germans can just go ahead and prove your case to the judges without my cooperation or confession! You will not get me to cooperate and self-convict myself, nor any of my friends!" Philippe shouted in loud defiance.

"Now, Mr Baucq, the case and evidence against you are strong, no? Your network associates are also implicated in serious crimes against the state of Germany, people like the Prince de Croy, Princess de Croy, Nurse Head Mistress Cavell, Mlle Louise Thuliez and all the others. Even as we speak, your friends are making their confessions and these implicate you and very deeply so, I am afraid to say, Philippe! Do not make a fool of yourself before the German Court, and confess and make things easier on yourself! You will get a much more lenient sentence!" von Kirchenheim lied with a convincing smile. He possessed no power or input into a Military Court's decisions or sentencing.

"So if the others have talked, you do not need my cooperation, now do you?" Philippe retorted with defiant satisfaction toward the arrogant velvet tongued Captain von Kirchenheim.

"No, no, no, Monsieur Baucq, you confess not for us Germans – you do it for yourself, for your own sake and so that justice may be fully served!" von Kirchenheim replied as he was about to play his trump card in this simple interrogation.

"Your defiance is both admirable and very foolish! Very well, Monsieur, naturally you do not have to talk! We Germans are not barbarians and we do not use torture to extract confessions from our prisoners! Yet I need to make you aware that my superiors in Berlin have chided me on my lack of efficiency in this whole ugly affair. It seems that I was remiss in not bringing into confinement all of the suspected guilty parties in this network, so I have the privilege and duty to inform you that in a few hours, we will be re-arresting your wife and two daughters! Yes, after all they were all found at your apartment assisting in preparing copies of the underground newspaper La Libre Belgique! Your family was actively preparing copies for distribution of that traitorous newspaper and other subversive pamphlets, so they are guilty along with you. We simply cannot leave the wife and young girls alone as street orphans, so to St Gilles they will be brought, rest assured Monsieur Baucq. Then they will be placed on trial along with you and subject to harsh court interrogations. If they are lucky enough to escape a prison sentence, their torments will not be over either. They will be unemployable. Oh and I must also add that since your home was the location of deliberate and blatant anti-German underground activity, it will be confiscated and closed-up, leaving your family as street peddlers – that is, if they ever get out of St Gilles. Your girls may even be placed into German custodial care and who knows with what type of lecherous family they will be quartered?" Captain von Kirchenheim announced confidently as the grinning Lt Pinkoff and Lt Bergan looked on with great admiration. Captain Joel remained silent and observant as usual.

Philippe could not believe his ears and his heart sunk like a lead weight! His wife and children were to be brought to the hideous and filthy St Gilles prison, to rot in filthy cells with faeces and rats and all sorts of perverted criminal types! Philippe was going to do anything to avoid this. The Germans had indeed pressed the right button on Philippe Baucq. "You can't do that, you bastards cannot do that to my innocent wife and children. You dirty German bastards!" he cried out as Lt Pinkhoff threw Philippe forcibly back down onto his hard wooden cot.

"No, no, Monsieur Baucq, it is your insolence and silence that have brought your wife and children to this dilemma; your rebellious actions against the state helped bring them here! You do understand, don't you?" Captain von Kirchenheim replied in a velvet soft rational monotone voice.

"They are innocent and I will not betray any of my friends," Baucq sobbed bitterly.

"Yes, of course, Monsieur Baucq, you are a brave and loyal Belgian. If the entire nation were made of the same fabric such as you, we Germans would not be standing here now and occupying Belgium. Now be smart and save your wife and child. Please confess your deeds to us!" Captain von Kirchenheim implored of the emotionally distraught father. When faced between patriotism and family, most captives chose their family's welfare first. Philippe Baucq was true to his word, he implicated none of his friends and no one in the network and he took full blame and responsibility for everything that had happened in the Brussels network cell.

Within a few hours, he had verbally confessed his underground newspaper distribution and helping Allied soldiers to flee Belgium and on into Holland, yet he hesitated to sign a confession that implicated anyone else and he did not read German in which all confessions were annotated. He stubbornly held off signing a full confession, but the Germans were allowed to make statements on their own behalf relating to all that Philippe Baucq had told them verbally. Although Baucq refused to sign anything, his oral confession was enough for the German interrogators for now; Baucq's words had just damned him! If anyone was to suffer, Philippe wanted it to only be himself, he had been caught dead cold with the insurrection newspaper processing centre in his apartment – it was utterly useless to lie any further, he surmised. With one verbal confession completed, the Germans now proceeded to arrange the other confessions.

\* \* \* \* \* \* \* \* \* \* \* \*

"Welcome, Princess de Croy, to our humble offices. We hope that your stay at the Kommandantur has been satisfactory, although we know that any accommodations provided will be far below those to which you are used to at Bellignies Chateau," Captain Joel noted in polite deference to his royal prisoner.

"I'd rather be at my home, dear Captain and may I ask when I shall be there again? I have an eighty-five year old English grandmother; she needs my attention and I am most worried about her!" The concern in Princess de Croy's voice for the plight of her grandmother Mrs Parnell was self-evident.

"Well I'm afraid that desire cannot be entertained presently. You see, both you and your most absent brother Reginald are complicit in leading an underground and subversive anti-German network your Highness!" Captain Joel calmly explained.

"You must be mad. My brother and I are of royal Belgian blood. Where is your proof? What means do we possess to do this? Why would we become involved in such an enterprise?" Marie demanded in rapid succession of the confrontational questions being directed at her person.

Captain Joel looked at his interrogation companion, Lieutenant Pinkhoff, who, unlike Lieutenant Bergan, was fluent in French and English. The Princess refused to answer any questions in German, even though she was fluent in the language; she was not going to give her German captors the benefit of interrogating her in their native tongue.

"We regret to inform you, Princess de Croy, that there are two main pillars of proofs against you: first, there is sufficient evidence from the raids on the residences of Edith Cavell, Philippe Baucq, Herman Capiau and the other network agents that clearly conspire to point a guilty finger at you and your brother; second, we have the sworn confessions of many of your network agents stating that you and your brother are the ringleaders of this anti-German network," Captain Joel replied without answering all of the Princesses specific questions.

"I denounce both of your assertions and I will not be swayed by any of your flippant lies!" Marie vehemently voiced back with anger.

"Facts do not lie, Madame and I think that your friends do not lie either. It will be better for you in your trial if you confess; this will make for an easier sentencing, as the court will look more favourably on an accused person who cooperates with German officials," Lieutenant Pinkhoff added as a means of 'good cop' persuasion.

The Princess was stubborn and wise, so she was having none of the Germans sweet-talking.

"Where is your brother, Princess and who were his contacts in The Hague and in London? How often did he travel overseas in the past year? What instructions did the British War Office give to you? How were communications managed?" Joel and Pinkhoff each asked in rapid machine-gun-like fashion. The Germans wanted the Princess to realize that they knew the details of the de Croy network liaisons with foreign entities and that lying was futile.

However, the Princess refused to be swayed by the intimidating vocal demands of the two imposing men. She was indeed a brave and strong willed woman just like Edith Cavell.

"Please try to understand that I do not know where my brother is presently, nor did I know of his comings and goings. He is a mature man who does as he wishes without notification to myself or anyone else. I know of no contacts or orders from the British or anyone else for that matter. I love my brother dearly and I will do nothing to betray him, even if it means my own life. Now gentlemen, what about arranging an escort pass for me to visit my aged grandmother?" Marie de Croy replied with grit and resolution.

The Germans were impressed by her spirit, but not by her defiance and lack of cooperation.

"Well, Madame, we do not usually grant 'favours' to uncooperative captives, but we shall ask our superior about your visit request. We Germans are humanitarians after all," Captain Joel replied in smug self-assurance.

"Your brother has a price on his head, Princess – 20,000 German marks and that's for being either dead or alive! How does that make you feel, Princess? Better that he give himself up and face a trial – at least he would have a chance!" Captain Joel remarked in hopes of persuading the Princess to reveal her brother's whereabouts.

"I think that you both underestimate and under-value my brother; a Belgian Prince is worth at least three times your German bounty on his head and you'll never collect it! He is too clever for any of you! Besides, I told both of you previously that I do not know anything of my brother's location and if I did, gentlemen, I am his sister and my loyalty runs with my bloodline, not the betrayal of a Judas! Given his chances in a German trial, I'd say my brother has a much better chance running the frontiers with all its machine guns and guards than facing a packed panel of German judges!" Marie responded back with a defiant candour that stunned the German officers. It was rare that anyone, especially a woman, stood up to them during an interrogation like this.

"So you will not make a confession, Princess de Croy?" Lieutenant Pinkhoff added in a vain quest hoping for some level of achievement with this stubborn prisoner.

"Absolutely not, gentlemen! You'll have to prosecute me with what you possess, as feeble as that may be!" the Princess snapped back.

The Germans knew that this stubborn woman was not going to be swayed by any of their threats or cloaked promises. "Guard, take this prisoner downstairs into the vehicle and have her transported back to her room at the Kommandantur barracks!" Captain Joel shouted as the conference door opened and two German privates appeared and escorted the Princess downstairs. No further words or social niceties were exchanged; this woman was not talking anytime soon, if at all. The next time they were going to see the Princess de Croy was at her trial.

"That's one tough, proud lady! I bet she rarely loses an argument!" Lieutenant Pinkhoff remarked in frustration. It had been a hot, fruitless interrogation and they had nothing to show for it.

"Yes, she is a royal and she's a stubborn woman too! Is it any wonder that she is forty years old and has been unable to find a suitable husband among the royals in Europe! I bet no one will have her!" Captain Joel noted with both bitterness and a laugh that was shared with Lieutenant Pinkhoff. They knew that they could compensate for the lack of any confession by the

Princess with another one made by another prominent prisoner, Directress Edith Cavell.

Unbeknownst to the Princess, while she was being kept in detention, a German raiding party had once again made a foraging raid on the Chateau Bellignies. This time, there were no de Croys or family friends there to stop them and they requisitioned the last of the Chateau's wine and champagne from the wine cellar. The soldiers also ransacked the house and in the melee, the nervous grandmother happened to slip and fall down the grand stairway, where she lay collapsed on the floor unaided by the marauding Germans. They callously left the old lady where she had fallen at the bottom of the grand staircase. Florine, the lone remaining housekeeper, was away for a few days and upon her return she called two doctors from Bavay; however, despite their best efforts the old lady died a few days later without having uttered another word. Later, just before the start of her trial, the Princess learned of this personal tragedy from a visit made by her appointed legal counsel, Mr Braun. The Princess was devastated by the news and went into a period of depression. It seemed that indeed the Iron Princess had a chink in her high moral armour: her family. If her grandmother had lived, the Germans surely would have exploited this weakness. She was now alone and quite independent in the world and perhaps this was best for the time being.

\* \* \* \* \* \* \* \* \* \* \* \*

Directress Nurse Edith Cavell, being an Englishwoman, was represented through the auspices of the US Legation located in Brussels with the Minister or Head Consulate being that of Mr Brand Whitlock. While the US Legation was informed of Edith's arrest a few days after the fact, the Americans had only received official word back through the Brussels German Political Minister Baron Oscar von der Lancken, that Edith had indeed been arrested by the German military police for unspecified and unpublished charges. The arrest was a concern, but it was not unusual either – the US Consulate had dealt with many similar type situations and these had ended with the prisoner either being released or deported. The US Consulate First Secretary, Mr Hugh Gibson, tried to arrange a personal visit and legal representation from a Belgian lawyer named Mr Guy de Lavel, who was on a contract retainer to represent US interests and those of the US Consulate in Brussels.

The Germans responded to the US offers of inquiry and legal representation with utter silence and this was not at all unusual for the

Germans. The US Consulate periodically continued to make 'good faith' efforts on Edith's behalf; however, until a trial was announced there was little they could do. It was not unusual for captives to sit for many weeks or even months in jail or prison until a trial was conducted and this was at the pleasure of the German military. If a trial suited their purposes, it was conducted rapidly and efficiently; conversely if it aided their purpose to delay any formal charges or a trial, then this course was pursued. In a case such as the de Croy espionage network, delay and uncertainty served the Germans quite well, as people tended to forget the euphoria and sensationalism of an event just a few weeks after its occurrence. For the time being, Edith Cavell was on her own and at the mercy of the cunning, lying German military police. There was no inherent right to legal representation prior to a trial under existing German military law and if an individual was not savvy like Princess de Croy, the Germans were able to bring pressure for confessions most easily from the prisoners. The interrogations of Edith Cavell continued until the Germans had obtained their information.

"Well, Directress Nurse Cavell, you have quite the reputation according to the tales of your many network friends; they all say such nice and flattering things about you." Lt Pinkhoff led off his questioning with a lying, flowery compliment that he hoped was going to loosen up her lips into the desired confession. He walked about the small, hot interrogation room at St Gilles prison, while Edith sat at a plain oak table dressed in the constricting and layered clothing of the day, while Lt Bergan, Captain Joel and a German private recorder sat in chairs aligned against a far wall of the dimly lit room.

"I cannot comment on the words of others which are said about me, I can only speak for myself and my own actions. As for my character, I am a simple, patriotic English nurse and Directress of the Berkendael Institute for the education of Belgian nurses," Edith stated in a clear, concise, medium-toned elegant tone in perfect French.

"Oh I think you are being too modest, Madame Cavell. You are not ordinary in any sense of the word. Let me see if I can summarize your life: unmarried, no friends male or female, forty-nine years old, a distinguished career in England and Belgium as both a governess and nurse, daughter of a Anglican Vicar, close friends with Dr and Mrs Depage, noted beneficiary of the Prince and Princess de Croy and finally a member of an underground network that repatriates Allied soldiers to fight against the Imperial German Army," Captain Joel quickly summarized Edith's life in one short sentence.

Edith refused to reply to the verbal indignity with any sort of a response as she stoically sat upright on the hard wooden chair furnished to her.

"So why did you not return back to England, your home country, when the war began and when Belgium became occupied? Did you not know of the German directive for citizens of nations at war with Germany to be repatriated to their nation of origin?" Lt Pinkhoff inquired with a tone of genuine curiosity in his voice.

This was a question that Edith wanted to answer desperately, as it defined her character and motives.

"Yes I could have easily left Brussels; the opportunity was there for me to leave. But as Directress of my nursing Clinique, I had the responsibility to stay and operate the Berkendael Institute, especially in time of war; there were many German and Allied soldiers to help. Leaving Belgium would have been so terribly easy for me to do, but staying was the real challenge. As medical staff left to help in the war, there were fewer and fewer nurses to assist those Belgian citizens left behind. The Depages were increasingly involved with other war activities and so, by default, they left me in charge of the institute or as I refer to it as my Clinique," Edith responded with reserved contentment.

"Yes, the Depages are very patriotic Belgians and very anti-German I may add. When Dr Depage went off to help the Allied medical efforts and Marie Depage was raising war funds in America, both you and the de Croys decided to become enemies of Germany, is all of this not true, Madame?" Lt Pinkhoff stated in a monotone voice.

Edith again decided to remain silent.

"About your Clinique, Nurse Cavell: who else among the nurses were involved in helping with assisting Allied soldiers escape to Holland?" Captain Joel calmly inquired, He knew that the Berkendael Institute was most close to Edith's heart; it was her passion in life.

"No one! There was absolutely no one else involved except myself! I deliberately kept all of my staff ignorant of my affairs and actions, if there is anyone to blame, it is I alone," Edith bravely replied.

The Germans were not distracted by or believing of this response – it clearly contradicted all of the facts to date.

"That is very commendable, Nurse Cavell, you're a brave lady, but you had to have some help and accomplices. Please tell us who else you were in league with in this de Croy network?' Lt Pinkhoff cajoled with an empathetic inflection in his voice.

"I told you, I had no accomplices, I did this all alone – no one else helped me!" Edith deflected back to the ears of this most unsympathetic audience.

"Do you know the persons called Martin and Fromage?" Captain Joel announced with a smiling sneer.

"No, I never heard of those people," Edith responded resoundingly.

"Bring them in!" Captain Joel shouted as a guard opened the door and prisoners Philippe Baucq and Louise Thuliez were brought into the doorsill of the room. They both looked pathetically demoralized and physically dejected. Their eyes were bloodshot and they looked as if they had not slept soundly in many days. "Now take them away!" Captain Joel shouted, as the two prisoners were quickly ejected from the room without having uttered a single word, yet no words were necessary. Edith's face was filled with horror and shame. It was obvious to everyone that she knew the prisoners and they knew her. She knew that the Germans had cracked her friends.

"Yes Edith, Philippe Baucq is 'Fromage' and Louise Thuliez is 'Mlle Martin'! Now do normal people go about using code names? Do they publish underground newspapers like La Libre Belgique? Do they use cipher books and codes to mask information on German munitions trains and depots? Do everyday Belgians assist in operating a network cell that repatriates Allied soldiers back to their homelands?" Captain Joel sparked out rhetorically in quick succession. Again Edith sat quietly and looked straight ahead at the wall saying not one word.

"I compliment you, Nurse Edith, you played a good game, but it is all over, Edith! They have talked! Others have talked! We know everything. Take a burden off your shoulders and make it right with your soul, confess! You will only look foolish in court if you say nothing! Any sentence you receive will be much easier with a signed confession – you may even be given an expedited deportation order to go back to England and do good for your own country!" Lt Pinkhoff argued very persuasively to the distraught English Iron Matron.

"You have all the answers, do you not? Well I suppose if you know of all of this, it is of no use that I further delay saying those things that I know to you – after all I am quite well trapped," Edith stated in a matter-of-fact reply, as the three German military officers smiled with satisfaction on finally getting a verbal confession from the second major network member.

She was brought a glass of water. As she related in French to the German interpreter named Corporal F Neubaus he recorded her self-confession exactly as she spoke the words without hesitation, stumbling or evasion. The words she spoke were clearly true and accurate, the Germans already had information and confessions from other prisoners and Edith's words perfectly complemented all this data. She first stated that she was an English woman under the citizenship of the United Kingdom and that from the period of October 1914 through July 1915, she had freely of her own will lodged and financially assisted soldiers of Great Britain, France and Belgium to cross the frontier into Holland. She also admitted to later assisting Belgian young men of military age to flee Belgium and go to Holland to volunteer in the Belgian army under their King Albert.

Edith acknowledged that the mining engineer Herman Capiau and Mlle Louise Thuliez had brought at least forty stranded soldiers to her Clinique in Brussels for temporary lodging and that she helped served as a coordinator for the frontier guide rendezvous points in Brussels. Libiez's name was mentioned as the primary source for false identification papers, while the de Croys provided civilian clothing for the soldiers, as well as being a source of network funding for procuring frontier guides, supplies and general operating expenses. She further identified specifically the identification of the English Colonel Percy Chatsworth (Slim), the Earl of Derbyshire and Sergeant William 'Billy' Taylor as being the first Allied soldiers that she, Capiau, Libiez and the de Croys had assisted. She noted in keen detail the drop-off point in St Mary's church, where Allied prisoners awaited the rendezvous with the various frontier guides that were sent by Capiau, Baucq, Severin or another network member. All of the soldier escapees were given 25 francs that came from Edith's own funds or from money provided by Georges Hostelet or the Prince de Croy. Lodging in Brussels was provided by herself at the Clinique or by Ada Bodart, Louise Thuliez, Philippe Baucq, or George Derveau. By name Edith acknowledged the transmission of Allied soldiers and able-bodied, young Belgian men with the Prince and Princess de Croy, Philippe Baucq, Louis Severin, Herman Capiau, Albert Libiez, George Derveau, Louise Thuliez, and Ada Bodart.

"You have been most thorough and cooperative! Thank you, Nurse Cavell, your soul will now be at peace! Guards, return Nurse Cavell to her cell and show her the greatest of courtesies," Pinkhoff stated with a courteous smile, as he added the send-off remark: "You have done well for yourself and the others I assure you."

Edith said nothing in return, as she slowly arose from her chair and was escorted back to her private cell number 23 on the ground floor, at St Gilles prison.

Edith was too distraught to do anything but pray, as she opened up her Bible and read a passage from Psalms to better calm her nerves. Alone in a cell, one's mind was tempted to seek mental voyages of despair and regret, as she now wondered about the unholy act of confession that she had just been persuaded by the Germans to perform against her friends in the name of truth and justice. Had the clever Germans played her as a fool? Was she merely being a victim or a realist? she pondered as she read the verses that rapidly filled her mind with quiet contentment and inner peace. It was too late for remorse or second thoughts, the deed was done and her words had already been spoken and from these the other prisoners were to be cajoled into making successive damning confessions much like a cascading waterfall.

The listing of names and activities was a disastrous admission to make and Edith's admission helped to seal the subsequent fates of all those that she mentioned in her confession. Later, after her verbal conversation had been typed out and carefully written down in German, her confession was slowly read back to her in French. Edith listened carefully to the transcript and she noted no flaws in the perfect transcription of her words. She signed the confession and it was witness countersigned by Lt Pinkhoff and the interpreter F Neubaus.

The German authorities now possessed in writing that which had to date only consisted of mere speculation and to make their victory all the more satisfying, this confession came from one of the leading de Croy network cell operators. With this information in hand, the Germans derived confessions from Louise Thuliez and some of the other accused; once signed and witnessed, a confession was deemed as a primary admission of guilt before a court of law. The arrest and interrogation phase of the Germans had been completed; now came the final stage of the trial in which the prisoners were going to face the strong hand of German judges. Yet none of the outside world knew any of the sinister workings that occurred inside St Gilles prison.

* * * * * * * * * * * *

While some of the de Croy captives remained quiet and obstinate, like Herman Capiau and Princess Marie de Croy, in maintaining their silence about the operation of the underground de Croy network, the confessions of those who did confess like Edith Cavell and Louise Thuliez, provided enough details for the German officials to start the legal proceedings against the thirty-five detainees out of the one hundred initially arrested, to begin to initiate a case against them. While Philippe Baucq did verbally confess under the threat of having his family imprisoned in St Gilles prison, his details were only of a general nature that only indicted himself and he also did not formally sign any confession. But the Germans wanted to squeeze this important prisoner for greater details of his culpability in the de Croy network.

Cleverly, the Germans placed a man named Maurice Neels as a stoolpigeon, or 'mouton' as the Belgians called it, into Baucq's cell for a night and Philippe was most eager to speak with a fellow Belgian. He eagerly confessed the more sinister details of his involvement in underground activities to include spying on German military activities, the distribution of the underground newspaper La Libre Belgique, the recruitment of civilian young men to join King Albert's army, the Holland frontier passage points and the transmission of German military information through the hidden shoe soles and inner clothing linings of the escaping Allied soldiers. The Germans did not have the confession of the exalted regal Prince Reggie, Princess Marie or Countess Jeanne de Belleville, yet they had something just as good: the detailed information furnished by Edith, Louise and Philippe. The Germans could not prove or allege that there was any implicit or direct support of foreign powers like the British War Office or The Hague to the de Croy network, yet such a liaison no longer needed to be proved beyond a shadow of a doubt; instead, the Germans had the confessions and informant information that provided the detailed working of the de Croy network and that was good enough for them! A skilled prosecutor could lead the Germans' judges by the persuasion of inference and logical deduction concerning any foreign liaisons.

With full approval of Field Marshal Erich von Falkenhayn, the head of the German General Staff and arguably the fourth most powerful man in Germany aside from the Kaiser, Field Marshal von Hindenburg and Field Marshal Ludendorff. Field Marshal Erich von Falkenhayn issued orders that went forth to Lt General Baron Moritz Ferdinand von Bissing, Governor General of all of Belgium, German Political Minister in Brussels General-major Baron Oscar von der Lancken and to the newly appointed Lt General Baron Traugott Martin von Sauberzweig, German Military Governor of Brussels to proceed without haste to prepare an iron-clad case, conduct an expedient secret trial and rapidly perform an execution of sentences.

The preliminary findings of the case against the de Croy network were to be prepared by those who knew the facts most intimately: Captain Hans von Kirchenheim, Captain Joel, Lieutenant Bergan and Lieutenant Pinkhoff. As trained and experienced military officers with extensive analytical minds and police experience in the case of Bergan and Pinkhoff, they were able to perform an accurate version of the network node reconstruction of the key players and activities within the de Croy network, aside from missing the details about the Belgian religious order ancillary support provided to the network. The Germans were brutal and arrogant, yet still prudent enough to know that the persecution of the Belgian religious and the resulting ostracizing of the Belgian general public, was a situation to be avoided at all costs. While they suspected some level of religious personage involvement in the de Croy network, they amply made due with the abundant group of captives that they had in-hand.

While the Germans were busy diligently preparing the tenets of their prosecution, the thirty-five prisoners, save that of Princess de Croy, sat in the restricted confines of the St Gilles prison for a span of eight hot stressful weeks from early August through to the first week of October 1915. The St Gilles prison complex was of a massive latter nineteenth century medieval inspired affair that sought to convene an architectural balancing among the elements of modernism, practicality and efficiency. Its dark ruby red bricks were periodically and tastefully accented with carefully positioned masonry veins of white chiselled stone, which gave the observer a feeling of both strength and tenacity. The main entrance was the administrative part of the structure and its architecture attested to an imposing regal Hampton Court-like design visually boasting a huge stone faced twenty-foot high edifice that contained the main front gate portal flanked by two massive medieval fortress-like stone towers that arched skyward forty feet high. Behind the massive stone front, the visitor was greeted to the architecture of the modern day, brick edifices arrayed in neat, symmetrical spoke-like pattern several storeys high, each red brick building artery led unto the central spoke or centre, which formed the main prison forum from which any of the five connecting perfectly symmetrical building wings could to be most easily reached.

The St Gilles prison was originally charged to function solely for the imprisonment of mere criminals; however, since the war, the Germans had quickly deemed it necessary to place within the St Gilles confines, various political prisoners and potential troublemakers to the German army occupying forces. Both men and women, and on occasions even children, were placed within the womb of the cold red brick beast whose hunger grew daily to feed its increasingly greedy appetite. The German authorities interred all resistance members, hostages, acquaintances and relatives for a period of confinement as they saw fit. In small groups or in solitary confinement, the prisoners were kept in dirty, grim, dimly lit cells, each measuring some fourteen feet by seven feet wide. Each cell had visual access to a window located twelve feet above the floor, providing light but denying visualization of the world that lay beyond the cells. In the solitary cells such as that inhabited by Edith Cavell, a specially designed bed-stand was converted into a bed and a small cupboard served to hold any small amount of personal items so allowed by the prison regulations and staff. Open cells were framed with the traditional heavy metal bars through which the guards could easily observe the prisoners, while the private cells had a large heavy metal door into which a peephole was engineered for stealthy observation of the prisoner.

The smell of vomit and urine filled the air, which became stale and acrid especially in the summer months. Whether it be a private or a public cell, ventilation in either was non-existent. Twice a week the prison administrators saw fit to allow the prisoners the luxury of thirty minutes of exercise in any format so desired by the prisoner, most of whom chose to simply walk about in the fresh air, as showers were provided only once a week under guard supervision. The food was merely adequate and sanitary in both form and preparation, nothing more, thus providing the prisoners with daily subsidence. St Gilles, nor any other wartime prison, did not tend to place weight upon anyone's bones. Although it was not generally encouraged, the prisoners were allowed to receive food from their visitors; however, this was not a daily occurrence and it could not be relied upon as a routine means or source of daily nourishment nor as an expected dietary supplementation.

During the two months since their arrests, the prisoners of the de Croy network were left mostly alone to meditate and to double and triple think about their fates, decisions and lives. The Germans deliberately wanted each prisoner to become psychologically unstable and vulnerable for the trial to come. If the Germans were lucky, a desperate prisoner asked to speak with the German interrogators, if only to have someone to speak with after long periods of isolation. A few visitors on specified occasions were permitted, but these were under strict German supervision with only personal details to be discussed and absolutely no touching was permitted. On certain Sundays, Edith was visited by Nurse Wilkins who brought her some personal items and some home-made stew, which she fondly relished. Philippe was visited by his family and seeing them raised his heart, while their all too soon departure sank his soul. Countess Marie de Lichtervelde visited Marie de Croy and informed her of her grandmother's fall down the chateau's grand stairway.

The Countess, however, also gave the Princess some good news – through a cryptic name she was able to successfully convey that Reggie was safely in Holland. This was a relief to Marie, but she still worried about her grandmother. The Princess pleaded with the Germans for a permissive visit, which the Germans placed into indefinite consideration. In detention everybody worried about something or somebody. Edith worried about the Clinique, Philippe worried about his wife and daughters and Princess Marie worried about her ailing grandmother and brother Reginald. Each prisoner also examined the possibility of their worse-case fates. Philippe was resigned that his destiny was sealed and that a death sentence awaited him due to his underground newspaper distribution activity and his role in passing secret German military secrets to the Allies. Princess Marie de Croy figured that her royal bloodline and fair sex was protection against a capital offence; however, her association with her brother in running the network was going to incur some level of capital level German retribution. Edith judged that her nursing work with helping the German wounded after the Mons battle granted her some measure of clemency, yet her English blood and escape assistance merited her some sort of sentencing, probably exile or imprisonment in Germany for the duration of the war.

The interrogations continued periodically, especially for Edith Cavell. She had confessed to the Germans about her role and that of the other de Croy network members; however, they wanted more! Specifically, they wanted testimony of the role of Countess Jeanne de Belleville. In utter exhaustion during one of her interrogation sessions, Edith merely admitted that her friend the Countess de Belleville had brought to her Clinique several Allied soldiers on a handful of occasions and that the Countess had offered her Brussels urban mansion as a temporary safe-house in sheltering the soldiers before they went on their journeys to Holland. Edith's admission was enough for the Germans to seek a charge against one of the last remaining de Croy network prisoners for whom they needed definitive information for a trial. Lacking the custody of Prince Reginald de Croy, the Germans made do with the satisfaction of having his sister Marie and the Countess in their clutches. The stage was now set for the trial to begin.

* * * * * * * * * * *

"Everyone get up! Get ready! Your trial begins in two hours! Rise and shine everyone!" announced a energetic German guard, as the prisoners were suddenly and callously ruffled from their cozy prison bunks, as the guard clanged along the cold steel bars to render a rudimentary, yet effective metal alarm clock for the slumbering prisoners.

"What in the hell is that ruckus?" Philippe Baucq uttered in a groggy half-asleep tone.

"That German bastard guard is telling us that we have a trial today – can you believe that shit!" Herman Capiau shouted from his cell that was located a mere twenty feet away from Philippe's.

"How can we have a trial when we have not been formally charged or met with our legal counsel?" another voice belonging to George Hostelet sang forth from another cell.

"I'm afraid that none of you understand! The rights which you had as Belgian citizens under a lawfully authorized Parliament are gone, a thing of the past! The Boche do not abide by Belgian law; they imposed German military law and we are to be judged under the procedures of a German military tribunal, so get ready for the shock of your lives, gentlemen!" Herman Libiez the lawyer shouted from his cell as he wearily tried to compose himself as a squad of German police and Belgian guards arrived to unlock the cells and have the prisoners shower, shave and dress for their appearance before the German tribunal.

"Miss Cavell, wake up! The trial finally begins today! Awake and get ready! I'm here to escort you to the bathroom for your bath and cleaning up; we want to make a presentable appearance before the military court!" a female matron guard stated as the guard opened up her solitary cell number 23.

"Well mercy me, this is a bit sudden and unusual! I did not even get to speak with any legal counsel on this matter. Who will act as my barrister?" Edith inquired with some bewilderment in her voice

"You will be defended by those so appointed by the German court, just like everyone else. No one is special before the German military court, now get your personal items and let's go get a bath," the Belgian female jailer instructed with the unsympathetic firmness of authority in her voice.

The same early morning awakening routine was being repeated in all the cells of St Gilles prison and at the Kommandantur German officers' quarters for the Princess de Croy. It was a mild, pleasant sunny Thursday, yet 7 October 1915 stood as a bleak day of reckoning for the de Croy captives and everyone was shocked at the suddenness of the reality announcement that they were all finally going to trial and learn their fates. Shock soon gave way to anxiety and fear, as each man and woman began to realize that they were to go from the regularity of St Gilles prison to what amounted to a formal German inquisition. Belgian courts were totally transferred to special military tribunals. The German military laid out the form and function of the military tribunal, which originated in the Imperial Military Penal Code for countries that the German military occupied. Under the code, both

German soldiers and civilians in occupied countries were liable to the same types of crimes to include that of treason. The new Military Governor of Brussels, Lieutenant General Baron Traugott Martin von Sauberzweig, had just replaced General Richard von Kraewel on 20 September 1915, as Berlin thought that the latter general was not being strict enough in dealing with the Brussels populace.

Lt General von Sauberzweig was a fifty-two year old career soldier from the Prussian cavalry and he was 'old school' through and through; he was not going to be easy or soft on the citizens of Brussels as his predecessor had been, he was determined to suppress any subversive activity and he had in his employ Dr Eduard Stober, the lead German military prosecutor to assist him in this new campaign. Already every resident in Brussels was required to register with German authorities and carry identification papers on them at all times under penalty of immediate arrest and house searches became routine. The US Consulate in Brussels, Mr Brand Whitlock, noted in his journal that when von Sauberzweig became Military Governor of Brussels, 'no one smiled anymore on the streets or in the cafes…they hoped only because it was the only virtue left to them…a black and monstrous silhouette had been cast over Brussels and it seemed, over the entire world'.

At promptly 6:15 am all the prisoners less Princess de Croy, thirty four of them, were assembled into the main hallway near the entrance of the St Gilles prison to await their transport to the German court, which was located a mere fifteen minutes away at the former Senate Chamber of the Belgian Parliament. Speaking was strictly forbidden or 'verboten' as the German guards shouted whenever a captive even tried to speak to another person standing next to them. Some of the prisoners recognized one another and presented a silent head nod or wink of the eye, while other prisoners remained unknown, such was the nature of the de Croy cell organization and compartmentalization of information, activities and people. Edith was anything but dangerous looking, having a mild face of a forty-nine year old matron and standing only a trim 5'6" tall. She was modestly dressed in a plum coloured coat and matching shirt and a light grey full-length plain dress and topped off her ensemble with a dark royal blue sailor hat complete with two large colourful ostrich feathers that stood straight up high. Edith refused to appear in her official grey Red Cross uniform; she did not want the Agency to fall into disrepute due to her actions and she also did not want to solicit any unwarranted sympathy of the court martial members. She was determined to represent only herself and not that of a recognized organization. She might be the type of person to help her fellow countrymen escape a German occupied country, but could anyone believe that she was a secret foreign agent who couriered forth secret information that resulted in German Zeppelins being bombed by the British? All the prisoners looked at one another; it was the first time they had seen one another since their arrests. Everyone looked like scared little chickens and they all had a right to be scared too! The Germans were notorious for their brutality ever since the invasion of Belgium began and none of the captives expected any mercy from the Germans.

A loud shout echoed through the cavernous prison hallway. "When I call your name, acknowledge it and step promptly onto the bus. Remember there is no talking, touching or exchanges of any kind between prisoners. Is that clear?" a German shouted out with a rough and rudimentary command of the French language. The names Cavell, Baucq, Severin, Hostelet, Bodart, Capiau, Libiez, Thuliez, Bull, Derveau, Mathieu, Pansaers and the lesser network members were called out, as the German sergeant checked off each prisoner's name. A guard dutifully accompanied each person and in only ten minutes everyone was accounted for and seated in the buses. The café owner Pansaers wept uncontrollably as the procession of black buses started out towards the Brussels parliament building. The Princess de Croy was conversely being transported in a private automobile from the Kommandantur building directly to the Belgian Parliament building.

By 6:30 am the parade of black buses had made their way to the backside of the Parliament House, sometimes referred to as the National Palace. Lt General von Sauberzweig personally endorsed this venue for the trial – he wanted a grand affair that prominently put the enemies of Germany on public display and as many German officers as possible were encouraged to attend the event. Officers needed to see the swine who were dressed as the harmless lamb, but who acted as jackals against the German occupying forces, or so von Sauberzweig believed with all his heart. The Senate Chamber was opulence finished to excess. There were the rich carpetings, fine enamel emblems of the royal line, polished marble pillars, 24K gold leaf plated frames of oversized frescos and gilded gold metalwork and vibrant silk wallpapering in shades of luscious reds and pastoral blue colours framed the entire chamber with the hue of wealth, power and intimidation. From the gold-plated grand balcony railings, German officers adorned in gold shoulder braid and chest filled medals were stretching out to see the forthcoming march of prisoners who had been the rage of gossip since their arrests some two months previously.

One-by-one the prisoners with guards at their sides strode down the red-carpeted aisle, trying to avoid the curious and sometimes hostile looks from the uniformed spectators who lined their way as in a gauntlet fit for a wild, sacrificial beast. The Senate Chamber was ordered with seating to the right that was reserved for the prosecution and to the left side of the aisle where the defendants and their counsel sat. On a small raised platform there was positioned a large oak table covered atop with a lush green velvet cover, there were five ornate high back red silk embroidered chairs behind the central table and facing both the prosecution and defendants – this was the seating place for the five German military tribunal members – the military judges.

The unintelligible mutterings of the officers were raised to higher decibels when they saw and were awed by the dramatic entrance down the main aisle of the regal Princess Marie de Croy, a woman adorned head-to-toe in black crepe as a sign of and respect for the mourning of her grandmother who had died a week earlier from her injuries sustained during the fall down the Bellignies main stairway during a German looting party. The Princess had only been told of her grandmother's death a few days ago. She was not allowed to attend the funeral, so she requested that Florine bring her black crepe mourning clothing as a sign of respect and sombreness. Numerous Belgian men bowed in deference to her regal status; however, the German military officers stood erect and non-responsive to this lady, who was now humbly subservient to German military laws. She was seated prominently in the first row directly in front of the five judges, flanked on both her sides by two German soldiers armed with Mauser Gewehr rifles affixed with eighteen inch long highly polished bayonets. An attending German court military physician stooped over and whispered in Marie's ear, "Princess, this trial should teach you a lesson, Madame, that women should have nothing to do with war; women should remain in their own homes!"

The Princess was not amused by this uninvited verbal intrusion and personal insult, but she was not to be belittled either and responded with tenacity immediately back at the German doctor. "Well I suppose that the women of Europe should then be thankful to men like you for bringing about all the deaths and misery you have brought to the land too! We Belgians were content to be in our own homes looking after the affairs of our own people, yet it was you German people who tore this tranquility away from us, it was the Germans who invaded Belgium, the Belgians did not invade Germany, so thank you very much, Monsieur to keep your arrogant opinions to yourself!"

The anonymous and rebuffed German military doctor peeled away quickly, speechless by the Princess's remarkable candour.

A few short feet away and separated by the guards, Princess Marie could see Edith Cavell sitting stoically and without visible emotion. Drawing up her back face veil, Marie de Croy was able to make a fleeting eye contact with Edith and the two women exchanged soft smiles between them. The Countess Jeanne de Belleville was dressed in a plain cream-coloured dress and she sat calmly with the look of resolve and calmness. In a crumpled up, plain black suit, Philippe Baucq sat with a blank stare on his face with a look that was detached from the reality of his surroundings.

A dapper, tall, late thirtyish, elegant, jet black-haired man complete with a classical glass monocle emplaced in his left eye was the centre of activity on the prosecution side of the aisle – this was the infamous Dr Eduard Stober. Into the Senate chamber strode the defence attorneys who were going to represent the thirty-five de Croy defendants, with groups of prisoners being assigned to one given lawyer. The Belgian lawyers were Messers Dorff, Kirschen, Brafford and Braun, while the German assigned supplementary defence lawyer consisted of Lieutenant Thielman. As per German military law, the lawyers took seats immediately behind their clients, making any face-to-face contact or communications quite impossible. The defendants were seated in the scarlet red plush chairs of the former Belgian Senate members; each chair was embroidered with the national symbol of Belgium, the Lion of Flanders. A German sergeant yelled out loudly, "Achtung", which meant attention and everyone in the Senate chamber stood up and waited as the five German military judges entered the front of the room from a side anteroom. They entered in their German military grey service dress and when they were seated, everyone in the room followed their lead and sat down in imitation of the judges.

All of the five German officers were middle-aged; they were Colonel Werthmann, President Judge of the Tribunal; Captain Baron von Cornberg, Captain Eck, Lieutenant Slenger and Lieutenant Pault completed the German court. The men were drawn mostly from the German Army Reserve listing, save for the President. The language of the military tribunal was naturally conducted and recorded in German; however, a French interpreter was made available, as this was the language of all the defendants. Each of the thirty-five defendants' names, along with the charges were read aloud in German by Dr Stober and each person was required to stand as their name was called. The charges were aiding and enabling enemy soldiers as a general charge with specific, individual charges being assigned later. Suddenly, the Court was cleared of all civilians, then all of the other defendants except Edith Cavell were cleared from the room. Unbeknownst to any of the prisoners or their appointed legal counsels, this was an onerous sign that signalled she was the most important prisoner and she had confessed so fully and with such detail that she was to be the first defendant examined and thus anything she stated could, and would, be used against the remaining thirty-four defendant-prisoners.

The military President Judge Colonel Werthmann pounded down a heavy wooden gavel forcefully onto a hardwood oak sounding-block, which enhanced the echo of the pounding sound that reverberated harshly and distinctly throughout the vaulted chambered court. Three times he pounded the gavel and yelled out in German the words 'order, order, order'. He then pronounced in a loud, clear voice, "Let the proceedings begin, this Court is now in session!" Immediately Dr Eduard Stober stood up; he was attired in a form-fitting German army uniform with the rank of Major, for which he held a Reserve commission.

"Nurse Edith Cavell, please stand up with your attorney to be in receipt of the Court's questioning in this case!" Stober remarked loudly in German, but which was immediately interpreted and translated back by a German army officer Lieutenant into French, which Miss. Cavell spoke fluently.

"Please state your name, age, nationality, religion, marital status, profession and residence to this Court, please!" he commanded in a loud inflective voice. Stober appeared and sounded like a thespian on a stage and, in a manner of speaking, he was, if only in his own egotistic mind.

"My name is Edith Cavell, aged forty-nine, English woman, devoted member of the Church of England, single, a Nurse-Directorate of the Berkendael Institute in Brussels and I live at that institution on the Rue de la Culture in Brussels." Edith spoke in a soft, but clear voice.

"For how many years have you been in Belgium and why are you still here as an English national, whose country is now at war with Germany?" Stober slowly verbally manoeuvred his key and frail looking witness.

"I have been here since 1908, about seven years since Dr and Mrs Depage recruited me as the Directress of the Berkendael Institute Clinique, which was the first establishment of its kind to professionally train Belgian nurses," Edith replied with obvious pride in her accomplishment. Stober was not satisfied with her response at all.

"You never fully answered my question, Madame Cavell. Why did you stay in Brussels when the war started? Did you not take notice of the German warning to leave or register yourself with the authorities? Technically speaking, you, Nurse Wilkins and anyone else on your staff who is not registered with the German authorities are illegal aliens and subject to imprisonment and deportation, so please answer my question with a proper answer, Madame," the prosecutor demanded, this time in a higher pitched voice.

"Yes my apologies, Monsieur, I stayed because I felt that my staff and nurse trainees were needed more than ever with the war and we did help to care for many hundreds of German, French, English and Belgian soldiers, along with some civilians as well. As for registering with the German occupation authorities, this issue quickly receded to the back of my mind, as we were busy with the onslaught of war wounded, my staff and I were working 16-hour days, sometimes more – I suppose we were overtaken by the war events."

"This is all very good, even noble I might dare say, except that you and your friends did more than that, didn't you? From November 1914 through to July 1915, you lodged numerous healthy, Allied soldiers and helped them to escape into Holland and rejoin their units and fight against the German Imperial Army? Was not one of the first soldiers a prominent English aristocrat named Colonel Percy Chatsworth (Slim), the Earl of Derbyshire and his aide Corporal William (Billy) Taylor?" Stober accused in a raised voice that brought some melodrama and sounds of hushed voices from among German officers in the room, especially those watching from the lofty and prestigious balcony visitors' gallery.

A simple "yes", was returned back with a soft, gentle voice. Again hushed murmurs from the visitors filled the Court, as Judge President Colonel Werthmann threw down the gavel and yelled for silence three times with the words 'Ruhe, Ruhe, Ruhe'.

"Thank you for being honest, Madame, now please tell the Court with whom did you collaborate, Madame Cavell?" Stober asked as he led his witness to incriminate the other de Croy network members.

"Maurice Capiau, Louise Thuliez, George Derveau and Albert Libiez," Edith confessed clearly and without any emotional hesitation. She had, after all, admitted this all to the Germans in her confession, so she felt no reason to hesitate as this was all a matter of record.

"Who was the Chief or Chiefs of your little underground organization?" he coaxed in a rather toying leading voice.

"I'm sorry did you say chiefs? I'm afraid there was no such thing that existed, it all just happened and everyone played their parts!" Edith announced with an innocence that brought forth laughter and denials from the spectators. Stober was ecstatic by the spectator feedback which merely inflated his voracious ego, as he continued to play to his audience by subjecting the helpless witness before him. The defendants were enjoined to merely answer the bullying prosecutor's questions directly and without elaboration or justified explanation. The legal defence attorneys were also prohibited from making any objections on behalf of their clients. Both the defendant and the defence attorney simply had to stay standing like mannequins during the prosecutor's most one-sided inquest.

"Come now, Madame Cavell, you are obviously an intelligent lady, one who is most capable of running a complex Institute for training nurses. Do you think that your Berkendael Institute operates seamlessly by itself? Do you think the German Army operates on its own? Or maybe even all the modern factories? I fear, my dear lady, that you are either not telling us the truth or you have been reading too many books by those fellows Marx, Engels and Dostoyevsky!" Stober chided with deep sarcasm at the absurdity of Edith's remark. Stober hoped that he was making positive points with the judges by invoking the names of prominent radical Communists and starry-eyed authors dreaming of a worker's utopia.

"Let us be truthful, why is it not the Prince Reginald de Croy himself, also abetted by his loyal sister the Princess Marie de Croy, who acted as the network chief and brains? Did he not visit the British War Office, The Hague and the US Consulate in Brussels to work his little espionage and saboteur network?" Stober suggested to the helpless witness as she struggled to remain truthful and answer the questions honestly. Edith, like the other network members, remained ignorant of the independent activities of the Prince and Princess; she knew little of the travels abroad, nor the transmittal of secret information. She and the others kept cloaked the details of their individual activities by invoking the 'need-to-know' axiom.

"No, no that's not true, it's not true as I know these things to be! I only know that the Prince and Princess de Croy helped stranded Allied soldiers and sent theses helpless men to Brussels to me! The de Croys provided some communications, some guidance and some money, that's all!" Edith sparked back with a slight tone of defensiveness at Stober's allegations.

"So, Madame Cavell you admit freely to this Court that the de Croys provided 'communications, some guidance and some funding' to your cell of agents. Well, I may be naïve, but that sounds like organization and leadership to me!" Stober remarked in jest as the entire room burst into laughter and the Judge President Colonel Werthmann was again forced to call the Court room to order.

"We have from the details of your confession the methods for how you accomplished your escape operations; however, far less clear is your motive.

Let's get to the heart of this matter for you – why did you do it? Why did you help these soldiers? Why did you continue to assist in this network almost a year after Belgium was occupied?" the dapper-appearing German prosecutor inquired with a inflection of curiosity in his voice.

"I only wanted to help my English countrymen, then my sympathies spread to those soldiers of other Allied nations, then to civilians who wanted to flee. We all believed that the Germans were going to shoot the soldiers," Edith replied with no attempt at evasion. Her body was feeling the strain of standing while testifying, just as the Germans had intended. A fatigued witness was liable to make mistakes in judgment and testimony.

"That is the most insane claim that I have ever heard. We Germans do not shoot soldiers who surrender! In fact, Madame Cavell, you and your conspirators placed these soldiers' lives in grave danger by placing them in civilian clothing, using them as carrier pigeons for secret information transmittals and trying to pass-through the guarded frontier with Holland. By trying to help Allied soldiers, you actually placed their lives in great danger!" Stober announced matter-of-factly, as the panel of German judges took their copious notes of the significant words being spoken.

"I did nothing in these terms as you have just expressed, Monsieur," Edith merely replied back.

"Did you receive correspondence back from any escaped Allied soldiers?" came his next question.

"Yes, on several occasions I did," Edith responded without realizing the implication of the prosecutors' inquiry.

"Madame Cavell, correspondence from France and especially England does not just show up through the normal postal system. There is a war upon us and no nation allows for the mails to be exchanged freely with a belligerent nation. So how did you get these correspondences that originated from a belligerent nation?" Stober snapped back and this time with a theatrical-like scepticism for all the Court to hear.

Edith said nothing; she was dumbfounded by the question. She had never thought to ask the Prince or Princess about the origins of the soldier's letters to her or how letters were transmitted out to England. Maybe ignorance was not truly bliss, as the saying went. "Monsieur, I do not know, I did not think upon such things!" Edith replied tersely.

"Maybe the postal fairy delivered it to you!" Stober remarked with blatant ridicule as the court visitors broke out in laughter.

"I'd like to suggest to the Court to entertain the very plausible idea that Prince Reginald de Croy both transmitted and received correspondence from escaped soldiers and also correspondence with the British War Office and The Hague, through his liberal travel authorization. I further suggest that he used his travel pass and documents to travel to Holland and England and that he was in contact with the US Consulate in Brussels using sealed diplomatic pouch courier services for receiving and transmitting various correspondences," Stober roared out for everyone to hear, as a wave of applause rose up from the chamber, again forcing Colonel Werthmann to pound his gavel at least a half-dozen vigorous repetitions.

"Madame Cavell, do you know the man named Fromage and the woman calling herself Martin?" he continued on with the questioning, digging an ever deeper hole from which Edith had faint chance of extracting herself.

"Well yes, I now know them to be Philippe Baucq and Louise Thuliez, but I never knew them by those false names though!" Edith responded, meekly.

On hearing this response Dr Stober's voice cracked if ever so faintly.

"Of course Madame, people use fake name and aliases every day. It is a favourite employ of cheating husbands and spies and you are no cheating husband, so you must be connected to an espionage network! Normal, trustworthy people use their real names not aliases; false names are used to hide the guilty and the devious and you, Madame, are both!" Stober noted with glee as he spotted the judges again taking note of his accusations onto their writing paper, a good thing for a prosecutor. Edith could only reply with her silence; she knew that Stober was gunning for her and that he took every one of her confessed interrogation responses and turned these around to use against her. In this starkness of the staged prosecution's questioning, she now deeply regretted making her jailhouse confession to Lt Pinkhoff and Lt Bergan some weeks earlier, but it was too late – her words had been transcribed and personally attested by her own signature endorsement.

"Madame Cavell, let us proceed back to Philippe Baucq – how well did you know him? How many times did you meet with him?" Stober returned to asking the tenet of his original line of questioning.

"Yes, I knew him a little, we met on a few occasions. I kept to my own business and I did not dabble in his affairs, Monsieur," she calmly answered without fully divulging any information that the Germans could use to implicate Philippe or Louise Thuliez. Yet any subterfuge was now pointless – the Germans had all of her answers; they merely wanted a confession or implication to be on the Court record.

"Let us not bicker over your knowledge of Baucq and Thuliez; you do stand by your signed confession back in mid-August concerning your underground work with the De Croys, Baucq, Severin, Capiau, Libiez and Ada Bodart? You also acknowledge that your activities aided the enemies of the German state?" Stober asked as he started to wrap-up his questioning.

"I merely want to acknowledge my association with those that you mentioned and those confessed by me during my interrogations; however, I do not admit to helping the enemies of Germany out of a military purpose, I only wanted to get these soldiers and young men out of danger in Belgium. After they crossed into Holland it was up to them to seek sanctuary asylum or try to get back to France with their units," Edith responded fully and with a tone of self-righteousness. The judges and Stober himself were impressed with Edith's voracity and patriotism. Behind her back they referred to her as that 'Iron Matron Englishwoman'.

"Well Madame, noble intentions sometimes turn into cold facts and the facts are that every soldier and young man whom you assisted went back into war against Germany," Stober accused as he raised his voice as he indicted Edith's answer back to the Military Tribunal Judges. He melodramatically pounded his hand on the table and peered directly into Edith's cool grey eyes.

A strange new voice arose from within the cavernous courtroom. "Madame Edith Cavell, now exactly how many men in total did you assist during the past nine months since your enterprise began?" the President Judge Colonel Werthmann calmly asked from his front bench. In such a tribunal, a judge could ask anything deemed as being necessity for clarification or inquiry; so too could the other tribunal members.

"Your Honour, about two-hundred or maybe two-hundred and fifty. We did not keep detailed records, especially during the last several months, such was the volume of soldiers and young men. We were going to close down our operations. Many were English soldiers, but a few French and Belgian soldiers too! Some youthful male civilians as well toward the end!" Edith sighed out as if a great weight had been taken off of her shoulders. The President Judge and the others whispered among themselves that helping non-English soldiers made a great deal of difference; it distinguished a mere patriot from the dedicated enabler. Again the German judges wrote down notes on hearing this fact confirmed publicly by Nurse Edith Cavell.

"Your Honour, with your permission, I'd like to dismiss this witness, I think she has told this Court quite enough! I desire to bring forward two expert witnesses in this case, Lieutenant Bergan and Lieutenant Pinkhoff," Stober announced as he faced the Military Tribunal Court with a deference slight bow.

"Yes, of course, please do!" President Judge Colonel Werthmann replied, hoping that these two military police officers could bring a conclusion to this witness, as the prosecution log was a lengthy one, and other prisoners needed to be examined. The Germans seemed to be in a hurry. Edith sat down in her chair, as did her legal representative Sadi Kirschen, who was the German court appointed defence lawyer for Edith. He was a mere puppet before the German Military Tribunal; he could offer no objections or cross examinations under German legal protocols in a time of war. If he had any new information or witnesses, he could bring these forth, but he had nothing! No preliminary meetings with his client were permitted and attempts of the US Consulate to provide legal representation by a contracted Belgian named Mr Guy de Leval were denied by the German authorities. Every other defendant was in the same precarious situation. Going before a German military court was a less than 50-50 probability of being found innocent; every factor was in the Court's favour.

Edith, like all defendants being questioned before the German Military Court Tribunal, was obligated to stand-up, along with their defence attorneys directly behind them, then to remain standing throughout the duration of their questioning by the prosecution and judges. Disguised as a form of deference and reverence to the law, this technique was a deliberate court inspired procedure that was designed to favour the prosecution's case against the defence, as this physical posture greatly fatigued a defendant, especially during a lengthy questioning process, which was also deliberately employed by the German prosecution to 'wear-down' a defendant, especially the frail and weaker sex. Before long, a defendant soon tired of this ordeal and they were now conditioned to admit or say careless words posed to them by a skilled, long-winded prosecutor. The only physical and mental relief that came to the helpless defendant was that of being dismissed by the prosecutor and thus allowed to resume the contented sitting posture once again.

"My name is Lieutenant Henri Pinkhoff, age thirty-five, German military police counter-intelligence section," the soft spoken, tall man replied as the judges unconsciously focused on the prominent purplish birth mark upon his face . His voice was soft, articulate and his words were well spoken in an upper class German accent.

"My name is Lieutenant Ernest Bergan, age thirty-six, German military police counter-intelligence section, previously assigned as the Kommissar of the Dusseldorf police," the raven-haired, onyx-eyed averaged framed man stated. Both men had their hands raised in testimony before the judges.

"Now, you are two trained and experienced policemen and military officers of fine repute and reputation. I shall not burden the Court's precious time in outlining any of your credentials and experiences; however, I want to immediately bring forth the fact that both of you, under the direction of Captain Joel and Captain von Kirchenheim, prepared and witnessed the confession of Edith Cavell on 12 August 1915 – correct, gentlemen?" Stober announced smartly.

"Yes, sir," was the immediate reply of both men.

"Will one of you be good enough to read through and provide the highlights of Madame Cavell's confession made that day?" Stober requested of the two German officers. Lt Bergan nodded to the slightly junior time-in-grade Pinkhoff, that he was going to read aloud the confession highlights of Directress Nurse Edith Cavell.

"Yes, Dr Stober and distinguished judges, here are the highlights of the confession: Nurse Edith Cavell freely admitted over the course of one year to assisting in helping Allied soldiers and military-aged men from Belgian into Holland using recruited frontier guides. The personages of the Prince and Princess de Croy, Madame Thuliez, Mr Capiau, Mr Libiez and Madame Bodart, all of them brought soldiers and young men to Brussels, some to Edith Cavell's Clinique and to other Brussels safe houses. With the assistance of Baucq, Severin and Capiau, soldiers were provided temporary lodging, false identification documents and then paired up with the border crossing guides. Money to pay for the guides and to the soldiers came from Madame Cavell and the de Croys, in addition to Georges Hostelet. The chemist Derveau provided escaped assistance to Allied soldiers by couriering them to and from Nurse Cavell's Clinique and he also furnished soldiers a safe haven in the form of lodging on certain occasions."

"Thank you very much, Lieutenant Bergan. Was there anything said about Countess Jeanne de Belleville?" Stober probed carefully as a knitter closing a knot loop.

"Yes, Herr Stober, Madame Cavell did confess that the Countess Jeanne de Belleville was the initial catalyst in bringing allied soldiers to the de Croys with the assistance of Louise Thuliez. The Countess then became increasingly involved in hiding several Allied soldiers on a handful of occasions and that the Countess had offered her Brussels urban mansion as a temporary safe-house in sheltering the soldiers before they went on their journeys to Holland. The Countess also assisted on several occasions to escort soldiers to Madame Cavell's Clinique in Brussels," Lt Bergan noted with perfect recall to the delighted Dr Stober.

"Herr President Judge, the prosecution rests its case as far as this defendant Edith Cavell is concerned. The two witnesses are dismissed. I now desire to call forth Philippe Baucq to the stand.

"Call forth the prisoner Mousier Philippe Baucq," yelled a boisterous German Sergeant who was serving as the de facto court crier. The court chamber doors opened and Philippe, accompanied by two German soldiers complete with rifles and fixed bayonets escorted him down the aisle of the chamber and he was stopped at a seat almost directly in front of the judges. He was instructed to remain standing.

"Please state your name, age, occupation, marital status and place of residence!" Dr Stober instructed in a monotone, unemotional voice.

"I am named Philippe-François-Victor Baucq, thirty-five years old, married with two lovely daughters, architect and currently I am residing in Cell number 72 at St Gilles prison," he announced with a tone and reference of stubbornness. The German judges took exception to the remark and so did Dr Stober. Low verbal rumbles of disapproval were voiced from the court visitors.

"Your tone and manners are not reverent! Don't be so disrespectful to this Court, you comical little man! Answer my question without any sarcasm! Now you answer me, are you Belgian and Catholic?" Stober asked sternly.

"Very well, I live at Avenue de Rodebeek 49 Brussels and in regard to my nationality and religion, let me say simply that I am a loyal Belgian, a lapsed Catholic and a good patriot," Philippe noted with a defiant smile. None of the Germans were amused by Baucq's amplifying remark. If Baucq wanted to make enemies of the German judges, he was succeeding admirably.

"You state that you are an architect, so for whom are you employed and what else do you do with your time, Monsieur Baucq?" the ever agitated prosecutor asked.

"There is minimal building work for an architect since the war began – the Germans are more concerned with destruction than construction! I try to keep myself busy. I proudly admit to be the leading distributor of the free newspaper La Libre Belgique and I freely admit to working with the de Croys, Nurse Edith Cavell, Louise Thuliez and Ada Bodart. I helped Allied soldiers and military age men reach the border of Holland. All I did was to take some refugee soldiers to and from Edith Cavell's Clinique and arrange rendezvous for the soldiers to meet the border guides," Philippe argued with honesty, boldness and sincerity.

"So do you want to admit to this court that you are guilty and change your plea from innocent to that of guilty, Monsieur Baucq?", Dr Stober coaxed loudly before the court, as this defendant had just admitted his crimes and his sentence of 'guilty' was most assured, especially given his defiant and disrespectful behaviour before the stiff-backed German military officers.

"No, not at all, sir! I want to admit to being a Belgian, a loving father and a devoted patriot. If I am guilty of anything, it is only these things and not those things labelled as offences by the German occupying forces!" Baucq shouted back, as the court room full of senior German officers broke out into jeers of disgust and an inaudible chorus of hated, rude verbal remarks.

"Ruhe, Ruhe, Ruhe," the German judge yelled again as he hammered his gavel onto the oak sounding-block. "Now you see here, Monsieur Baucq, you answer the questions stated to you and nothing more! This is not an open forum for you to spread your propaganda and you have a hostile audience in this chamber. The country of Belgium, all of its occupants and yourself are now under the authority of German military law since the defeat of your country last year – that, my rebellious friend, is a fact and it is also an accepted precept under international law as well. This is a court of law even if you do not approve of it being so, yet such is life. You shall not acquire in this Court that which was denied to you and your countryman on the battlefield! This is not a street-corner or the Speaker's Square in Hyde Park, London, where one can say whatever one pleases and without consequence. Now you behave as I have instructed you or you will either be physically gagged or removed from this courtroom without a chance of further defence. Is that clear, Monsieur?" Judge President Colonel Werthmann angrily scolded the rebellious defendant as he wagged and pointed his finger aggressively at Baucq's face.

Philippe was obviously humbled as he meekly nodded his head in vertical affirmation of the judge's instructions and his obedience thereto. The visitor's gallery rose as one and applauded in a roar of obvious approval at the President Judge's remarks, to which there was no call for abatement from the judge's mighty gavel. One-by-one the members of the de Croy network were being sequentially vanquished by the prosecution.

Dr Stober smiled faintly with delight at the President Judge's verbal reprimand of the bellicose little Belgian architect. "Let us proceed back to my questioning. What about the secret information on the German military that was conveyed to the Allies? What about the border crossing points? What about the cryptic notes and the mention of German munitions sites and trains? What about the bombings of the German aerodromes and Zeppelin sheds outside Brussels?" Dr Stober argued with a thunderous voice.

"Of these things I know nothing," Philippe replied with a resigned voice, which none of the Germans believed. The Germans had found very incriminating evidence in Baucq's house the night of the raid and he could not explain it to the Court.

"Ah a funny thing it is, that so many obviously intelligent and accomplished people come before this court to make testimony and suddenly they know nothing about any evidence or facts presented to them! Everyone must have courtroom amnesia! This is simply astonishing! With such ignorance, I am surprised that both you and Nurse Cavell made it through your professional schooling, which is quite demanding if I am not mistaken," Stober bombastically remarked for the judges and court audience to hear.

"You're a very bad liar, Monsieur Baucq. You used a code name, you had German military information in your home, your residence was found with cipher and encrypted information in it, you distributed an illegal underground newspaper and you acted as a processor and enabler of Allied soldiers to Holland. I think that is quite enough of a resume for the Court to ponder. I have no more questions of this prisoner!" Dr Stober remarked as he quickly rested his case on Philippe Baucq.

"You may move on with the next accused," the President Judge announced without even looking up from his writing paper. Philippe wearily took his court seat and sat motionless in silent humility. Stober glanced at the German Sergeant and simply nodded his head. "The Court calls forth Madame Louise Thuliez," he thundered in a trumpeting voice.

Down the long corridor of hostile, staring male faces, the dowager, plain-looking woman proceeded into the court attired in a simple, dull, dark blue dress under watchful double-guard escort, Louise Thuliez proceeded until she was directed to her appointed place directly before the panel of German judges. Her long brown hair was pulled back and her head was draped in a plain bonnet hair, she truly looked like the typical school mom. She looked much older than her physical age suggested, she was a lady of simple decorum and the stressful weeks in St Gilles prison did not contribute to one's physical beauty. Like the others, she looked distressed, anxious and tired.

"Madame, please, for the Court record, state your name, age, nationality, religion, marital status, occupation and living address. Please do not follow Monsieur Baucq's poor example in answering such a simple question with either hostility or sarcasm," Stober directed and warned the defendant, who was blissfully ignorant of the proceedings that had just occurred in the court chamber prior to her summons.

"I am Louise Thuliez, thirty-four years old, Protestant, Belgian patriot, single, a school mistress and I live in the city off Lille just across the border in France," Louise replied with a tone of clarity and fortitude in her voice.

"Ah at last, the first honest woman in this proceeding thus far and I am glad that you are not using your alias name of 'Martin' today either. Now you have already confessed and pleaded guilty in writing as some other defendants have thus pleaded, so I shall not go into any lectures of a general indictment; however, perhaps you can provide some details of the de Croy network, such as how many soldiers did you assist and have you heard back from any of them?" Stober asked in a very friendly tone. Louise had heard none of Edith's or Philippe's testimony, so she knew not that the information being requested was to further damage Louise's case before the Court, as it would serve as self-incrimination.

"Personally, I assisted with about one hundred and twenty-six men and I do not recall any of them writing back to me or at least I do not remember receiving any letters from them," she replied with a most reserved modicum of honesty.

"Who was the head or leader of this network?" he asked in a gentle coaching voice.

"I cannot attest that there was an actual head or leader; from my perspective we all did what we could to help the soldiers, who were in a desperate, starving state. In hindsight, I would be hard pressed to even acknowledge the existence of a formal organization at all," she replied as the sunlight flickered off of her wire-framed glasses that presented her with an appearance of old age. Hushed whispers gently echoed throughout the Court upon hearing her words.

"Did you know or ever meet any of the frontier guides?", he pressed in vain interrogation of the seemingly helpless woman.

"No, I'm afraid not, I never met the guides, I merely brought the soldiers to Edith, Philippe and the de Croys," Louise unhesitatingly responded in a most innocent reply that sentenced both herself and added to the guilt of her friends. Truths told in good conscience and faith before this court was akin to immediate self-incrimination without mercy.

Stober deftly continued to lead this lamb unto the judicial slaughter. "Money, Madame, let us speak of money. Money is the lubrication for all things in man's affairs and this includes espionage. Now who and how much money was paid to you to run this little side-business of yours? Things must have been slow at the school for you to take on such extracurricular activities, Madame Thuliez," Stober noted in an obvious tone of mockery. Yet Louise was true to her benign character and she took no offence; she merely continued to answer Stober's questions as these were asked of her.

"There was very little money that I saw. Prince de Croy did give me 500 francs once for food, clothing and some incidentals, but that was the extent of the funding. All of us did this because we are humanitarians and patriots," she responded with an air of indifference. Stober was getting frustrated: she was guilty, but he wanted more incriminating admissions.

"You and the Princess de Croy are friends and as such you both assisted each other and that included the photography of taking pictures for the soldiers' fake identity cards, correct?" he queried, again sniffing around for a damning response against the Princess de Croy.

"Yes you are correct, the Princess and I, along with Albert Libiez were all involved in the photography of Allied soldiers and young civilian Belgian men," she replied without hesitation or reservations.

"Well excuse me for being bold, but the last time that I checked the German Penal Code, the deliberate falsification, transmittal and possession of false official German mandated documents was considered to be a capital offence to which you now shamelessly admit of yourself and implicate those of your underground friends!" Stober quickly interjected boldly and to the utter amusement of the military courtroom visitors as whimpers of laughter were heard. Louise stood there and did not respond to Dr Stober's verbal ridicule.

"You also knew Philippe Baucq and you assisted in the distribution and preparation of the illegal newspaper La Libre Belgique – is that not also correct?" Stober stated as his patience with this defendant was growing short.

"Yes, you are correct once again, Monsieur," Louise retorted.

"Who were you waiting for past the curfew hour in the café operated by Pansaers?" Stober demanded harshly.

"Just some friends who never showed up, so I left after waiting perhaps too long a time," Louise remarked plainly.

"Were these illegal allied soldiers again?" Stober inquired with deeper inquisition.

"No, just a male acquaintance who never showed up," Louise flatly remarked.

"That must be some friend that you had to stand you up like that, very ungentlemanly of him. I suppose you don't have a name and address of this acquaintance do you, Madame Thuliez?" Stober remarked with mordant accusation. Louise Thuliez stood and did not utter a reply back; she knew that she could not state the true purpose of her meeting with the Belgian miners.

"I suppose that you also know nothing of those foreign letters, code book and encrypted address book and frontier maps that were found in your large hand bag the night of the raid on Baucq's residence?" Stober inquired of the wavering defendant.

"That was not my hand bag. I never saw it before!" Louise lied poorly.

"Well that's another strange coincidence in that your name was noted on an identity tag within the recess of the lining of the hand bag, so I suppose that it must belong to another Louise Thuliez," Stober shouted loudly, as he was clearly frustrated by this obviously lying woman who had been caught red-handed with contraband espionage items.

"I do not suffer fools graciously and I pray neither does this Court. If it so pleases the Court, I have no more questions of this witness. May I proceed with the next defendant?" Stober asked the President Judge.

"Please yes do so, Dr Stober, but only one more before a mid-day break," Colonel Werthmann responded as he too appeared to be getting jittery about the series of prisoners who all seemed to have the same story and all of whom seemed guilty in varying degrees.

"The Court calls forth her Highness Princess Marie de Croy of Belgium," barked the Sergeant again in a trumpeting voice. There was again a curtain of silence, almost reverence as the black veiled Princess descended once again into the Senate chamber from an awaiting side anteroom reserved for VIPs of which the Princess certainly ranked. Dr Stober met her with a slight bow and a devilish smile, but not one of admiration, but of eager posturing contempt.

"Please state your name, age, occupation, marital status, nationality, religion, and place of residence!" the prosecutor reiterated in now rote manner for the Court recorder.

"I am Princess Marie de Croy of Mons, Belgium; I am Catholic, a patriotic Belgian, forty years old. I have no employment status aside from my philanthropic and charity work and I live at my family's ancestral home of Bellignies Chateau in Mons, Belgium. During the beginning of the war, my brother and I offered up the Bellignies Chateau as a military field hospital and I was trained as a nurse, so I assisted in that endeavour as well, but those times have since long passed," the Princess replied with candour and pride.

"Please take a chair and sit down, Princess, a royal person such as yourself should not be made to stand as these other prisoners!" Stober remarked as he made a forced-smile to the Princess, while conversely making a masked insult to the Princess's exalted position and denigrating those of her co-conspirators. He aimed to destroy her flawless character in short order.

"Thank you, Princess de Croy, your family name is a long and regal one to which our Court is familiar. Now, can you tell us the status of your siblings?" Stober inquired directly. He had wanted to come to the leadership issue quickly and to identity the mastermind of this criminal organization.

"One moment please, Herr Stober. First I'd rather like to inform the court of the tragic status of my beloved eighty-five year old grandmother, who was left to die at the bottom of our stairway after being half-frightened to death by a German raiding party on my ancestral family chateau, Monsieur Stober! She is dead, dying like a dog on the floor and helpless and you beastly Germans did it. You should be on trial for this, you are murderers!" shouted out the outraged Princess in alternating French and German.

The agitated and angry prosecutor was having none of this guff from another defiant defendant and he quickly acted to mute this unsolicited outburst against the court and the German state. "Be quiet, shut your mouth, Princess or I shall be forced to have you forcibly gagged or taken from this chamber and judged in absentia! Do you understand me, Madame Princess? Your Belgian Royal rank holds little influence over a German Military Tribunal, understand me?" the President Judge Colonel Werthmann stood up from his seat and yelled loudly and with anger at the black crepe draped woman standing directly before him.

Princess Marie gazed at Stober with steely-eyed utter contempt. "You Germans killed my old, helpless grandmother! Murderers!" the Princess shouted out angrily.

"This is your last warning! Now you be quiet, Princess or you shall be dragged from this courtroom kicking and screaming, black veil or no black veil; woman or no woman; Princess or no Princess!" Werthmann shouted out vigorously, as a room full of angry German military officers rose-up and shouted loud reinforcing jeers in support of the judge's remarks. He was a regular German army professional officer with thirty years of hard service in the Prussian cavalry and this experience had instructed him to be hard, disciplined and authoritative; he was also having none of this woman's feminine emotional nonsense and verbal insults in his strict German military court proceedings.

Marie knew that she had met her match in this Prussian officer; she decided that her fate was pre-determined as well. She wanted to be strong, but not caustic to her case and sentence, which promised to be a difficult one. She immediately sought to make benign verbal amends to the court. "I apologize to the Court and your personage, President Judge; I am a loyal Belgian woman of some position in my country and I am outraged by the acts that I see being daily committed unbeknownst to some of the Imperial German Army officers. If I do not plead for the wrongful death of my grandmother, who else will?" she replied, hoping to add some rationalization to the outraged Colonel Werthmann's conscience.

"Your apologies are accepted, dear Princess, but please remember who you are and where you are! The abuses of the German Army 'rank and file' such as you have so accused, exist in all large armies in time of war; however this is not the time or forum to address these issues. These matters will need to be addressed through the Governor General of Belgium, General von Bissing and Military Governor of Brussels, General von Sauberzweig and I submit that you make appeals to these entities for any wrongs done to you. Are these things now clear to you, Princess?" the President Judge asked of the recently ridiculed and humbled accused.

"Yes, Monsieur President," Marie sounded back clearly and without any tone of tears or trepidation.

"Please answer the prosecutor's questions, Princess," the Colonel ordered.

"I am the older sister of two Belgian Princes; the older brother is Prince Leopold and he is gallantly serving in the Belgian army with King Albert of Belgium. My younger brother Reginald's whereabouts I am not certain of – he disappeared from my life in August," Marie de Croy noted straight away. She was not bothered that she had told a 'white lie' to the Germans; she knew her brother had crossed into Holland and she guessed from there travelled to London. This speculation was to remain her secret. Stober remained undeterred.

"Did you and your brother assist Allied soldiers during the past nine months by lodging them, providing them with food, civilian clothing and taking pictures of them for false identity cards to which escape was made from Belgium into Holland?" he indicted the Princess and her brother in a loud voice.

"First, Monsieur Prosecutor, I am unable to answer for the actions of another, so the question about my brother I cannot attest; however, I did personally help some Allied soldiers – how many I do not recollect – these Christian acts of mercy are not counted on one's fingers! Yes I took the photographs of some of the Allied soldiers and I did this for my personal scrapbook. Someday this war will be over and I wanted to capture some memories of the fine young boys that I helped, as foolish and incriminating as that action may now appear to you!" the Princess cleverly deflected back to the bold prosecutor. Stober was furious, he knew that the Princess was up to her eyeballs together with her brother Reggie in running this operation and now neither she nor her brother were mature enough to live up to their responsibilities. Her brother had fled and she covered-up and lied.

Stober was not to be so easily deterred. "Why did you assist these soldiers at all? If they surrendered to the Germans they would be treated safely and be taken care of by the German army, thus leaving you and everyone else in your network innocent to this day. You could have spared yourself and all these other defendants the agony of this trial!" Stober stated. He hoped to instil both guilt and a motive for the Princess and her brother.

"No, that contention of yours is wrong. If I did not help these stranded Allied soldiers, I would not have spared myself of a guilty conscience for not helping those in dire need of my assistance, Herr Stober. We Belgians are under the impression that the Allied soldiers' lives were in danger, as we were continually hearing reliable stories of soldiers being taken out and shot, notably at the town of Hiron. We also heard that a dozen Allied soldiers were shot to death there after they had raised up their hands to surrender by German infantry troops. There was another situation that was not a mere story; it involved the arrest of our Mayor, who had prior knowledge of Allied soldiers being maintained by Belgian civilians in his town and for his honesty, he was jailed by the Germans. The mayor was also threatened with his life and forced to pay a fee to the Germans. After hearing of this innocent incident, few Belgians turned over any Allied soldiers in their care to any German official and so the same townspeople came to me and anyone else who could help them!" Marie noted boldly.

"Your statement is peripheral to the issue of aiding young men back to Germany's enemies. Let us move on to other matters. Please inform the Court of the procedures and the extent of your involvement with assisting Allied soldiers escape from Belgium," Stober continued in his questioning of the Princess.

"Both myself and my brother Prince Reginald de Croy, along with Louise Thuliez on occasion, escorted them! We took the soldiers to Brussels. I cannot know for sure who took care of them while they were in Brussels and I will not speculate on that either. Sometimes not knowing the full details is a blessing – 'ignorance is bliss' as the saying goes! I performed my deeds out of my own volition and without any undue influence or pressure. My actions were performed because I believe in helping the destitute and the helpless; it is a dogma of my Catholic faith. I could have placed this entire burden on my brother – after all, he is now missing and blame falls easy upon the shoulders of those not present to defend themselves. I firmly believe that the individual alone must answer for one's actions and not place the blame on others due to convenience of circumstances," Marie answered with preciseness and nobility of character, and incurring a venial sin of not implicating Edith Cavell or anyone else in the Brussels cell.

"What about funding for the network? You and your brother gave money to some of your colleagues? To whom and how much please?" he asked with keen interest of hearing her answer.

"You are correct, Herr Stober, yes I did give out some small amounts of pocket-money! I provided some small amounts to Louise Thuliez and only a small amount, maybe forty or fifty francs, for the soldiers' food and such things," the Princess replied again with another white lie of exaggeration. She and her brother both gave hundreds of francs to pay the guides and the food and clothing was not cheap either as the war inflated the prices of old clothing and especially food. The British navy blockade of Germany was indeed a dual edged sword that cut both the German army and the innocent Belgian civilians equally sharp.

"Let's get into the foreign connection of your network: how many times was your brother Reginald visiting London and The Hague?" Stober probed ever deeper into the 'brains' of the de Croy operation.

"Once again, Monsieur Prosecutor, my brother's travels and meetings are of his own affair; my siblings and I are all adults and we respect each other's privacy. Those things, which he did or is alleged to have done, belong to him alone. If you want to implicate his actions to those of mine, I cannot stop you, but I shall not betray my family – they were with me throughout my earliest years and I pray they will remain with me through my end times," Marie stoutly remarked with pride.

"One more thing, Princess, why did you refuse to sign a confession while some of your other compatriots had no reservations about doing so?" Stober inquired, as much out of personal curiosity than anything else.

"Simple: my religion," she smartly replied.

"Religion – what do you mean by that, Princess?" Stober was startled.

"You asked me my religion. I am a devout Roman Catholic and a tenet of our faith is that confession is to be reserved between a priest and the penitent. I see no Roman Catholic priests in this Court, Monsieur!" Marie sparked out in public defiance to both the laws of man and the laws of the Imperial German Empire. These words were dangerous and the Court knew it! These were the words of individual conscience and such faith was more dangerous in a solitary, determined woman than a battalion of German infantry.

"For an observant Catholic, you take great liberty with the eighth Commandment about making false witness, dear Princess! It seems that like most people, you are quite selective in the practice of your sins and virtues. I draw the Court's attention to the fact that this woman evades the truth when it is so convenient for her to do so. She skillfully toys with the Court and her left and right hands do not know what the other is doing!" Stober muttered loudly in German, his frustration and anger being self-evident to the entire assembly.

"You are an obstinate woman! Pity the man who marries you, Princess! I can see that I am getting nowhere with you on this and I will not have you use this forum as a propaganda platform either, so now on to the next question, Princess. For the final time I ask you: what did you do with your Allied soldiers? Where did they go? To whom did they go?" Stober fired back in rapid succession. His impatience with the Princess was clearly visible. She was not cooperating with his verbal razzmatazz.

"I'm afraid that I have already given you my responses to these queries, the responses of which clearly displease you, so you get angry at me and ask these again! I have already given my answers and these remain immutable," Princess Marie de Croy replied back in a cool and rational manner. Her response and attitude drove Dr Stober to an uncontrollable outburst.

"This woman is clearly a hostile party to any query to which I hope to explore in this case; her verbal banter merely deflects and delays the prosecution's progress. I will take no further indulgence with her and with the kind court's patience. Unless there are any objections or questions from the Tribunal, I request dismissal of this defendant," Stober barked out in vulgar disgust. There was not a word of objection from the German military judges. The Princess had exhausted the best legal offence that the German prosecution could throw at her and she remained afloat like a sturdy battleship. With a nod of the judges, she turned and was escorted to sit back in her chair in the front row of primary defendants.

The Court was recessed for two-hours, during which time the prisoners were held in a common atrium area that was well populated with German soldiers and their own guards. While the military men were provided rations by the canteen, nothing was given to the prisoners. Was this intentional or a mere oversight? The issue was irrelevant; it did not matter, as hunger knows no distinction between intention and omission, it merely exists. Half-way through the lunch period, some soldiers took pity on the prisoners and they left them the food that was not consumed; however, no eating utensils were provided, this being an obvious security precaution and instruction which every German soldier had been drilled on since their initiation into the German Army. The prisoners none too proud of their circumstances, merely used their fingers or tried to tilt the containers back far enough so that the food dropped down into their mouths through the grace of gravity.

The afternoon session brought the same degree of inquiry by Dr Eduardo Stober as in the same manner of questioning of those of the morning's defendants. Everyone admitted to having done something within the de Croy network. Albert Libiez, Herman Capiau, Severin – all admitted to assisting fugitive Allied soldiers in getting them food, clothing and lodging. George Derveau admitted to being a liaison between Edith Cavell and Herman Capiau, while George Hostelet freely admitted to assisting Edith Cavell's cell operation with funding for food, clothing and the passage of the soldiers north into Holland. The two café owners, Oscar Mathieu and Maurice Pansaers, merely admitted to having 'looked the other way', when the de Croys, Edith Cavell, Philippe Baucq, Louise Thuliez, George Hostelet and the Countess Jeanne de Belleville wanted to stay past curfew hours for a meeting or used the café as a rendezvous point for strange men to meet and leave. Ada Bodart admitted to harbouring over thirty-four Allied soldiers in her home. The Countess de Belleville only admitted to having permitted her Brussels mansion to be used as a lodging safe-haven for Allied soldiers, but nothing more.

This short questioning wrapped up the first day of testimony; all the major de Croy network players had been questioned by the prosecution. It was now the defence team's turn to make a summary defence for each of their defendants. Sadi Kirschen was one attorney with multiple clients to defend. These included Edith Cavell, Bodart, Severin, Derveau, and other minor players. He asked for the German secret police files and dossiers for each of his clients, but these were denied by the judges on the grounds of security. Sadi had only his wits and that information to which he had heard in the Court with which to defend his clients – it was a farce! Attorney Sadi Kirschen affirmed that Edith Cavell stated that she was too devoted a nurse to have been guilty of all the charges levied against her. He pointed out too that she had helped many German soldiers, who otherwise would have died. He further pleaded that the Allied soldiers came to her, she did not go out seeking them, so as a humanitarian, she could hardly refuse them her kindness. Kirschen also emphasized the point that Edith Cavell, along with the other defendants, were in fear for the lives of the Allied soldiers.

A similar defence was made on behalf of Ada Bodart, Severin and Derveau – all with similar passion and all to the same fate – the denial of each item of defence so raised in objection to the Court. The prosecution dismissed each and every defence as irreverent. The fifty-two year old Mr Pansaers was visibly sick, his skin ashen grey and his limbs trembling from overtaxed nerves. Attorney Kirschen pleaded that he be released – both he and Oscar Mathieu were mere 'observers' to the actual network actors; if they were guilty, it was by ignorance alone. Stober countered with a cocky reply that 'ignorance was not a valid excuse for obvious unlawful and mysterious activities' and that as grown men, they had a responsibility to bear in this affair.

Attorney Braun rose to defend his two clients, Princess Marie de Croy and Countess Jeanne de Belleville. The evidence against both of them was so strong that he could not deny all of their guilt. Instead, he put forward the same arguments for the Princess as she had made in her own defence. He noted that the Princess assisted the Allied soldiers under the undue influence of her brother and out of mercy derived from her Catholic faith. She gave care, food and lodging – she did not convey any soldier to actually escape directly to Holland. As a humanitarian act, she opened up the Bellignies Chateau as a temporary field hospital for all soldiers, Germans included. She was a nurse and she cared for the soldiers personally. This action naturally followed through to helping the refugee Allied soldiers. As for the Countess, she only provided lodging and food. He argued that the Countess should not even have been charged and brought to trial. The flustered words met with scant visible sympathy from the German judges.

The second day of the secret trial was conducted later in the morning about 9:00 am Friday, 8 October 1915 with only the more menial, low-level personages such as miners, farmers and Dr Bull. Instead of being held in the ornate Senate chamber house, the second day's venue was moved to the more sedate lower house Chamber of the Representatives. The audience was also a fraction of that witnessed at the previous day's trial. The change was probably because the theatrics of the grand first day were not so warranted in the second day of the trial. Before the prosecutor and Court, Dr Bull, like Princess de Croy, confessed nothing. He pawned himself off as a close friend of many of those in the de Croy network, but nothing more. He also, wisely, never signed a confession, nor did he admit anything verbally to the German police during his interrogations. His only crime he stated was performing minor oral surgery and examinations on some men at Edith's Clinique, the origin and nationality of which he confessed to have no idea. He and his wife had wisely burnt all incriminating evidence of Dr Bull's espionage activities as soon as Philippe Baucq was arrested on 31 July and the Germans had no evidence or witness to expose the major espionage personage within the de Croy organization.

Dr Bull wisely kept his mouth shut and answered only those specific questions posed to him and then with only a simple response. He knew that the more a person spoke on the stand, the more likely the person was to betray a confidence. A wise man, he had learned early in life the correct time to speak as well as those instances where silence was a virtue. No one in the network had even mentioned his name in connection to the activities of the de Croy network; he was merely scooped-up as part of the large German raid and his arrest was by mere association by being an on-call dentist to the Berkendael Institute. Reggie de Croy knew of Dr Bull's activities, but he kept such confidences to himself, again to spare other members in the network if any of them were arrested. Save for intensive examination of the primary culprits during the first day of the trial, by the end of the second day on 8 October, all thirty-five defendants had been quickly questioned and very meekly defended. As intended by the German Military Tribunal and the German General Staff, the trial was over quickly and secretly. The 'eyes of Berlin' were on this trial and these defendants.

Dr Stober read the prosecution's summary entirely in German; only Marie de Croy and Herman Capiau who were fluent in German fully understood him. He gave a passionate speech that praised the German Army and military secret police for their efforts in the case. Again for the Court's edification, he summarized the major players involved and the critical roles that each person played. The 'leaders' of the network in the Lille-Mons area were largely French or regal; these included the Prince and Princess de Croy along with the Countess de Belleville. The other important person who assisted them was Louise Thuliez.

The yeomen of the network consisted of Capiau, Libiez, Derveau – the Borinage group, the men who were the hands behind the forged identity papers and without which the unfettered movement from rural areas of Belgium to Brussels could not be safely accomplished by the Allied soldiers themselves.

Finally, there was the issue of the critical Brussels cell, which received the soldiers, provided critical financing, lodging, feeding, transporting and arranging for the frontier guide pick-ups. Some members also were involved in the notorious La Libre Belgique underground newspaper and couriering of secret German military secrets – this cell consisted of Edith Cavell, Philippe Baucq, Louis Severin, Ada Bodart, and George Hostelet.

The legal charges were unexpectedly changed without notice from the initial charge of aiding and abetting of enemy soldiers to those of capital crimes and only announced now during his court summary. Calmly and with some obvious delight, Dr Stober asked for sentences against all the named capital players to be charged for treason. A chill immediately came over Princess de Croy's body. She knew treason was a capital offence. She waited until she heard that the prosecutor's sentence demanded for Cavell, Baucq, Thuliez, Severin, Capiau, Libiez, Derveau, Countess de Belleville, and Bodart was to be that of death.

The Princess de Croy, was recommended for a fifteen year prison sentence instead of death. To her great astonishment, the Princess de Croy had expected even greater leniency from Dr Stober in his recommendation of sentencing, then she keenly recalled how each capital offence witness had rebuked him publicly with rebuttal and verbal ridicule, especially by herself. For some unknown reason she was being treated with deference and mercy. The other lesser prisoners were recommended for terms of imprisonment or hard labour ranging from one to fifteen years in duration. Not to be forgotten, the Prince de Croy was recommended in absentia to death as well, along with a wanted 'dead or alive' bounty of 20,000 German marks on his head. Georges Hostelet was recommended for a prison term of ten years imprisonment. Everyone was visibly upset; in fact, Pansaers fainted down onto the hard floor on hearing his recommended sentence of five years in prison and he had to be revived with smelling salts quickly provided by the German court physician. Pansaers was obviously not going to be able to survive even one year in a German prison, let alone multiple years. The President Judge asked the defence and the individual defendants for any closing arguments to be made before the Court adjourned.

Some like Edith Cavell simply stated, "I have nothing to say" – she knew that argument against a closed-mind was futile. Baucq tried to shout out some anti-German rhetoric, but the President Judge slammed down his gavel and silenced him immediately as two huge guards escorted and ejected him from the court chamber with Baucq yelling profanities all the way down the aisle and out into the hallway. Ada Bodart was the emotional one and she cried for mercy from the Court justifying the lives of her two children and recently widowed status as mitigating factors. Severin was so choked up with emotion that he could not utter a word. The Princess took the high road by stating that she 'stood by her own actions' and she tried to argue that

Edith Cavell should receive a lesser sentence because she was not a major element in the de Croy network. Yet all these punishments were merely recommendations only by Dr Stober; the judges were going to decide the actual sentences. All members came to attention, as the President Judge rose and ordered an end to the trial and that he and the other judges were going to deliberate and take all views and evidence into consideration. The Court was cleared and the prisoners were taken back to their respective cells to contemplate their newly imposed morbid recommended sentences.

\* \* \* \* \* \* \* \* \* \* \* \*

It was Saturday morning, October 9, 1915 and the de Croy network prisoners sat sullen and retrospective in their prison cells with utter angst; none of them had ever imagined that the Germans would recommend the imposition of nine capital offences with executions and scores more with long terms of hard labour. Was it all lambast of the very extroverted Court showman Dr Eduard Stober or were the sentences a reflection of the actual state of affairs that the Germans were seeking? It was not unheard of for harsh sentences to be publicly heralded and demanded, only to be substantially reduced within the cloister of the private Court chambers. Given the stoic temperament of the Court, the British blockade and the battlefield stalemate – could anyone expect the German military to be in a generous mood? Only five men now possessed in their hands the ultimate fate of the accused: the German Tribunal Court judges. Appointed by the new Brussels Military Governor von Sauberzweig, it was their duty to bring a quick justice to these defendants and their marching orders from von Sauberzweig was that they be thorough and stern with the defendants. They had heard all the Court arguments, they had read the confessions and they had looked into the eyes of each defendant. They had calmly listened to the narcissistic, arrogant Dr Stober make his grand speeches and courtroom theatrics and they also heard of his long, severe recommended sentences as well and they were not appreciative of his personal 'demands' for all of these executions. All of them were professional military men. They were men of honour, tradition and discipline. Finally, they were men who were confused and divided on the prosecutor's recommendations.

"It's all up to us now, gentlemen! The Belgian Governor General von Bissing, the Brussels Military Governor von Sauberzweig and the German General Staff – are all waiting anxiously for our verdicts and soon! We'll work all weekend and make sure we get these sentences correct. This

Court is no 'rubber stamp of the prosecutor'; we will arrive at our decisions independently without any external influence regardless of rank or social standing, then we'll forward these off to the appointing and approval authority – Military Governor von Sauberzweig – for his modification and final approval. Once we arrive at our decision and recommendations, the matter rests with the Military-Governor. We will satisfy both our honour and duty, our conscience will be well served. Any questions, gentlemen?" the President Judge Colonel Werthmann announced with directness, as the five men gathered in a secluded and guarded chamber within the Belgian Parliament building.

"We need to keep the following three things in our minds during our deliberations and these instructions come to us from Berlin. In all our discussions and findings on these prisoners we must strive to maintain and preserve the following: first, German justice must be seen as swift and efficient; second, German justice must be seen as unfaltering and universal; and finally German justice must be seen as totally impartial. Does everyone understand these operating parameters?" the Colonel slowly and deliberately inquired of his fellow judges.

The four German officers all either immediately responded 'yes' or nodded their heads in vertical affirmation. "Good, then gentlemen, let's begin the discussions. Put your rank aside and be honest in your deliberations. Now, does anyone have any first thoughts about the defendants and the recommended sentences of Dr Stober please?" he encouraged to the subordinate officers, trying to encourage an informal discussion among the group.

"Yes sir, I think that the pompous and prettified prosecutor Dr Stober is an arrogant and crazy man! He is demanding nine death sentences, a good percentage are women, one of them an old maid English nurse, one a widowed school mom and another a French Countess! What is the world going to say about the noble German people who kill women such as these? I do not like this one bit, Colonel!" Captain Baron von Cornberg's candid opening remark offended some of those present.

"Sir, I do not concur with Captain von Cornberg at all! Germany is at war, a modern war, a war of attrition, a war in which soldier and civilian alike are profusely engaged – the combatants are both men and women!" Lieutenant Pault retorted back immediately.

"Some of these accused must die! Germany cannot afford to be seen as weak or faltering; we have thousands of young German troops dying every day in France and Russia! Can the lives of nine civilians really matter so much in a world where tens of thousands are dying daily?" Captain Eck chimed in without hesitation.

"I agree, sir, these are capital crimes! Over two-hundred and fifty soldiers and young men escaped, espionage was committed, secret information was transmitted to the enemy and that rag of an underground newspaper was distributed throughout Brussels! Someone must pay for these acts!" Lieutenant Slenger angrily spoke out in self-righteous indignation.

"Yes, someone must pay indeed! I do not think that we can merely approve all nine death sentences, nor do I think that we can commute all nine death sentences either. As there were nine recommended death sentences, perhaps we can meet somewhere in the middle, maybe only approve four or five capital sentences and in a rank-order of precedence, gentlemen," Colonel Werthmann spoke softly with a tone of resigned concession reverberating in his voice. It was a judicial strategy designed to 'cut the baby in half Solomon-like solution' and it sounded fair to everyone present. They all nodded in affirmation with silent head nodding.

"That fellow Baucq, that bastard Philippe Baucq! That man obviously deserves the death sentence if anyone does; without any doubt this man needs to pay for his outright treason! If he feels so strongly, why is he not fighting in uniform? The man is a coward! His guilt and defiance are disgusting – did you all see how he tried to use his precious Court time for propaganda purposes? It was not to plead for the Court's mercy. I recommend a death sentence for Philippe Baucq!" Lieutenant Pault barked out intensely with visceral hatred.

"I will second that," Lieutenant Slenger echoed.

"Make that a third," Captain Eck immediately followed.

"Yes, I too vote for his death," Captain von Cornberg stated flatly.

"I shall make it unanimous," Colonel Werthmann concluded with a slight huff in his voice.

"Well, that verdict was determined most easily. Now what unfortunate soul is next, gentlemen?" Colonel Werthmann suggested in a rather democratic and un-Prussian-like manner. This high-ranking Prussian was accustomed to issuing orders, not soliciting advice from others, especially from junior Reserve list officers; still, he was mature enough to endorse this collegiate forum and not demur against it.

"I am not pleased with the innocent little grieving Princess de Croÿ's testimony – she was obstinate, defiant and so very proud! Both she and that cowardly brother were the leaders of this network! She was mocking the Court and she was too damn smug! She is proud and stubborn, too good and noble to sign a confession or admit her guilt except where she could not avoid doing so! Her answers danced around every question too. The Princess deserves to die!" Lieutenant Slenger remarked with obvious contempt for the woman.

"Yes, I know that she is guilty too, but I did enjoy the way she fenced back and forth with that arrogant Stober. If his thoughts could kill, the Princess would already be dead! Did you see that pompous man all made-up like a dandy? I think he visited a hair salon just before the trial," von Cornberg replied with a laugh as he sipped on some coffee and puffed on his elaborately carved Meerschaum pipe. All the other four German officers followed in with a hearty laughter and the sombre mood of the group was finally broken and discussions proceeded along in a less formal atmosphere.

"I do not precisely understand the reason why Dr Stober asked for such a lenient sentence against the Princess? I think she was a co-conspirator with her brother, but there's nothing concrete to align her involvement from either facts or testimony from the other prisoners. All I can find her guilty of is helping feed, shelter and move-along the Allied soldiers to others in the network. Stober recommends only a sentence befitting a fringe role. I know she deserves a greater sentence, her guilt is highly suspected, but she made no confession and her involvement is most circumstantial at best. If there was greater guilt on her part, then she hides this most well and with utmost decorum. I think she deserves a capital sentence in my heart, but the facts and testimony do not support her receiving a death sentence – damn it!" Captain Eck pronounced.

"Ah, Captain Eck, there's the sticking point: we all suspect her transgressions, but only she actually knows the truth of these! She is convicted by the accusations of others and not of her own volition! She made no confession and that was her brilliance; without it, there is a shadow of a doubt! That is where the others made their mistakes; the Princess de Croy is a clever, brave lady in spite of her crimes," Lieutenant Pault chimed in with his concerns.

"There is also the fact that she is a Belgian royal and it is easier to imprison a Princess than it is to kill her. We want justice, but we want to avoid public protests and more sabotage too! After all, only the French and English kill their royalty!" Colonel Werthmann half-joked in reference to the French Revolution and Cromwell's execution of Charles I in England. Again there was a torrent of laughter among the German judges; they each thought that the Germans were most superior in breeding and behaviour to that of their older, more established European neighbours. An alternative not even contemplated in their psyche was that they feared that they were inferior to their enemies. The Germans mocked that which they feared.

"The Princess's sentence that I recommend is for a ten year term in prison and hard labour – that is a more fitting sentence for a royal than an execution by firing squad; besides she can always be executed later," Werthmann stated almost as a de facto decision. "Are there any dissenting opinions, please speak up if you have any now?" the Colonel asked of the forum.

No one had any objections; they did possess a slight degree of enmity for the Princess yet they believed the Princess to be under the undue influence of her brother the Prince de Croy. Their rigid Prussian intellect could not fathom the fact that a spinster woman could be so independently minded and clever to be involved in such masculine schemes as spying, espionage and treason, especially for a lady of royal upbringing. This was not the first time in history that the underestimation of one's opponents ironically resulted favourably for the aggrieved party.

"Good decision, gentlemen. The Princess will be 'well-aged' and perhaps less caustic a woman in ten years' time. Now let us proceed to speak about that Cavell lady, that English nurse!" he directed with a tone of some bitterness in his voice.

"She's a weird one, a real cold fish! I felt as if she was hiding something within herself!" Lieutenant Slenger muttered aloud.

"A strange one, to be sure! An Englishwoman, unmarried, a nurse in a foreign country and in a time of war, then she gets herself involved in matters beyond her own affairs," she needs to pay for that! Her actions went far beyond the mere act of patriotism!" Captain Eck volunteered his opinion without waiting to be asked.

"The war makes for strange actions in most people. Yes, pay with prison time or expulsion out of Belgium, but to kill her? I think that is too harsh and Germany will suffer if she is executed!" warned Captain von Cornberg with logical acumen.

"Edith Cavell was the heart and soul of the Brussels cell – without her, none of the planning could have been executed and she concealed herself behind the International Red Cross emblem and the Berkendael Institute Clinique. She is a matronly old English woman and she was involved in affairs outside her profession; she is obviously guilty, but I am unsure about the recommended death sentence too!" Lieutenant Pault argued with concern.

"I believe that you have a point there; after all, if she only helped English soldiers, one could argue her actions were based solely on patriotism, but she helped all Allied soldiers and civilian young men – that is called active recruiting for the enemy. Those actions go beyond patriotism; it points to treason! Still, she helped German wounded soldiers too! She was a naive woman caught up in the tempo of things! I think a death sentence is too strict. Perhaps we should show compassion and entertain a suspended sentence for her!" Lieutenant Slenger added in strident pragmatic reasoning.

"All good points, gentlemen, your arguments have swayed me! Yes, I am forced to go along with all of you. Edith Cavell is guilty of treason against Germany; we can endorse a sentence of execution with the consideration of leniency to commute to prison with hard labour or exportation, we'll let the Military Governor von Sauberzweig make the final endorsement," Colonel Werthmann announced, to which everyone else nodded in agreement.

"Now, let's discuss Mlle Louise Thuliez, the helpless widowed school matron from Lille who became the right-hand of Philippe Baucq and Edith Cavell," Werthmann calmly directed to his fellow judges. "She was caught on 31 July with Baucq and his family throwing copies of La Libre Belgique out of the second floor balcony and frantically ripping up copies of it! We spied her at the café owned by Maurice Pansaers late at night well past curfew and probably waiting for a soldier rendezvous! There is the evidence of espionage, as witnessed by the Allied soldiers' letters, an encrypted message and a codebook in her purse. That is guilt if I ever saw it!" the Colonel lambasted to his fellow officers.

"Most definitely, sir, I have to concur; this woman, in spite of her unfortunate personal circumstances, is guilty of a capital crime and worthy of the sentence of execution. I can see no room for mercy, her guilt is too great and the preponderance of evidence is considerable. In fact, I think she is more guilty than Nurse Cavell," Captain von Cornberg seconded the Colonel's verdict.

"I too hate to see a widow with children executed, but she is guilty and we have her signed confession. Her crimes and guilt are even more self-evident than that of Nurse Edith Cavell's; after all, she had all that coded information in her purse and she was a conspirator in that illegal newspaper with Philippe Baucq. At least Edith performed good works as a nurse, whereas Thuliez did no acts of mercy or charity. Guilty with execution, perhaps with the consideration of leniency to commute to prison with hard labour the same as we recommended for Nurse Cavell to Military Governor von Sauberzweig," Captain Eck remarked to counter the definitive sentence of an outright execution.

"I agree with that too!"

"So do I," Lieutenant Slenger and Lieutenant Pault announced quickly.

"As President Judge, I will concur with that recommendation as well," Colonel Werthmann smiled as he jotted down the judges' tally decisions onto a piece of paper.

"Proceeding along, what are your views on Monsieur Louis Severin?" the Colonel pronounced in a mundane manner as if he were simply reading down a grocery-shopping list.

"My opinion is that he is as guilty as Nurse Edith Cavell, maybe more so; that long-bearded man is a die-hard Belgian patriot. I can see nothing that negates or mitigates his recommended sentence," Captain von Cornberg announced straight-out.

"He is more guilty than Edith Cavell, he was an enabler with the frontier guides and I saw no remorse in his court demeanor – he was bold and defiant," Lieutenant Pault added with vehement contempt for the man.

"I will second that!" Colonel Werthmann coolly replied.

"As do I...include me!...I concur too!" Eck, Slenger and Pault followed in quick verbal successive concurrence. So went the terminal verdict for Louis Severin, for whom there was little pity for a middle-aged, sombre looking Brussels chemist.

"So now we come to the next noble, or should I say aristocrat, the accused, socially prominent, the French Countess Jeanne de Belleville of Lille." Colonel Werthmann ran his pen down the list of prosecution names annotated neatly on the paper before him.

"Sir, you mean the evil partner of Prince and Princess de Croy and Mlle Louise Thuliez? Well, I for one would like to endorse her execution sentence without dissent as recommended by Dr Stober," Lieutenant Pault verbally lambasted at the mention of her very name.

"I do not share those sentiments! In fact, I would like to have the Countess's sentence exchanged for the rather lenient sentence that we just applied to that of the Princess de Croy's – ten years of hard labour!" Lieutenant Slenger fired back quickly. "The Countess de Belleville may have been one of the first enablers to assist the Allied soldiers, but that's about the extent of her culpability, along with providing residence and refuge to refugee soldiers and able bodied young men," Slenger quickly amplified in his justification and audible protest at the capital sentence being sought against her.

"I understand your concern, Lieutenant Slenger and your point is well taken and logical, yet we are also involved in the web of politics. This trial and these verdicts are as much political, as military crimes. For your guidance, we need to show that no one in occupied German territory is above the law, even royals and the aristocrats. In this discussion, no aristocrat has yet been condemned to a capital sentence. Aside for Princess de Croÿ, we have been dealing primarily with working class women and men. So the burden rests on us to decide this woman's case; though she be a fringe player, she is an aristocrat and she is the only one thus presented to us!" Colonel Werthmann so counselled his fellow judges. It seemed that he too had been given 'guidance' from Berlin and the Brussels Military Governor to which he was now subliminally conveying to his fellow judges. Men of experience and education, they could read 'between the lines' of the Colonel's short judicial homily.

"Guilty it is then! For the Countess," Lieutenant Pault shouted out, as Captain Eck quickly endorsed and seconded his verdict. The reality of democracy being freely exercised within the stewardship of the President Judge's supervision did have definite limitations.

"I can endorse a sentence of execution with the consideration of leniency to commute to prison or a sentence of hard labour and then let the Military Governor make the final decision; our consciences will be satisfied!" Lieutenant Slenger strongly voiced out quickly.

"I will second that option," Captain von Cornberg quickly added his vote.

"I think we can agree with that caveat," Colonel Werthmann replied with a smile that betrayed the inner irony that he was playing the role of a Solomon-like figure from the Bible in deciding other people's fate based on pure argument and personal judgment. Yet so too was the process of justice in democracies.

"Congratulations, gentlemen, we have just deliberated on the top five defendants in the de Croÿ network trial; there are four other characters left, not including the ring-master Prince de Croÿ. These other capital crime defendants are accused of offences that fall below even those crimes committed by the Countess de Belleville. We then have all of the other 'minor' defendants, many of whom we are going to have to let go for lack of confessions or collaborative evidence. What are your views, gentlemen?" Colonel Werthmann magnanimously announced as an invitation to a collegiate discussion instead of an authoritative manner.

"Thank you, sir, for this open opportunity to discuss these remaining cases. As per your previous recommendation, I'd say that these other network actors like Capiau, Bodart, Libiez and Derveau – they are all most likely guilty of some level of collaboration, but only of crimes of a lesser personal involvement. We can best do these people justice by giving them long prison sentences, fifteen years each," Captain von Cornberg wearily sighed as he stood up and got up from the table, lit a cigarette and stretched his legs by pacing about the room.

Captain von Cornberg continued his thoughts on the remaining capital sentences: "Thus far we have decided on the imposition of five capital sentences of execution with some of these sentences requesting commutation to prison terms and this is very fair. As to the remaining capital offences recommended by that mad man Stober, I personally think that prudence and justice are well served by the imposition of varying degrees of prison, along with a few of these sentences requesting complete commutation is both reasonable and judicial. It should satisfy our superiors in Berlin and the general public – after all more civilian death sentences will not necessarily bring about greater justice," the captain sighed with both a breath of exhaled cigarette smoke and that of wisdom as he gazed out aimlessly into oblivion with thoughts of the greater war on his mind.

"Very interesting, very enlightening and very astute! Yours is a most sobering and non-traditional Prussian outlook, Captain von Cornberg. Your words are the insights of a man who has lived long and seen much! There are five death sentences, then four sentences for fifteen years of hard labour and finally the dear Princess for ten years of hard labour. Not too bad of a breakdown either; we will have a representation of women, men, middle class, one aristocrat and one royal –- that, Captain von Cornberg, is a very sobering and democratic representation of sentencing that I have ever seen, congratulations! Now what about the others, like Dr Bull, Georges Hostelet, Oscar Mathieu and Maurice Pansaers?" Colonel Werthmann sighed, looking for some interesting suggestions on these sentences.

"We do not have the evidence to convict any of them of more than token crimes, yet we strongly suspect that they were complicit in knowing about the de Croy network activities and they all 'looked the other way'; yet we cannot legally prove any of this, aside from the two café owners, who obviously broke curfew on a few instances and this is merely a fineable offence!" Captain von Cornberg acutely pointed out.

"Five years of hard labour?" Captain Eck responded back in suggestion.

"Prison with suspended sentences?" Lieutenant Pault countered back his reply.

"Deportation or exile?" Lieutenant Slenger added as his own recommendation.

"I think Lieutenant Slenger has a point there – for at least some of these characters. I think we can get the prominent Dr Hostelet off of our backs by sentencing him to a few years in prison with the option to commute to exile," Colonel Werthmann remarked with glee.

"Dr Bull, that English pain-in-the-ass dentist, should be deported back to England – the same fate that I wish we could have imposed on Cavell, but she had signed the confession and verbally indicted herself and everyone else in open court! The faster we get all these expatriate English citizens out of Belgium, the better off we will be. I'm for getting his ass out of Belgium quickly and without publicity! It is bad enough that we are placing a capital sentence on Edith Cavell; we should avoid imprisoning an aged English dentist – let us be rid of him!" Captain von Cornberg echoed out boldly for the fate of the still anonymous de Croy network espionage mastermind.

"You make good sense, von Cornberg, you should be in the diplomatic corps!" Colonel Werthmann toyfully mocked back with a rare grin.

"And to what end of those café owners, Mathieu and Pansaers?" Captain Eck questioned with great concern, though no one else seemed to share his concern for these two lowly men.

"We could give them nominal sentences of two-to-five years in St Gilles prison," Lieutenant Pault noted very casually and without much thought.

"These men are small potatoes, we throw them back into the Belgian population and we show our humanity and leniency, while these two men will wildly spread all of the horror stories of their trial and imprisonment which will strike fear in their fellow Belgians and result in fear and less cooperation with any Allies and their paid agents!" Captain von Cornberg reasoned with skill and calculation.

"For the café owner Mathieu, we should impose the short prison sentence just discussed; however for that decrepit, sickly Pansaers, I think we should cut him loose and have no further bother with him. My God, did you see that mass of nerves shaking in the courtroom? He even fainted! We are better served by letting him go than burdening our prisons with another sick man. His café will be placed permanently 'off-limits' which is itself a harsh punishment. Call me lenient, but my vote is to commute that poor fellow's sentence and let him die at home with his family in destitution," Lieutenant Pault announced in defence of the obviously physically dejected Pansaers. There were no objections to Lieutenant Pault's lenient recommendation or rationale. Pansaers was to be mercifully spared it seemed.

"Ah I knew the German Army possessed some of the wisest men in Germany and there's no doubt in my mind that we will win this war with men and judgment as sound as yours," Colonel Werthmann praised the efforts of his tribunal members.

"Excuse me, sir, what of the other accused prisoners?" Captain Eck asked with eagerness and some ambiguity.

"Excellent point, Captain Eck, we'll have to write up our findings of the capital sentences and send these off immediately to both the Belgian Governor General von Bissing and the Brussels Military Governor von Sauberzweig. Naturally a copy will go directly to the German General Staff, based upon the approval of the German General Staff, who are free to modify any of these capital sentences. As Lieutenant General von Sauberzweig appointed this Military Tribunal, he will have the final authority to sign any execution warrants and then order the initiation of the sentences at a time and place of his own discretion. All the other minor defendant sentences, we can decide tomorrow on Sunday. I am inclined to impose short jail or forced labour time or outright commutation of sentences at this point; we need prison space for more serious offenders. We'll have enough to keep us busy for the rest of today in our final reports on the capital prisoners," President Judge Colonel Werthmann announced with authority.

Over the weekend while they awaited their verdicts, the St Gilles Kommandant thought it wise to give the prisoners a last visit with friends and family before the sentences were announced, after which immediate imposition of the sentence was to be imposed. Edith Cavell was visited by several of her Berkendael Institute Clinique staff nurses, to include now Acting Directress Elizabeth Wilkins. They exchanged some quaint stories, some laughter, hugs and a group prayer. Philippe Baucq, who was sharing a cell with George Hostelet at this time was depressed, nervous and a complete emotional wreck as he hugged and kissed his wife and children for probably the last time on this earth, so certain was he about his impending execution. He thought himself a fool for having ventured so far and being radical in his rebellion against the German occupation. He wished that he had kept his resources confined to only one element against the German resistance instead of the several in which he had dabbled. The other prisoners shared similar tears and farewells with their families.

On Sunday 10 October, the German Tribunal Judges met again to discuss the lesser sentences of the minor players within the de Croy Network and again the judges thought themselves enlightened and lenient men by recommending only sentences of short terms of imprisonment and hard labour that ranged from two through to eight years' duration, while another eight prisoners were fully acquitted not by their innocence, but by the lack of evidence and confessions. Unsurprisingly, the major network figure, Prince Reginald de Croy, was found guilty 'in absentia' and issued a death sentence of immediate execution if ever he was to come into the hands of the Germans.

The verdicts were thoroughly reviewed, processed and sent up through fast courier channels to the German General Staff, Governor General of Belgium and Military Governor of Brussels that same day. The judges' work was now finished; they merely awaited a courtesy reply to their verdicts. However, a reply was also going to be sent to the German prosecutor Dr Eduard Stober and the Kommandant of the St Gilles prison where the majority of prisoners were being maintained. The five de Croy members sentenced to death now had their final fate to be determined by the Military Governor von Sauberzweig, the convening authority of the judicial proceedings against the de Croy network.

* * * * * * * * * * *

The weekend passed and every prisoner was on 'pins and needles' concerning their fates. A sentence could be reached and validated in a day, weeks or months. Each one of them in their minds wondered how disparate the actual sentences were to be from the recommended sentence of Dr Stober. The measure of duration was dependent upon the pleasure and exigency placed upon a trial by the German officials and this trial was indeed an important one of keen interest to the German General Staff in Berlin. The US Consulate in Brussels was still operating under the innocent illusion that no trial had even taken place and that the accused were still awaiting a court date, to which Consul General Brand Whitlock had wanted a Belgian national attached to the US Consulate in Brussels, Mr Guy De Leval, to be Edith's court counsel.

Minister Whitlock was suffering from a severe fever and respiratory upper chest congestion issues and he was on the verge of mandatory bed rest convalescence, yet he managed to send off a diplomatic 'eyes-only' cable to the Ambassador Walter H Page stationed at the US Embassy in London informing him of the Brussels US Consulate efforts in contacting and representing English Nurse Edith Cavell in her defence and that efforts were underway to try and break the German communications 'black-out' involving this entire de Croy Network incident and to pass this status update to Sir Edward. Grey was the British Secretary of State for Foreign Affairs posted in London. Whitlock further directed his second in command, Mr

Hugh Gibson and the US Consulate Belgian legal advisor Mr de Leval,
to immediately contact the German Political Minister in Brussels, Baron
Generalmajor Oskar von der Lancken, and request an immediate audience
and update on Nurse Edith Cavell's imprisonment and status. The Germans'
secrecy had been total.

Late Sunday evening when the Germans were performing their ritual
mid-night cell check at St Gilles prison, they discovered a tragic incident.
The emotionally distraught and temporarily mentally imbalanced café owner
Maurice Pansaers had, in his despair and forgone conclusion of being found
guilty, hanged himself in his prison cell with pieces of improvised clothing
tied together into a make-shift noose. The news of his suicide spread like
wild fire throughout St Gilles prison, yet Monday brought even more
definitive and dreadful news.

"Everyone get up, make yourself presentable and be ready in five
minutes to be marched down to the main assembly area, now get dressed
and make it quick!" the various guards shouted aloud into the numerous
cells of the de Croy network prisoners. The early Monday morning arousal
was unexpected and it could only mean ominous news for the prisoners of
the de Croy network. Meanwhile Princess de Croy was already transported
from the Kommandantur barracks and standing in the mail hallway under
the watchful eye of two huge guards with their prescribed Mauser Gewehr
98 rifles with fixed carefully polished bayonets. With utmost German
military efficiency, within twenty minutes, every prisoner was assembled and
silence was the enforced order of the day as the thirty-four prisoners looked
nervously at one another. Each one of them was prepared for the German
prosecutor's court recommended sentences, yet each of them secretly hoped
for less-than-prescribed, merciful reduced sentences. They all were sombre
due to the announcement of their final sentences and from hearing of the
tragic suicide of Maurice Pansaers.

Dr Eduard Stober, looking perfectly groomed and meticulous as ever,
strode proudly and confidently down the main prison corridor and into
the St Gilles assembly hall located just inside the front gates of the prison.
Stober looked fit and trim in his form-fitting German military uniform
despite his fortyish middle-aged frame and sedentary desk-bound lifestyle.
Amazingly also accompanying him were Captain von Kirchenheim, Captain
Joel, Lieutenant Pinkhoff and Lieutenant Bergan. Despite the completed role
that these German military officers had played in uncovering the de Croy
network, they personally wanted to see closure on all those people who,
in many instances, had existed only as names within the recesses of their

memories and dusty files.

"Good morning everyone, the German Tribunal has sent their capital and de règle sentencing recommendations to the German Command authorities for review and approval. I'm only going to read out the final sentences of the major, capital sentences, I will defer the other rulings to the Sergeant Major to read the remaining of the lesser sentences," Stober noted in his loud German voice that was immediately translated by his translator into French. Always the egotist, Dr Stober really did not want to be bothered with reading out the entire, long list of thirty-five verdicts of the 'small fish'; he was only interested in the major prisoners.

"Let me have everyone's attention! Under the auspices of the German Penal Code paragraph 58 which states that, 'Any person who, with the intention of aiding the hostile Power or causing harm to German or allied troops, is guilty of one of the 'crimes' of Paragraph 90 of the German Penal Code, will be sentenced to death for treason'. The specified 'crime' listed in paragraph 90 as applied in the Military Court and trial against these indicted capital crime prisoners are the charge of 'conducting soldiers to the enemy'. Such charges are applied against and have been levied upon the name of the people I am about to announce," Stober heralded out like a bloated show master at a circus performance. Every capital defendant's heart pounded like a drum and each of them quietly prayed theirs was not among those names to be announced by the German prosecutor whose original recommended capital crime list was shy of a dozen names. Stober continued to the finale of his boisterous monologue.

"The sentences of death under the charge of treason and without any consideration for commutation or extenuating circumstances are: Philippe Baucq, Louise Thuliez, Edith Cavell, Louis Severin and Jeanne de Belleville. The sentences for fifteen years of hard labour are: Herman Capiau, Ada Bodart, Albert Libiez and Georges Derveau. The sentence for ten years of hard labour is Marie de Croy. For George Hostelet five years in prison. These sentences are effective immediately and to be carried out at the pleasure and determination of the Military Governor Baron Major General von Sauberzweig. All capital cases are automatically subject to appeal to the Military Governor, but these appeals for leniency or commutation do need to be written out by each condemned prisoner immediately and I will take these myself to General von Sauberzweig. I shall be leaving here in three hours, so do not waste any time!" Stober remarked in a loud voice. The recommendations for leniency of the Military Tribunal had been ignored and overturned by a higher German military convening authority.

There was an eerie silence as Stober rolled up the list and placed it back into his flat black leather valise. He handed another piece of paper to the Sergeant Major to read the lesser sentences to the assembly as he and the German officers left the room. Everything the Germans were doing was perfectly legal in accordance with existing international law and German national sovereignty. The fate of Philippe Baucq was set in stone from the beginnings of the trial; he was guilty by his own action and by his police interrogation responses, not to mention his outrageous court room antics! Someone had to pay with a life for this network and with the Prince de Croy being absent, Philippe was to receive no mercy. Philippe was a good substitute for the Prince de Croy. He was definitely guilty of operating an illegal underground subversive newspaper and he was a guide and recruiter to many Allied soldiers. Strong evidence existed that he was also in communication with foreign Allied elements and that he also conveyed secret German war activity data to the Allies.

Edith's sentence was also immutable and her crimes were confessed and endorsed with her own signature. The Germans wanted to send a clear message that women who interfered with the German war effort were subject to the same harsh punishment as those of men. The Germans noted that women had played at least an equal, if not superior, role in the de Croy network operations and they needed to send a strong signal to other women not to follow their example, lest they too were going to suffer the severe consequences of German justice. There were no free passes in the German military justice system during The Great War. The fact that she was an English, unmarried, childless woman made the imposition of the sentence more tolerable to the Germans. The Tribunal's request for mercy had been deliberately ignored.

Philippe cusped his face in both his hands and cried out and wept in despair. "What shall become of my poor wife and two daughters? What a foolish thing I have done! What a foolish man I have been!" He sobbed like a helpless child. The prisoners were barred by the guards from physically touching one another and Edith could only imagine the fear that Philippe was experiencing, not for his own life, but of his soon-to-be-widowed wife and fatherless daughters.

Georges Hostelet slowly spoke from a distance six feet away. "Edith, are you going to appeal the decision? You have nothing to lose!" he uttered with a tone of urgency and expressing his own intentions. Edith looked pale and unemotional as usual; she looked sadly back at Georges and stated, "Such an action on my part will be useless! You see I am English; the Germans despise the British for entering the war and spoiling the German plans for a quick victory. They want and need for an English woman to be executed; since I am here and obviously guilty, I am their prized trophy victim."

Georges looked back at her and thought that he spotted some tears in Edith's eyes. The trial and verdict had finally taken a toll on her strong English Iron Matron's resoluteness; she resigned herself to her death sentence and made no written appeal.

"No more talking there, you two, you are now convicted prisoners!" a lean German guard shouted in German with verbal satisfaction in his dictatorial voice. Georges looked back at the guard with contempt. "So what are you going to do to me, Boche bastard? Imprison me! I've been in your filthy prison for two months!" he remarked sarcastically in French. The German guard looked at Hostelet with utter contempt and he dearly wanted to strike the Belgian across the face with his pistol, but there were too many other prominent people present.

All the other capital offence prisoners were too shocked to say anything. Marie de Croy merely stared straight ahead in emotionless anticipation of her fate to labour long and hard, probably somewhere in Germany and under dire conditions. She wondered if she was ever going to see her family or her beloved Bellignies Chateau again. The Princess was surprised and relieved that she was not going to be immediately executed for being one of the ringleaders of the de Croy network, but she then guessed correctly that the Germans had wanted her alive for their own propaganda purposes and while executing a French Countess was one thing, it was quite another to apply a capital sentence against a Belgian Royal family Princess. It seemed that even the German military knew certain limits and niceties to be followed.

Pastor le Seur of the St Gilles prison staff slowly and with almost crouched caution and reverence approached Edith Cavell and requested that she escort him to a nearby small room. She nodded her head to silently affirm his request. The Commandant nodded his head to Edith's German guard and she and the minister were escorted into a small room, while the other prisoners were dismissed to further ponder their fates. Few of them received any really good news this day. Maurice Pansaers had prematurely killed himself but some lower level defendants were lucky enough to be pardoned due to lack of evidence. Those receiving prison terms were not fortunate either – a prison term in Germany was physically tough and challenging; many a prisoner died from illness, injuries and malnutrition, and for some a prison sentence was merely an execution of death under a polite disguise.

"Madame Nurse Cavell, I must regretfully inform you that things are not going well for you. I fear, in fact, I have it on good authority that your death sentence will be successfully fulfilled shortly – within a day or maybe two at the most," Pastor le Seur whispered sadly. Tears filled Edith's eyes as he continued to speak. "There will most likely not be any delays or commutation of your execution. I know that you are a woman of loyalty, faith and of Almighty God and I want to be there for you until the end of your mortal life – that is, with your permission! Please do not see in me any of my German blood, see only a poor churchman trying to assist his fellow Christian meet such a barbaric fate in these supposedly modern times."

A few tears welled up for the first time in Edith's soft porcelain white face as she realized that she was to be in this world only another half-day or less. Pragmatic reality often trumped reserved idealism. Edith gently wiped her eyes and forced a gentle smile upon the beleaguered minister. "No Pastor, I am fine; however if you can act as a courier to my poor eighty year old mother in England a note that I shall write to her later today, I shall be forever in your debt. You see I told her and my entire family that when this war began, that I was going to be safe and that if one had to do one's duty in this war, let it be with the poor soldiers at the front and that is where I have stayed for better or worse! Thank you, Pastor." Edith gently smiled. With these words, it was now time for the Pastor to weep and he did so, as he sadly bid Edith a short farewell before seeing her later in the evening.

Suddenly an extemporaneous thought engulfed the old Pastor's mind – 'perhaps I can arrange for an English minister to visit you this evening, Madame Cavell. I shall do my best to do this for you and I'd like to minister to you up through the end times!' the distraught Pastor sincerely resolved. Edith's eyes responded back with an immediate positive response.

"Thank you Pastor, I'd greatly appreciate that effort and there is nothing else that you can do for me. You see, my fate, like every other person, resides with the Almighty," Edith replied as her guard escorted her back to her solitary cell. The Pastor had never seen so courageous a woman and one so willing to die for her country – this was indeed a woman of substance and character. For the first time in his life, the Pastor felt ashamed to be a German – 'what sort of a country kills a woman such as this English nurse?' he embarrassingly thought to himself.

True to his words to Edith and with some fancy finagling, Pastor le Seur finally contacted a British chaplain who had also remained in Brussels to minister to the diplomatic and international community that had still remained in the capital when the war began.

Pastor le Seur also spoke to Philippe Baucq and asked him if he had desired the company of clergy and Philippe stated with red teary eyes that later in the evening he desired a Catholic priest to visit him and administer the Catholic sacraments in preparation for death: confession, holy communion and extreme unction. The Pastor agreed and he speedily departed to make contact with both the Anglican minister and a Catholic priest. The de Croy network had finally been vanquished along with all of its members. Those network members who were presented with the opportunity of escape had wisely chosen this option. There was no honour in merely making oneself another target for the German firing squad – to the Germans it mattered not if one nobly gave oneself up for surrender, one's fate was already sealed. All that remained was the final consummation of the imposed death decrees and this event was happening with rushed imminence. The only people with any chance of a commutation were those capital defendants who appealed their death sentences – Louise Thuliez, Louis Severin and Countess Marie de Belleville. Until these petitions were carefully reviewed and processed, these three condemned could not be executed. Making no appeals, Edith and Philippe were consigned to their fate.

The German Military Governor Major General von Sauberzweig physically signed the execution warrants for Philippe and Edith late on Sunday 10 October, after carefully reading and rejecting any commutation of the five capital sentences submitted to him by the discerning military judges. The other three capital sentences were still under appeal and so no execution warrants could be completed against these other three capital prisoners. There was no reason for any delay in the two sentences not to be consummated. He had made his determination that these two prisoners were to be immediately executed on Tuesday, 12 October at dawn. Von Sauberzweig had carefully coordinated with the German General Staff and they had no objections to his final decision – he was the sole military authority in Brussels and his word on this matter was now final. The execution decision and death warrants lay in the exclusive authority of the Brussels Military Governor and he dismissed any recommendation for any leniency that was recommended by the judges for any of the condemned capital crime convicted prisoners, especially for the English woman Edith Cavell. For an unknown reason von Sauberzweig disliked Edith Cavell – ironic for the fact that he did not personally know of her, just the crimes of which she had been accused, tried and now convicted. Time was of the

essence before any rumours leaked out and any serious diplomatic efforts
were initiated to block the executions. At all costs, no word of this action was
to spread beyond the city of Belgium. Communications of the day restrained
the speedy transmittal of any news by electronic means to multiple days
now that the war had severed many key communication organs. This was to
remain strictly a military matter and not be allowed to morph uncontrollably
into a political issue.

The Belgian Military Governor General von Bissing was informed
of the execution orders by von Sauberzweig as a matter of professional
courtesy alone, yet ironically by the German military chain-of-command,
the Belgium Military Governor had no authority over the Brussels Military
Governor; in the German military hierarchy, these were two totally separate
and distinct postings neither of which had predominance over the other, nor
did that of superior military rank. Both the trial and de Croy network was
aligned geographically to the district of Brussels, thus everything relating to
the trial and sentencing lay in von Sauberzweig's hands.

Both Baronial Military Governors ordered all of their subordinates to
remain silent on all details and inquiries regarding the matter of the trial
and especially the sentencing. It was imperative that the executions be
kept secret upon peril of military discipline. Orders were issued to ignore
or stall any external inquiries on the trial or the prisoner's fates, regardless
of the party making the inquiry. The Germans were going to release
information as it benefited them, not others! The US Consul-General Brand
Whitlock was never informed of the trial or recommended sentences by
the German military defence lawyer Captain Kirschen, despite Whitlock's
previous personal requests in August by for this information. As with
the usual efficiency, there quickly arose a rumour of a secret trial, but no
German official confirmed any information. In the days before electronic
multi-media, verbal stories and the spreading of gossip was rampant for
both women and men as a means of social convention to pass along the
mundane events of the day. The guards at St Gilles prison were among the
most voracious of gossip mongers – it not only passed their time, but they
used such privileged information to inflate their male egos to their wives,
girlfriends and male acquaintances. If the story was juicy enough, a guard
usually received a free drink from his saloonkeeper or a fellow drinker. It
seemed that it paid to possess 'boasting rights' for the guards at St Gilles
prison.

From discovery, arrest and prosecution, each stage of the counter-
espionage process was carefully monitored at the highest levels of German

military and political authorities. Berlin was keenly interested and involved, demanding to be kept informed of every salivating detail. There was a pragmatic reasoning to the speedy German trial and rapid execution of the death sentences. Germany could ill afford the posting of valuable soldier and financial resources in the maintenance of huge counter-espionage operations and more of these were going to be needed unless the civilian population of Belgium and any other German occupied country was brought to their knees into obedient and quiet submission. Clearly, this example of a few hundred recruited and escapee Allied soldiers was merely the start of bad things to come; success only begged for a replication of more underground networks and activities across the entire western front. A bold, public example was mandatory to counter any imitators. A harsh and determined sentence needed to be applied and quickly. The threat of mere prison or deportation was not an ideal solution either, as it still bred positive propaganda for the Allies and it showed potential copycats that there was not the ultimate price to be paid for treason to the German state. A mere slap-on-the-wrists could no longer be a satisfactory solution. Death by German military firing squad or hanging was a much better and clear solution; it solved many issues in a very terminal single fashion too.

The Germans had no qualms about killing civilians, especially a woman; in fact, they needed to kill some woman in the de Croy underground, if only to illustrate that German law was impervious to one's given sex. The Germans wanted to discourage any similar copycats among the fairer sex. They knew that they also needed the 'correct' woman. The Princess was a public and royal figure – killing her could bring about a great uprising among the Belgian population. Additionally, the Princess had signed no official affidavit of confession and every witness testified that she had only assisted in feeding and lodging some Allied soldiers and nothing substantially more.

The German judges deemed her death off-limits and instead they imposed a long term of hard prison, the ruggedness of which might indeed carry its own death warrant. No the Germans needed another woman entirely, someone equally culpable yet not as prominent as the Princess. Mlle Louise Thuliez was a primary co-conspirator along with Philippe Baucq and she was a network courier and assisted in running the underground newspaper too. Surely she was worthy of execution, yet the testimony in court clearly showed that she had not shown the obvious signs of being a leader of any sort – if anything, she was a foolish follower; besides she had filed an appeal and this motion had to be entertained and this meant a delay in her execution. The Countess de Belleville was a possible execution candidate; still her crimes and involvement were not prominent enough and she too had also filed a death sentence appeal.

There was only one readily available woman to execute: Nurse Edith Cavell. Edith showed intelligence, defiance, courage, determination and actual leadership. Heading up the Red Cross Clinique rue de la Culture, she demonstrated natural management qualities for personnel, funding, food, housing, transportation and planning. The Germans also remembered that her Clinique was one of the major points of network recruiting and escapee operations. She was also English, a major Allied enemy, middle-aged, stoically detached personality and she had the added advantage of being both unmarried and childless – she was the perfect second execution candidate to share the firing squad with the traitor Philippe Baucq. Unless von Sauberzweig intervened, Philippe Baucq and Edith Cavell were to be the first two prisoners executed by German military firing squad, followed by Mlle Louise Thuliez, Louis Severin and finally Countess Jeanne de Belleville.

* * * * * * * * * * *

# Chapter 10:
# The Rifles in October

*"Well my dear Baron von der Lancken, if you do not know the Kaiser well, you can simply make a phone call to him right now and get to know him better by discussing Edith Cavell's execution!"*

"A secret trial! Verdicts! Executions! Edith Cavell's execution! Just what in the hell are those bastardly Germans trying to pull here? This is an outrage, a blatant attempt to upset the modern judicial order behind a veil of deceit and dark secrecy!" Consul Brand Whitlock angrily bellowed forth from the sick-bed of his bedroom in the US Consulate in Brussels. There was a heavy, congested, gravelly tone to his voice, as the thick mucus in his throat struggled to free itself from his vocal cords and his throat was raw-red from an infection and the strenuous coughing. The Consul was fighting the mid-stages of influenza and his three visitors were mindful to keep their distance, lest the primary staff of the US Consulate become infected. The three men prudently remained at a safe distance near the door entrance.

"When did this travesty happen? How did you come to know this? We've heard nothing back from the German political office – not a damn thing has been conveyed to us despite our previous requests, nothing from this Generalmajor Baron von der Lancken or his side-kick boot-licking lackey, Mr Conrad. Silence, nothing but silence from the Germans! Excuse my language, but those German bastards are hiding something from us!" Whitlock hoarsely shouted out in a strenuous monologue outburst with both obvious anger and discomfort.

"Sir, we just heard the news about ten minutes ago from Acting Directress Nurse Elizabeth Wilkins of the Berkendael Institute, Edith's right-hand assistant at the nursing school Clinique," First Secretary Hugh Gibson replied back to the Consul's original query. "Nurse Wilkins and two other nurses are frantic that the rumours from some of the St Gilles guards indicated that the execution sentences were read today at noon and that the executions are scheduled for tomorrow morning," Gibson added with an anxious filled voice.

"This is outrageous! It's like vigilante justice! The Germans are sneaking this entire affair under the wire, hoping that the sentence is carried out before any knowledge or protests about this dastardly event can be officially challenged. Son of a bitch!" Whitlock shouted out from his bed in utter disgust and anger; a mild mannered gentlemen, he hardly ever used off-colour language.

"Time is too short, sir, we need to intervene now! There's no time for cables from Presidents or Prime Ministers. If we do not intervene, Edith Cavell will die in a few hours!" Mr Guy de Leval, a US Consulate employed Belgian attorney stated urgently.

"The rumour is that the Germans are also going to execute the Belgian Philippe Baucq and we know nothing about the other people who may also have death sentences on their heads," Gibson added in quick summary.

"Get me up! Get me up out of this damn sick bed quick! I don't care how sick I am. I represent US President Woodrow Wilson and I'm writing out a letter to that old cantankerous bastard, that Prussian Military Governor von Sauberzweig, an official letter of appeal for the commutation of execution for Edith Cavell – she's our prime responsibility as a citizen of the United Kingdom; those other unfortunate souls are not, I'm sad to say," Consul Whitlock replied as he wearily threw off the warm bed comforter and sat up wearily on the side of his bed. He was obviously tired, congested and sore. Every bone in his body ached to include his jaws and teeth. Guy de Leval quickly draped a thick terry cloth robe over the Consul. "I had the unfortunate task of meeting von Sauberzweig and he is obstinate, grumpy and has a sour look on his face that matches his disposition! His grumpy personality reinforces the negative image of the Germans," Whitlock remarked as be slowly placed on his bedroom slippers.

Whitlock slowly strode over to his small, convenient bedroom table-desk, opened the centre drawer to withdraw official US Consulate embossed writing paper and jotted down a short, sincere appeal to stay Edith's execution. He wrote two letters: a longer one to the Military Governor von Sauberzweig and a shorter letter to German Political Minister von der Lancken. A professional diplomat, Whitlock was literate in French, the international language of statesmen. He was mindful to compose the two short correspondence letters in both English and French, this precaution to circumvent any misunderstandings or delays on the part of the Germans.

With the possession and clarity of prudent thought, the one page letters took only ten minutes to compose. He addressed the letters and envelopes to the respective German officials and then from a nearby lit candle, he sealed the back of the envelope with the customary official seal of the US Consulate to prove the letters' authenticity and physical integrity. This type of 'old world' formality was also a distinction greatly appreciated by the stuffy and tradition-bound Germans, who were known to simply throw-away official correspondences that were not properly presented to them. He hoped that Baron von der Lancken, who he had known since 1914, could intervene with the newly installed Brussels Military Governor Lt Gen Baron Martin von Sauberzweig.

"It's finished and let us hope that this works. I have composed two appeal letters, but go to see the German Political Minister first, the Military Governor refuses all visitors without an appointment and he's probably in bed by now anyway", Whitlock remarked.

"What time is it anyway?" Brand Whitlock inquired, as he had forgotten that he had previously removed his wristwatch from his left hand after his wife and physician insisted that he be confined immediately to his bed.

"It's 9:15 pm, sir," Hugh Gibson remarked nervously.

"Damn it, this remark is of no disrespect to you gentlemen, but a character like Lt General von Sauberzweig or Generalmajor Baron von der Lancken are a bit arrogant and straight-laced – they're both Prussians, you know! Being such, they are not going to fancy seeing or entertaining any execution appeal from Consulate staff; the proud Germans want to see the top-man and I'm too damn sick. It's damp and raining like hell outside and I'll catch pneumonia for sure if I even try to move from here," Whitlock stated with naked resignation as he handed the sealed appeal envelopes to his First Secretary Hugh Gibson.

He thought for a few seconds while climbing back into his bed. "Call the Consulate driver and get a car quickly. I want both Hugh and Guy to go directly to the Spanish Embassy. I want both of you to pick up the Spanish Ambassador, Foreign Minister Marques de Villalobar. The Marques is a very accommodating man, he speaks several languages and he speaks frankly and with the power of the King of Spain – he's a good man to have with you and I'll contact him immediately. Now go you two and don't be too diplomatic here; a brave English woman's life is in our hands!" Whitlock noted as he picked up the telephone receiver as Gibson and de Leval quickly departed the room to get their hats and overcoats to protect them against the pouring torrential rains now soaking Brussels. The ride over to the Spanish Embassy was a modest ten-minute affair.

"Hello gentlemen, I am Marques Rodrigo Saavedra de Villalobar, but just call me Rodrigo. Consul Whitlock briefed me about Nurse Edith Cavell. It's a terrible injustice! What are those stupid, damn Germans thinking?"

the Marques stated with obvious displeasure and agitation. He was a tall handsome man with rich, thick black hair, warm brown eyes and a well-developed muscular frame. "We have no time to lose, gentlemen," the Marques stated with a hurried voice as he grabbed his coat and hat, and the three men quickly ventured out into the waiting American Consulate automobile.

"Quick driver, let us be off to the German Political Minister's office!" Gibson shouted out to the driver in a tone of urgency. "Let's get going and put on the gas, driver!" Guy de Leval shouted anxiously in the informal American vernacular that was popularizing the modern world. In less than ten minutes, their vehicle pulled up to von der Lancken's private house. It was an urban pocket mansion that doubled in both form and function as his private residence and official private office for high-level visitors and private social functions as so benefited his official duties. The baron's playhouse was a beautiful three storey, dark beige marble structure that occupied a quarter block of prime Brussels real estate; its previous owner had been a top Brussels banker who was overseas when the Germans invaded and neither he nor his family returned to the mansion. Many wealthy Belgians were in exile and equally waiting-out The Great War.

"Yes gentlemen, may I help you?" a tall, lean, aged butler about fifty years old inquired of the three men in a thick German tone, as they stood in the pouring rain holding black umbrellas over their heads.

"Do you speak French or English?" Ambassador Rodrigo Saavedra quickly inquired in acceptable German.

"Yes, I speak both, please state your names and business. This is a late hour to be calling on anyone," the German butler interjected with a stone chiselled face.

"Good, speak English then, so my American friends understand our conversation. I am the Spanish Foreign Minister Marques Rodrigo Saavedra de Villalobar and this is the American Consulate First Secretary Hugh Gibson and Attorney Guy de Leval. We are here to see the Political Minister von der Lancken," Ambassador de Villalobar demanded forcefully.

"I'm most sorry, gentlemen, the General and his staff are not here! His Excellency is out to the theatre, 'at the Le Bois Sacre' with his staff! I do not know when they will return. I suggest you make another visit tomorrow morning like any sane person!" the arrogant German servant announced without fear or hesitation in his voice or mannerisms.

"Who in the hell do you think you are talking to here! You're a rude, arrogant little man and a servant at that! A brave woman's life is at stake;

neither she or ourselves have the luxury of a 'tomorrow', so we're coming in and waiting for the Baron to return and return he must, correct?" Ambassador de Villalobar announced as he brushed aside the butler and the three men walked into the ornate marble encrusted vestibule of the Political Minister's residence. It felt good to be out of the cool downpour of rain. Both Gibson and de Leval were impressed by the Marques's no-nonsense attitude and they were both glad that Consul Whitlock had wisely asked for his assistance.

The strict-laced German butler was astounded at both this rude action and the insult to his position as being a mere servant. "You cannot, you must not do this, it is 'verboten', not permitted!" cried the German butler in alternating German and English responses.

"Well there 'Fritz', murdering a helpless, middle-aged English nurse is 'verboten' too!" Hugh Gibson spat out in both obvious mockery and insult. The butler was flabbergasted as his eyes bulged out in self-indignation of this breach of German territory by three uninvited brash uninvited foreigners.

The three men unburdened themselves of their heavy rain-soaked outer garments onto a conveniently available ornate wooden coat rack. Small puddles of water immediately formed on the floor. It was 9:30 pm and time was burning down fast; they needed German action on the Cavell matter, not the attention to manners.

"Look here, my good man. I know my problem is not of your personal concern, but you are still going to help us whether you want to or not! I want for you to go to that theatre where the Baron von der Lancken and his aides are being entertained and tell him that the Spanish and American representatives are waiting to see him on an urgent matter and we are not leaving his residence until he returns to speak with us, do you understand me?" de Villalobar announced, not as a request, but as a formal demand. Immediately taken aback by the rude words, the German butler looked at him with a gaze of contempt.

"Don't just stand there, do as I say, you awkward man! Call for a car and get going and show us to a room where we can await His Excellency's return," de Villalobar added to remind the German butler of his obviously forgotten manners afforded unto foreign diplomatic visitors. Ambassador de Villalobar knew from experience that most people succumbed to demands that were made in a tone of self-righteous behaviour, bellicose outbursts and unflinching confidence. His bombast worked!

"Follow me, I'll take you to the yellow sitting salon, gentlemen, come right this way!" the butler replied as he led the three strangers into a lush, golden coloured room that was decorated in Louis XVI white and gold furniture, light gold threaded silk wallpaper and honey-coloured Persian silk carpets. Gold gilt mirrors strategically adorned the walls, as did the huge ornate painting that depicted scenes from the Napoleonic era.

"Please wait here, I will inform the Baron and come back to inform you of his reply," the butler slowly muttered, as he closed the tall white doors to the ornate golden yellow salon. The three very frustrated men waited in the ornate room while the butler journeyed to the 'Le Bois Sacre' theatre to convey the urgent message that he had been given. A period of about thirty minutes had passed and the German butler finally returned again to the Baron's home with an answer.

"Excuse me, gentlemen, I have done as you have requested, despite my better judgment may I add, and the Baron von der Lancken stated that he will see all of you when the theatre play is completed," the butler announced as he opened the salon door and just as quickly closed it after making his pronouncement. The butler was proud and he was not going to be tongue-lashed again by these obviously socially inferior men, who possessed titles greater in excess than their individual manhood. The news was sobering to the three anxious emissaries; the Germans were deliberately stalling – they didn't care about Edith Cavell's pending execution. For over two hours time passed like a stalled glacier, then suddenly a sound was heard at the front door and the Baron and his two rain-soaked aides entered the foyer of the residence in a cheerful, careless mood oblivious to the three visitors awaiting for them.

"Well I see that I still have three unannounced guests and at such a late hour too! This is most irregular," the Baron loudly announced as he opened the yellow salon doors. His English was perfect. He was tall, physically trim and handsome with brown hair and in his early forties.

"Herr Baron von der Lancken, we just learned a scant few hours ago that Edith Cavell and Philippe Baucq are going to be executed tomorrow morning at sunrise! We represent the British interests and we represent the sovereign nations of Spain and the United States. We plead for the life of Edith Cavell with either a stay of execution or a commutation of the death sentence to a term of hard labour. Any leniency for Philippe Baucq is also gratefully requested," Ambassador de Villalobar pleaded directly.

"I cannot believe this outrageous statement. A trial needs to take place before a sentence can be levied. I have seen no public proclamation of any trial verdicts nor have you, gentlemen!" the Baron arrogantly proclaimed although he possessed the summary details of the trial and impending death sentences.

"There are no known verdicts, Baron, it was a secret trial!" Guy de Leval shouted out unceremoniously without any pretense of diplomatic politeness.

"Who are you, sir, what is your name and position please?" the Baron replied as he looked snobbishly down his nose at this loud-mouthed man with the Belgian accent.

"Excuse my abrupt manners, but time is of the essence. My name is Guy de Leval. I'm with the US Consulate, I am Belgian, but I represent the US Consulate in all their Belgian legal affairs," he replied back straightaway.

"We've heard rumours that there was a trial and execution verdicts!" Gibson chimed in, "and I am the First Secretary at the US Consulate, Hugh Gibson is my name, Herr Baron!" Gibson wanted to ensure that the Baron remembered his name and position.

The Baron smiled with condescendence at Hugh Gibson's remarks. "My dear First Secretary, the German government does not operate on rumours! I hope that the American government does not either or am I wrong Mr First Secretary?" the Prussian replied with veiled contempt at the blunt accusing words being spoken to him at this hour by an obvious inferior ranked diplomatic officer, not to mention that of Gibson's commoner status. The Baron surmised that this was just another brash, uncouth, fumbling American bureaucrat.

"We heard this information from someone employed in the St Gilles prison!" Guy de Leval interjected suddenly. He took personal and professional offence at Baron von der Lancken's casual, smug attitude and the obvious belittling of a professional colleague.

"Well sir, prisons are full of rumours and stories; there is nothing else to do in confinement except to make up these little play fantasy things; besides, gentlemen, it is a late Monday evening and all the government offices are closed and the Kommandant is gone for the day as well, tomorrow will be a better time to investigate this matter further and with a clearer, refreshed constitution too," the Baron added with a dismissive air.

"No, no, hell no, Baron! Tomorrow will be too damn late, Edith and Philippe may well be dead by tomorrow morning or maybe that is your intention! I insist that you start making phone calls right now to investigate this matter!" Mr Gibson stated in an agitated, raised voice of concern.

The Baron immediately had a look of anger and disgust in his eyes. Who were these uninvited barbarians to come barging into his residence and demand anything of a German general officer in time of war and a titled Baron to boot? "I'm afraid that you are in a position to demand nothing of me in my own private residence and offices. It is true, you Americans are as brash as those cowboys depicted in your novels and moving picture shows!" the Baron announced with obvious sarcasm and disdain.

"This is murder!" Guy de Leval shouted out as he lost his temper. "A civilian woman and man are going to die because you are pretending ignorance of an evil, foul deed that is about to be performed," he burst out angrily. This outburst was a professional and personal insult to which the Baron was not going to passively tolerate.

The Baron stood up erect and walked over to Guy de Leval and looked him squarely in the eyes. "Sir, if you were in the German army, I would personally shoot you for those words! Sometimes I wish that the institution of dueling was not abandoned; I would take personal satisfaction from you and these other men." The men stood there visually loathing each other, yet nothing was being resolved. Gibson and de Leval almost wanted to physically throw a punch at the arrogant Baron's face, but their discipline ruled over their emotions.

"I think the time for anger and proud words lie elsewhere and for another time. Action is needed here, gentlemen, not words," Ambassador de Villalobar interjected. He needed cooperation, not confrontation to save Edith's life. Spain indeed had a wise man as their representative in Brussels.

"I believe that you gentlemen may think these 'allegations' to be true; however, it cannot be so, I cannot believe that such a sentence could be executed so quickly and especially against a woman and a foreign woman at that!" Baron von der Lancken lied with contrived emotion, as he argued adamantly to his hostile uninvited late evening guests.

"Please, Baron von der Lancken, I'm asking that you simply call the warden at St Gilles prison and verify the status of Edith Cavell personally. If they deny the execution, then we only made an error of over-reacting; however, if her execution is confirmed, we can take steps to save her. I implore you, Baron, to make the simple phone call and to make it now!" Hugh Gibson pleaded passionately.

The Baron was moved by Gibson's logic, but he already knew all the facts involved in the de Croy network trial and the execution verdicts. He decided that he could no longer stall his unwelcome visitors any longer, so he merely placated them. "Very well if you'll excuse me, I have a phone call to make, gentlemen," he replied politely and he left the room. General von der Lancken's two aides, Captain Count Harrach and Major Baron von Falkenhausen, stood aloof and spoke between themselves in a far corner of the room. The US and Spanish Legation men nervously paced the polished oak floor that was covered with a massive, lush red and yellow coloured expensive Persian rug; the three men paced anxiously back and forth with nervous trepidation.

Five minutes later, Baron von der Lancken returned back to the elegant yellow salon with a non-descript look upon his face. "Gentlemen, that which you have purported to be true is in fact going to occur tomorrow, I'm sorry to say. Excuse my ignorance in this matter!" The Baron spoke with well-staged humility for the first time this evening.

The American and Spanish Legations were aghast to say the least. Either Baron von der Lancken was totally ignorant of the execution decision or he was a very good liar. Ambassador Whitlock had a note that he had given Mr Gibson to convey to the Baron. The Baron opened up the short letter and he read it silently. It simply stated:

*Honorable Baron von der Lancken:*

*My Dear Baron:*

*I am too ill to present my request to you in person, yet I appeal to the generosity of your heart and that of the German nation, to support and to save this unfortunate woman from death. Have pity on her in the name of President Woodrow Wilson and the American public! I trust that German mercy will outshine German justice in this special appeal.*

*Yours sincerely,*

*Consul-General Brand Whitlock*

*United States of America*

"Baron von der Lancken, I have another correspondence from the United States Consul General for the German Military Governor von Sauberzweig. It's a letter for a stay of execution in the name of the President of the United States. Baron von der Lancken, can you make an appeal to the Brussels Military Governor?" Gibson requested flatly.

The Baron said nothing; he knew that any appeal was fruitless. He merely gazed straight ahead into empty space.

"So what are you going to do about this situation?" demanded the Spanish Ambassador Marques de Villalobar, as he spoke in a exasperated tone to the astonished Baron von der Lancken. An answer was needed and quickly.

"Whether I personally approve of it or not, I am a professional German Army officer and a German military court has rendered its decision. We all have our orders and this unfortunate duty must be carried out, so I see no illegal or immoral situation here and I see no problem with this verdict, as unpleasant as it may be to me personally," the Baron responded soundly and without a visible concern for any foreign diplomatic interference in the matter.

"Now just wait a minute, Herr Baron. This may be an 'open and shut' case for the German military authorities, but I can assure you that this decision and its ramifications have not been given adequate consideration. Speaking for the neutral United States, I can assure you that killing two civilians, one who is also a elderly woman and a Red Cross nurse of some fine reputation I might also add, is going to hurt the image of Germany across the world. If you must demonstrate German justice in a time of war, then please consider imprisonment, hard labour or exportation for Edith Cavell. You can use a live breathing prisoner better for your propaganda more efficiently than you can a buried corpse that will immediately resurrect in the form of a martyr," Mr Gibson carefully and shrewdly argued to Baron von der Lancken, hoping that logic may persuade the emotions of the moment.

Yet the insanity of war itself was not the substance of logic; it was instead fed by the animalistic and base human elements of hatred, power, revenge and blind prejudice. The Baron's head turned slightly away from Mr Gibson, for in his heart and judgment he realized that Mr Gibson's argument was most logical and likely correct. The discipline of the German General, however, dominated over the man's more submissive compassionate nature. "I am sorry, Herr Gibson, this is now a German military matter and I am serving as the German Political officer and thus this matter is entirely out of my chain-of-command, there is absolutely nothing that I can do. A decision has been made and it will be carried out by the German Army tomorrow morning at sunrise," Baron von der Lancken replied without emotion.

"Herr Baron von der Lancken, you are an intelligent man and I want to bring to your attention the fact that the German image in the international community is not too good and it has gotten a lot worse of late with the burning of the Belgian town of Louvain, the sinking of the passenger ship

Lusitania and now the execution of a helpless matron English nurse," Hugh Gibson tried to set forth his case calmly.

"Do not think to preach of national image to me, sir! We Germans do not give a damn about what others think; we only care about that which we think and do! It is the strong who rule the world, not the compassionate and the weak!" the arrogant Baron fired back carelessly and in a manner most irregular of a high level political officer, such was the German mindset.

The three visitors stood there with their mouths aghast and with incredulous facial expressions for a few pregnant seconds. They could not believe their ears at the Baron's brazen, callous reply. The Germans were putting a loaded gun to their heads and committing international political suicide, yet in this aberration of a world war, could any deliberate action be termed 'insane'. The war itself was an unholy insult to the very word 'sanity'; there were countless thousands and tens of thousands of soldiers being slaughtered each day on such a monumental scale that perhaps the Germans and the world had become immune to the folly of two civilians being executed against a backdrop of untold thousands.

"As the official minister and representative to his Majesty the King of Spain, I say to you that the Spanish Government does not look kindly upon Germany and her allies in this rushed judgment and I officially implore you to please pick up that phone and contact the highest German political officials in Berlin – and that includes the Kaiser himself!" Marques de Villalobar strenuously voiced as he pointed his arm to the phone that sat naked upon a nearby desk.

"How dare you speak like that to me in my very house! You come here uninvited and make late night demands of me that are outside my responsibility and then you not only threaten, but cajole me to call the Kaiser himself on a matter of settled military business! Well sir, I can inform you that Berlin is advised of this entire matter, as they have been since the arrest of those traitors and their decisions are final! I cannot and will not jeopardize my position, upset the German chain-of-command or insult the Kaiser by making an inappropriate personal communiqué to Berlin on this matter. Besides I am not on familiar terms with the Kaiser and my calling him would be deemed inappropriate and even rude! Now, this matter is concluded in my opinion, gentlemen," the Baron resolved with a terse, elevated voice.

"Well, my dear Baron von der Lancken, if you do not know the Kaiser well, you can simply make a phone call to him right now and get to know him better by discussing Edith Cavell's execution!" Ambassador Rodrigo Saavedra de Villalobar shouted back in a belligerent and insulting tone.

Baron von der Lancken was insulted by this remark and he thought for a second to have the three men physically thrown out of his residence. Captain Harrach and Major von Falkenhausen clearly heard all the arguments among the parties. Captain Harrach cast a belligerent, hateful look at the Spanish Ambassador; he hated these pretentious, fancy mannered foreigners interfering in German military affairs and he thought his superior officer had been far too polite to these men who were visiting the Baron both unannounced and uninvited at a very late hour of the evening.

Captain Harrach was a young officer and he had lived a sheltered life. The world simply consisted of that which he had seen and experienced, which was little. He was full of naïve German patriotism and he stunned the room when he made an uninvited bold remark that, "the life of one German soldier seems to us as being much more important than those of all these old English nurses. In fact, I think that the only tragedy here is that there is only one old English traitorous nurse to shoot instead of several more!".

The three visitors were stunned at the callousness of the young German officer, yet von der Lancken did nothing in the way of discouraging the young man. Major Von Falkenhausen was in his mid-thirties; he had studied at Cambridge in England and he was touched by Edith Cavell's fate. He thought it pointless and poor policy to execute her, yet he was not a senior officer of course and he was powerless to either influence or alter her fate. He kept his counsel and silence to himself.

After another thirty minutes of arguing ensued, the Baron became irritated with the entire situation and he thought that the only measure short of physically throwing these three men out into the street was to make a amenable offer to them. "We're getting nowhere in all this arguing, gentlemen, so I am going to call my driver and go visit the German Military Governor Baron Lt Gen Von Sauberzweig and I hope that this satisfies the last option that I can exert in this request of yours. Give me that damn letter from Consul Whitlock," the Baron remarked to Hugh Gibson, as he threw on his heavy wool grey German overcoat and ventured out into the rainy cool night accompanied by Count Harrach and Baron von Falkenhausen.

The hour was now shortly past midnight of 12 October and Edith and Philippe had but a few sparse hours to live unless a stay of execution was granted by either the Military Governor or his superiors in Berlin.

The Political Minister von der Lancken took his two aides and went to go pay a late night visit to Lt General von Sauberzweig. However before making any such visit, the Baron von der Lancken took the precaution and courtesy to call him before coming over for an in-person visit. The fifty-two year old

General was not at all pleased about being awoken, but he gave General von der Lancken the civility of the visit anyway.

"This had better be a good reason for awakening me at this hour, von der Lancken! What is so damn important that the matter could not wait until tomorrow morning at a time when all sane people are awake!" the greying-haired, over-weight man with a prominent black handle-bar moustache groggily remarked as he met General von der Lancken in his private study still dressed in his bedroom slippers, pajamas and night robe.

"I am terribly sorry for this most inconvenient interruption at such a late hour, but the American and Spanish officials are pressing me to request to see you regarding a stay of execution for the two prisoners Englishwoman Edith Cavell and the Belgian Philippe Baucq – both are to be executed in a few hours. This is from information that I confirmed from the St Gilles prison officials," von der Lancken summarized in a succinct description of events.

"I am surprised at your impetuous actions regarding this incontestable matter, Baron! This is all settled business, van der Lancken! The prosecution has made their case, the judges have made their decisions and sentence recommendations and I have, with some modifications, endorsed the sentences! These two prisoners were convicted soundly and by their own words and actions, the nurse even signed a full confession that implicated all of the other de Croy network members and their actions. She had a chance to get out of Belgium and she did not take that opportunity; she could have only assisted English soldiers, but she extended her assistance to recruiting young Belgian men to flee and join the Belgian army. They assisted 250 men – that's equivalent to a German infantry company!" the Military Governor gruffly replied with a tired, resigned voice as he sat down in a comfortable reading chair, while General von der Lancken thought it better to remain standing.

"I have for you a letter of personal appeal from the American Consul Brand Whitlock to stay the execution of Edith Cavell in the name of the President of the United States! The Spanish Ambassador Marques Rodrigo Saavedra de Villalobar, in the name of the King of Spain, also requests leniency from Your Excellency as well!" von der Lancken added, while deftly handing von Sauberzweig the American Consulate's personal letter of appeal. The still groggy middle-aged general took a 18K gold rimmed monocle from his robe pocket and placed this firmly into his left eye socket to so permit his reading of the US Consulate letters; middle-age was taking its inevitable toll on his aging body and eyesight was one of the first bodily organs to manifest itself with the aging process. Von Sauberzweig reluctantly took the letter, broke the envelope's back wax seal and read the one-page letter of appeal. He carelessly tossed the letter onto a nearby nightstand. "Rubbish! Sheer and utter rubbish!" von Sauberzweig muttered as he stared ahead with a distraught look upon his winkled face.

"Those two condemned are quite bold and proud; they showed no humility or remorse for their crimes. I was there at the first day of the trial. I hid myself in the recesses of one of the viewing balconies and I saw them standing there like proud peacocks; it was disgusting and I was forced to leave the courtroom chamber. The other three prisoners convicted of the capital crimes of treason and providing aid to the enemy have all filed appeals against their executions and I am presently entertaining these appeals. That Belgian bastard Baucq and English old bitch Cavell were too damn proud to submit a motion of appeal, so by their own stubbornness, they have thus condemned themselves!" von Sauberzweig dryly stated.

"So I take it, sir, that you reject these diplomatic appeals to suspend or even delay the executions of Edith Cavell and Philippe Baucq this morning?" von der Lancken asked with an air of uncertainty in his voice, which couched a second attempt for a verbal appeal.

"My dear friend von der Lancken, for security reasons you are ignorant of certain aspects of this secret trial and how the verdicts were determined, but let me assure you that leniency has already been granted in the sentencing. There were nine original recommended death sentences excluding that renegade coward Prince Reginald de Croy. After careful deliberations, we ended up with only five prisoners being recommended for execution. We even spared his sister the Princess de Croy – instead of execution, she and others are going to get hard labour terms and some of the lesser prisoners are even being freed, so do not lecture to me about leniency! The German Military Court and I have given much leniency, more than those English deserve!" General von Sauberzweig spat out in an obvious bitter tone. His hatred of the English was particularly intense and unknown.

General von der Lancken was not without some sympathy for the plight of the Englishwoman Cavell. He decided to make one final appeal to the Military Governor's humanity, that is if the old General still had any of it left in his personal constitution. Experience had made him a bitter man; the war had changed him over the past six months, yet few knew the reason.

"Then there is to be no mercy for Edith Cavell, no delays in spite of the American and Spanish appeals?" von der Lancken asked in a last gesture to save Edith's life.

"Mercy! Mercy for our enemies! Mercy for this old matron Englishwoman who helped to recruit over two-hundred and fifty Allied soldiers and civilians out of Belgium to fight against our brave German troops! Let me tell you something. My son Peter was a soldier serving in the infantry in France six months ago when he was shot by an English soldier, whose bullet struck his head and caused him permanent blindness! He is only twenty-five years old and his life was all before him; now he is an invalid with a bleak future and he will need constant life-long care. His prospects for a military career, decent marriage and children are ruined and his mother cries daily for him. His future is ruined and so is that of me and my wife! That bullet that blinded him could well have come from one of those men that Edith Cavell helped escape! Mercy for this spinster Englishwoman – never! She and Baucq die at dawn by firing squad as so prescribed. Good night, General von der Lancken!" the angry old general shouted out loudly as he rose and walked out of the room.

General von der Lancken had gotten his final answer and he had perhaps learned more about the reason for Edith's execution than he had ever wanted to learn. Sometimes ignorance was indeed bliss. In any event, there was zero chance of Edith Cavell getting her sentence commuted or delayed; she was General von Sauberzweig's 'special project' and he was not to be denied his form of personal justice. Revenge blinded even the most exalted of men. Knowing that he had no further chance of affecting Edith Cavell's fate, General von der Lancken and his two aides made haste from the Military Governor's residence and back to his own quarters. The hour was now 12:30 pm and he was dead tired. The whole night had been filled with melodrama that had not changed the status of any state of affairs.

Some twenty minutes later Baron von der Lancken returned back to his residence accompanied by his two aides. Upon hearing the door open, the three men rushed from the drawing room to meet the Baron, not even allowing him the time to remove his well saturated heavy wool coat, so anxious was their concern for Edith and Philippe. "What was Lt Gen von Sauberzweig's response? Did he call Berlin or issue a stay of execution on his own validation?" the Marques de Villalobar inquired with agitated exasperation in his voice. The Baron looked tired and weary; he wore no smile or friendly frown, just an expressionless, tired face.

"Gentlemen, I truly did all that I could to appeal to his better nature and I think he has none in this matter of mercy for Nurse Edith Cavell. I am sorry to say, gentlemen, that the visit, the letter and my appeals were of no success. The Military Governor has informed me that he has instructions from Berlin High Command to carry out the executions and that at this point not even the personal intervention of the Kaiser could stop it!" the Baron wearily sighed with weary resignation. It seemed as if the German ship-of-state once in motion lacked the agility to quickly make any sudden change in course or even to be able to stop abruptly. This same type of inertia had ironically led to the unstoppable mobilization of the German war machine about one year earlier and motions once set into action were sometimes impossible to alter without a concerted level of effort. No one in authority wanted to exert such efforts no matter how bad the eventual outcome might be for Germany and those associated with this execution process.

"You cannot allow this injustice and insanity to happen. I implore you to stop it, Herr Baron!" the Marques de Villalobar demandingly shouted to the stunned Baron as he emotionally grabbed the general and pulled him up by his coat lapels.

The Baron was both astonished and caught off-guard by this invasion of his personage by a mere Minister from a neutral weak military country. "Get your damn hands off of me, Herr Villalobar or I shall place you under military arrest and have you exiled from Belgium on the next train!" the Baron threatened in a low rumbling voice, his eyes full of hatred. The Baron's two aides came quickly to their superior's defence and they grabbed the Spanish Foreign Minister backward, pulling him quickly away off the Baron.

"Go, get out of my house now! There's nothing left to be done, maybe you can say some prayers for those two wretched souls!" the Baron cried out as his aides brought the coats and hats of the three men and escorted them out of the front door of the Baron's residence.

The three men had attempted all that could humanly be expected, yet they had to try or forever be haunted with the thought that they had not tried their best. Upon arriving back at the US Legation residence, the three men were met in the foyer by three familiar women dressed in the distinct grey uniforms of the Red Cross – these were three of Edith's nurses. Mrs Whitlock had been kindly, and nervously, entertaining them for the past several hours. The faces of the men quite evidently betrayed their mission failure in meeting with the German Military Governor and altering Edith's and Philippe's fate of execution.

"I am sorry, ladies, we were unsuccessful. The German machinery for the execution of Edith and Philippe is in motion and no force short of the General von Sauberzweig himself can stop it! No appeals are possible and no visitors will be allowed at the Tir National firing range. We are sunk in this matter, my dear ladies, I'm very sorry!" Mr Gibson stated as the three Red Cross nurses started to weep uncontrollably. Nurse Elizabeth Wilkins, now the de facto Matron Nurse at the Clinique rue de la Culture, was sobbing uncontrollably. She silently wondered how a mere innocent act of kindness to some stranded British soldiers could escalate into a full blown underground movement to which they all had played a part and for which Edith and Philippe were to pay the ultimate price.

The hour was now almost 1:00 am 12 October 1915 and the night of last-minute argument and appeals was to fruitless avail. The heavy persistent downpour of the proceeding night had exhausted itself now into a gentle mist. Several miles away, Edith and Philippe were awake in their private cells, not being able to sleep; there would be time enough for eternal repose in just a few scant hours.

\* \* \* \* \* \* \* \* \* \* \*

During the parallel hours in which Ambassador Marques de Villalobar, Mr Gibson and Mr Guy de Leval were valiantly pleading and arguing with the obstinate German officers, Nurse Edith Cavell and Philippe Baucq were spending their last hours on earth in their solitary prison cells in pensive self-reflection. Edith sat in cell number 24, while Philippe was located a short distance away in cell number 72. They both rested quietly on their hard, sturdy wooden chairs with the solace of their thoughts of contrition and omission of the 'ifs' and 'might have beens' in their lives. The soft glow of pale yellow incandescent light bulbs made any plans for sleeping quite impossible, as did the sheer physical nervousness of the impending termination of their lives; even brave people had a hesitation about dying. The lights were intentionally being kept on, so as to discourage any additional suicides like that of Maurice Pansaers. The German officials anxiously wanted this matter to be placed behind them; they only wished that they had all five of the capital sentence prisoners ready to shoot altogether at one time and thus settle this matter once and for all. For additional security, each prisoner within a private cell was physically monitored every thirty minutes by a roving guard, who uninvitingly peered into the private cells via a small metal sliding slot located within the recess of the main sturdy cell door. Each time the metal observation slot was opened, it created a most distinct and audible annoying metal-on-metal sound, which became insultingly more intolerable upon each successive opening. Even in their last few hours on earth, the two condemned prisoners could not obtain a respite of quiet solitude. The Germans were not to be denied these two executions and they wanted to ensure that the final proceedings were conducted with Teutonic efficiency. They cunningly calculated that an exhausted, unrested prisoner suited their planning perfectly.

The hour was 8:00 pm and Edith and Philippe both eagerly awaited the arrival of their respective religious ministers. Being terribly alone in the sole company of one's terminal thoughts was becoming sheer madness with myriad contemplations racing wildly within the deep recesses of their minds. To maintain their composure and thoughts, they each busied themselves with composing final letters of farewell and appreciation to both family and friends. Philippe wrote letters of regret and love to his wife Marie and to his daughters Yvonne and Madeleine. He could hardly imagine the reality of the cold fact that he was not to be in this world, or his family's lives, for another night and he became filled with great despair.

Edith tried to place any morbid thoughts aside by composing letters to those she was leaving behind. It weighed on her that these were to be the last tangible remnants in her life and her soul became mournful. In the past her letter writing had been an easy means of personal conveyance to her family and friends; now such writing became a final burden for things that could never be properly placed into emotionless words scribbled onto an inanimate piece of paper. Still she valiantly soldiered on as she had throughout her solitary life. She wrote to her mother, her siblings and to Nurse Elizabeth Wilkins, the sole friend that she had outside of her family. She then composed one final letter that was not to a friend, but to a struggling young woman whose life was only beginning, a woman who was young, impressionable, pretty, naïve and one who had made a tragic mistake. Her last letter was to Nurse Trainee Anne Shepardton, the person who had betrayed her, the Clinique and the entire de Croy network to that scoundrel agent provocateur Gaston Quien. She wanted Anne to know and believe that everything was forgiven and to put any past transgressions behind her and to move forward with her young life.

*'My Dear Nurse Anne:*

*I know this vocation has been especially difficult on you. Nursing is never an easy calling and I know that you are seeking more out of life than being a mere housekeeper or factory worker back in our beloved England. Yet destiny has imposed an even greater challenge on the nursing profession by the accidental occurrence of this horrible war, during which you have been professionally baptized. Your young eyes have witnessed more pain, destruction and death than any young lady may be expected to endure. Yet through this all, you have stalwartly remained with the Clinique, and myself; this is a dedication for which I am eternally grateful. I am also appreciative of your youth and its wandering soul in these times of uncertainty and I do not judge you one way or another unless I too have journeyed in your own shoes. In retrospect I think we have both strayed off our chosen paths, yet our lives are not of a chartered, known course as that of a ship, as in this life unforeseen obstacles face us suddenly and we must live up to the challenges and opportunities presented unto us. Let us both place the past behind us and instead look toward the future of a new brighter world, a vastly changed world that will hopefully emerge from the ashes of this hellish war and for which I pray will be both kinder and wiser, than to one in which we currently find ourselves cast. May the future offer you the better things of this life and I hope you realize your full potential in either the nursing profession or another worthy endeavour."*

*Forever Yours,*

*Edith'*

Edith placed down her pen, folded the letter and placed it into the envelope with the simple name of 'Anne' signed onto the front of the envelope. She knew that Anne was young, innocent and striving to break out of her dull existence. Once upon a time in her youth, Edith had felt such youthful yearnings as well, yet she lacked young Anne's natural beauty and vibrant personality. In the solitude of her thoughts, Edith reviewed carefully all the phases of her life; in quiet retrospect she wondered if the decisions of her life had been the right ones, if she had ever made much of a difference to anyone in this world. Never having been the target of romance in her life, she imagined as she had many times before during her existence, the alternate vicarious life she might have had if she had chosen other paths in her life – a life with the traditional comfort of 'hearth and home'; the life of being happily married with the traditional husband, playing children and barking dogs, all amidst the lush green English countryside in a small rural cottage setting. Such was the thing of dreams for her.

Suddenly her inner most thoughts dissipated instantly, as she was unexpectedly interrupted by a harsh hand knocking on the door and interrupted Edith's pleasant thoughts and she responded a simple 'yes' in a pleasant, non-remarkable tone. No one would have suspected from this brave woman's voice or physical countenance that she was facing her own mortality a scant few hours in the future. To her surprise and delight, in walked Reverend Stirling Gahan from the English Church of Brussels. True to his promise to Edith, the St Gilles Pastor le Seur had quickly contacted a British chaplain who remained in Brussels to minister to the diplomatic and international community that still remained there when the war began. Pastor le Seur had written a short note to Reverend Gahan, which tersely read:

*Reverend Gahan:*

*Please come at once, an English woman in dire consequence desperately needs your ministerial support, to include confession and Holy Communion. Present the enclosed pass to the St Gilles guards and request to see me immediately!*

*Very Respectfully Yours,*

*Pastor le Seur,*

*St Gilles Prison Minister*

The note was short, serious and lacking in any additional specific details, yet it succinctly distilled the essence of Edith's personal religious desires. Still Rev Gahan never knew pastor le Seur exaggerate or panic and this note sounded true of both elements. He knew that he had to act quickly and he called for his car and was off to St Gilles prison. The drive was a short and wet one, the sky having released a steady torrent of cool drenching water to cast further gloom upon the already Gothic filled evening. The note from Pastor le Seur disarmed every glaring stare and objection from the plebian, often-gruff, prison guards.

"Good evening, Nurse Cavell, I'm Reverend Stirling Gahan of the English Church. I'm sorry for my late arrival, but I just received Pastor le Seur's urgent note, which was lacking in details, yet seeing you now in this prison cell, I know that you are in formidable trouble. However, I do fondly remember your kind face from the congregation at the 8:30 am Sunday services. I'm sorry that we never got to know one another better, but I am at your disposal this night for as long as you desire," Reverend Gahan explained

with a soft, gentle comforting voice as Edith rose and gently took his hand
with a soft smile.

"Thank you for coming, Reverend. I am condemned to death and the
Germans are going to shoot me in the morning. I need your help and that of
the Lord's! I have been found guilty of assisting a few hundred English and
Allied soldiers escape from Belgium into the safety of Holland and now I
am condemned to die because of that act!" Edith remarked with teary eyes,
the few that she had ever openly displayed in her life. Reverend Gahan was
flabbergasted by Edith's sudden remarks; he had no idea that this strict-
laced, English Victorian bred gentlewoman could have committed any act
worthy of a firing squad. Rev Gahan looked intensely with astonishment at
the grey haired woman and her possible capital crimes. Yet he had no luxury
of time to further ponder such selfish probing thoughts about her crime and
criminal circumstances; as a minister of the Lord he had a soul to shepherd.

"Come Edith, let us sit down and recite the Lord's Prayer together,"
Reverend Gahan spoke with a comforting smile as the two sat down
together, made the sign of the cross and slowly recited he universal Christian
'Our Father' prayer most slowly and reverently. Edith felt more resolved and
peaceful after the prayer recitation.

"I'd like to take the Eucharist as well, Reverend," Edith requested softly, as
the Reverend said some prayers and the two partook of the unleavened white
wafer to commemorate the last meal of Christ with his apostles before his
crucifixion. They recited more prayers and again they made the sign of the
cross in unison. A look of virtual complete calmness descended over Edith's
face, a situation that was common among those possessing strong religious
faith and inner spiritual fortitude.

"If it's not too much trouble, I'd like to unburden my soul fully and
before I meet the Lord. I'd like to talk with you very frankly about things
that I even feared to closely examine myself, Reverend. These are the most
coveted intimacies, such things I hide in my soul like a budding butterfly in
its metamorphic cocoon, secrets that I have kept to myself all my life and to
which I have never revealed to another breathing soul. Some things should
not be taken into the grave," Edith softly whispered to Reverend Gahan.

"Yes, of course, Edith, we call such talk as referred to as 'one's final
things', but such talk is strictly voluntary – you know that we Anglicans do
not practise the formal sacrament of Confession as the Catholic so profess,"
Reverend Gahan replied as a reminder to Edith. He did not want her to say
or do anything that was against her will, especially in her last hours on earth.

"Where do I even begin?" Edith spoke softly, her eyes focused on a point of infinity straight ahead before her eyes. Reverend Gahan gently grasped her hands, providing emotional comfort to a gentle soul who was about to reveal her inner most secrets, fears and desires.

"It has been with me since my earliest childhood memories. The loneliness, the feeling of being somehow different, apart from the other children, even my siblings. I was 'the serious one', the 'good little girl', always obedient to God, family, my country and my ideals. I always felt myself somehow predestined to be alone, to merely mingle with others, but always apart and remote from them. I have tried my best to change, but I could not make myself to be like those idyllic women depicted in the Jane Austen romance novels. I feel cheated, yet I feel guilty too! I am full of self-pity for myself, yet when I see the wretchedness and the plight of mankind around me, I am saddened all the more because I feel an empathy for my fellow human being and I want to help them, so I became a nurse. I have lived a pleasant gentle life; however, a life without personal love, the love of a man and children…yes wonderful rosy-cheeked playing children – these were not to be mine. I hated myself for not having obtained these womanly things. Yet I am fortunate too, I've had the blessings of a loving and religious father and mother, loving siblings and remarkable health. Yet I always wanted these other things, this is one of my personal sins and my dearest secret regrets," Edith confided with a sadness in her eyes.

"Edith these things are only…" the Reverend was speaking to retort Edith's words before he was interrupted mid-sentence by her and he dared not interfere with these most personal confidences.

"No, that is not all! I am not finished, there's more to tell you, Reverend Gahan. I've been uncomfortable with people and even formal authority throughout my life. I am somehow selfish. I always wanted to do things in life my own way and possess self-control over my fate; that is the reason I became a Governess and it's the primary reason that I lobbied to be the Directress of the Berkendael Institute too. This is the sin of the ego and that of love of one's self. I realize that physically I am a plain woman and my personality is best described as being pensive. I knew these things about myself, I tried to change but could not, so I chose God's will for myself and I decided to devote myself to those with whom I could relate: the poor, the lonely, the destitute, the children and finally the sick. My calling was to give back to the Lord and this meant to those who were suffering and less fortunate than myself," Edith spoke from the deepest recesses of her soul.

The Reverend comforted Edith with all his resolve; he had heard similar stories from other people to whom he ministered during their final hours.

It seemed that most souls had regrets in life for things that a person wished had been different. "Edith, don't you realize that all people fall short of their dreams and ambitions? You are not alone in your feelings of your perceived short-comings! We are all flawed humans and we each think at times that we fall short of some artificial ideal; you are not being very fair with yourself. Each of us have different talents and paths in life – the real test is how well we each live up to these challenges. While some embrace these, others flee," Reverend Gahan tried to counter-back on her self-condemnations.

"I don't really know about my life anymore, Reverend. Did I make the correct choices? Should I have pursued other options? Should I have left Brussels when the Germans invaded or should I have even returned back to Europe when the war began? I was selfish and ambitious; I wanted to operate my own nursing Clinique with minimal interference or oversight. I was granted my 'dream job' and for my sins, I also was caught up in this prisoner escape plan and I did not run from it, I wildly embraced it! This was my sin, the sin of both fallen angels and mankind – the selfish sin of pride! Pride in my independence and ambition and in being accountable to no one, I rebelled against the German occupation law and the neutrality charter of the Red Cross. These are my confessions and these are my sins, may the Lord forgive me and have mercy on my soul!" Edith sobbed tearfully as she clasped her face into her two hands for several seconds. Reverend Gahan was humbled in his own heart from hearing these most personal confidences of Edith. She was one fine and brave woman and England and the world was going to soon lose one of the nobler personages to appear on the world stage, he thought to himself.

"You are so very wrong, Edith! Many, if not most things, in this life lie beyond any person's control and most of us are not the fair-haired lucky ones so depicted in romance novels and dreams. You have lived a very good and worthy life, a life lived without the distractions of extreme wealth and high social birth. The person you are is the person who you have forged throughout your life; you owe your merits to no one except the Almighty. The good things you have done in your remarkable life - and these are many – are yours through your hard work, dedication, a strong resolution and the grace of God. You have lived a rigid, moral and purposeful life, a life of selfless caring. There are no deficiencies in you or your character or in your life; if only others had done equally as well as you have! Can you imagine the joy that you and all the others gave to those hundreds of Allied soldiers and to their families? Those families and England would be a much poorer place without your coming into this world and the decisions that you rightfully made. All of England and the world will be proud of you, Edith!"

"The fond memories of pre-war Brussels, these are so cruelly witty to me now, Reverend Gahan. I can remember it all so clearly and in rich detail, as in slow-motion fashion, how beautiful it all was before the war. I remember how green the grass looked, the sweet fragrant smell of the flowers and the radiance of a honey coloured sun on my face, the summer of 1914 was like a soft, fragrant and delicate flower that was born to die. I can so fondly recall the first pleasant encounters with my new band of Belgian acquaintances gained by my being named the Directress of the Berkendael Institute Clinique; I possessed personal authority and a position of some recognition and respect from many people above my station in life and I loved it. I silently delighted in my position and for the first time in my life, I developed friends. We used to meet in the quaint cafes of Brussels, we talked and laughed – it all seemed so harmless. Suddenly the war erupted and we all foolishly thought that it was to be over soon, how wrong we all were about that assumption. Yet with the war came an opportunity to help others, first the wounded soldiers and later the stranded Allied soldiers. My little group and I used to meet and plan in the quaint cafes of Brussels. I recall meeting with Philippe Baucq, he was so strikingly handsome and charming – I perhaps even envied his wife Marie; she had the idyllic life of husband and children. I recall that this past spring Philippe, Louise Thuliez and Herman Capiau walked along and stopped to watch a sidewalk puppet show 'Dance of the Puppets', a play that satirized the conduct of people in life and life's predestined qualities. The show ironically depicted the marching in of soldiers and innocent people being killed. Do you believe that life is predestined, Reverend? Are people really only puppets in this world – what difference did it all make?" Edith confessed a slight feeling of doubt and desperation to her unofficial confessor.

"Predestination is the power and prerogative of the Almighty, Edith. God does not use the plights of men and women for amusement; we are placed here to see if we are up to these fleeting challenges of this most temporal life. We get to see the world and ourselves only fully in the next world. Bravery, initiative, good works, faith, prayers and love are the weapons in our war chest of life and you have used your arsenal of weapons in a most skilled manner, Edith. A boat that travels along without a rudder, a map and a good Captain soon finds itself adrift at sea, while the other vessels complemented with all of these elements finds itself on a straight course and a sound destination. We as individual souls are the rudder, the Holy Bible is our map and the Lord is our Captain," the Reverend provided in maritime parable symbology.

"You are a brave woman, Edith. I know little of the charges brought against you except that you helped many English and Allied soldiers back to their homes. As a religious man I am bound to neutrality; however, as an Englishman I am proud of your actions," the Reverend replied. He was impressed with Edith's character and countenance.

"No! No, it is far easier to be brave when you have nothing to lose. The brave are those who have everything and risk losing it all! You know that out of the five of us condemned to death, Philippe got the short end of the stick. That poor man has two lovely daughters and a beautiful wife…my dear sweet Lord, his anguish tonight must be unbearable," Edith deflected back with moistness forming in her eyes.

"Edith, with brave people such as yourself and Philippe and all of our brave soldiers in the trenches fighting on the side of righteousness, then goodness will surely triumph one day! It has happened before in history; it can happen again. You all did what you needed to do, even in the face of death," Reverend Gahan exclaimed as he provided perspective to Edith's belittlement of herself. He needed to strengthen Edith's spirit further for her to face the firing squad with dignity and bravery.

"Death is but a word to many; to me it is an all too real daily reality. It is not a stranger to me, dear Reverend – in my profession and especially in this awful war, I have witnessed it many times a day, although I do not welcome it, I do not fear it as the final end either. It is a reality of life and a final equality we all will one day face and today is my day. May the Lord forgive me my trespasses and grant me eternal life with Him," Edith remarked with a calmness often seen in those who have made their peace with the Lord. Reverend Gahan comforted Edith as he continued to hold her hand and provided soothing reassurances of her life's work.

The words of Reverend Gahan helped to calm Edith. She was going through the final stage of death – the step of final acceptance. "Thank you, Reverend! I only acted on those opportunities and decisions presented to me and for which I had a certain penchant. I have no regrets in helping any of those poor young soldiers whose entire lives lay before them. As for myself, well I am no longer young and I have lived much of my life; I only hope that this ordeal does not overly weigh upon my old mother and siblings! You see they all wanted me to leave the war zone, but I, being naturally stubborn and wanting my own way, refused to leave a situation where nurses were needed most critically – the war zone. I hold no bitterness to the Germans, 'they are who they are' and they cannot help being blinded by a culture of hate and militarism. Some fear death and are angry and sad by all that they will have to relinquish in this life; however, I am not a woman of great wealth, power, beauty, intelligence or creativity, but I do have the rewards of faith, good works, fine friends and the opportunity to have assisted others even if only in a small way. I do not welcome death, but life has not burdened me down with tangible things to which I have no attachment or desire for possession. My long wait to face the inevitable will soon be relieved and by my faith I pray, rewarded," Edith concluded. With such pious words, Reverend Gahan was speechless. Edith had said it all and she had said it to perfection.

"Would you extend to me the honour of reciting the Lord's Prayer one more time with me, Edith?" the Reverend asked softly while clutching Edith's cold hand.

She smiled back at him and then she started to softly utter the words: "Our father, who art in heaven, hallowed be thy name…" The Reverend joined in and they completed the prayer several times in unison. Edith had never said or felt the words to the Lord's Prayer as deeply as she had that early morning of 12 October 1915.

The Reverend and Edith stayed and prayed together until the morning unavoidably arrived and, with it, the inevitable German prison guards and the familiar clinking of heavy metal keys and locks. Soon Pastor Paul le Seur would be there to escort her out of her cell. "All that matters in this world, and that which remains, is love. One day love will conquer all," Edith sadly stated.

"Edith, when the time comes, shall I be there for you?" Reverend Gahan had inquired.

"Thank you kindly for asking, Reverend, so few men have asked anything of me in this life! My answer is a simple 'no'. I want to spare you that indignity that those Germans are going to do to me. I want your last thoughts to be of me as I am now. I want you to always remember me and my last night of discussions with you. I shall not permit these remembrances to be sullied and insulted by my shattered body and blood! That indignity I shall leave for those who most want to take my life in the morning at the Tir National shooting range!" Edith responded in a voice that was both compassionate and still defiant.

"I will naturally respect your final wishes; however I shall always pray for you daily, Edith and the memory of you will never desert me. Thank you for this time with you. I did my best and I hope that it was adequate," Reverend Gahan softly concluded. He had exhausted all his words and he was emotionally exhausted.

"You did very well indeed, Reverend. You surpassed all of your Sunday sermons and this was the best one yet," Edith smiled back, and giving the Reverend a small dose of emotional reprieve. "Oh, I have some personal letters here. Could you please take these and distribute them to Directress Wilkins at the Clinique? She knows the people to whom I have addressed the letters and the means necessary to courier these as well," Edith asked with almost modest embarrassment, such was her personality for self-reliance and never wishing to impose on the good graces of others if at all possible.

"It will be my pleasure and it will be done," Reverend Gahan smiled as he tried to hold back his own tears of remorse. He had been with her such a short time, yet so candid were her confidences that Reverend Gahan could not seem to forget the final impressions of Edith Cavell. He knew that she was right to spare him the tragic scene of her execution; no one present was going to forget it and Edith did him a great favour by relieving him of this burden, providing that, of course, the Germans would have even permitted Reverend Gahan's attendance – which they would not. This execution was to be strictly a German affair, to which outsiders were to be emphatically enjoined from attending.

They said another few sets of prayers together. As a rumbling of guards could be discerned walking the corridors of St Gilles prison, Edith uttered her final words to him, "Patriotism is not enough... I must have no hatred and no bitterness toward any one," she added as the female matrons approached and assisted Edith to make ready for her final walk out of St Gilles prison.

\* \* \* \* \* \* \* \* \* \* \* \*

Edith was not the only prisoner in deep self-reflection and confession this evening. In cell number 72, Philippe Baucq sat with a Catholic priest discussing the regrets of his life and actions as well. Having seen his wife and two daughters this past weekend, he could not bear to see them on his last night on earth.

"It is no good, Father. I cannot bring myself to make a full and complete confession! My sins are too many, my faith too fragile! My spirit too weak! I'm probably destined to hell and deservingly so! I was so stupid, so patriotic, so full of myself that I let my own ambitions get away from me. I, myself, a petty little powerless man thought he could take on the entire German army! Who in the hell did I think I was fooling? I only fooled my own ego; the Germans knew just about everything except the La Libre Belgique newspaper. German bastards!" Philippe Baucq cursed out in obvious forgetfulness of the Belgian priest's presence.

"None of us are free from sin, Philippe; until we die, it stays with each of us! We do our best to live each day a little bit better – that's how life is, my son," the middle-aged Catholic priest replied.

"These acts of being an underground patriot are for the young and single, not for a married man. I was selfish, proud, egotistical and I acted like a crazy young rebel, Father and now both my family and I will be paying the ultimate price for these insane acts," Philippe cried tearfully.

"A proud Belgian patriot, that's me! I did no one any good with any of my actions," Philippe cried out in utter self-disgust and mockery.

"Pride, ego, rebellion! Be honest with me, are these words really your moral moniker, Philippe?" the priest inquired rhetorically. "You use these words incorrectly."

"What are you saying, Father?" Baucq answered back, puzzled by the priest's doubting words.

"Think carefully, Philippe. Was it pride that showed its ugly face the hundreds of times that you risked capture and death by personally assisting helpless soldiers get back to their own people and families? Was it ego or rebellion that led you and your friends to publish the truth about the Germans when everyone else remained passively silent and complacent? I think not, Philippe. You and Edith and all the others performed all of the things for a good and righteous cause, not that of personal gain or selfishness. You did it all with great risk and from the depths of your hearts," the Belgian priest retorted back compellingly. Philippe was not dissuaded by his acts of defiance against the Germans that had led him to ruin.

"Nothing matters! What makes us different from our enemies, the Germans? I thought we were better than them, now I think maybe we are of the same cloth!" Baucq stated wearily. He hated himself and the entire world at this moment in his life.

"You're so very wrong, Philippe! Unlike the Germans, your actions saved many military and civilians lives alike. You did not hurt or kill anyone like the Germans do to both soldiers and civilians. Remember you gave life, you did not take it. You and the other underground members are good people and very conscious Christians; you risked your life and freedom so that others may gain theirs; you acted while others merely wished or stayed ashamedly silent. You have lived the Christian creed, not in a passive way, but as active foot soldiers of Christ. If it were not for the actions of yourself, Edith and the others, the lights in Europe really would have been extinguished at the start of the war; now a dim light has been lit and it continues to grow brighter as others see your example and follow in your lead. The torch of tyranny is being exhausted and replaced with the candle of freedom," the priest wisely countered Baucq's argument.

"No, we are failures, we got caught and placed many other innocent people in great danger. No one else in Belgium is foolish enough to do the things we have done," Philippe replied back with resigned disbelief of the attending priest's words.

"No, Philippe, these things are done every day. I hear of ordinary Belgians helping many other refugee soldiers and also fellow Belgian citizens! You and the others killed no one, you tried only to help others escape from Belgium. The example that you and the others set is being replicated across Belgium and other occupied countries." The priest attempted to placate Philippe's conscience.

"Help soldiers escape! Father, I did a lot more than that! I distributed that underground newspaper and I passed along German military information! Who knows what secondary harm these things caused – Germans with families probably died because of my actions," Philippe yelled out in obvious regret.

"People cannot remain passive lest evil triumphs. The work of the Lord resides not only in the passivity of the lamb, but also in the roar and actions of the lion! Belgium and many other countries are at war and sadly people die in war, just as people die crossing the street or getting sick with pneumonia. Such are the affairs of men, yet I am here to shepherd you in the matters of your soul," the priest carefully reminded this young man.

"Yes, of course, Father, forgive me, you are right. I don't know how long it was since I was in church, probably when my little girls were baptized or received the First Holy Communion," Philippe stated bluntly back to the best of his recollections.

"Sins…of course! Where do I even begin?" Philippe sighed as he paused a few seconds before continuing. "Let's see, I've lied a lot, mainly to the Germans! I gambled and cheated at cards. I had sexual intercourse with many women, many times before my marriage! I have not been a regular churchgoer in years. I drink and smoke too much! Every now and then I use strong words, even the misuse of the Lord's name," Philippe confessed.

"I am still no saint, Father, but I have changed! Marriage and fatherhood changed me – for the better too. I saw life as something more than my pleasures…more than just myself," Philippe eagerly volunteered in defence of his reformed lifestyle.

"The priest uttered some mysterious words in Latin and made the sign of the cross over Philippe's forehead. Philippe had just made a final Act of Confession in the Roman Catholic rite, an abbreviated format that was authorized in Cannon Law for those in exigent circumstances, such as imminent death.

"Would you like to take Communion with me?" the priest asked.

"Yes, I would and thank you, Father," Philippe replied as the priest administered the blessed sacramental wafer of the Catholic Eucharist believed by the faithful to be the 'incarnate blood and body' of Christ. The priest said some more prayers, lit some candles and anointed Philippe's forehead with blessed oils. The priest had just administered the sacrament of Extreme Unction, the last Catholic sacrament to be administered for those in danger or anticipation of immediate death.

The Catholic priest made ready to leave, as per Philippe's request. He wanted some quiet time to himself. He asked for a final blessing and this he received from the Belgian priest, who then got up from his chair and knocked on the cell door – a signal to the waiting guard that he had completed his ministerial duties.

Philippe took out the Bible that was placed in his cell and he began to read through the passages and take to heart the meanings of the stories that were inspired to his spirit. Like Edith Cavell, he made peace with his own spirit and Lord Almighty. He was ready for his death, but he did not by any means relish it.

It had been a night of great distress and grave melodrama for all parties attached to the impending executions of Edith Cavell and Philippe Baucq. None of those involved could ever forget their actions this past night and it would forever live in the memories of the survivors involved in the last-minute attempts to save the lives of the two desperate souls. It was a watershed moment. The only saving grace was that the other three condemned prisoners were not also sharing the mutual fate of Edith and Philippe.

\* \* \* \* \* \* \* \* \* \* \*

The early morning of Tuesday October 12, 1915 was dark, dreary, overcast, cool and wet from the previous night's drenching rains. Sunrise for this day was to occur at 6:59 am with 'full dawn' being thirty minutes later and thus the aimed time for the execution was planned to be 7:30 am and the Germans meant to keep to this schedule. It was as if the weather had conspired with the Germans to create the perfect morbid weather environment for a firing squad. It was 6:00 am and a heavy handed knock was initiated on the cell doors of both Edith Cavell and Philippe Baucq. "Make ready, get fully bathed, dressed and prepared," sounded forth a heavy throated male voice in French.

Neither of the two condemned had slept all night, their nervousness and preoccupation of their impending fates prevailed over any bodily necessity or regimen. The natural urge to eat was absent as well. Sleep and food had become moot appetites for the condemned. Both Edith and Philippe bathed and performed their respective personal hygiene tasks, Philippe was even allowed to be shaved by the prison barber and given some Bay Rum aftershave lotion, which generously diffused throughout the prison bathroom and later his prison cell. No food or drink was afforded the prisoners; they may become sick and vomit their stomach contents and the Germans wanted none of this mess or any related bodily issues.

By 6:45 am they both were dressed and ready. They came for Edith first; ever the gentlemen, the Germans made sure that the English lady was treated with social deference. At last the nervous waiting was over as the heavy metal St Gilles door to cell number 23 opened wide and with a rustic metallic tone that befitted a horror play. The door opened to reveal a stoic faced group of several men, to include two prison staff clergymen, a prison administrator and two Army escort guards.

"Please Lord, give me strength in my final hours and have mercy upon those who are prosecuting me," Edith whispered as she again made a silent prayer and asked for the Lord's mercy.

"Are you ready, Madame Cavell?" the St Gilles prison guard inquired in tepid monotone sounding voice.

"Yes I am quite ready. Before we leave, I want to say that although you are my enemies, you have all been kind and civil to me here at St Gilles. We have both done our jobs well, there's no bitterness on my constitution. Make no mistake, I do not want to die, but I have lived my life and it has been a good one. I'm ready. Shall we go and get my dear friend Philippe?" she remarked with a brave, confident voice.

With those words Edith arose and the group moved slowly down the St Gilles hallway to retrieve Philippe Baucq in cell number 72. The door creaked slowly open and he stood up and said nothing. He looked at Edith with a resigned tired look and then a short grin appeared on his face. His eyes were bloodshot from crying and lack of sleep.

"Well hello, Philippe, my dearest friend; it's been quite a while since we last spoke," she remarked.

"No talking, remember!" a brash German guard interrupted with a barking voice.

Philippe ignored the order. There was little to be done to a condemned man, he thought to himself.

"Thank you, Edith, I couldn't sleep or eat at all last night. I made my peace with the Creator, so that is it," he uttered with a flat-line tone to his voice.

"I did the same as well!" Edith replied in kind.

"We must go now! I said no talking!" the German military guard rudely snapped out as he escorted Philippe out of his cell doorway and down the dimly lit prison corridor that was arrayed with numerous guards. Executions always drew a huge audience of faces behind prison door ports and from the guards. It was another story that they could take to the lunchrooms, family tables and taverns about seeing another prisoner shot and relate the gruesome details of how the condemned reacted on the morning of their sentences. This was an especially prominent prison scene, as this time a stoic English nurse was to be shot and not some mere Belgium woman of less esteemed character.

As Edith and Philippe walked slowly down the main St Gilles elongated corridor, the prison guards and military officers paid her silent homage by either gently bowing as she passed them or they conversely removed their hats and nodded their heads in respect. Walking out into the outdoors, the two condemned were greeted by foul, cloudy chilly weather and the sight of three nasty looking, despicable men: Dr Stober, Lt Pinkhoff and Lt Bergan. Their long, expressionless faces were not a welcome sight. The array of several dark grey German uniforms formed the ideal complement to the overcast gloomy weather. Edith and Philippe glanced at one another before being separated into two vehicles. No touching or forms of expression were permitted; even in their executions the Germans proved themselves to be cruel control masters. Edith's face was fixed, stoic and thinly drawn; the tiredness from a sleepless night was betrayed in her weary, slightly reddened eyes.

In an ironic gentlemanly gesture of the occasion, one of the guards gently acted as her shoulder brace for her entry up into the waist-high elevated sedan. Yet German decorum necessitated that all formality and dignity be maintained in the closing of this affair; there were to be no errors or impropriety. Before she stepped up into the automobile, she noticed and nodded to the figures of two nurses in the darkness some short distance away, the faces to which she was unsure. Upon being seated in the elevated rear passenger seat, she came to recognize the two nurses and she was filled with both joy and sadness. It was Nurse Elizabeth Wilkins and Nurse White, who were observing her for the final time this side of eternity. It was 6:59 am – sunrise as the first glimmer of light in the sky appeared and the executions were scheduled precisely for 7:30 am at the Tir National firing range, only a ten minute journey by automobile from St Gilles prison.

Several miles away in the Brussels suburb of Schaerbeek, the Tir National lay in quiet green slumber awaiting its early morning visitors. The blackened orb of morning was slowly surrendering its daily soul to the new day's new sunrise. In half an hour the lighting conditions would be sufficient for full unimpeded visibility even with a clouded sky – good visibility was an obvious prerequisite for any execution by firing squad. The Tir National was a firing range used before the war by the Belgium Army for target practice and now the Germans were using it for their own nefarious devices to include the execution of prisoners. The Tir National had been a busy location since the war had begun with scores of accused persons meeting their demise there. At the Tir National firing range a seasoned German infantry Lieutenant and two 'short squads' of German infantry soldiers were getting their gear, uniforms, rifles and ammunition in precise German military order. These German infantry soldiers were recent veterans from pitched hand-to-hand trench battles on the western front in France, not rear echelon garrison troops. Their hearts and souls, if they had any left, had been hardened after seeing both friend and enemy soldiers alike killed or mutilated by having their faces and heads exploded by impacting high velocity bullets, while others had witnessed limbs of soldiers cut off by artillery shrapnel. Still others saw stomachs disembowelled by machine gun fire and bodies blown to hand-sized pieces by high explosive shells. Such despondent soldiers were impervious to the mere act of shooting and witnessing two people being shot at close range. Still the German Lieutenant was taking no chances, so he again prepped the sixteen soldiers about the task at hand. The Imperial German Army played no firing squad 'tricks' such as having every other man use blanks instead of real 7.92 mm Mauser rifle ammunition to give 'psychological comfort' to the soldiers in thinking the 'other guy' was responsible for the fatal shots. The German Army was a militaristic one that embraced war and all the tenets of such; this included every German soldier doing his duty no matter how distasteful, and so every German in the squad was going to be a professional killer this day.

"You soldiers 'fall-in'," shouted the German Lieutenant. The sixteen grey clad soldiers came to immediate attention forming a single straight line composed of two sections of eight soldiers each. The symmetrical arrayed line of young soldiers were identically adorned with the Imperial German Spiked helmets called the 'Pickelhauben' or painted-black lacquer helmets, long German Mauser Gewehr rifles, black boots and thick wool grey wool overcoats. Each man was lean and clean-shaven and stoic in his demeanour; none of them were nervous or put-off by the execution duty – this was just another type of military obligation for them and any day not spent in the madness of the muddy, stinking trenches was pure heaven to each of them.

"Listen-up close! In about twenty minutes you will be ordered by the German military authority to perform a sentence of execution upon two civilians convicted under proper German Military Tribunal proceedings to the capital offences of treason and espionage against the German state and army. One person is a Belgian man, the other is an old English national woman. Do your duty in this affair and have no mercy on them, as their actions helped many hundreds of Allied soldiers and young men escape Belgium and to fight against you fine young soldiers. Remember that some of these same escaped soldiers may have killed some of your comrades as well. As far as shooting a woman goes, be not concerned, you should not pity her! She is a matronly English woman with no husband or children, so you will not be killing a mother who leaves behind any orphans!" the young German officer shouted out in a very callous voice to the sixteen executioners. The soldiers' reactions were nonchalant.

"Soldiers, position of rest-in-place! You are permitted to smoke or stand easily in place, but go nowhere else – our 'guests' will be here shortly," the Lieutenant announced as he handed over the immediate supervision of the firing squad detail to the German Sergeant Major. The seasoned Lieutenant knew that having soldiers stand at the position of attention was both unnecessary and fatiguing; he wanted to ensure that each man was relaxed and confident in their aim.

By 7:15 am the two condemned were at their ultimate location. Few civilians were awake and walking the streets of Brussels and the sky was only beginning to radiate with the back glow of the rising sun that radiated a soft glow behind the dark grey skies. Those few pedestrians present gave scant notice to the small procession of black automobiles making the rapid transit through the uncluttered cobblestone streets of the clean modern city. The Germans wanted no witnesses or onlookers at this clandestine scene. The picturesque city of Brussels still lay half-asleep and this was the best scenario for the Germans – they wanted no public notice of these two traitors being led off for their executions.

The three black motorcars drove up to the Tri National front gate; it was another architectural period-piece of late nineteenth century ruby-red brick edifice accented with the traditional white stone order accent position above and below the windows, doors and corners of the two-storey structure. Upon arrival through the front gate the vehicles stopped in a courtyard quadrangle, where the vehicles were parked and immediately several guards exited the black sedans. The Protestant, Pastor Le Seur from St Gilles prison, was attired in the distinct scarlet-purple coloured robes of a German Lutheran Protestant clergyman; he was visibly evident against the mundane flock of grey coated military men. Father Captain Leyendecker, a German Roman Catholic priest was attired entirely in black vestments, save for that of his purple neck-draped vestment called a stole. He was to serve as Philippe Baucq's religious minister.

The entire ensemble of personages walked in a moderate pace down the Tir National visitors' hall. The tiled floors echoed with the footsteps of Edith and Philippe along with the thunderous pounding of heavy black German army hobnail soled boots. The main corridor was lined with the sober grim faces of the 250-soldier company complement of the Landwehr German infantry soldiers, who were all dressed in medium grey coloured uniforms. Some of these soldiers saluted or came to immediate attention upon Edith's and Philippe's entrance and passing, so great was their repute throughout he German garrison community. There was a more realistic explanation for the presence of all these soldiers – that of curiosity – and to make matters worse it was morbid curiosity. As per human nature, everyone present wanted to tell the tales of 'I was there' or 'I saw them last' type accounts. The sight of the two frail unassuming civilian figures amongst the stoic strong phalanx of neatly arrayed young German soldiers was ironic and pitiful at best. How could these two innocuous figures be so threatening to the great and victorious Imperial German Army?, many pondered silently to themselves. Down past the long main corridor, the duo was escorted unto a small enclosure with a veranda that was located at the rear of the Tir National visitors' hall.

A party of select German officers awaited the condemned pair: Kommandantur William Behrens, German commander of St Gilles prison, Captain Benn – a medical officer and two other regular German army officers as assistants to the Tir National Commander. Without any undue delays or social niceties, these German personages immediately escorted Edith and Philippe out to the actual firing range located at the rear part of the Tir National building. The firing range consisted of a plain green field of some 100 yards distance, now punctuated with muddied patches of ground, nature's gift from the generous downpours of the preceding night. A twenty-foot high simple dirt embankment served as a convenient bullet-trap for the projectiles that passed through both paper targets and gelatinous human tissue with equal ease.

The two German officers led Philippe and Edith to a distance of a mere eight paces away from the veranda and out across the muddied field to where the sturdy wooden firing posts were arranged and firmly moored into the ground. With diligence, they were fastened with tied hemp rope, so as to sufficiently affix and anchor both Edith and Philippe's bodies to the sturdy wooden firing posts, this measure to ensure that their bodies would not be defiled by falling over into the voluminous muddy field. More care was devoted to the future deceased than they had been accorded over the past two months of imprisonment. The pair were carefully fitted with blindfolds. One of the German officers assisting in placing on the blindfolds noted that Edith's eyes were filled with tears and this distressed him greatly. Dr Stober was in charge of the execution proceedings and he took almost delight in addressing the assembly on hand of which there were many. He cited the German Penal Code and paragraphs 58 and 90, which specified the 'sentence of death for treason'. Dr Stober loudly read out the sentences in German with an obnoxious high pitched voice.

The two clergymen were given several minutes to provide any last minute words of conciliation and a short prayer was whispered of the 'Our Father' to both Edith and Philippe. Philippe's Catholic rite blessings took a little bit longer than Edith's Lutheran Protestant administered prayers, but this posed no major impediment to the proceedings. Dr Stober dutifully noted the time and after a few minutes, he nodded to the firing squad detail officer. With youthful eagerness, the German Lieutenant drew forth his sword and raised it high into the air. It was the first, and probably the last, time that he would ever do so again in his life and he wanted this macabre distinction to be his and his alone. Every one of the sixteen infantry soldiers had been previously issued one 7.92 x 57 mm Mauser bullet by the German Lieutenant. He loudly shouted and ordered the soldiers on command to take their single bullet and load one bullet into their Mauser 98 Gewehr rifle spring-loaded magazine well, which was accomplished in precise drill-order fashion. The next order shouted by the young Lieutenant was the command to 'Load' the bullet into the rifle chamber, which was again performed to preciseness and this time with a single chatter of sixteen rifle bolts rubbing metal-against-metal sounds upon the contact of the rifle bolts to the rifle chamber area. The rifles were now at instant-ready state for firing, requiring the mere pull of the rifle trigger, of which every soldier was only too familiar. Each soldier knew that he was going to kill either a civilian man or woman and they did not care. The war had robbed them of any remorse.

In unison, the veteran German infantrymen followed in rote, precise military manner the commands of the firing squad Lieutenant with exact perfection. "Ready! Aim! Fire!" the German Lieutenant yelled forth in a loud German voice, as the sword that was raised high over his head, swung immediately downward toward the ground in one short, rapid vertical arching motion.

"Long live Belgium and patriots!" Philippe yelled out in a final act of defiance before being instantly shattered by the eight powerful rifle shot salvo. Philippe had exercised his last expression of free earthly speech. In a coherent instant, sixteen powerful Mauser rifle volleys were simultaneously unleashed in a perfect chorus that sounded as one singular roar, so well choreographed was the firing squad's discipline and marksmanship skills. So close were the soldiers to the executed that they saw the visible sprays and gushes of vibrant crimson blood spurt from the two bodies, which were immediately saturated with enormous amounts of blood. With minimal effort, each of the riflemen was true to his aim and both Edith and Philippe were riddled with eight powerful German 7.92 x 57 mm rifle bullets. Each Mauser bullet was unleashed with the muzzle energy of 3,000 foot pounds; both Edith and Philippe's bodies were immediately dealt a massive dose of 24,000 pounds of raw kinetic energy, most of which merely transgressed effortlessly through the soft body tissue with no relative bodily resistance. A light momentary cloud of light grey rifle propellant smoke filled the air in the front of the firing squad, as the hot projectile gas and smoke immediately condensed against the cool misty air.

Edith had a few spastic, reflective body convulsions, which lasted but a second or two and which appeared to falsely illustrate the illusion of ebbing life. Both she and Philippe, however, had died instantly. One powerful rifle bullet had impacted Edith in the forehead just above her blindfold and the blood gushed and splattered upon her face and drenched the blindfold that was now soaking wet with warm crimson coloured blood. So destructive was the power of the Mauser rifles that puddles of blood collected on the dew soaked ground beneath the feet of Edith and Philippe. Huge wounds had been carved into their bodies and many vital organs had been traumatically exploded by the energy of the projectiles. All eyes stared with great single attention to the now bloodied, lifeless and limp bodies. Their lifeless torsos immediately slumped slightly forward with the force of total dead body weight; only the strong hemp rope bindings affixed to the firing posts kept the bodies from falling unceremoniously downward onto the red spattered ground. The Lieutenant gave the command and the German soldiers brought their rifles down to the right side of their bodies in unison. The acrid smell of cordite rifle propellant filled the moist damp air. Every one of the observer's eyes were fixed on the bloody gruesome scene, yet not one of them could bear to look away, so captivated were they by the morbid scene before them. The human psyche was a strange web of contradictions that deplored violence on one level, yet it was strangely attracted and fascinated by gore and the visibility of death.

The defined protocol for firing squad executions mandated that a medical officer confirm the deaths of both Edith and Philippe. Captain Doctor Benn rushed forward to the bodies, accompanied by Pastor Le Seur and Father Leyendecker. Doctor Benn brought out a stethoscope and he listened for Edith Cavell's heartbeat – none existed. He then quickly rushed over to Philippe and he also had no heartbeat. A quick visual examination of both Edith and Philippe's bodies revealed to the German officer witnesses and Doctor Benn that multiple fist-sized gaping wounds were evident in each of their backs, a forensic indication of the destructive force that was inherent in the newly introduced powerful smokeless powder cartridges. These same powerful bullets were killing soldiers on both sides of the war at a distance of several thousand yards. No human could easily survive the impact of just one of these deadly projectiles, much less eight of these apiece. There was no doubt in Dr Benn's mind that their deaths were immediate and painless. He looked down at his watch; it was precisely 7:30 am 'first full light' and both Edith Cavell and Philippe Baucq lay dead. The Germans had met their timeline and completion of the execution orders signed by General von Sauberzweig.

Two rather non-descript and plain wooden coffins were brought forward on a horse drawn wagon and Edith and Philippe were dutifully and carefully placed within the rather makeshift wooden coffins. A scant fifty feet away, a makeshift cemetery was maintained by the German authorities and it was well-populated with the victims of other German military justice and this place too became the resting place of Edith Cavell and Philippe Baucq. Two small simple wooden crosses inscribed with their names and date of death served as their only worldly testimony of earthly existence. The ground of Belgium was to be further consecrated by the blood and flesh of many millions of lives in the years to follow. By 11:00 am all of Brussels had heard of the execution of Edith and Philippe. The Germans themselves in bright red posters announced the death of the two traitors and the fate that awaited those foolish enough to follow in their footsteps. Also announced on the warning posters was noted the death sentences of the other three convicted prisoners. The Belgians called it murder and assassination, yet there was little else they could do, being under the eyes of the German secret police and the harsh heels of the German occupying Army. In Britain and around the world, there were cries of injustice and murder, yet the Germans neither sought nor gave any mercy; instead they mounted their own propaganda war which stated that Edith, Philippe and the others were traitors, spies and active agents of the Allied forces. The world moved on as the tragedy of Edith and Philippe was eclipsed by ever-greater battles and human suffering.

The US Consulate was in shock and disbelief – they had expected a 'last minute' stay-of-execution for at least Edith Cavell. The Nurses at the Berkendael Institute Clinique were crying and in great grief. All of England was in an uproar and this brazen act increased enlistments into the British Army with untold thousands of new recruits. Those in utmost grief were those who knew and served with her in the de Croy network. Louise Thuliez, Louis Severin and Countess Jeanne de Belleville were still on death's row and only their appeals had saved them from the immediate fate that had befallen Edith and Philippe that morning. Yet even the German General Staff was not totally immune from the outrage of enormous negative public opinion. The other three condemned de Croy network members sat in their cells for two weeks awaiting their fates, until the personal intervention of President Woodrow Wilson, King Alfonso of Spain and Pope Benedict XV were made to Kaiser Wilhelm II to spare their lives and commuted sentences of prison or hard labour were granted.

Those serving non-capital sentences like Princess de Croy were sent off to do hard labour in various locations in Germany about a month after Edith and Philippe's execution. Louise Thuliez, Louis Severin and the Countess de Belleville would not be granted freedom until the end of the war in November 1918, some three years later. The old Berkendael Institute Clinique was abandoned soon after Edith's death and a new alternative established in its place; however, the original Clinique nurses were scattered to other Belgian hospitals and duties, while the remaining English nurses were deported from Belgium and eventually sent back to England. A new clinique was established and re-instituted after the war in Nurse Edith Cavell's name and memory.

* * * * * * * * * * *

# Chapter 11:
# Briefings and Billiards

*"Muuumm…I confess that I don't like either option, Brand! Maybe one day the Europeans will realize the fruitlessness of making war among themselves and instead channel their energies and talents into living the good-life of peace and prosperity," William shot back with an immediate off-the-cuff parlour reply. Both men smiled at one another at the close bonds that they had formed in the short amount of time that they had spent together"*

"Do you have any questions? Mr Donovan? Excuse me, do you have any questions?" Consul-General Brand Whitlock remarked as he leaned forward in his chair.

"Oh I'm sorry, my apologies, Mr Whitlock, my mind was racing about the details of the de Croy network. It's really a remarkable story of sacrifice, initiative and courage. That execution of Edith Cavell and Philippe Baucq was tragic! It's hard to believe that the Germans did that!" Donovan remarked with a sadness in his voice.

"Yes, well, the Germans are brutal, the war is dragging on with no end in sight and the German patience is long since exhausted. In fact, their humanity probably died after they were stopped on the Marne over a year ago. It's hard to believe that they were killed about eight months ago; we tried our best to stop the executions, but the Germans were determined to have their way and they certainly got it with these two executions," Consul Whitlock replied, his disbelief still evident in his voice.

"So how are the other prisoners doing – Capiau, Bodart, Countess de Belleville, Libiez and Princess de Croy?" Donovan asked.

"For God's sake I wish the hell I knew the answer to that question," Whitlock answered back contemptuously, as he pounded his hand on the chair. "I make inquiries and the Germans simply ignore these. I hope that they are all still alive and healthy, but such information cannot be obtained."

"Did you get all the information that you needed, Mr Donovan? Is there anything else that I or the Consulate can provide for you?" the Consul-General asked earnestly.

"No, I think that I have seen and learned enough. That pile of documents

330

was a real eye-opener, as were your personal recollections. I want to thank you for taking the time to sit down with me and relate these stories to me. I still have difficulty believing such monstrous things happened. Naturally we heard some of this news back in the United States, but it only becomes real once you are in the country itself and you have spoken to those who were actually a part of it! I'll be leaving in a few days to start the other legs of my European trip. I still have a lot of research and coordination to do with the other countries on my travel itinerary," Donovan confessed with a broad smile on his face.

"One final inquiry and this one is strictly off the record, Brand: what do you think about the military situation here and the prospects for Germany winning this awful war?" Bill Donovan plainly asked of the man who had seen the war in Belgium since its inception.

There was a pregnant pause before Brand Whitlock's reply, as he gazed into oblivion in obvious gesture to some in-depth critical thinking.

"Well Bill, in the beginning of this war I thought as many Americans did, that we needed to keep out of European wars that were not our concern. Each side made stupid mistakes for a war that did not need to be fought over the killing of some Archduke and his wife in a small corner of Europe which few Americans could even place on a map. A war that began as a simple European squabble has now metastasized into a cancerous growth that has eclipsed any sort of rationality for its continued purpose. I greatly fear that governments and generals are clueless to stop the insanity, so it continues without an end in sight. Should America get involved? I frankly do not know, Bill. The United States is protected by the Atlantic Ocean, but is this a valid enough reason to stay out of a future fight? I see one of two possibilities: one is where each side fights itself to exhaustion with no clear military victor; and the other is that by some miracle Germany wins and becomes more belligerent like a dragon whose appetite cannot be satisfied. Perhaps the tipping point in our decision will be if there ever becomes a direct threat to the US interests or a clear threat to our sovereignty, then we'll get involved and the US public will endorse it, but I do not see involvement in the war as things now remain," Whitlock concluded with some exasperation in his breath.

"Muuumm, I confess that I don't like either option, Brand! Maybe one day the Europeans will realize the fruitlessness of making war among themselves and instead channel their energies and talents into living the good-life of peace and prosperity," William shot back with an immediate off-the-cuff parlour reply. Both men smiled at one another at the close bonds that they had formed in the short amount of time that they had spent together.

"Oh look at the time, Bill, we've been talking or rather I've been talking, for over two hours! It's almost time for dinner too! I'm afraid that the dining fare in the Consulate is a bit barren given the local food shortages – this is mainly due to the British embargo, so you and Mr Hoover really need to ramp up that food programme being sponsored by the Rockefeller Relief Commission." The two men got up from their chairs and walked toward the library door.

"That, sir, is quite a relief. I think that I need to lose some weight anyway; sitting around preparing legal briefs and estate paperwork does not tend to burn off a lawyer's weight after a hearty lunch. There are some great clubs in which to dine in Buffalo and if you are ever up that way, I want you to look me up, Brand," William replied with a honest invitation.

"Well thank you, Bill. You should have been here in Brussels before the war began, Bill, we had the fanciest parties around with eight course meals and fancy balls as well. Each Embassy and Consulate tried to out-match the other in terms of food and entertainment. I fear that after this war concludes itself, we shall never go back again to that grand type of living. A lot of people's lives are going to be changed by this war and that includes the aristocrats and nobility too," Brand replied back with a smile.

"Oh Mr Whitlock, I hope that you do not think this as an out of place question, but I feel as if I got to know Edith Cavell and Philippe Baucq in some personal sense, even if it is only vicariously – is it possible for me to visit their graves?" William Donovan requested of his pleasant host .

A look of sadness befell the Consul-General's handsome face. "I'm afraid that request is not possible, Bill! The nurses at the Berkendael Institute Clinique tried in vain to get possession of Edith's body to re-inter her at the new institution's location in a more rural setting; however, the Germans denied the request – they feared that Edith's and Philippe's grave could become objects of homage and maybe even inspiration to other Belgian patriots. Both myself and the nurses also tried to visit their graves at the Tir National firing range, but the Germans again refused our request and the Tir National is off-limits without express permission of the German military officials and they are not in a accommodating mood as you well realize. After the executions, the US Consulate became even more estranged from the German political officials. I guess they think that we are too chummy with the British and that we are not true neutrals like the Swiss and Scandinavians," Whitlock replied with a tone of regret.

The two men walked out of the library and prepared for dinner, over which Bill had the pleasure of meeting Mrs Whitlock, Guy de Leval and Hugh Gibson, names heretofore that only previously existed in the context of dry diplomatic dispatches and Consulate summary notes. They were all delightful personages and they relayed more details and actors in the de Croy network than was possible in the multiple days of reading dry diplomatic summaries and cables. Despite his previous reservations, William Donovan was most glad that he had made this journey to Brussels and he made it a personal vow to someday pay his respects to those brave patriots Edith Cavell and Philippe Baucq.

In two days' time, Donovan ventured forth on his pre-planned travels to the other European countries noted on his visa; these included: Holland, Denmark, Germany, Austria Turkey, Bulgaria, Norway and Sweden. He was greeted with the utmost of cooperation and courtesy, even in Germany, which realized the growing importance of the role of the United States in the world and given the pragmatic fact that Germany wanted as many civilians in Europe to be fed through the Rockefeller War Relief Commission, this to alleviate the strain on its own domestic food supply and to mitigate mass rioting from starving European civilians. Germany could ill afford to fight on both the battlefield and the breadbasket.

At each US Embassy or Consulate, William Donovan filed a summary specific 'country-by-country' field report to his superior Herbert Hoover. The food situation in Europe was desperate. Hoover made the appropriate country negotiations for the food relief agreement, to include a strict outline of the policies and procedures to be followed for grain transport, storage, distribution and invoice tracking. Each country authorized that bona fide agents of the US War Relief Commission be granted safe letters of passage for workers involved in the distribution and transport of designated US War Relief food parcels and grain sacks. The grain sacks were an important end-item, as these were carefully controlled, tracked and distributed to the various identified war stricken countries to be used for controlled commercial purposes such as civilian clothing and essential textile purposes. The European war was making continental civilians both hungry and increasingly unclothed.

By July 1916, Donovan had completed his findings concerning both the food relief situation, as well as his personal mission of investigating the social, political and military posture of both Allied and Austro-Hungarian forces. His conclusions were realistic and bleak. Military victory was impossible for either side; modern war technology and the modernized industrial state had made the conduct of war almost limitless. Neither side could breach the defences of the other to any great degree. The manpower losses were having an impact on the industrial and social order of the warring countries, as there were fewer and fewer men to work the fields and perform the other forms of labour taken for granted before the war. Despite modern advances, agriculture and farming in Europe was still a manual, not a mechanized affair and as men went off to war, agriculture production fell and more people went hungry.

The war also meant that there were fewer marriages and births; consequently the populations were starting to decline. Standards of living fell as incomes dropped, fewer civilian goods were produced and there was both less money and people to spend any money that existed. More and more resources were diverted from the civilian sector to the various war industries for every country involved in the war. Due to the product shortages, prices of consumable and durable items rose, as did inflation rates. As the military and economic elements of the warring nations stagnated and fell in capacity, the socio-political demands of the common man and woman rose, but were not able to be met by the resource-constrained national governments.

There was social unrest; people began to question the wisdom and very authority of their governments and leaders who led them into this so-called 'fast war' that was now in its second bloody year. The tenets of Communism began to challenge the rule of monarchs and the aristocrats across Europe. If the common people were noble enough to spill their blood for their countries, they were so entitled to have a say in the governments that led them. The landed gentry and aristocrats lost more and more of their labourers to both the war and the factories; soon the masters of the land had only a fraction of their former workers. A war that relied on volunteers soon found a drought of such eager young men, who had seen many badly wounded or killed without any sign of even a partial victory. Forced conscription led to sporadic resistance and sometimes outright rebellion and the very fabric of the nineteenth century social paradigm was being slowly torn by the distresses of war.

\* \* \* \* \* \* \* \* \* \* \*

Bill arrived prematurely back to the United States after an urgent summons by President Woodrow Wilson. He prepared a brief one page summary of his findings concerning the status of the war in Europe with ample supplementary in-depth data reports to be included within a separate correspondence for either the President's further reading or that of his personal advisors. It was early July 1916 and the nation had just completed celebrating its annual Independence Day – the tattered remnants of red, white and blue decorations lined many a shop window and public building edifices. It seemed surreal to Bill that a mere ocean separated the free, carefree people of the United States from the wretched starving masses in Europe and he hoped that geography could keep his nation from this maddening war, yet he realized that an ocean some day was not going to be enough to shelter his country from the chaos that reigned outside its physical domain.

As befitted the weather of a southern urban city that had been constructed upon a once marshy swamp area, the July weather in Washington, DC was uncomfortably humid and the physical temperature was most smothering, especially given the prevailing social necessity for gentlemen and ladies to be 'dressed to the nines' in layers of constrictive, non-breathable Victorian-era cotton and wool suits and flowing pastoral dress ensembles complete with sun parasols. Men and women sweated profusely. Huge doses of fragrant perfumes and colognes were used by both sexes to mask the pungent smell of human body odours. Adding olfactory insult to the entire sweat-doused affair was the relentless ordure of horse manure deposited by horse carriages that still prevailed upon the concourses and streets of the nation's capital, to include the most unwelcoming flying pests of prominent large green flies that assaulted the innocent denizens along every major transportation artery within the hot urban centre. The major sport of the day was trying to ward off these nasty flying germ carrying flies that seemed to be of Biblical proportions throughout the city and it was only the daily prevalence of dusk that provided a temporary, but most welcome, respite from these small flying demons.

As per his previous visit protocol, William Donovan presented his name to the man dressed in neat civilian clothing posted in the small white stone guardhouse that was positioned adjacent to the Executive Mansion. Donovan's name was noted on the White House visitors' log, but still an inquiry to the President's aide was required to determine the suitability of such a visit at the present time; emergencies and other unforeseen distractions were becoming the increasing bane of the US President and his schedule was to become increasingly inflexible with the march of time and the advent of the rising importance of the United States in world affairs. Once again a phone call inquiry was made to the mansion for the determination of Donovan's further physical progression.

"You are cleared to proceed, Mr Donovan, I'm sorry for the delay. An aide will greet and escort you at the side door," the serious, but courteous broad-framed man stated in a rigid business-like manner. 'Another stern looking Secret Service agent, I suppose that the seriousness of their job precludes the gesture of smiling,' he thought to himself. Bill was greeted by a hand-off Secret Service agent at the door and the two men took a familiar stroll down the elaborate palm planted corridors to the once again familiar Presidential billiard room. The agent knocked on the closed door and again waited for permission to enter.

"Come in please," echoed the familiar voice of the President Woodrow Wilson, his voice clearly resounding through the thick wooden white painted doors. The agent gave a silent head nod and William Donovan slowly turned the door handle, while presenting his hat awkwardly to the agent who placed it on a nearby hallway chair.

"Well how is my little spymaster?" Wilson exclaimed with a jovial smiling face. "Welcome back, Bill, job well done, very well done indeed!"

John O'Brien smiled with a complimentary pat on Donovan's back.

"A drink Bill?" the President cordially offered.

"No thank you, sir, my personal constitution does not tolerate alcohol graciously, it wreaks havoc on my body – I try to avoid it!" Bill politely replied.

"Ah yes, that's right, John had previously informed me about that issue with you, no offence is taken, Bill," Wilson remarked.

"I've been reading your reports along with those of Mr Hoover's and I must say that things are a shambles in Europe and the war comes closer to America with each passing day," Wilson signed with a depressed voice. He had campaigned for President on a platform of outright non-involvement and the vast majority of the American public was in overwhelming concurrence with this sentiment.

"I have cables and reports from Mr Hoover that he has had quite a few nasty and heated confrontations with the cantankerous Germans, especially that detestable, malicious Lt General von Sauberzweig, the same fellow that executed the Belgian and English civilians whom you had written to me about – now he is trying to interfere with the American food relief programme! That man must be crazy to do that, he's cutting off the hand that is feeding millions of starving civilians that will become the problem of the Germans!" President Wilson scowled angrily in frustrated self-rhetoric bombast. "Ah, why am I getting upset over matters that are in a crazy German General's mind! Well Bill, what do you have for me?" the President continued forth.

"Well yes, sir, Mr President, I have a short summary letter which outlines my thoughts on the issues that face America concerning the war. If you don't mind, sir, it's a one page general summary if you so desire to read it." Donovan handed the President a neat standard-sized business envelope.

"Yes I sure do want to read it. I like the way you cut to the chase in your communications and being a Princeton University man, I greatly admire good writing. It reflects the clear thinking and essence of a person, don't you agree?" President Wilson smiled and rhetorically replied back to Bill Donovan as he carefully placed his wired-frame glasses onto his face. President Wilson sat down on a comfortable soft cushioned reading chair and looked at Donovan's letter, which was composed in carefully crafted, elegant Spencer script handwriting.

*Dear Mr President:*

*The mission to which you have charged my personage to investigate in detail the conduct of the war of the European Powers has been completed. I have seen much suffering and I can see no quick end to the violence, as a military solution remains elusive and the prospect of peace seems impossible given the intractable nature of the belligerent parties. The warring sides have invested too much sunk capital in the elements of suffering, death, resources and national pride for there to be anything but a continuance of the military campaigns and the goal of all parties remains that of ultimate military victory by both the Allied and Central Powers; peace is not an option even being contemplated by either side. The insanity of this war cannot be mediated – both sides are too psychologically entrenched along the entire western front to entertain anything except for a military victory, yet both sides are not equally morally depraved either. I have personally witnessed the physical destruction and human suffering – it is of the greatest magnitude the modern world has yet witnessed and I fear that starvation in both the neutral countries and Germany will continue unless the US continues and increases the amount of humanitarian aid that is presently being afforded via the Rockefeller Foundation.*

*Furthermore I personally recommend that should the decision be made for the US to become engaged in this struggle, that it side with the Allied Forces. This judgment is based on my personal investigations into the military conduct of the war and in particular the gross physical abuses and destruction of German Imperial military power directed against the city of Louvain and the senseless executions of civilians,*

*to include the unwarranted exigent execution of English nurse Edith Cavell and the*
*Belgian patriot architect Philippe Baucq.*

*The arrogant and brutal German military war machine is a cancer upon the face*
*of Europe and indeed I fear for the stewardship of Europe should Germany emerge*
*victorious in the war. All the US efforts must be made to either end or influence the*
*war to avoid this very real possibility and in the words of nurse Edith Cavell, "it is no*
*small prudence to keep silence in a time of evil". If I may be of further assistance to you*
*or your administration, I am humbly at your immediate disposal.*

*Respectfully,*

*William Donovan, Esq*

*July 6, 1916*

President Wilson's face looked intensely at the contents of the letter. He kept
his eyes on the letter and said nothing for a full five minutes. Finally he tilted
his head up, removed his glasses and looked off into oblivion for another
minute.

"Well, well, that's some analysis that you have done there, Bill, once
again it was a thorough analysis. Are things really that bad over there?" the
President remarked with a hope of scepticism that perhaps too dark a picture
was being painted by Bill Donovan.

"I'm afraid that it may get even worse, Mr President – at least that is
my opinion on the reading of the facts. I think that Consul-General Brand
Whitlock will reinforce my findings, Mr President. I've seen reports on the
destruction of the Belgium town of Louvain, starving civilians everywhere,
the sinking of the Lusitania and many civilians being murdered by the
German military for almost petty, hyped-up infractions against an imposing
German military occupation ordnances," William Donovan added as he
awaited a response from his Commander in Chief.

"No, no that will not be necessary, I just wanted to hear your reply with
my own ears. You see Bill, I've had the same personal reports back from
Consul Whitlock and Mr Hoover – yours makes it a third confirmation and
all your reports point the same way: Germany is the aggressor and she will
not cease until exhausted or defeated. The question is, 'Can America stay out
of the war for much longer or does America merely face a more menacing

risk of a powerful Germany becoming ever more menacing with the nectar of a military victory?'" the President wearily questioned.

"Sir, I'm afraid that's a political question; however, I can offer my analogy on the European war: it's like two men playing poker and neither side has the fortitude or wisdom to call the other guy's hand, the stakes on the table are too high for either side to capitulate. Neither side wants to lose, yet militarily no one can win! So the war and killing go on and on, as each side raises its military victory bets with higher and more costly military battles and campaigns! Sir, the killing over there is ten times the ferocity and death toll of the US Civil War. I'm not sure the American public can tolerate such bloodiness for a foreign war about which they know practically nothing," Donovan added, as his friend John O'Brien presented to him a look of obvious disdain for making such a political interjection to the President.

Wilson was disturbed by the remark, not for its contention, but because the US Civil War was still fresh in the soul of the American public and that war was much closer to home for Americans to grasp, while few Americans could relate to the affairs in Europe or could even find it on a map. "Well I do not intend to be another President Lincoln either; besides Europe is an ocean away and there is no way that I can couple Europe's interests with those of the United States – neither the American public or Congress will endorse such a idea! I am receiving cables from Mr Walter H Page, our Ambassador to Great Britain, and he has informed me through diplomatic cable about a great battle that started a few days ago near a place called the Somme. He said that in just the first day of the battle, British casualties there amounted to 60,000 British soldiers with over 20,000 being killed. My Lord, can you just imagine that amount of American boys killed in one day? That is more than three times the number of men killed at Gettysburg by both Union and Confederate forces! I think there would be riots in the streets if I were to take America into such an engagement at this point in time. Unless there is a drastic threat against America, I'm afraid that we're riding this war out, gentlemen," the President concluded with a tone of finality in his voice. The room was eerily silent, the President had made up his mind and that was the end of the conversation on the issue of the US getting involved in the European war presently.

"We sit here over three thousand miles away in our splendoured seclusion of isolationism and we think ourselves to be better than the other poor slobs slogging it out in the muddy trenches in Europe year after year and to endless avail. A lot of brave people have been dying over in Europe for years and now the war comes ever closer to us. Germany is aggressive and dangerous and I fear for our country if this wild beast continues to grow. I think the hardest thing for any political leader or anyone for that matter in this life is to make a self-admission that a long-held belief or pursuit was in error. Human nature and its inherent stubbornness has been the bane of man's existence since time immemorial and I realize that I am not immune from this very human weakness as well! I'm not so sure that if I were in that terrible position of any of the European combatants, that I could have made any better decision in the war than they have done. It's easy to play poker without using your own money," the President replied with a shallow introspective voice.

Donovan and O'Brien knew that the President had campaigned to stay out of the war, yet in less than a year's time the reality of the increasing submarine warfare and the interception of the Zimmermann Telegram presented a real threat to the national security of the United States. Reality dictated that any action had to wait for future calamitous events to unfold. For the moment, all that the Administration could effectively do was to rush more grain and food to Europe and keep a watchful eye out for any onerous war encroachments that could pose a danger to the United States.

President Wilson rose up from his chair and Mr O'Brien and Donovan followed in kind. "Thanks for the report, Bill, that was quite a good job. You should keep your finger in intelligence analysis – you have a rare talent for it. As far as America's role in the war, I think for the moment that we should stay focused on the War Relief food effort and getting those stranded American citizens back from hostile foreign shores. I'll let Herbert Hoover run with that ball; he has a 'knack' for such organizational efforts – he's an engineer by trade and talent." The President shook Bill's hands and bade him farewell.

* * * * * * * * * * * *

Over the next eight months, despite President Wilson's deliberate intention to remain neutral in the war in Europe, incremental and steadily escalating unfavourable belligerent actions by the Germans forced him from neutrality to the eventual declaration of war on the side of the Allies. The Germans seemed ignorant of and intent on defying one of the tenets of foreign affairs, 'make no enemy where one does not exist'.

In November 1916, the ocean liner and sister ship of the RMS Titanic, and now a converted hospital ship, Britannica, was torpedoed by a German submarine in the Aegean Sea. There was by the sake of Providence only a token loss of life, but the point of German military brutality against the war wounded on a hospital ship drew immediate analogies and recollections of the sinking of the Lusitania. Germany continued to fumble and make diplomatic mistakes. Also in November 1916, the Germans increased the attack sorties by both Zeppelin and bomber raids over London. A telegram intercepted on January 19, 1917 sent shock waves through the heart of United States neutrality. Known as the Zimmermann telegram, named after the new German Foreign Minister Dr Alfred Zimmermann, the diplomatic cable was sent from Germany's Foreign Minister Zimmermann to the government of Mexico, in which the Germans offered the repatriation of the territory that the United States had gained from Mexico during the US-Mexican War of 1845, this in exchange for Mexico declaring war on the United States and subsequently invading the southwestern United States. This was a very sensitive issue as the bandit and revolutionary Pancho Villa had invaded some US territory in the state of Texas in 1916 and General Pershing had been sent to weed out the renegade without any success. Captain Donovan had served on General Pershing's staff during this Punitive Expedition.

To add oil to the diplomatic fire, on February 1, 1917, the Kaiser pronounced a resumption of unrestricted submarine warfare against any flagged vessel and any type of cargo carried, including War Relief foodstuffs. Shortly hereafter, President Wilson broke off diplomatic relations with Germany and every other Central Power country, which included Austro-Hungary and Bulgaria, as well as countries within the Ottoman Empire. On March 1, 1917 the Zimmermann Telegram became public and the American public went from neutral to anti-German when the German Foreign Minister publicly confirmed that the terms of the communiqué were genuine. This was an act of war through a third party as far as most Americans were concerned. Yet Wilson still stoically avoided war calls. The American vessel Algonquin was torpedoed on March 5, 1917, but President Wilson was resolved he was not going to be driven into a bloody war over a few US ships being sunk.

The United States continued to lose vessels to German submarines throughout March. Next, the American public and President Wilson had had enough of these German aggressive acts and the Germans refused to listen to reason. He realized that William Donovan, Herbert Hoover and other counsels had indeed been correct about the Germans. On April 4, 1917 the United States finally declared war on Germany by a vast majority Senate vote of 82 in favour of war and only 6 senators voting no. The US lower chamber, the House of Representatives, had a similar lop-sided vote in favour of war as well. On April 6, 1917 the United States declared war with Germany and by de facto the Central Powers. It took a full year of mobilization and training for US military forces to see any significant military campaigns under General Pershing.

\* \* \* \* \* \* \* \* \* \* \*

Being a Reserve Captain in the United States Army National Guard, Bill transitioned from Buffalo Attorney Bill Donovan to becoming Major William Donovan and the Commanding officer of the 1st battalion of the newly formed composite Infantry Division of the New York National Guard known as the 69th Division, more popularly to be known as the 'Fighting 69th'. This was quite an honour for William Donovan, as he was only a Major and by rank a battalion was normally commanded by a Lieutenant Colonel. Yet he possessed active military service witnessed by his recent stint in General Pershing's Punitive Expedition to Mexico while most other US Army officers had no field experience at all. His division shipped off to France in October 1917, after the 69th Division had undergone the necessary recruitment, fitting-out and training.

He and his unit fought in the Battle of the Ourcq, which was fought from July 27-31, 1918. During this battle, he led his unit to successfully engage and defend against superior German attacks on his unit. In the hard hand-to-hand fighting his unit lost sixty percent of its strength as casualties. In October 1918 he was wounded leading an infantry attack against a German defensive position. Ironically during his convalescent stay in a Paris hospital, his old friend Herbert Hoover visited him. Hoover was still administering the War Relief Commission to provide food to the European allies and neutrals. The two men spoke of old times and stories. Donovan was now a full Army Colonel and a decorated war hero with a Distinguished Service Cross (DSC), the Distinguished Service Medal (DSM), the French Croix de Guerre and Purple Heart medal. Later, after the war, in 1922, he was to be awarded the Congressional Medal of Honor in recognition of his valiant service during the Ourcq and Kriemhilde battles.

The last German major 'break or make' offensive of the war started in March 1918 and it was appropriately named the 'Ludendorff Offensive' after the German Field Marshal, the new Chief of the German General Staff who engineered and approved the military operation. The German military campaign was a 'last gasp' for the Germans to win the war and it was all that the French and English forces could endure before the bulk of American army forces arrived to finally turn the war inevitably in the Allies' favour. The

German attack lacked specific strategic objectives to which to narrowly focus their assaults and after heavy losses in April 1918, the attack stalled and great waves of American military forces arrived to reverse the course of events and ironically it was the Allies attacking and the German army went on the defence. General Pershing wanted to drive further with the US military attacks right into Germany proper; he felt the need to decisively and militarily defeat the German army completely and without question, yet the stomach of the other European armies and politicians was that there had been enough fighting and that an Armistice at the earliest possible date was sufficient.

The Europeans had been in the war from the first shots fired and they had lost several times the amount of military casualties as the United States forces. The fresh American forces and huge amounts of war material were too much for the Germans to resist and on November 11, 1918 the armistice was signed and the Great War ended favourably for the Allies. The German Army retreated out of Belgium into Germany, taking with it much of the information and data files on controversial and questionable activities conducted during their occupation of the country, to include any incriminating evidence on the de Croy network and the prosecution's case of its primary members to include Edith Cavell and Philippe Baucq.

Some good things good did come out of the ending of The Great War. One of these was that the military and civilian prisoners were set free and this included Princess Marie de Croy, Louise Thuliez and Countess Jeanne de Belleville and all the other imprisoned de Croy network prisoners. Under a faltering German government and much disorganization, they had all been released from German territory confinement and made their way back using whatever means possible, through to Belgium through myriad rebellion, street riots and public anarchy, as the veneer of German central military authority collapsed under utter exhaustion to that of Communist and Marxist agitators. By late November 1918, they were back in Belgium and they were reunited with their respective families. Reginald de Croy arrived back from London and Leopold was granted time to make a marriage that had been delayed by war for the past four years.

The ancestral family estate of Bellignies was in dilapidated condition and found to be in great need of urgent repair, as was to be the case of all other Belgian noble and middle-class homes. The chateau had suffered the indignities of war and weathering, several artillery shells had struck it, and there was not an unbroken window throughout the noble structure and various small creatures had made nests for themselves given this wide-open convenience. Retreating German troops also looted the structure and destroyed anything in sight. Inside the chateau, the furniture was either broken or badly soiled. During the chateau's long abandonment, all the servants save for a lonely gardener had left – there was nothing for them to do, nor wages to be paid to them. Many hundreds of German troops made the chateau their temporary bivouac and the entire inside was in desperate need of complete repairs. Family papers, photographs and other heirlooms littered the hallways and rooms, while other more valuable or attractive items had simply been looted. Now English troops became its temporary occupants, for which none of the de Croys had objections. Baron de la Grange had died sometime in 1916, shortly after the Princess had been exiled to prison; however, the Baron's son remained to care for the old man's estate which had been left to him.

With the return of peace came the return of fond memories of the dearly departed loved ones, including Edith Cavell and Philippe Baucq. In May 1919, Colonel William Donovan and about a dozen other English, Belgium and French officials assembled in the Tri National firing range. Along with them were brought two ornate wooden caskets and several photographers. William Donovan was adorned in the olive drab uniform of an Army Infantry Colonel; across his left chest was arrayed the prominent war ribbons of valour. Slowly and carefully, the two graves of Edith and Philippe were disinterred by a half dozen workman; they carefully used pick axes and shovels to dig up the two coffins. After about 40 minutes, the shovels hit the distinct wooden objects that had been the resting repose of Edith and Philippe for the past three years. Very gently, the diggers brushed the dirt from atop the cheap, soiled coffins. Sturdy ropes were placed under both of the heavily earth encrusted oblong objects and a team of men strenuously brought up the wooden caskets from the dark earth. Both of the coffins were encapsulated in a surrounding encasement of solidified dirt that stubbornly clung to the coffins and which could not be immediately or easily removed.

The grave diggers took small garden tools to the caskets and after about 20 minutes, the distinct outline of a wooden European-styled casket was revealed. As visual confirmation of the deceased was required, the coffins were opened for the normal and formal purpose of visibly identifying the remains. As the crowbars squeakily worked to ratchet up the lids of the coffins, a small crowd of official looking onlookers gathered more tightly around the coffins. A morbid curiosity was part of the human condition that conversely breeds curiosity and disgust. As the coffins were carefully opened, those gathered closed-in around the coffins, as the lids were carefully removed with iron pry bars. Immediately many observers were sickened and nauseated by the decomposed corrupted sight now confronting them.

Before them lay with their arms laid across their torsos in careful repose was the decomposing brownish corpses of Edith and Philippe. Their features despite discolouring were true to their likeness. Some people turned away in utter disgust at the normal sight of bodily decomposition, while others simply bowed their heads and said a short prayer. Those with recent battlefield experience merely looked on with intense curiosity, so numb had their senses become to decomposed and rotting human flesh; they had lived with it for many months and in some cases, several years.

The camera crew carefully photographed the corpses to illustrate to the world the reality and horror that Edith and Philippe had endured. The authorities wanted to ensure that both they and the public had physically attested to the authenticity of the two deceased to prevent any false rumours of there being either empty graves or substituted corpses being exhumed from the graves. Colonel Donovan with a saddened face looked on and whispered in a low and sombre voice: "Well Edith, today you are finally going home to England. You have both done well, very well. I'm sorry it took us so long to get here! Let's see if your countrymen can't find you a more fitting resting place upon the quiet green fields of England."

Military and diplomatic officials from the United Kingdom quickly took control of Edith's remains, while a similar party of Belgian officials performed the same stewardship for Philippe Baucq's remains.

The corpses were carefully transferred to the new ornate wood caskets with great reverence. The St Gilles officials and clergy verified the remains and several clergy prayed over the remains and sprinkled the corpses and caskets with Holy Water. The coffins were draped with the respective flags of Great Britain and Belgium. Philippe's wife and now adolescent daughters met his coffin at a Brussels catholic church, where it laid in requiem for several days before a solemn mass and burial. Edith's casket was taken by a British delegation across the European continent to France and then back to London, England. A horse-drawn gun carriage paraded her ornate wooden coffin through the streets of London for a memorial service at Westminster Abbey. Later a train took her remains to Norwich Cathedral for final honours, memorial and a grand final interment. She rests there to this day in peace, only five miles from her childhood home.

* * * * * * * * * * *

# Epilogue

*"The sole reason that the war ended was that the Germans ran out of soldiers before the Allies, yet the fundamental causes of the war remained intact and a mere generation later, another greater war started to finish off where the last war had failed. Perhaps the greatest errors of the war are the human ones and these remain with us to the present"*

The Great War had many consequences on the world, some good and others bad,which remain consequential to this very day. In its transformational impact, it was the most consequential war since the time of Napoleon some one hundred years previously; it even dwarfed the larger, succeeding Second World War in its impact and many historians claim that the Second World War was merely a continuation of the Great War and that the twenty-one years of peace in between was merely an abbreviation gap for the warring countries to refresh, rearm and re-invent their armed forces. The three great Empires of Russia, Austro-Hungry and the Ottomans collapsed and the monarchies of Europe were largely replaced by either democratic or Communist ruling bodies. Germany, although debated by some as not being a true empire, nevertheless lost many of its foreign possessions and had severe external military and economic covenants imposed upon it through the Versailles Treaty.

President Woodrow Wilson's attempt for fair, but prudent war repatriations from Germany was over-ruled by European nations that wanted mere revenge at any price. Thus the seeds of a new war had been planted. The hostility and vindictiveness of the victors over the humiliated defeated Germany directly led to a boiling political caldron in Germany that led to post-war nationalism and the rise of the Nazi state to take revenge against their same enemies of The Great War. If old generals fight using the young soldier's experiences, then Adolf Hitler and his generals fought WWII using the same military objectives and grand strategy envisioned in The Great War, but with a reversal of victories and defeats on the respective Western and Eastern Fronts.

Just as the military and the political leaders did not see the dangers of the industrial-military advancements being made before the Great War, so too did another generation of generals and politicians fail to appreciate the advancements in the technological-military developments taking place after the Great War and into the 1920s and 1930s. As in all wars, the victor and the vanquished learned vastly different lessons from their respective war experiences. The victorious French became convinced that huge defensive barriers and fortifications were an optimal solution to any future offensive attacker, since their dreadful and costly experiences gained through fruitless insurmountable human-wave offences had proven to be indecisive in The Great War. The French curtailed much of their defence spending, save for building up the huge concrete line of massive fortifications located along its eastern border facing Germany, known as the Maginot Line.

The defeated Germans took an opposite position to that of the defensive-minded French. The Germans learned that their military offensive had worked up until the time that it became stalled by a stubborn defence early in the war and later the Hindenburg Offensive was working until the United States armed forces arrived to stop the German Army momentum. Consequently they were determined not to repeat the same mistake twice; they developed a strategy, tactics and weapons that could negate and roll-over any defensive measures made by man. The Germans still believed in the offence, but it needed to be notched-up for the modern technology available. The Germans kept a keen eye on developments in modern machinery and emerging technologies, they threw away the old rulebook and developed greater battlefield mobility strategy and armaments in the form of tanks, airplanes, motorized infantry mobile artillery and radio communications – the combined symmetry became known as 'Blitzkrieg' or lightning war strategy.

Great Britain and the United States adopted neither a vast defensive or novel offensive military post-war strategy; instead both nations withdrew to positions of splendid isolation and pacifism. Great Britain never had keen political and military interests on the European continent and thus devoted itself to governing its increasing burdensome colonial possessions, whose inhabitants were seeking self-rule and independence from an Empire that most of them would never see or truly comprehend. America looked inward, secure in the fact that two oceans protected it, yet the Japanese air and maritime attack on Pearl Harbor cruelly and irreparably shattered this safety illusion.

The strict class differences that were the vestiges of the previous century were largely vanquished, as class distinctions proved to be largely illusionary as to the merit of individual men and women. Ability not birth was a better proven barometer of competency as witnessed in the disastrous elite leadership failures during the Great War. Industry and markets were the new masters of society, not the landed nobility. Yet modernity was a two-edged sword: the benefits it produced for betterment of living was equally counter-balanced by its destructive ability to kill vast amounts of humanity in the form of new weapons of warfare to which no one realized the true potential. Without the horrors of the Great War and the resulting 'lost generation', there arguably might never have occurred the Roaring Twenties Jazz Age, the rise of universal suffrage, modern labour unions and collective bargaining, and the rise of the modern consumer class. It was the average man and woman who bore a disproportionally heavy burden in resourcing the war in term of human sacrifice on the battlefields, which had an equal civilian converse for the same human capital employed in the factories and war industries.

Having bitten out of the apple of equality, post war men and women demanded their political rights from their governments in which they had falsely placed all their confidences before the Great War. They now rightfully demanded their equal rights in terms of voting, working and education opportunities. A new social compact had been forged. The public in a more sceptical perspective viewed political and military leaders with a jaunted eye and sometimes outright contempt. The masses of middle and lower classes withdrew from the dialectic discord with their national leaders and a wave of isolation swept the world and this paved the way for potential despots and demigods to take advantage of a disillusioned electorate. England and many other countries suffered great losses in their male populations and this inevitably led to a 'generation of widows', who furthered endorsed the call for pacifism at a critical time during the 1930s when military intervention against fascism was needed most. Once again, nations failed to fight the wars that were vitally necessary and avoid the wars that were peripheral and trivial.

Some contend that the Great War directly led to the rise of Communism, Fascism and ultimately the Second World War. Others argue that the world would have been better off had Imperial Germany won the war to become the leader of a united Europe. Yet there is no definitive answer to these alternative history speculations; the multitude of factors and probabilities that determine great events is so vast as to tax the imagination of the average lay person and the aim is hopelessly pointless and best confined to other venues. We can, however, appreciate that many brave men and women gave their lives to their countries and ideals without any second thoughts in pondering any sort of alternative reality or 'what-if's'.

In many ways, innocence and hope generated by the promise of a new modernity was tarnished. The modern industrial-scientific era which brought forth changes in engineering, chemistry, transportation, communication and consumer goods also brought forth the horror of modern destruction to include aerial bombing, mechanized and mobile warfare, deadly rapid fire machine guns, submarine warfare, poison gas usage and artillery and an almost endless supply of munitions which only became exhausted when there were to be no more soldiers to kill. The countries had fought each other into exhaustion and sheer manpower annihilation. The sole reason that the war ended was that the Germans ran out of soldiers before the Allies, yet the fundamental causes of the war remained intact and a mere generation later, another greater war started to finish off where the last war had ended.

Perhaps the greatest errors of the war are the human ones and these remain with us to the present. The fallacy of human nature is that it is a victim of its own preconceived ideas and perceptions. Human nature cannot easily accept folly or the ability to make a drastic change to existing ideals and thinking, even when faced with irrefutable facts and logic. We are a slave unto our own ego, ID and vanities. The Great War could have been stopped at multiple points during the conflict, yet the individual leaders and the public masses could not bear to see their nationalistic cause and objectives in any other perspective or viewpoint from their own. Ironically, the more soldiers that were killed, the more stubborn and politically entrenched became the political postures. It is a bit amusing and fascinating to think about the soldier-level inspired 'Christmas Truce' of 1914, in which thousands of individual soldiers on both warring sides had simply laid down their guns to peacefully celebrate the Christmas season – had this truce continued onward indefinitely and on a more massive scale, just how different the war could have been changed.

Concerning the fate of Edith Cavell, there was lack of support and consensus to bring forth a post-war investigation into her trial and execution. The official German records were conveniently 'lost' and post-war riots and political unrest made any attempts quite difficult to bring about a high level investigation with international representatives. The German Government refused to cooperate with any further investigation on this matter from the victorious allied forces. The official files and data on this case have subsequently disappeared and have been deemed as lost to history. Lt Bergan admitted after the war that the German secret police used lies and subterfuge to get Edith to make a confession and that many of the other network prisoners never made or signed confessions. Although personal in his guilt, it was a collective German militant government that bred his actions and that of so many fellow Germans. Perhaps Edith Cavell's best legacy is the goodness and nobleness of character that she left behind as an inspiration for others to dwell upon and even emulate. She may have thought her own life's accomplishments as being small or inconsequential; however, individuals, especially great ones, do not possess the objectivity to make a realistic assessment of their own lives and in their own times. History sees best when it views from a distance and from today's historic lens, Edith Cavell and Philippe Baucq are true patriots for their countries and free people everywhere. The Second World War saw the further destruction of any German records that had not been previously destroyed.

History is replete with incidents in which the ruling governmental power was conclusively more responsible for more deaths collectively than was ever attained by individual criminal acts, thus remains the bane of mankind to this day. The loss of life was monstrous and it can only be approximated, with the Central Powers losing over 3.5 million soldiers, the Allied Powers lost over 5 million soldiers and another several million civilians killed through bombardment and starvation. The Great Influenza of 1918-19 killed as many people worldwide as the war had inflicted with bullets and shells. The Middle East and its incipient troubles to this day, are a direct result of the collapse of the Ottoman Empire and the rise of European powers in the area.

* * * * * * * * * * * *

The post-war fate of the noteworthy characters and personages depicted in this novel are briefly summarized below in alphabetical name ordering.

**Edith Louisa Cavell**. In May 1919, after her exhumation, an exalted national service was held for her which was attended by the King and Queen of Belgium. She was returned to England with great reverence and ceremony. After a memorial service at Westminster Abbey, her body was taken by special train from Liverpool Street to Thorpe Station, Norwich. She resides in perpetual repose outside of the east end of Norwich Cathedral referred to as Life's Green, just several miles from her childhood home.

**Philippe Baucq**. Along with Edith Cavell, he was disinterred from the Tir National grave in May 1919 and given a hero's memorial and burial in Brussels. He is remembered as a favourite son to Brussels and Belgium.

**Lt General Baron Moritz Ferdinand Freiherr von Bissing**. He continued to serve as the Brussels Military Governor until his death in 1917. The old Prussian cavalry officer who tacitly condoned the de Croy secret trials and sentences died on 18 April 1917 at the age of 73 years old.

**Prince Reginald de Croy**. After the Great War, he served as the Belgian First Secretary to the Belgium Embassy in Washington DC. He was instrumental in helping Belgium and Brussels during the post-war reconstruction period. He died of natural causes at the age of 83 years old in 1961. He is fondly remembered in the city of Mons, Belgium.

**Princess Marie de Croy**. After three years of imprisonment in a German prison, she was reunited with her two brothers. She died of natural causes in 1968 at the age of 93 years old.

**Dr Antoine Depage**. After the war, he continued to be a leading surgeon in Belgium becoming the department head of the Brugmann hospital and he also became a prominent advocate of the Boy Scouting organization. In August 1925, he died at the age of 63 years old.

**William 'Wild Bill' Donovan**. He returned to his legal practice in Buffalo, New York. He was awarded the United States Congressional Medal of Honor in 1922 for his heroic actions in the Great War. During WWII, he was appointed by President Roosevelt to lead the United States Office of

Strategic Services (a forerunner of the Central Intelligence Agency) as a Major General. In 1953 President Dwight Eisenhower appointed Donovan Ambassador to Thailand. He died on February 8, 1959 at the age of 76 years old.

**Field Marshal Erich von Falkenhayn**. He remained as the Imperial German General Staff leader until the stagnation of the war and lack of victories led to his replacement in August 1916. He was replaced as Chief of Staff by Field Marshal Paul von Hindenburg. He served as the German Commanding General in Palestine and he retired from the German army in 1919 and wrote several military books including his memoirs. He died at his German estate in 1922 at the age of 60 years old.

**Dr Georges Hostelet, DSc**. He continued to be active in mathematics, physics, chemistry and social sciences. He was appointed in 1932 as a member of the International Statistical Institute in The Hague. He is the author of numerous books and articles on mathematics and statistics. He was an advocate of integrating science with social development and activities. He died in 1960 at the age of 85 years old.

**Herbert Clark Hoover**. His efforts in the Great War brought over 120,000 stranded American citizens back from Europe without incurring any financial debt to the US Government. The Commission for Food Relief in Belgium supported over 10.5 million civilians with food aid. His leaderships to provide emergency food relief to post-war Europe helped untold more millions of people avoid starvation in the early 1920s. He became the 31st President of the United States in March 1929. He presided over a period known as the 'Great Depression'. Failing to provide a quick economic recovery, he served only one term and retired to private life in 1933. He lived his life in quiet seclusion with his wife and he died on October 20, 1964 at the age of 90 years old.

**Hugh Gibson**. He became US Minister Plenipotentiary to Poland on April 16, 1919 with succeeding postings as the Minister to Switzerland in 1924; Ambassador to Belgium and minister to Luxemburg in 1927; and as the US ambassador to Brazil from 1933-1937. He died in 1954 at the age of 71 years old.

**Victor Gille**. One of the chief frontier guides employed by Edith Cavell's cell, he escaped Belgium and joined the Belgium Army.

**Armand Jeannes**. In 1921, he was observed by one of his former victims and shadowed by Belgian police for some months. He was arrested in March 1922 and taken to the city of Mons for further witness identification, police interrogation and trial. Mlle Thuliez, Herman Capiau, Countess de Belleville and Albert Libiez all testified that Jeannes was part of the German 'agent provocateur' infiltration of the de Croy network. The Court President found him guilty of high treason and sentenced him to death. Belgium eliminated its death sentence; consequently he was imprisoned to twenty years confinement.

**Maurice Neels**. This secondary 'agent provocateur' provided secret testimony against Philippe Baucq and the de Croy network. In January 1916 a patriotic and sympathetic Belgian national who worked in a Belgian café spotted Maurice Neels and followed him along the backstreets of Brussels, where Neels was confronted and stabbed to death in a darkened ally. On his body was found a carefully forged passport with an alias identity and the neutral country of Switzerland. Neels was still an active 'agent provocateur' at the time of his death.

**George Gaston Quien**. The primary 'agent provocateur' within the de Croy network and who Philippe Baucq suspected of his betrayal was arrested while wearing a French army uniform in May 1919 and he was tried in Paris in June 1919. With an impartial court, the judges found him guilty of treason. A death sentence was imposed, and then commuted to twenty years imprisonment to French Guiana, the infamous 'Devil's Island'. He served his full fifteen years and returned back to France in 1934. He vanished into obscurity.

**Ambassador Rodrigo de Saavedra**, The Marques de Villalobar, continued to serve throughout the war as Spain's representative to Belgium until the time of his untimely death. He tragically passed away as a result of peritonitis on July 9, 1926 at the age of 62 years old.

**Lt Gen Baron (Colonel General) Traugott Martin von Sauberzweig**. Shortly after the execution of Edith Cavell and Philippe Baucq, he was relieved of his posting as the Brussels Military Governor and assigned as the Chief of Staff to the 8th German army stationed in Ukraine. He was awarded one of Imperial Germany's highest military awards, the Pour le Merite. He died in bitterness and never renounced or regretted his decision for the executions of Edith Cavell and Philippe Baucq. He died on April 14, 1920 and he was 57 years old.

**Consul Brand Whitlock**. He continued to serve as the US Consulate to Belgium throughout the war and in 1919 he became the first US Ambassador to Belgium when this posting was elevated to an Embassy level. He became a commercial author and wrote fifteen books. He died on 24 May 1934 at the age of 65 years old.

**Elizabeth Wilkins**. Nurse Wilkins was identified as a persona non-grata by the Germans and forced to leave Belgium in November 1915. She returned back to England along with the remaining Clinique English nurses.

**President Woodrow Wilson**. After the war, President Wilson went to Paris to help shape the League of Nations and draft the Versailles Treaty. For these efforts, he was awarded the Noble Peace Prize in 1919. The strain of lobbying for the US entry into the League of Nations led to an incapacitating stroke in September 1919. The US Senate rejected the League of Nations and he left office in March 1921. He died on February 3, 1924 at the age of 68 years old.

## THE END

\* \* \* \* \* \* \* \* \* \* \*

CPSIA information can be obtained at www.ICGtesting.com
Printed in the USA
BVOW05*1920020515

397954BV00002B/2/P